BUSINESS/SCIENCE/TECHNOLOGY DIVISION
CHICAGO PUBLIC LIBRARY
400 SOUTH STATE STREET
CHICAGO, IL 60605

W9-CXP-865

TF
197
.G67425
1993

Greenberg's guide to
early American toy
trains.

$59.95

DATE			

BUSINESS/SCIENCE/TECHNOLOGY DIVISION
CHICAGO PUBLIC LIBRARY
400 SOUTH STATE STREET
CHICAGO, IL 60605

BAKER & TAYLOR

GREENBERG'S® GUIDE TO

EARLY AMERICAN

TOY ★ TRAINS

CARLISLE & FINCH
W. Graham Claytor, Jr.

HAFNER
Paul A. Doyle

DORFAN
Carlton Norris McKenney

Greenberg Publishing Company, Inc.
Sykesville, Maryland

Copyright © 1993
by Greenberg Publishing Company, Inc.

Greenberg Publishing Company, Inc.
7566 Main Street
Sykesville, Maryland 21784
(410) 795-7447

First Edition

Manufactured in the United States of America.

All rights reserved. No part of this book may be reproduced in any form or by any means, including electronic, photocopying or recording, or by any information storage system, without written permission of the publisher, except in the case of brief quotations used in critical articles and reviews.

Greenberg Publishing Company, Inc., publishes the world's largest selection of Lionel, American Flyer, LGB, Marx, Ives, and other toy train publications as well as a selection of books on model and prototype railroading, dollhouse building, and collectible toys. For a complete listing of current Greenberg publications, please call 1-800-533-6644 or write to Kalmbach Publishing Co., 21027 Crossroads Circle, Waukesha, Wisconsin 53187.

Greenberg Shows, Inc., sponsors *Greenberg's Great Train, Dollhouse and Toy Shows*, the world's largest of their kind. The shows feature extravagant operating train layouts and a display of magnificent dollhouses. The shows also present a huge marketplace of model and toy trains for HO, N, and Z Scales; Lionel O and Standard Gauges; S and 1 Gauges; plus layout accessories and railroadiana. They also offer a large selection of dollhouse miniatures and building materials and collectible toys. Shows are scheduled along the East Coast each year from Massachusetts to Florida. For a list of our current shows, please call (410) 795-7447 or write to Greenberg Shows, Inc., 7566 Main Street, Sykesville, Maryland 21784 and request a show brochure.

Greenberg Auctions, a division of Greenberg Shows, Inc., offers nationally advertised auctions of toy trains and toys. Please contact our auction manager at (410) 795-7447 for further information.

ISBN 0-89778-230-5 (Hard Cover)

Library of Congress Cataloging-in-Publication Data

Greenberg's guide to early American toy trains / introduction by Bruce
  C. Greenberg -- 1st ed.
       p.   cm.
    Includes index.
    Contents: Pt. 1. Carlisle & Finch / by W. Graham Claytor, Jr. --
pt. 2. Hafner / by Paul A. Doyle -- pt. 3. Dorfan / by Carlton
Norris McKenney.
    ISBN 0-89778-230-5
    1. Railroads--Models.   I. Greenberg, Bruce C.   II. Claytor, W.
Graham (William Graham), 1912- Carlisle & Finch. 1993.
III. Doyle, Paul A. Hafner. 1993. IV. McKenney, Carlton Norris.
1923- Dorfan. 1993. V. Title: Guide to early American toy
trains.
TF197.G67425 1993
625.1"9'0973075--dc20
                                                    92-41600
                                                       CIP

R00978 09144

BUSINESS/SCIENCE/TECHNOLOGY DIVISION
CHICAGO PUBLIC LIBRARY
400 SOUTH STATE STREET
CHICAGO, IL 60605

CONTENTS

★

INTRODUCTION by Bruce C. Greenberg 5
ACKNOWLEDGMENTS 7

PART I ★ CARLISLE & FINCH by W. Graham Claytor, Jr. 9
PART II ★ HAFNER by Paul A. Doyle 71
PART III ★ DORFAN by Carlton Norris McKenney 159

GLOSSARY 230
CARLISLE & FINCH INDEX 231
HAFNER INDEX 232
SUMMARY OF HAFNER TYPES 234
DORFAN INDEX 236
SUMMARY OF DORFAN TYPES 238
ABOUT THE AUTHORS 239

INTRODUCTION

★

by Bruce C. Greenberg

This guide focuses on early twentieth century American toy trains. The American toy train industry, although relatively small, was in fact well established by the late nineteenth century. A number of toy train manufacturers were mass producing a variety of floor trains designed to be rolled on the floor without rails. These were cast-iron, lightweight metal, or even wooden trains covered by elaborate printed paper labels, mostly hand-powered, but occasionally powered by clockwork. In addition there were several manufacturers — including Beggs and Weeden — of alcohol-fired steam toy trains operating on tracks. Carlisle & Finch and Hafner helped change and develop an existing industry, and Dorfan made a comparable contribution a generation later.

The differences between these three companies are as revealing and significant as — or even more significant than — their similarities. The fact that each flourished for a time suggests the complexity of the industry and its market; in other words, there were different ways to compete effectively and each manufacturer played its strongest suit. These companies differed in many ways: in their production techniques, their distribution networks, the price range of their toys, their advertising and promotion techniques, and in their relative capabilities to innovate (or their lack thereof).

The three companies differed in the size and type of trains they produced and their production techniques. Carlisle & Finch, already established as a producer of electrical equipment, entered the limited existing toy train market by offering a small streetcar with three attractive new features: it was electrically powered (as were real ones), it modeled the latest urban transit technology, and of course it ran on track. Carlisle & Finch's toy streetcars were an immediate hit and encouraged the firm to establish a full line of trolleys and trains. The company initially made its trolleys and passenger cars from polished sheet brass with a wooden base, and its use of wood for locomotives throughout its history set Carlisle & Finch apart from most other toy train manufacturers. The passenger cars were eventually made of enameled thin tin-coated steel ("tinplate"), with the lettering hand-painted or embossed, but early Carlisle & Finch production used paper labels for its first mining and road locomotives and freight cars. This of course harkened back to the earlier tradition of paper labels affixed to wooden forms.

As the line expanded at the turn of the century from streetcars to steam-outlined power, locomotives were constructed with thin tin-coated steel boilers and cabs on wooden bases were electrically powered. As further developments occurred, top-of-the-line Carlisle & Finch equipment was premium-priced, and more elaborate construction techniques were used. Some of Carlisle & Finch's trains were large, almost in the scale-model category, and quite expensive, but all tended to be realistic and relatively costly for the time.

According to William Hafner's sons Robert and John, William Hafner started train manufacturing as early as 1905 with very limited production. It entered the low-price end of an established market for trains on O Gauge track which was dominated by Ives in Connecticut and several German companies. Hafner used simple two-part iron castings for its locomotive chassis powered by clockwork mechanisms. Its manufacturing techniques were consistent with its low prices. The steam locomotives pulled cars made from lightweight stamped steel designed with fewer rather than more component parts. These cars were decorated with exceptionally colorful and detailed lithography — the same low-cost technique used for tin food packaging — which distinguished it from Carlisle & Finch's construction methods. The lithography process was also used by Ives across its diverse line and by American Flyer. It was used by Dorfan as well as by most low-end toy train manufacturers until the advent of plastic trains. Furthermore, Hafner rolling stock was outfitted with one-piece couplers, as was most Dorfan, except for its Wide Gauge and very late O Gauge equipment, which had more complicated couplers. Hafner's main emphasis was on economical production of rugged and colorful toys.

Dorfan started production in 1924, twenty-eight years after Carlisle & Finch and nineteen years after Hafner. At that time, Dorfan entered a very well-developed market for electric trains on track dominated by Lionel, American Flyer, and Ives, accompanied by Hafner, Bing, and other European trains. Its founders, Milton and Julius Forchheimer, brought years of previous German toy industry experience with Fandor to their new company. Dorfan sought market share by innovation in design, manufacturing, and promotion. Dorfan pioneered in the use of large die-cast parts to form the locomotive body. The die-cast parts added more surface detail than was present in stamped-steel or cast-iron locomotives. Previously, detail such as piping and handrails was added by expensive hand assembly. The new heavier die-cast locomotives also had enhanced traction.

Dorfan led in the development of easily assembled and disassembled locomotives, and featured its construction techniques in a series of effective advertisements that promoted the educational play value of Dorfan toy trains. Its "take-apart" locomotives afforded young engineers the excitement of building their own trains as well as giving them firsthand exposure to the workings of an electric motor. Perhaps no other company after Carlisle & Finch can claim as many firsts. One of the most significant was the introduction of a reversing mechanism.

Dorfan's manufacturing techniques were related to both cost constraints and to marketing considerations. Die-cast locomotives were less expensive to manufacture than were stamped-steel locomotives, with fewer parts required. Detail was accomplished economically as it was included in the castings. At the same time these die-cast parts provided marketing advantages: Dorfan advertised in print and on film how its heavy engines could pull more cars than its competitors' stamped-steel bodies. Dorfan's premium locomotives came with cars of heavy-gauge stamped steel, which costs more to buy and to stamp and form; these cars were substantially overbuilt and as such were similar to the top-of-the-line cars of its principal competitors — Lionel, American Flyer, and Ives.

The three companies also differed in the ranges of products they offered. Consistent with its low-cost niche, Hafner offered the narrowest range of items, Carlisle & Finch a medium range, and Dorfan the widest. Carlisle & Finch trains were relatively expensive and realistic; Hafner trains were inexpensive and toylike; Dorfan's were less realistic than Carlisle & Finch's but certainly as realistic as those of its important competitors. Dorfan's line and those of Lionel, American Flyer, and Ives offered a range from short stubby toys to sleek, more realistic models. The realism of the line relates to why people buy the trains and the price they are willing to pay: realism attracts adults as buyers of models for their own use.

The three companies differed in their advertising and promotion and in their catalogue documentation. Carlisle & Finch produced elaborate catalogues with considerable descriptive information. No doubt due to its experience as a manufacturer of electrical goods, its line was much better documented than most others of the period. In contrast Hafner produced the least documented line of any long-surviving company, even when compared with the frugal Marx. Dorfan provided substantial documentation in the form of consumer catalogues, consumer instructions, and informative trade and consumer advertising. Of the three, Dorfan was by far the most promotion-minded company. Promotion of new ideas was Dorfan's tool in working to enter a well-established market. Dorfan ran with its new ideas.

The advertising and promotion practices of the three companies relate to their pricing structures and the realism of their products. Carlisle & Finch trains were relatively expensive toys with a major adult following and therefore its thorough documentation appealed to its buyers. Hafner trains were built for use by children and bought by adults for children based on low price and color. Consumer advertising was neither necessary nor economically efficient and few catalogues were made. Marx, the most important producer of inexpensive American toy trains, also chose not to invest in consumer-directed advertising, which would ultimately increase the cost of their products. Dorfan trains ranged from moderate to high-priced but were sold primarily on the basis of new features which differentiated them from the competition, so its substantial efforts at promotion included detailed consumer catalogues.

The three companies departed the industry for different reasons. Carlisle & Finch had by 1915 essentially lost much of its market share to Lionel and Voltamp. This loss of market was probably due to Carlisle & Finch's lack of response to its competitors' technical innovations. Sectional track was much easier to use and more reliable than strip track, but Carlisle & Finch persisted in emphasizing its older form of track, although it introduced a flimsy sectional track. Lionel and Voltamp offered operating headlights which made exciting night operation, but Carlisle & Finch did not. Although its history reveals its use of simple and cheap methods of solving problems such as insulation, it is still ironic that a company that had been a technological pioneer left the market in part because it failed to continue to innovate. As it turned out, Carlisle & Finch's timing was poor:

they left the market just as the American toy train market began to grow rapidly due to the end of German imports, as the result of World War I. But because of increased demand from the onset of the first world war, electrical goods manufacturer Carlisle & Finch chose to focus on marine searchlights, an area in which it was preeminent and which brought greater profits.

Why did Dorfan disappear? Although Dorfan enjoyed costs advantages due to its die-cast locomotives, its engineers clearly over-designed its rolling stock, particularly its passenger cars, which were assembled with too many eyelets and tabs. Its engineers designed and carried out low-cost locomotive production, but failed to apply critical analysis to their rolling stock. Hence rolling stock production costs were probably higher than competition would allow, and this no doubt reduced profit margins to low if not unacceptable levels. Another factor was the unintended consequences of Dorfan's innovative die-cast technology. Significant die-cast part failure probably occurred within two or three years of manufacture, and unhappy consumers turned the company's technological advance into a very expensive problem. If parts were replaced in quantity, profit would greatly suffer. If parts were not replaced, consumer dissatisfaction would soon cause the distribution network to fall apart. Beyond all this, Dorfan faced the twentieth century's most severe economic decline, the Depression. Most of the toy train industry experienced significant losses; Dorfan and several others closed down.

Hafner was the longest-lived of the three companies. It started manufacturing toy trains in 1905 and finally terminated in 1951. Its line was continued by Wyandotte until 1956. Hafner did not innovate technically. It did not advertise to consumers; it consistently advertised with a modest budget and only to the trade. Its trains were toylike and were not intended to appeal to adults for their own use. The company did make a successful management transition from founder to son, it successfully weathered two wars and the Depression, and it outlasted nearly all of its competitiors. The company sought a narrow niche at the low end of the market and continued to fill this niche. That it met its end was most likely the result of the desire of its successful owner to retire early and of very aggressive competition from Marx for its low-end niche.

The American toy train industry has been a vibrant and exciting industry for about ninety-two years. Its vitality and innovation have largely been the result of the small firms that have entered the industry and challenged its leading firms. Usually the small firms do not survive, but they always leave their mark. Today the industry is bubbling with action, as literally hundreds of small firms compete for the adult toy market. In fact, adult toy train enthusiasts have never had such a marvelous selection of high-quality equipment to choose from.

About This Book

Each of the three parts that comprise this book was researched and written independently and each takes a slightly different approach to descriptive listings of specific items. As is especially true with early toy train manufacture, there are variances in systems of numbering. Each part begins with a preface by its author to explain in detail the approach used. For example, Graham Claytor employs catalogue numbers, since catalogues exist for every year of production save one, and car numbers are infrequently present. Paul Doyle and other Hafner collectors cite side-of-car numbers because few catalogues are available and cars are normally numbered. It was possible to include both catalogue and side-of-car numbers in one sequence for Dorfan listings without being unduly confusing. The listings throughout this book include all types of numbers in some way, and all numbers are listed in numerical sequence in the index for that part (all three indexes are printed in the very back of this volume, for handy reference). Note that the complete description of a item will be found only once in a chapter's listings, under either catalogue or car number.

Note also that there is a composite glossary of terms pertaining to early toy trains in the back of the book, immediately preceding the indexes. For your convenience summaries of types of Hafner and Dorfan items are not only provided within those sections of the book but are repeated after the appropriate indexes.

Just as the numbering system used for listings varies from section to section, the approaches to establishment of values differ. Greenberg Guides strive to include complete and updated ranges of values as general guidance for collectors, but always with a few caveats. The actual price you can expect to pay for an item is affected by a number of variables — such as the region of the country (in some areas certain lines are more avidly collected than others, and the Northeast is known for prices generally higher than those in other regions); the point in the run of a meet at which you negotiate a purchase (asking prices generally drop toward the end of a meet); and, most importantly, the condition of a piece. The ranges of values included in this book are meant as guidelines only and require a few words of explanation. First and last, however, we urge novices not to make major purchases without the assistance of friends who have experience in buying and selling trains.

The quantity of items from the three manufacturers covered here which are offered for sale varies widely. There is, comparatively speaking, much more Hafner traded than Carlisle & Finch. Hafner expert Paul Doyle, living in the metropolitan New York area, is able to attend meets virtually every week and has been filling notebooks for over ten years with asking prices (ignoring the obvious aberrations of inflated prices), examining mail-order lists, and compiling standard guidelines of expected prices for Hafner items in both Good and Excellent condition (using the standards set forth by the Train Collectors Association).

Widely viewed as the eminent Carlisle & Finch collector and authority, and recognizing a rather small trade in Carlisle & Finch items, Graham Claytor did not wish to set down or endorse values. The publisher asked Nicholas Ladd, who had recently catalogued a Carlisle & Finch collection, to research sales activity and prepare a market report. Consulting every major auction house that handles toys and trains in this country and in England, as well as individual collectors from various parts of the country and his records of observed sales, he has provided a general range of values for items; in some instances these are educated estimates. Because of the rarity of Carlisle & Finch items and other situations pertaining to the condition of pieces, he had to devise standards of evaluation not exactly parallel to TCA's. This is explained in a note to the Preface of the Carlisle & Finch section.

Providing values for Dorfan items presents its own special challenges. There is trade and interest, and in fact prices, especially for its Narrow Gauge, have been increasing steadily in recent years. But the often deteriorated/deteriorating condition of many Dorfan pieces, because of its special alloy, affects prices markedly. We include a range of prices for Restored, and several other factors enter in. It is not uncommon, for example, for a Dorfan item to now have a truck from American Flyer or some other substitution to have been made. If it is a completely original piece, of course the price expected will be much higher. Or you might find pieces already crumbling being offered for sale, but a realistic price might be what the parts would bring. Or if a piece was made with a spring coupler, it will be worth more than otherwise. In the very tricky area of establishing Dorfan values, it is especially true: when starting out, seek the advice of an experienced collector.

General Acknowledgments

Each section's preface concludes with thanks to collectors, readers, and others who have assisted that particular author. Here we wish to cite the members of the Greenberg staff who have worked over a period of several years to make this new publication possible.

The enthusiasm and support of **Bruce Greenberg** has been supplemented by the guidance of managing editors **Samuel Baum** and **Allan Miller**. The first versions of the manuscripts were processed, edited, and circulated to readers by **Wendy Burgio**, **Marsha Davis**, **Terri Glaser**, **Andrea Kraszewski**, and **Eugenia Purman**.

Elsa van Bergen edited and coordinated the final phases of the total project and was assisted by **Donna Price**, who went far beyond proofreading to check that the sections of text and art functioned together, and by **Richard M. Watson**. The cover was designed by **Norm Myers** and **Maureen Crum**, who also assisted in inside art preparation. **Wendy Burgio** was pasteup artist and designer. **Al Fiterman** and Bruce Greenberg took most of the photographs and **Bill Wantz** printed photos and stats for the book. Production manager was **Cindy Lee Floyd**.

THE CARLISLE & FINCH COMPANY.
CINCINNATI, O.
U. S. A.

W. Graham Claytor, Jr.

With contributions by
Franklin O. Loveland

Market report by
Nicholas Ladd

CONTENTS

★

PREFACE 13

ACKNOWLEDGMENTS 14

ONE ★ AN INTRODUCTION TO CARLISLE & FINCH 15

TWO ★ TROLLEYS, TRAILERS, AND INTERURBANS 23

THREE ★ COAL MINING LOCOMOTIVES AND CARS 31

FOUR ★ STEAM OUTLINE LOCOMOTIVES 34

FIVE ★ PASSENGER AND BAGGAGE CARS 42

SIX ★ FREIGHT AND WRECK CARS 46

SEVEN ★ TRACK, SWITCHES, BRIDGES, AND STATIONS 52

EIGHT ★ POWER SOURCES 58

NINE ★ RELATED CARLISLE & FINCH ELECTRICAL TOYS 61

TEN ★ 1934 PREPRODUCTION SAMPLES by Franklin O. Loveland 63

GLOSSARY and INDEX appear at the back of this volume

PREFACE

★

Most senior train collectors today were born after World War I and many more came along after World War II. To most of these, the name "Carlisle & Finch" is not in the real world of Lionel, Ives, and American Flyer which most of them know well, but belongs at best in a footnote in a history book. Yet the electrical repair and products firm of Carlisle & Finch, of Cincinnati, Ohio, was the first successful American manufacturer of toy electric trains — six years before Joshua Lionel Cowen's Lionel Mfg. Co. started in business — and for a dozen years or more was by far the largest and most successful toy electric train maker in this country. While some of its products are now ninety-five years old, they are still collected and operated, and its top-of-the-line items are not surpassed in design or operation by anything made since. Although relatively rare, Carlisle & Finch equipment can still be found and is eminently collectible.

The chapters that follow describe known Carlisle & Finch toy train products. The Publisher's Introduction to this book has explained that, especially with early American toy trains, it is often difficult to decide whether descriptive listings should use the manufacturer's catalogue number, or the number appearing on the side of the car. In the case of Carlisle & Finch, we use catalogue numbers exclusively, because catalogues were regularly and frequently issued, and the numbers sometimes appearing on the sides of Carlisle & Finch cars and locomotives are both unrelated to the catalogue numbers and cannot reliably be used for identification of the particular piece of equipment. Side-of-car numbers are listed in a box at the beginning of the chapter's listings, which are, as explained above, entered by catalogue number.

Occasionally, a number will consistently appear on a car or locomotive and not be duplicated elsewhere, but in many cases different numbers will be used on the same car or engine from time to time, and one or more of these numbers will often be used on entirely different pieces of equipment at the same time. Finally, many, if not most, of the cars and locomotives carry no number on them at all. Thus catalogue numbers are the constant in describing Carlisle & Finch items, and to clearly cite the number given at the beginning of a listing as a catalogue number, I have chosen to include the label "No.". Note that the Index appearing at the back of this volume does contain side-of-car numbers where they exist, as well as the more reliable catalogue numbers.

Even more than most other toy train manufacturers, Carlisle & Finch tended to keep each item in production for a number of years, but it made frequent variations in it from year to year. In the Carlisle & Finch listings, a year or a span of years is the organizing principle of the variations. Because the chronology of Carlisle & Finch production is so important, occasionally listings are ordered by year of introduction of the item rather than by catalogue number. As is typical of the labor-intensive style of production of early manufacturers, some *production* variations exist, even within the same time frame, and — when known — these are also noted. It is very likely that some other variations exist, and we hope that our readers will report these.

It is important to understand that each distinct item for which multiple variations exist will initially be described with measurements and other characteristics common to *all* variations; this will be followed by variations that have occurred from time to time, listed as (A), (B), (C), etc. Unlike the products of many other toy train manufacturers, these variations occur in an order or progression which can be identified and at least approximately dated with some assurance. To obtain all of the characteristics of any particular variation, it will usually be necessary to examine the several previously listed variations, as well as the common characteristics given at the beginning of the particular listing.

When a really major change in a particular item occurs, even though the catalogue number remains the same, a new listing of the item will be made that will include subsequent variations in similarly lettered subparagraphs.

CATALOGUES

Carlisle & Finch toy train catalogues (called their "Catalogue B") were issued annually from 1896 through 1915 (with the exception of 1910 when for some inexplicable reason there was no catalogue) and were serially numbered, apparently with 1896 as No. 1. Many were published with dealers' names on the covers rather than Carlisle & Finch's name. This was a common practice; Lionel catalogues often have the name of a department store on them. The catalogues themselves have become collectors' items, and copies of all of them, except for the elusive 1896, have been examined during the preparation of this book. Reproduced excerpts from many of them appear throughout the chapters that follow.

Because Carlisle & Finch often retained the same catalogue illustration from year to year in spite of substantial product changes, the catalogues' illustrations, although frequently helpful, must be used cautiously when dating various product changes. Changes in the text are frequently more helpful in this respect. Unless otherwise stated, descriptions in this book are based on observed samples as well as catalogue changes, but the dates given must all be taken as approximate rather than exact. In many cases a change in a model may have been made before it was indicated in a catalogue, and similarly it is clear that both Carlisle & Finch and its dealers continued to sell models remaining in their inventories after later models had been introduced. Train sets often have been found that consist of late locomotives with earlier cars, and vice versa. It is probable that at least some of these sets were made up at the factory or put together by the dealer to use up old stock.

SCALE

Carlisle & Finch trains, like those of later tinplate manufacturers, are toys, not scale models. Since they are designed for 2-inch gauge track, which is just ⅛ inch narrower than Lionel Standard Gauge,[1] they generally fall into the same size category as the many well-known "standard" or "wide" gauge trains of Lionel, Ives, American Flyer, Dorfan, and some European manufacturers. Like them, they vary in size from small to quite large, and in detail from rudimentary four-wheel cars to sophisticated detailed Atlantic-type 4-4-2[2] locomotives, such as the No. 45 and the later No. 34, described in Chapter Four.

CUSTOMER MODIFICATIONS

In a fascinating little hardcover book entitled *Miniature Electric Railway Construction*, published in 1906, Carlisle & Finch customers were encouraged to add overhead trolley poles to their streetcars and to make other modifications to Carlisle & Finch equipment. They were given detailed instructions on how to accomplish this. In fact, in several catalogues, Carlisle & Finch also listed individual wheels, motors with pinion gears, and complete motorized and trail trucks for eight-wheel cars. As was stated in the 1908 catalogue, "Anyone wishing to make his own double-truck car can do so" by using this equipment.

One locomotive used the motor and frame of an early No. 4 Carlisle & Finch locomotive — an example of otherwise hand-built models that use Carlisle & Finch components. The model was constructed around 1900 by a William Stone in the small town of Bedford, Virginia, and was part of his collection of Carlisle & Finch equipment.[3]

In this case, we know from the original owner's family that the modification was made by the customer, not the factory. In other cases, however, the modification could have been either an uncatalogued preproduction model or a rebuild by the customer or by someone else — especially when they are more than three-quarters of a century old. Two of these modifications in four-wheel trolley No. 1 have been located as examples.

The most interesting such example is in the Ward Kimball Collection and has a solid sheet-metal body that is covered with printed paper labels that simulate four windows on each side. A reversing lever on the forward platform indicates that this model is equipped with a three-pole reversing motor. (See Chapter One for a discussion of motors and power in Carlisle & Finch items.) This could be a preproduction model of the No. 1-R car that was introduced in 1899, or it could be a customer-built body with a Carlisle & Finch motor.

A second early example was reported by Frank Loveland in the October 1982 issue of the *Train Collectors Quarterly*, pages 11 and 17. This car has a body similar to the four-wheel No. 1 trolley described in Chapter Two, but it is labeled "N.Y. Elevated RR", and its motor and motor mounting are unlike any other No. 1 cars found. The label could well have been applied by a dealer or the owner, and the significant changes in the motor and motor mounting seem unlike anything known to have come from Carlisle & Finch.

Other questionable factory or customer modifications may turn up. It would be helpful if readers will notify the author c/o Greenberg Publishing Company, 7566 Main Street, Sykesville, Maryland 21784, of any that may be found.

VALUES

Publishers Note: As explained in the Introduction, the value guidelines included in the chapters that follow have been supplied by Nicholas B. Ladd. While with most other manufacturers' production one can cite values for pieces in several categories of condition as established by the Train Collections Association, collectors fortunate enough to locate any Carlisle & Finch pieces tend to rate them Good to Excellent. Nick Ladd points out that he has bent the description standards because the typical Carlisle & Finch piece is never found in mint or TCA excellent condition. In fact, condition of these items is often hard to describe due to age, construction, and materials employed. Thus "Good" condition is considered to be: intact and in running condition with paint or metal scratches, dents, and worn paper. "Excellent" would have fewer of these imperfections. In both cases the descriptions do not parallel those of the TCA because the items are so old and so rare.

NOTES

1. When Lionel "standard gauge" equipment was first offered in 1906, it was described as 2-inch gauge — which was indeed the accepted wide gauge in this country at that time. When it was found that the gauge as manufactured was actually $2\frac{1}{8}$ inches rather than 2 inches, and thus was an oddball size at the time, it may well have been decided to call it "standard" in the hope that this difference would not be noted — a smart and eventually successful marketing decision!

2. The conventional method of classifying steam locomotives uses what is called the "Whyte" system of three or more numerals separated by hyphens. The first is the number of small pilot wheels on both sides at the front of the engine, the next number represents the number of driving wheels, and the third represents the number of smaller trailing wheels. Most of these types also carried recognized names, such as "Atlantic" for the 4-4-2 arrangement and the "Pacific" for the 4-6-2.

3. Mr. Stone's collection included a now rare 1897 brass bridge No. 5, a mint 1899 or 1900 smooth-sided No. 1 trolley, and several very early coal mining cars.

Acknowledgments

I received a great deal of expert help and assistance from many friends in the Train Collectors Association and The Antique Toy Collectors of America. Especially among those that I would like to mention are Professor Franklin Loveland, whose great interest in Carlisle & Finch and extensive writing and research in company files have been a great help to me and to others interested in this field.

I should also particularly thank Dick Hopkins and his father, George Hopkins, for enormous help over a period of years. George Hopkins' great Carlisle & Finch layout, dating back to around 1909, is undoubtedly the finest and longest-lived C & F operation ever.

Along with every other toy train collector, I also owe a deep debt of gratitude to Louis H. Hertz for years of friendship, scholarly research, and leadership in this field. His landmark book, *Riding the Tinplate Rails*, resulted directly in my initial interest in Carlisle & Finch back in 1949, and his advice since then has been of enormous assistance.

Of course, Bruce Greenberg and his editors, particularly Elsa van Bergen, have not only helped correct my mistakes but have made publication of this book possible.

I shall not attempt to list the many friends who have helped me acquire my collection, answered my questions, and given me sound advice about the material in this book. To all of them I express my heartfelt thanks and good wishes for many years of successful collecting.

W. Graham Claytor, Jr.

CHAPTER ONE

★

AN INTRODUCTION TO CARLISLE & FINCH

In his article on Carlisle & Finch in the August 1971 *Train Collectors Quarterly*, Dick Hopkins described their model No. 45 locomotive as "the most perfectly proportioned classic ever produced." How is it that a company whose main concern is marine appliances came to produce such superb model trains?

The Carlisle & Finch Company was founded in Cincinnati, Ohio, on July 1, 1893, by Morten Carlisle and Robert S. Finch.[1] The founders were young men of about twenty-one years and their company was intended to deal with a young industry — electrical technology.

At the outset the firm was primarily engaged in repairing motors and other electrical equipment. Brent Finch recounts that in 1894, shortly after Carlisle & Finch moved to West 6th Street in Cincinnati, "it became evident that the company would have to enter product manufacture, in addition to their repair work, if it wished to grow." At the time, German-made clockwork toy trains were popular, big-selling imports. Robert Finch and Morten Carlisle conceived the idea of powering toy trains by electricity, using the tracks as "wires" to bring electrical power to the locomotive's motor.

Accordingly, in early 1896 the company designed and offered for sale a toy four-wheel electric trolley car. In his classic *Riding the Tinplate Rails* — a book that in 1944 really launched today's antique toy train collecting hobby — Louis H. Hertz wrote that the co-founder of Carlisle & Finch, Robert S. Finch, had told him that some five hundred of the initial four-wheel electric cars were produced for 2-inch-gauge three-rail track, but that orders for as many as a thousand cars were received. Mr. Finch added that the next cars designed were for two-rail rather than three-rail track. Early company files recently identified by Frank Loveland indicate that second and third runs of five hundred cars each were made in late 1896, in time for the Christmas season — probably to fill customer demand. It seems highly likely that this was the first production of the two-rail Carlisle & Finch railway equipment that then became standard and was first listed in their 1897 catalogue.

Carlisle & Finch's early success led to the decision to establish toy electric trolleys and trains as a major product line. Contrary to the impression prevalent today, however, Carlisle & Finch was not the first to enter this market; that honor must go to Jehu Garlick of Paterson, New Jersey. (See *Railroad Magazine*, December 1946, page 116.)

Garlick had been an employee of Eugene Beggs, who manufactured the first steam-powered toy trains in the United States in the early 1880s. By 1895 Garlick was in the business of making his own version of these steam trains. Fascinated by the Baltimore & Ohio Railroad's operation of electric locomotives in their Baltimore tunnels in early 1895, he designed a toy electric model of these engines, using driving wheels and some other parts from his steam locomotives. His locomotive used a permanent-magnet direct-current motor with overhead trolley, and operated on a fixed circle of 1⅞-inch-gauge track — the gauge used by Beggs. It has been reported that in late 1895 he made approximately two hundred of these toy electric engines. Sales were slow, however, and their manufacture was not continued.

The success that eluded Garlick was quickly attained by Carlisle & Finch. During the ten years following the introduction of their first car in 1896, they were the largest electric toy train manufacturer in the United States and soon dominated the field with their extensive line of two-rail 2-inch-gauge railway equipment, track, and accessories. Without question, they were the first successful American manufacturer of mass-produced electric trains.

The first known advertising of Carlisle & Finch toy trains appeared in issues of *Scientific American* in 1896. The 1897 electric toy catalogue, listed as "Catalogue B," gave the company's address as 828-830 West 6th Street, Cincinnati. Listed as sales agents were J. H. Bunnell & Co. of New York; Thos. Hall & Son of Boston; Electrical Supply & Manufacturing Co. of Cleveland, Ohio; W. T. Osborn & Co. of Kansas City, Missouri; St. Louis Electrical Supply Co. of St. Louis; The National Automatic Fire Alarm Co. of New Orleans; James Clark Jr. & Co. of Louisville, Kentucky; William Gumbley of London, England; Ortega & Oieda of Caracas, Venezuela; and R. W. Cameron & Co. of Sydney, Australia. C & F's extensive dealer network and marketing expertise, along with the simplicity and low price of their early products, may explain why they were successful and Jehu Garlick's earlier toy electric engine was not.

The 1898 catalogue listed twenty U.S. firms ranging from New York to California which sold a "full stock of our novelties." (Note: "novelties" has the specific meaning, "a small manufactured article intended mainly for personal or household adornment," according to *Webster's Seventh New Collegiate Dictionary*, but manufacturers of toy trains have generally been sensitive to use of the word "toy.") In 1899 and 1900 the catalogues included a 24-inch electric torpedo boat and an electric toy car, neither of which was continued in later years.

On April 17, 1897, the firm was incorporated and later moved to 228-231 East Clifton Avenue, where it stayed for about the next fifty years. As electrical technology advanced, the firm was innovative in several areas. Among other things, Carlisle & Finch manufactured the first horizontal arc searchlights and this led to their becoming preeminent in the marine searchlight field.

This photo, ca. 1906, is of the Clifton Avenue factory. Note the large number of No. 45 locomotives, later model No. 4s, and large freight cars.

TWO-RAIL CHARACTERISTICS AND PROBLEMS

As mentioned above, Carlisle & Finch's first production run of its initial four-wheel No. 1 trolley in 1896 used 2-inch-gauge three-rail track, but all subsequent production was for 2-inch-gauge two-rail track.

As those acquainted with two-rail HO, S, and I or G Gauge equipment know, the use of two-rail track presents both equipment design and operating problems, but it is far more realistic than the center third-rail system used traditionally in most tinplate toy train systems of various gauges.

With three-rail tinplate track, the current is transmitted to the car or engine motor through a contact with the center third rail, the return being through the car or engine wheels on the running rails, which for three-rail track would normally be electrically bonded together. In two-rail

track, however, the current is transmitted to the motor only through the wheels on the two running rails. This means that the two rails must be insulated from each other, *and* the wheels on one side of all rolling stock must be insulated from the wheels on the other side. With wood ties there was no problem in insulating the rails from each other, but metal wheels with steel axles could not be used without insulating the wheels from the axle, splitting the axle into two parts joined by a fiber insert, or by using no through axle at all.

In the course of its twenty-year production of two-rail trolleys and trains, Carlisle & Finch used all three ways of solving this problem. The simplest and cheapest method used during approximately their first eleven years of operation for their smaller passenger, freight, and trolley trail cars was to eliminate the through axle altogether. In the four-wheel equipment, 1-inch cast-iron wheels on each side of the car were allowed to turn on short nails driven into a wooden block that constituted part of the frame or base of the car. With eight-wheel equipment using two four-wheel "trucks" (or "bogies" as the Europeans call them), similar wheels were nailed on each side of a small block of wood that constituted the truck frame or "bolster," and this in turn swiveled on a wood screw or bolt that fastened each bolster to the wood or metal car frame.

Carlisle & Finch's powered trolleys, and locomotives whose driving wheels are connected to an electric motor by pulleys or spur gears, all use steel axles split into two parts that are connected by fiber tubes or bushings to provide the necessary insulation. These are referred to herein as "split insulated axles." The same type of split insulated axles are also initially used on the larger passenger and freight train cars.

Around 1908 Carlisle & Finch eliminated both the nails-on-wooden-blocks and the split insulated axles on all unpowered trail cars and substituted solid steel axles with fiber insulation between the wheels and axles on both sides. In fact, this system had been generally in use by the various other American manufacturers of two-rail toy trains and trolleys, including Lionel's 2⅞-inch-gauge equipment from 1901 to 1905, as well as subsequent 2-inch-gauge equipment by Howard, Knapp, and Voltamp. Only a few trolleys made by other manufacturers copied Carlisle & Finch in using split insulated axles.

A final problem presented by two-rail locomotives and powered trolleys is how to transmit the current from the wheels on each side to the motor. Voltamp and some other manufacturers using metal car or locomotive frames must do this by providing insulated sliding metal pickups or shoes pressed against the inside of insulated wheels on one side, the wheels on the other side passing current through the axle and frames. These pickups frequently cause power interruptions to the motor unless kept clean and under proper tension. By using a nonconducting wooden base in most locomotives and all trolleys, usually with brass plates or side frames attached to each side of the base through which the split insulated axles pass, Carlisle & Finch avoids this problem altogether. This extensive use of wood in steam-type locomotives is unique to Carlisle & Finch. Its top-of-the-line No. 45 locomotive of 1903–1908 is the only engine not using a wooden frame, and here the same result is achieved by having a two-piece cast-bronze frame with the two parts insulated from each other.

EVOLUTION OF EARLY MOTORS

The early two-rail trolley cars first listed in 1897 (four-wheel No. 1 and eight-wheel No. 2) were equipped with small two-pole motors connected with one set of iron wheels by a pulley or rubber band arrangement. Since their two-pole armature meant that these motors had a dead center, it was often necessary to start the four-wheel cars by hand. Possibly to avoid this problem, the early eight-wheel cars had two motors: the probability was that at least one of them would not be on dead center and so would start without a push. At the same time, the first No. 3 mining engine was equipped with a self-starting three-pole reversing motor from the beginning. The difference between two-pole and three-pole motors is illustrated in the reproduced excerpts from the instruction book entitled *Miniature Electric Railway Construction*, published by the company in 1906.

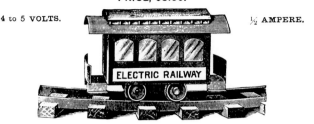

No. 1. Complete Electric Railway.

PRICE, $3.50.

4 to 5 VOLTS.   ½ AMPERE.

Early two-rail trolley, which had a simple motor, shown in C & F catalogue; the motor was illustrated in Miniature Electric Railway Construction, *shown below.*

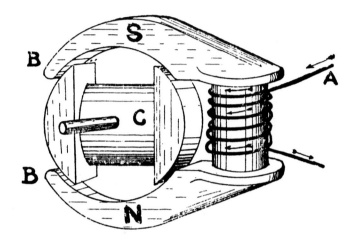

Motor used on small four-wheel car. Current of electricity flows along wire A, magnetizing the iron it is wound around. C is the armature which will become polarized.

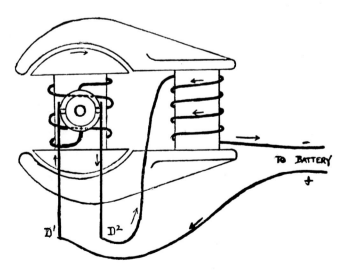

This shows the complete winding of a motor in which the "field winding" or wire on the field magnet and the armature winding are in series (the same current passes through both in succession).

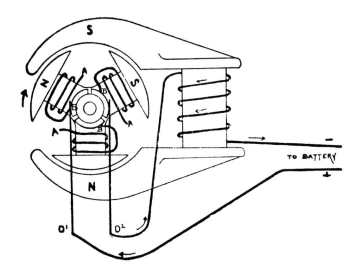

Three-pole armature, most commonly used as it has no dead center and will start to revolve as soon as the current is passed through the motor (the two-pole armature often requires turning to be started). The three-pole armature requires a three-part commutator so as to change the direction of the current in each one of the three arms or poles as they pass the pole pieces of the field magnet.

By 1899 the four-wheel trolley No. 1 was also offered with a reversing three-pole motor (see illustration on left) and was catalogued as No. 1-R, and both the No. 3 mining engine and the first 0-4-0 No. 4 road locomotive had their self-starting and reversing three-pole motors connected directly to the driving wheels by spur gears. In 1902 the first No. 42 trolley with spur gear drive was offered. This was followed in 1903 by a 19-inch-long double-truck interurban car (still designated No. 2), with all four wheels of its power truck driven by spur gears from a newly designed three-pole reversing motor within the truck itself.[2] In the same year a more powerful and advanced five-pole motor with a "Gramme ring" armature was included in a new No. 45 locomotive described below and detailed further in Chapter Four.

CARLISLE & FINCH: INNOVATION AND ARTISTRY

With the introduction of its most popular item, the No. 4 steam-type locomotive in 1899, Carlisle & Finch rapidly expanded its toy train line. In that year were added a gondola (No. 11) and a boxcar (No. 12), making up the company's first freight train, and in the next year, 1900, were added a No. 13 brass coach and a No. 13B baggage car to

Photo courtesy of Dick Hopkins

Photo courtesy of Dick Hopkins

1908 a second and slightly smaller handsome Atlantic-type locomotive, No. 34. No other company in this period offered such a wide variety of trains, trolleys, and accessories.

Operating Carlisle & Finch Layouts

In his historic book, *Riding the Tinplate Rails*, (pages 77–87), Louis H. Hertz describes one of the oldest 2-inch-gauge two-rail train layouts, started by George S. Lee of Hyde Park, Massachusetts, in 1904 with Howard and Carlisle & Finch trains and continued until dismantled and donated to Mr. Hertz for preservation in 1940. Without doubt, however, the longest-lived and most elaborate Carlisle & Finch model railroad system was the "Transattic and United Ry" of Mr. George Hopkins in Eugene, Oregon. This was started with a late model Carlisle & Finch No. 45 locomotive in 1908 or 1909, and expanded and continued by Mr. Hopkins until his retirement in 1991, when it was dismantled and preserved by his son, Dick Hopkins of Menlo Park, California — a total operation of over eighty years. The photograph on the opposite page shows the attic layout.[3] Mr. Hopkins took seriously the Carlisle & Finch suggestion that their customers experiment with modifications of their equipment. Being an accomplished technician himself, he scratch-built an improved No. 45 locomotive, making it a beautiful Pacific-type 4-6-2 engine, almost identical in overall appearance to the original late model (it is shown here, in the hands of George Hopkins).

Couplers

Carlisle & Finch trains employed two different coupler systems. (The single trolley of 1896 of course required no coupler.) In 1897, starting with the first mining engine No. 3, and for some six years thereafter, a *link and pin* coupler system was used on both locomotives and freight and passenger cars. Most trolleys remained without couplers, even though unpowered trailers were also listed. The link-and-pin-type coupler proved unreliable and it is puzzling that this arrangement was so long-lived. The link and pin worked satisfactorily when the engine pulled the train, but in a backing-up move, the links tended to cause the cars to jackknife and derail. In 1903 an improved coupler system

constitute a passenger train. Finally, in 1903, Carlisle & Finch produced what many believe to be the most beautiful and accurately detailed toy locomotive ever made by a United States manufacturer — the 4-4-2 No. 45. This nickel-plated Atlantic-type locomotive with its nickel trim and its black tender lettered "N.Y.C. & H.R." was about 27½ inches long. No. 45 was such an accurate copy of the locomotive hauling the newly inaugurated "20th Century Limited" from New York to Albany on the New York Central & Hudson River Railroad that Carlisle & Finch felt justified in using for two years an actual photograph of the prototype engine as the catalogue illustration for this locomotive. With this top-of-the-line locomotive and its companion 19-inch-long passenger and 15-inch-long freight cars listed in the next two years, Carlisle & Finch established itself as a world leader in the production of high-quality toy electric trains.

Other superb models followed: in 1904, two large and handsome four-wheel trolleys — No. 18 (closed) and No. 19 (open); a switch engine, No. 20; a motorized derrick car, No. 53; a freight-loading platform, No. 54; a large truss bridge, No. 56; and a glorious 36-inch-long No. 57 cast-iron suspension bridge — modeled after the nineteenth-century suspension bridge across the Ohio River at Cincinnati, Ohio. Later came a No. 87 six-wheel truck vestibule Pullman sleeping car, a huge 36-inch-long terminal station, and in

A comparison of a link and pin coupler with a bumper band coupler (see Chapter Three for further illustration)

was introduced. A half-round spring metal bumper strip, or *bumper band*, was fastened to the ends of each car and to the rear of tenders, and to some locomotive pilots. When equipment is coupled using this new system, bumpers on adjacent vehicles are held together by small U-shaped pieces of wire that are dropped over them.

While this system worked well in practice, it presented a new problem because the height above the rail of the bottom of the bumper bands varied with the type and size of the equipment: ¾ inch on mining engines and cars, 1¼ inch on locomotives Nos. 4 and 20 and their passenger and freight cars, and 1½ inch on the No. 45 locomotive and its much larger passenger and freight cars. This meant that these different pieces of equipment could not be readily coupled together.

In 1908 and 1909 Carlisle & Finch standardized all these couplers at a height of 1¼ inches above the rail, so that all equipment thereafter manufactured could be coupled in a train. For collectors and operators today, however, the problem remains because many if not most surviving cars and engines were made before rather than after the standardization of coupler heights.

Keeping the Trains Moving

Chapter Seven describes in some detail the various types of track and switches offered by Carlisle & Finch. Initially the track consisted only of strip-steel rails inserted in slotted wood ties. In 1905 brass tubular rail on wooden ties (called "Tee Rail") was offered. But like the strip-steel trackage, this type of track required assembly by the customer. This involved bending the rail to the desired radius and fastening the rail to the wooden ties with small nails. Not until 1908 was preassembled sectional tubular track produced, and then only with 15-inch radius curves. These sharp curves were too tight for the large No. 45 locomotive and its cars. The preassembled sections of track had wooden ties without any base to make them rigid. It is odd to reflect that, for all the clever innovations produced by Carlisle & Finch, their trackage should have been so poorly thought out. From 1906, for example, Lionel offered strong and rigid sectional track for its equipment. In 1907–1908 Voltamp also offered sectional track mounted on a firm wood base. Carlisle & Finch's failure to keep pace with its competitors in this critical area likely contributed to a loss of market share and eventually to its withdrawal from the toy market.

A satisfactory electrical power source was a serious problem for the operators of the products of Carlisle & Finch and other early electric train manufacturers. Many homes did not have electricity, and anyway there was initially no satisfactory means of reducing the voltage to a level usable for toy trains even when main service was available.

Chapter Eight lists the solutions sought for this problem. Initially, glass jar batteries using zinc and carbon electrodes and a chromite solution were recommended by Carlisle & Finch despite the menace to carpets and floors. Hand- and water-powered dynamos were also listed. Later on, dry cells were the only type of batteries recommended. Even after 1908, when a primitive cylindrically shaped transformer with a wooden handle and five stepped taps giving 10 to 15 volts was listed, the principal power source

recommended by Carlisle & Finch for their trains continued to be multiple dry cells. Once again, this seems to be an odd lack of "imagineering" on the part of Carlisle & Finch! Both Lionel and Voltamp emphasized superior and more convenient transformers as part of their product line, and development in this area gave these companies a significant advantage as more and more homes were electrified.

RETAIL PRICES

Carlisle & Finch's retail prices were remarkably steady over their entire twenty-year history, from 1896 through 1915. Their initial and cheapest trolley (without track or battery) started at $2.75 in 1897 and was reduced in 1902 to $2.25 until discontinued after 1907. Their most popular item — the No. 4 0-4-0 road locomotive — started in 1899 at $6.50 for the engine and tender only, and this price was never changed through the last catalogue in 1915, in spite of significant improvements in the locomotive itself.

Similarly, Carlisle & Finch's top-of-the-line deluxe Atlantic-type 4-4-2 locomotive No. 45 started in 1903 at $22 ($25 including track and batteries); this price was continued through 1909 and then reduced to $17 in 1911 and 1912 and to $13.50 in 1913 through 1915. These last price reductions were undoubtedly forced by increased competition and made possible by the substantial downgrading of this engine in 1909 and thereafter, with resulting lower manufacturing costs.

END OF PRODUCTION

Carlisle & Finch offered its largest variety of equipment from 1905 to 1908. Prior to that time, it had faced modest competition in the electric train and trolley field from Lionel 2⅞-inch gauge, from Knapp and Howard 2-inch gauge, and from European imports, but it held a clear lead over all of these. The rapid growth in the second half of the decade by the Lionel "Standard Gauge" and the Voltamp 2-inch-gauge lines, with their superior sectional track and transformers, plainly presented a much more serious challenge. This obviously put pressure on Carlisle & Finch's relatively stable prices, and this in turn required cost reductions. This became very apparent in 1909 and subsequent years.

First of all, a number of previously popular items were dropped, including the largest and most expensive 19-inch passenger cars No. 51 and 52 in 1909, the beautiful but costly No. 19 open trolley in 1911, and the fine but less complex No. 18 closed trolley in 1913. In this connection, it is interesting to note that Lionel's Standard Gauge line started in 1906 with three trolleys and two locomotives. By 1912, as the production of Carlisle & Finch electrical trains seemed to be winding down, the Lionel line had expanded to include nine trolley models, including one interurban and eight steam outline and electric-type locomotives.

Several remaining items were simplified to reduce manufacturing costs. This cheapening process, so familiar to collectors, was especially noticeable in the changes made in 1909 and later years. In 1909 these included the significant redesign and downgrading of the top-of-the-line No. 45 locomotive, as well as the early 19-inch-long No. 2 Interurban of 1903, and the substitution of a smaller and simplified No.

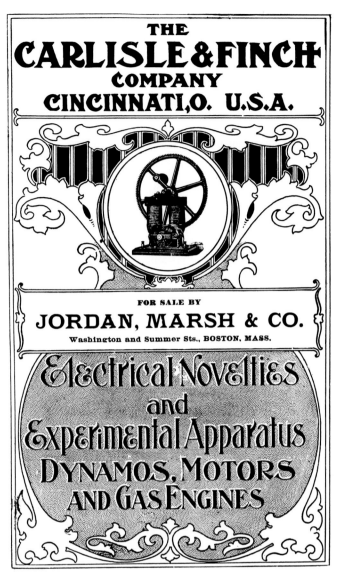

A 1900 catalogue for a dealer, before trains were featured on the covers, and the artistic back cover of the last catalogues, right

9 station. In 1911 the size of the handsome early Nos. 90, 91, and 92 freight cars was reduced, and in 1911 or 1912 the elegant early No. 42 single-truck 1902 trolley was replaced by a queer-looking substitute apparently put together from spare pieces of other cars.

In spite of the difficulties caused by competition in the electric train field, Carlisle & Finch would undoubtedly have continued in this business had it not been for the outbreak of war in Europe in 1914.

In 1915 Carlisle & Finch published its last toy train catalogue. The entire trolley and train line was discontinued the following year. The demand for Carlisle & Finch searchlights and other marine electrical products was growing enormously, and as American industry geared up for wartime production, toy train manufacturing gave way. According to Brent R. Finch, grandson of co-founder Robert S. Finch, just as the automobile companies received government contracts for engines for military vehicles, Carlisle & Finch was awarded contracts for marine

searchlights and similar products for the navy and merchant marine.

Finch said that after the war the company felt it was more practical to concentrate in the searchlight production field. It also occurred to him that the image of a firm that made toys might not be attractive when soliciting government contracts in the future!

Carlisle sold his share in the company to the Finch family on August 3, 1926. Brent S. Finch succeeded his father as company president at that time, and was followed by his son Brent R. Finch on March 11, 1966. Company founder Robert Finch died at age ninety-five on January 23, 1963.

With the cessation of train production, marine equipment became Carlisle & Finch's sole business. About 1934, however, several prototype models for a new line of toy trains were made at the factory. Each surviving prototype is unique. The whereabouts of a streamliner engine that was part of this collection is unknown. The story of this period is told in Chapter Ten.

By way of a footnote: In 1950 Carlisle & Finch moved to its present location of 4562 West Mitchell Avenue, Cincinnati. According to Brent R. Finch there were barrels of old toy train parts still in the old factory at the time of the move. These were to be transferred to the new location, but a fire destroyed the old factory building and its remaining contents. (The location of the old factory is now an urban playground.) All the toy train material was lost. Fortunately, some of the records of the old company were moved to the new location before the fire occurred, and Frank Loveland has been working with these records to provide a summary of the early operations of the company. Samples of the documents examined by Frank Loveland appear in Chapters Nine and Ten.

Carlisle & Finch continues to manufacture marine searchlights, navigational lights, and floodlights, and its customers include the U.S. Navy and Coast Guard. Carlisle & Finch–made equipment is found in such varied locations as aircraft carriers, submarines, tugboats, and lighthouses. Those who have occasion to ride on the Mississippi River cruise ship Delta Queen will find Carlisle & Finch arc searchlights, dating from the middle 1920s, on the wings of the bridge of this famous stern wheeler. While this is impressive, for collectors the Carlisle & Finch name will always symbolize important contributions to early American toy train production.

NOTES

1. The early history of this firm has been set out in detail in excellent articles in the *Train Collectors Quarterly* by Franklin Loveland and others, including Brent R. Finch, grandson of one of the founders and current president of the company. See TCA *Quarterly*, Spring 1980, pp. 4–6; Fall 1980, pp. 28–29; October 1982, pp. 10–16.

2. This was the largest mass-produced electrically powered model offered at this time. Voltamp built an 18½-inch model in 1909 while Lionel did not offer a 20½-inch car until 1910.

3. The author has also set up a fairly extensive train and trolley layout in his home from time to time. These operations were described in the January 1986 issue of the TCA *Quarterly*, Vol. 32, no. 1, p. 4, and have been filmed on video cassette, a copy of which is on loan to the TCA Toy Train Museum in Strasburg, Pennsylvania.

CHAPTER TWO

★

TROLLEYS, TRAILERS, AND INTERURBANS

Since Carlisle & Finch's toy train production was largely concentrated on trolleys and their trailers for the first three years of their entry into this business, it seems appropriate to begin detailed examination of their production with this category.

When Carlisle & Finch started in the toy electric train business in the late 1890s the electric trolley or streetcar was spreading into cities and towns all over the country. As such, it made a very popular toy. As noted in Chapter One, Carlisle & Finch soon offered trolley cars that were larger and more sophisticated than the rudimentary little cars with which they got started.

OVERHEAD WIRE TROLLEY OPERATION

Carlisle & Finch was the first successful American manufacturer to offer streetcars actually powered by overhead wires through a swiveling trolley pole on the roof of the car. The car body was insulated from the truck frame so that the current cannot flow from car body to truck to track but travels along the wire to the reversing switch and armature. Prototype practice was accurately followed; a small grooved wheel at the top of this pole contacted the overhead wire. This development occurred in 1905 when the beautiful closed and open trolleys Nos. 18 and 19 were wired for operation under live overhead trolley wire and recatalogued as Nos. 99 and 100. Cast-iron lineside poles to support the trolley wire were listed at the same time. (Further details are given later in this chapter.)

Since prototype streetcars and interurbans in most cities operated these true "trolleys under wire," these were far more attractive and realistic than cars that took their current only through the track (see catalogue illustration). While these were the only Carlisle & Finch cars actually catalogued for operation under wire, Carlisle & Finch's fascinating little book *Miniature Electric Railway Construction* explained in detail how any of their streetcars could be converted to operate with trolley-wire feed. I have made such a modification on a 1904 model of the No. 2 interurban with very satisfactory results; however, to have

the flexibility to operate the car from either track power or overhead wire power, I added a small single-pole double-throw switch under the car to provide electrical feed from either source (see photographs in Chapter Seven).

While Carlisle & Finch was first in successfully marketing streetcars designed to operate under wire, they were not alone in this. Voltamp Electric Manufacturing Co. of Baltimore also offered a number of trolleys and interurbans designed to operate under live overhead wire in the 1909–1915 period. While Voltamp plainly copied closely the Carlisle & Finch systems, it is clear from differences in the filigree work on their lineside poles that they did not merely purchase their poles or other equipment from Carlisle & Finch.

Although Voltamp was the only other 2-inch-gauge manufacturer to offer an overhead trolley wire system, there were several others who made and sold similar arrangements. Around 1905 Georges Carette & Co. of Nuremburg sold a handsome electric I Gauge trolley car with trailer, powered by an overhead trolley arrangement. Ten years earlier Garlick of Paterson, New Jersey, had used the overhead trolley system for his unsuccessful electric tunnel engine (as described in Chapter One). Finally, around 1910, Ives produced for a short time both clockwork and electric O Gauge streetcars with working trolley poles under overhead wires.[1]

Probably because of disappointing sales, Carlisle & Finch discontinued its overhead wire system after 1907, just before Voltamp picked it up. Voltamp in turn gave up its overhead system after its catalogue No. 4, around 1913–1915. In spite of its attractive realism, an overhead trolley arrangement for toy trains probably presented too many complications to the customer to become a commercial success.

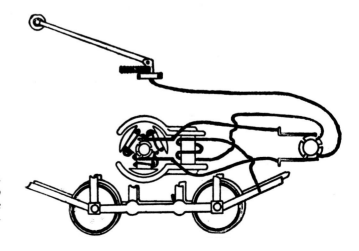

Carlisle & Finch catalogue text accompanying the illustration reproduced here indicates that the trolley pole is shown connected to the reversing switch by means of a separate wire; in actual practice this wire may be dispensed with and may only run from the reversing switch to the car body.

COMPLETE ELECTRIC RAILWAY, $3.00

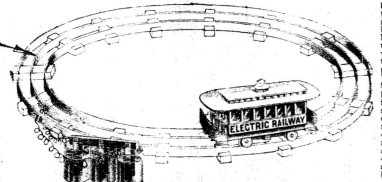

ELECTRIC RAILWAY, circular track 3 feet in diameter, 2-in. gauge. Car made of polished brass, 7 inches long, 4 inches high. Runs 150 feet per minute. Illustrates the practical working of the modern trolley car. Entire outfit packed in strong wooden box. Weight, ready for shipment, 5 lbs.

HAND-POWER DYNAMO. This is a powerful dynamo designed to give the greatest output with least weight of metal. It generates direct current, 10 volts, 2 amperes or more according to the power applied. Will run all kinds of electrical toys, charge storage batteries, etc. Weight in box, 16 lbs. Height 12 inches.

HAND - POWER DYNAMO,
Price, $6.50.

THE CARLISLE & FINCH CO.,

AGENTS WANTED.
830 W. 6th Street,
CINCINNATI, OHIO.

No. 100. Trolley Railway (Summer Car)

PRICE, $11.25.

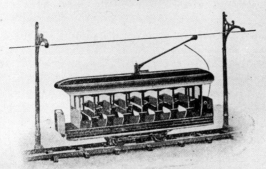

This railway has the same motor car as our No. 19 with the addition of the trolley. The reversing switch, trolley pole, and track are the same as with railway No. 99 shown previously.

The outfit consists of motor car, 18 feet of track and ties, 12 bracket poles and clamping ears, 18 feet of trolley wire and 5 batteries.

Length of car, 13½ inches. Height above rails, 6 inches. Width, 3½ inches.

Weight, boxed, 30 lbs.

Price of car and trolley only, $6.25.

Price of trolley pole and stand, 75 cents.

Diagram of Track and Poles for Railways Nos. 101 and 102.

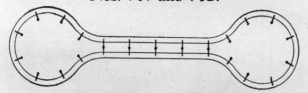

Book on Electric Railway Construction, Price $1 00. See page 76.

No. 61. Outfit.
PRICE, $10.30.

This railway is similar to the two last described but is more complete. It has a trail car and larger track in addition. The equipment consists of the following:

1 No. 1 Motor Car.　　　1 No. 9 Station.
1 No. 1 Trail Car.　　　　1 No. 43 Loop.
6 Dry Batteries.　Weight, boxed, 25 lbs.

No. 62. Outfit.
PRICE, $10.80.

Same as the No. 61 outfit, except that a No. 1-R Motor Car is furnished in place of the No. 1. Otherwise it is the same.

Weight, boxed, 25 lbs.

No. 63. Outfit.
PRICE, $13.55.

An Interurban Railway with track, station, crossing, switches and batteries. Everything furnished necessary for its perfect operation. Equipment consists of the following:

1 No. 2 Motor Car.　　　　1 No. 43 Loop and track.
1 No. 9 Station.　　　　　 7 Dry Batteries.
Weight, boxed, 26 lbs.

Book on Electric Railway Construction, Price $1 00. See page, 76.

Gd   **Exc**

DETAILED LISTINGS

We now turn to a detailed description of Carlisle & Finch's trolley and interurban cars and supporting equipment. The cars are categorized into four- and eight-wheel types.

As explained more fully in Chapter One, the first Carlisle & Finch toy train was a 2-inch-gauge trolley designed for inside third-rail operation. There is no formal listing of it since no 1896 Carlisle & Finch catalogue and no example of this three-rail trolley have been found, but there is no doubt that they were produced and sold. Several magazine advertisements, including the June 1897 sample reproduced here, clearly show a strip-steel three-rail circle of track and a fancifully drawn four-wheel trolley. Other contemporary advertisements described the three-rail car as having a brass body 7 inches long and 4 inches high. The body was probably similar to that of the early four-wheel two-rail trolley described below.

Note: After most Carlisle & Finch listings you will see a range of estimated values, which reflects the market report compiled by Nicholas B. Ladd, as explained in the Introduction to this volume and the Preface. Usually there is only one set of values for each type of car; some variations may be higher or lower.

Four-wheel cars

No. 1 FOUR-WHEEL TROLLEY (TWO-RAIL), 1897-1907: Four-wheel open platform motorized trolley, 7" long, 4½" high, 2¾" wide; a polished brass body with four cutout arched windows and wooden frame; 1"-diameter red cast-iron wheels are on split insulated axles. A two-pole motor is located inside the body on top of the wooden base or floor, with pulley wheel and belt drive to one pair of iron wheels. Roof has no vents (although these erroneously appear in the 1897 and later catalogue illustrations).

400 – 1000

(A) 1897-98. All-polished-brass body, roof, platforms, and platform ends; smooth uncorrugated body sides and ends; paper label "ELECTRIC RAILWAY" below windows in large block letters. Ward Kimball Collection.

(B) 1899-1901(?). Same as above, except that label below windows is smaller and better-known yellow and black; "ELECTRIC RAILWAY" paper label.

Note: We know from the 1899 catalogue illustration of No. 13 passenger coach that this label was in use by that time.

(C) 1902(?)-03. Same as above, but with three corrugated lines or ridges embossed on sides and ends of body. Date of this change is either 1901 or 1902.

(D) 1904-07. Same as above, but no paper label; "ELECTRIC RAILWAY" is embossed in large letters below windows. The roof, platforms, and platform ends are now of tinplated sheet steel instead of brass and are painted black.

No. 1 FOUR-WHEEL UNPOWERED TRAILER CAR, 1897-1907: The wheels are affixed to pieces of wood below the wood frame by nails instead of axles; except this, the car is similar to the two-rail No. 1 trolley, with generally the same variations as listed above.

Gd   **Exc**

No. 1-R FOUR-WHEEL TROLLEY WITH REVERSING MOTOR, 1899-1906: Similar to two-rail motorized No. 1 trolley, but is powered by a three-pole "self-starting" motor, with reverse lever located in center of front platform. Its variations are similar to those of No. 1 trolley. Discontinued after 1906; relatively few of these have survived.

600 – 1200

1902 No. 42 EARLY FOUR-WHEEL TROLLEY, 1902-09: Single-truck trolley, 8" long, 5" high, 2⅜" wide; polished brass body with five cutout arched windows on each side and three corrugations on sides and ends; tinplate roof is black and open platforms at each end have black single steps and black platform ends. A three-pole reversing motor powers one pair of wheels on split insulated axles through spur gears, the motor being mounted inside the body, with a partial wood floor only at the two ends; reversing lever is located on forward platform.

(A) 1902. Initial version; has the usual yellow and black paper label "ELECTRIC RAILWAY" below windows on each side; black cast-iron truck side frames attached to the end pieces of wood floor; red cast-iron wheels 1" in diameter on split insulated axles.

(B) 1903. Same as above, but with newly designed handsome cast-brass truck side frames similarly attached to the end pieces of floor; unpainted 1¼" brass wheels. This car is well proportioned and quite handsome.

(C) 1904-09. Same as above, but with no paper label; "ELECTRIC RAILWAY" is embossed below windows on each side.

No. 42 UNPOWERED FOUR-WHEEL TROLLEY TRAILER, 1902-09: Similar to No. 42 in this period, including side frames and 1¼" brass wheels on split insulated axles, but without motor. It had the same variations as those listed above. Not listed after 1909 catalogue.

350 – 900

1909 No. 42 LATE FOUR-WHEEL TROLLEY, 1911(?)-15: Although the catalogue illustration and description remains unchanged from the 1902 model, in the later years this car is quite different in many particulars. It has four instead of five arched windows, and these have embossed window frames with "ELECTRIC RAILWAY" embossed below the windows. Instead of cast-brass side frames and a large motor inside the body, the car's wood floor is mounted on a stamped-steel four-wheel truck with 1¼" pressed-brass wheels insulated from solid steel axles. The truck is powered by a small motor inside the truck itself which is geared to only one axle; truck identical to those on late 1909 No. 2 interurban (see below) and the late eight-wheel passenger and freight cars described in Chapters Five and Six.

Note: This car is simply ugly: although the overall dimensions are substantially unchanged from the 1902 model, the use of the four-wheel steel truck under the wood floor results in raising the body about ½", and this, with the absence of full-length cast-brass side frames, distorts the car's proportions and makes it appear too short and too high. It is impossible to ascertain from the catalogue the precise date of this change. Since this was plainly a cost-reduction measure, it obviously took place at or shortly after 1909. Since 1911 was the first year in which no No. 42 unpowered

Top left: No. 1 trolley, 1899–1901, smooth side, yellow paper label; two-pole motor with belt or rubber band drive. Right: Same as left but with corrugated sides, probably 1902–1903. Bottom: No. 1 trolley, 1904–1907, with embossed side, and matching unpowered trailer car of same period.

Top left: No. 18 closed four-wheel trolley without trolley pole, 1904–1915. Top right: No. 19, open or summer trolley of the same size, 1904–1911. Bottom left: No. 99, 1905–1907, same as car directly above but with trolley pole wired to motor car for operation under overhead trolley wire. Bottom right: No. 100 summer car, same as car directly above but again with trolley pole for operation under overhead wire. Carlisle & Finch produced the first lineside trolley poles starting in 1905 and discontinued these after about 1907. Voltamp, which did not start producing trains until about 1908, made cast-iron lineside and trolley poles that resembled Carlisle & Finch's but were not made from the same mold. The trolley poles on the cars shown are Voltamp poles, because the original C & F poles were missing.

Top left: The first model of the No. 42, 1902 only, with cast-iron frame on bottom and cast-iron wheel. Right: The improved car, 1903 only, with brass underframe, brass wheels, and same paper label, "ELECTRIC RAILWAY", under window, missing here. Bottom left: Same car, 1904–1911, but with embossed name. Right: 1912–1915 car with only four windows and steel-sided truck mounted under the floor.

Top left: No. 2 double-truck motorized trolley, 1897–1901, smooth sides, rounded-end roof, paper label; has twin two-pole motors, one in each truck and is thus usually self-starting. Top right: The same car, believed to be introduced in 1902, possibly 1901, with corrugated sides and square-end clerestory on roof (the paper label "ELECTRIC RAILWAY" is missing); it has two trucks, one powered (and with a three-pole self-starting motor) and one not. Bottom: This large brass-body interurban No. 2 was introduced in 1903 and replaced the earlier trolleys shown above. The two trucks have handsome cast-brass side frames. The motor is contained within the forward truck and drives all four wheels through spur gears. See photograph on page 30 for later No. 2s.

Gd   Exc

trail car was listed, this seems the most probable year when the hybrid car was substituted for the 1902 No. 42.

600 – 1000

No. 18 LARGE FOUR-WHEEL TROLLEY, 1904-13: Attractive single-truck motorized trolley, 13½" long, 6" high, 3½" wide; polished brass body; brass platforms and platform ends and brass roof painted black. The sides are gracefully curved top to bottom; each side has four 2"-wide stamped arched windows with embossed window frames; two corrugations along sides and "ELECTRIC RAILWAY" embossed under windows; sheet-metal bench seats along each side below windows; handsome cast-brass truck side frames. A three-pole reversing motor is located beneath the wooden floor; early model motors had solid cast-iron field magnets but after 1909 these were laminated to improve their magnetic field; motor connected by brass spur gears to one pair of unpainted pressed-brass 1¼" wheels, on the usual split and insulated axles; reverse lever is in form of a motorman's controller on front platform.

Note: One of these cars has been reported with a nickel finish, but none was so listed in any catalogue. No other variations have been verified.   **1200 – 2000**

No. 99 FOUR-WHEEL TROLLEY WITH OVERHEAD TROLLEY POLE, 1905-07: Same as No. 18, but with a car-top trolley pole that swivels (see illustration earlier in this chapter), wired to motor for operation under overhead trolley wire. For those who wished to add them, trolley poles were listed in the catalogue for 75 cents each.   **1200 – 2000**

No. 19 LARGE FOUR-WHEEL SUMMER TROLLEY, 1904-11: Handsome single-truck open or summer motorized trolley, 13½" long, 6" wide, 3½" wide; polished sheet-brass roof and platform ends; body, steps, and seven reversible bench seats of tinplated sheet steel painted yellow and orange with black trim; cast-brass truck side frames are fastened to wood floor. Reversible motor similar to that in No. 18 located beneath wooden floor, connected by spur gears to one pair of 1¼" pressed-brass wheels on split insulated axles. Reverse lever in form of motorman's controller is on front platform. No significant variations have been found.

1200 – 2000

No. 100 FOUR-WHEEL SUMMER TROLLEY WITH OVERHEAD TROLLEY POLE, 1905-07: Same as No. 19, but with car-top trolley pole wired to motor for operation under overhead trolley wire.   **1500 – 2400**

Eight-Wheel Cars

No. 2 EIGHT-WHEEL TROLLEY, 1897-1902: Two-truck open-platform motorized trolley, 12" long, 5" high, 3⅛" wide, in several configurations as noted below.

Note: A catalogue illustration shows car with braces from the four platform corners to the roof. Whether any car produced by Carlisle & Finch ever looked like this is doubtful; no example with this corner post configuration has been found.   **1000 – 1500**

(A) 1897-1901. Cars from this period that have been examined have sheet-brass bodies with smooth sides, brass roof, open platforms without roof braces, and no floor of any kind. The brass clerestory "railroad" roofs have rounded

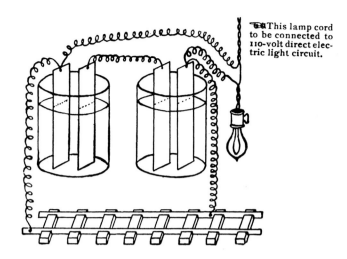

This lamp cord to be connected to 110-volt direct electric light circuit.

Gd   Exc

ends. A yellow-and-black paper label "Electric Railway" is under the seven cutout arched windows on each side. Prior to the 1899 model, these cars may have had a label in block capital letters as noted in No. 1 (A) above, but no examples have been found. Each of the car's two brass-framed trucks has four 1" cast-iron wheels on split insulated axles and a two-pole motor with belt and pulley-wheel drive to one pair of wheels. In 1897 a modification of this car was listed as catalogue item **No. 2-S** for operation on 110-volt direct or alternating current, primarily for show-window display. In 1898 this was corrected to limit the 110-volt operation to direct current only. In 1899 and thereafter, car No. 2-S was omitted altogether, with the explanation that any No. 2 car as well as other Carlisle & Finch equipment could be operated on 110-volt direct current by using the incandescent electric light and lead-acid battery arrangement shown in the 1897 catalogue and reproduced here. (This type of power source is discussed further in Chapter Eight.)

(B) Ca. 1901-02. Squared-off roof ends; three corrugations on body sides and ends. One production version of this car has a single two-pole motor in each brass-frame truck, and has been found both with and without a wooden floor. A second version has a single three-pole motor in one wood-frame truck. The latter car also has link and pin couplers on each end. There was never any mention in the catalogues of any of these changes.

Note: The 12"-long No. 2 trolley was discontinued in all versions after 1902.

No. 2 EIGHT-WHEEL UNPOWERED TRAIL CAR, 1897-1902: Wheels are attached to swiveling wooden bolsters at each end by nails serving as axles; except for this, similar to No. 2 eight-wheel trolley, with same variations as listed above. Almost identical with No. 13 passenger car (described in Chapter Four).   **600 – 900**

1903 No. 2 EARLY LARGE EIGHT-WHEEL INTERURBAN CAR, 1903-08: Billed as "entirely new in all respects," it nevertheless carries the same No. 2 catalogue number as the earlier eight-wheel trolley. 19" long, 6" high above rails, 4" wide; wooden floor and open platforms without roof braces; ten arched windows punched out on each side; three corrugated lines embossed on both sides and ends; platform doors cut out at ends. 1¼" pressed-brass wheels on split insulated axles are mounted on trucks with wooden

Gd   Exc

bolsters and handsome cast-brass truck side frames. A newly designed three-pole motor in the forward truck is geared to drive all four wheels of that truck, a major improvement in both acceleration and steady operation. The reversing lever is in the form of a motorman's controller on the forward platform. No couplers.

Note: Carlisle & Finch's largest powered car.   **1100 – 1800**

(A) 1903. Body, roof, open platforms, platform ends of polished sheet brass; brass wheels painted red; light yellow paper label 8½" long with "INTERURBAN RAILWAY" in black letters attached below the windows on each side.

(B) 1904-06. Same as above, with generally similar but improved gear drive between motor and wheels of forward truck; all brass wheels now unpainted; "ELECTRIC RAILWAY" embossed in large letters below windows.

(C) 1907-08. Same as above, but body, roof, and platform ends are described in catalogue as "nickel plated." All examples examined are formed from sheet zinc with a nickel finish. Windows of 1907 model continue to be plain stampings, but windows on 1908 model have embossed window frames.

Note: Several unpowered interurban trailer cars have been found, but none was ever catalogued by Carlisle & Finch. It seems likely that these cars were originally sold as power cars but were converted to trailers when their motors broke down. With the addition of some coupling device, these cars can be used as additional large coaches behind the No. 45 locomotive.

1909 No. 2 LATE LARGE EIGHT-WHEEL INTERURBAN, 1909-15: Same size and carries same catalogue number as the 1903 interurban, but it is a very different car in most respects. 19"-long sheet-brass body; five 2"-wide arched stamped windows on each side and round portholes with embossed edges at the end of each side as well as on either side of the end doors. Two corrugations run along the sides and across the end panels; tinplate roof, platforms, platform ends painted black; car body similar to but slightly larger than Pullman parlor car No. 87 of 1905-06 (described in Chapter Five). This interurban has the later type stamped-steel side-frame trucks, with insulated pressed-brass 1¼" wheels on solid steel axles. A much smaller motor than used in the 1903 interurban is mounted in the forward truck and drives only one pair of wheels.

Note: The small motor, single-axle drive, and steel truck frames represent a substantial downgrade from the handsome 1903 interurban. No subsequent variations in this car have been identified.   **1100 – 1800**

Related Equipment

No. 54 SUPPORT PIERS FOR ELEVATED RAILWAY, 1905-08: Cast-iron, each 10" high with cross tie for strip steel track attached to top.

No. 98 ELEVATED RAILWAY, 1905-08: Motorized single-truck trolley car No. 42 (described above) operating on a 3-foot circle of strip steel track supported by ten cast-iron support piers, 10" high. Very rare.

No. 103 LINESIDE TROLLEY WIRE POLES, 1905-07: Cast-iron single- and double-track wire lineside poles,

No. 54. Elevated Railway Posts.

PRICE, each, 30 cts.

These posts or columns are intended to support the track so as to make an "Elevated Railway." They are of cast iron and are very ornamental. Each one has a cross tie attached to it, ready to receive the track. Price does not include any track
Height, 10 inches.
Weight, each, 1 lb.

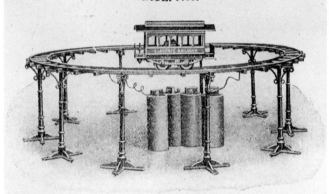

No. 53. Electric Elevated Railway.

PRICE, 7.60.

This is a very ornamental and practical railway. The track is supported on ten elevated posts and arranged in a three-foot circle. The car is our regular No. 42 motor car.
4 Dry Batteries make up the equipment.
We can highly recommend this railway.
Weight, boxed, 27 lbs.

No. 103. Bracket Poles for Trolley Wire.

Single Pole.   Double Pole.

Made of cast iron with brass "ears" for holding the trolley wire. Drilled, finished and painted.
Price, single poles, 30 cents each.   Price, double poles, 50 cents each.

Top: No. 2 interurban with brass body, 1904–1906. The body now has embossed "ELECTRIC RAIL-WAY" under the windows rather than having "INTERURBAN RAILWAY" printed on a paper label. This is the unit the author equipped with Voltamp trolley poles for operation since he could not find any original C & F poles. Middle: 1907–1908, exactly the same as above but finished in polished nickel plate and without overhead trolley. It is actually polished tinplated steel that is lacquered. Bottom: This 1909–1915 car shows major changes in design, with five large windows rather than ten smaller windows. A major change in trucks and motor, with new cheaper steel side-frame truck motor geared to only one pair of wheels rather than four, was part of C & F's drive to economize.

designed to support trolley wire as used for trolley cars Nos. 99 and 100, described above. Painted orange or black.

NOTE

1. Neither Carlisle & Finch nor any other known manufacturer made or even suggested a "wire frog" to enable a trolley operating under wire to negotiate a switch. It is not difficult to make one from a small piece of sheet brass or tinplate that will permit the trolley wheel to follow the wire as it divides above a right- or left-hand switch. The author has successfully operated both Carlisle & Finch and Voltamp trolleys through switches with such an arrangement.

CHAPTER THREE

★

COAL MINING LOCOMOTIVES AND CARS

The first locomotive made by Carlisle & Finch was a coal mining engine designed to pull very small cast-iron and wood four-wheel coal cars. A reason for choosing this type of engine for the start of their locomotive line may well have been the importance of coal at this time as the primary source of energy for industry, transportation on land and sea, and early electric power generation. On the other hand, more pragmatically, the choice may have been dictated by the fact that, like their four-wheel trolley, the mining engine was cheap and easy to manufacture.

LOCOMOTIVES

1897 No. 3 COAL MINING LOCOMOTIVE, 1897-98: 0-4-0; this first and very rare coal mining locomotive has body

of sheet-brass or tinplate, 6" long, 3" wide, 3½" high, covered with paper, lettering "ELECTRIC / COAL MINING LOCOMOTIVE" on both sides; link and pin couplers are fitted; three-pole reversing motor, reversing lever above body. One pair of 1" red-painted cast-iron wheels on split insulated axles, driven by an unusual double-reduction belt and pulley wheel drive system that gives the engine less speed but more power than the No. 1 trolley of the same period.   **400 – 750**

1899 No. 3 COAL MINING LOCOMOTIVE, 1899-1915: A significant improvement over the first 1897-98 model; longer (7") and more rugged looking. The three-pole reversing motor is connected by means of brass spur gears to one pair of 2" red-painted seven-spoked driving wheels on split insulated axles; all-wheel drive is achieved by brass side rods.

300 – 500

(A) 1899-1902. Body is covered with yellow paper; "ELECTRIC COAL MINING LOCOMOTIVE" printed in black letters on both sides; link and pin couplers attached on both ends.

(B) 1903(?)-04. Same as above, but with bumper band couplers (bottom of coupler ¾" above rail). Copy on yellow paper label shortened to "COAL MINING LOCOMOTIVE".

(C) 1905-07. Same as above, but body is now enameled in a solid color (red, yellow, orange, or green) with "MINING LOCOMOTIVE" embossed into sides of sheet-metal body.

No. 17.   Coal Mining Locomotive and Dump Cars.

PRICE, $6.25.

5 to 6 VOLTS.   ¾ AMPERE.

This equipment is the same as No. 3, but dump cars are substituted for the coal cars.

These cars are made so that they will stand upright and may be filled with sand, gravel, etc.

Each car can be dumped as desired. This train will be found of the greatest interest and will be a never failing source of pleasure and amusement.

Complete equipment consists of locomotive, three dump cars, 18 feet of 2 inch gauge track and four dry batteries.

Cars are made of cast iron, have wooden bottoms and cast iron wheels. Are very durable.

Locomotive is the same as the No. 3 locomotive.

Length of train, 20 inches.

Weight complete, boxed, 13½ lbs.

Locomotive Only, $3.50 each.

Dump cars, 40 cents each.   By mail, 50 cents.

Track and Ties in 9 ft. lengths, 35 cents.

Extra dry batteries, per cell, 25 cents.

Examine the 1906 catalogue and that from 1911, and notice the higher bumper bands that developed in 1908.

No. 17.   Coal Mining Locomotive and Dump Cars.

PRICE, $6.25.

5 to 6 VOLTS.   ¾ AMPERE.

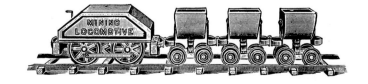

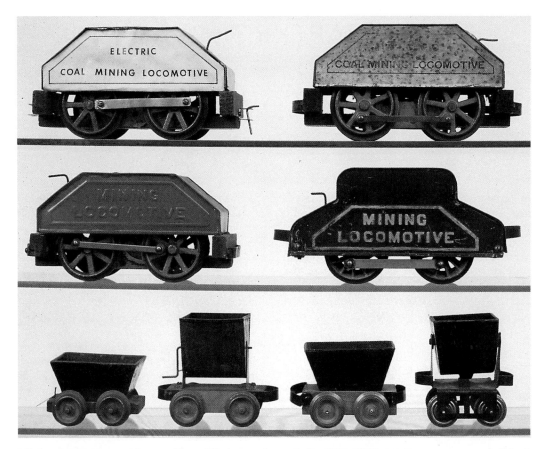

Mining locomotives and cars. Top: Mining engines. Left: 1899–1902, totally paper covered, 2-inch driving wheels, spur gears, link and pin couplers. Right: Bumper band couplers instead of link and pin couplers, condensed wording of label. Middle left: Same as above but without paper label and with side embossed lettering. Middle right: Locomotive shape significantly changed in the 1911–1915 version, with twelve-spoke driving wheels instead of seven, and with bumper band couplers significantly higher than previously. Bottom left: Fixed-bucket, four-wheel cast-iron coal car with wooden base and iron wheels, 1897–1903; coupling system consists of small nails in end of wooden floor and connected with loop of wire. Second: 1904 dump car with tinplate body and bumper band couplers, ¾ inch above rails, matching locomotive bumper band couplers. Third: 1905–1915, similar but with cast-iron body, brass wheels, and black outside frame; bumper couplers 1¼ inches above rail to match later mining locomotives. Fourth: Cast-iron fixed bucket, wooden floor, bumper band couplers ¾ inch above rail, 1904–1908.

Gd   Exc

(D) 1908-09. Same as above, but in this period the bumper band couplers are raised from ¾" above rail to 1¼" above rail. This change is shown by a comparison of the catalogue illustrations for the mining set No. 17 in the 1907 and in the 1908 catalogues. Height of couplers on this version of the coal mining locomotive matches those of coal cars of same period and those of the No. 4 locomotive and its cars, but will not mate with couplers of earlier mining engines or cars.

(E) 1911-15. Same as above, with approximately same dimensions, but shape of locomotive body is significantly changed, having rounded contours. The 2" red driving wheels now have twelve spokes instead of seven. The bumper band couplers are 1¼" above the rail. One example of this locomotive has been found in green with the embossed lettering painted orange on one side, but unpainted on the other side. Dark green is the most typical color for these "hump-type" locomotives.

COAL MINING CARS

No. 3 FIXED BUCKET COAL MINING CARS, 1897–1915:
Four-wheel cast-iron body cars, issued in various sizes from time to time. The earlier cars have wooden and the later cars have metal frames. There were several versions.   **75 – 125**
(A) 1897-1903. Cast-iron body 3" long, 2" wide, 1½" high, has sloping ends connected by iron strap at bottom, fastened to wooden base about 3¼" long, 1⅝" wide; red-painted 1" cast-iron wheels nailed into wooden base or frame. At some point, the cast-iron strap joining the ends was omitted and instead small cast-iron projections at inside bottom edge of ends were used to fasten body to wooden base. Cars are coupled by using links to small nails in ends of wooden base.
(B) 1904-07. Same as above, but with bumper band couplers, ¾" above rail.
(C) 1908. Same as above, but bumper band couplers are raised so that their lower edges are 1¼" instead of ¾" above

Gd Exc

the rail, to match No. 4 locomotive and its cars and mining locomotives of this period.

(D) 1909-15. Same, but cars have insulated ⅞" diameter brass wheels insulated from solid axles, and black-painted steel truck side frames attached to black-painted metal frame. Bumper band couplers are 1¼" above rail.

No. 17 SIDE-DUMPING COAL MINING CARS, 1904-15:
These first appeared in the 1904 catalogue and thereafter were produced in several variations: **85 – 125**

(A) 1904. Side-dump body, rounded bottom, made of tinplated sheet steel; 2¼" long, 3¼" wide, and 2½" high above base. Sheet-brass plates are fastened to sides of base to support split insulated axles and red-painted 1"-diameter cast-iron wheels. Car has bumper band couplers with lower edges ¾" above rail.

(B) 1905-07. Cast-iron side-dump body approximately 2½" long, 2⅛" wide, and 2¼" high, on wooden frame with red-painted 1" cast-iron wheels attached with nails as axles. Bumper band couplers ¾" above rail.

(C) 1908. Same as above, but bumper band couplers have been raised so that their lower edges are now 1¼" above rail to match the mine locomotives being produced at this time.

(D) 1909-15. Same as above, but with metal instead of wooden frame. Insulated ⅞"-diameter brass wheels are set on solid steel axles and black-painted steel truck side frames are attached to black metal frame.

No. 3. Coal Mining Locomotive and Train.

PRICE, $5.75.

5 to 6 VOLTS.   **¾ AMPERE.**

This represents a modern hauling plant as used in our large coal mines. The motor is self-starting, and on top of locomotive is a lever connecting with a reversing switch, by means of which the train may be run backward or forward.

Connection is made from the motor to the wheels by means of double reduction spur gearing with accurately cut teeth. The wheels are spoked, two inches in diameter, and made of iron.

The locomotive is very powerful. It will climb grades and haul the three cars heavily loaded. It will haul 10 to 12 empty cars on a straight, level track. The speed is somewhat less than that of the railways Nos. 1 and 2.

The equipment consists of locomotive, three coal cars, 18 feet of 2 inch gauge track, and four dry batteries,.

Coal cars are iron, with iron wheels. They will stand hard usage.

The track may be arranged in any shape. It is better to see that it is level, as the locomotive will run easier and be easier on the battery when track is in this condition. Oil all moving parts of locomotive and train frequently.

Length of train, 18 inches.

Weight, complete, boxed, 13½ pounds.

Coal cars, 25 cents each.   By mail, 35 cents.

Track and Ties in 9 ft. lengths, 35 cents.   By mail, 50 cents.

Extra dry batteries, per cell, 25 cents.

Compare the catalogue illustrations on page 31, which show the side-dumping cars, with this one from 1906, showing the fixed bucket car.

CHAPTER FOUR

★

STEAM OUTLINE LOCOMOTIVES

The first steam outline toy electric locomotive made in this country was the No. 4, first listed by Carlisle & Finch in its "Catalogue B" no. 4 in 1899. This is a small and inexpensive 0-4-0 engine and tender that became the centerpiece of the Carlisle & Finch toy train line; its $6.50 retail price continued without change until the toy train business was discontinued in 1915, and far more of these locomotives and the freight and passenger cars designed to go with them were sold than any other items Carlisle & Finch made.

Prototype road engines all had one or more pilot or trailing wheels, so this was not a good copy of the real thing. With only four driving wheels and no pilot or trailing wheels, however, it tracked very well and ran like a jack rabbit, even with a string of cars. In 1904 a generally similar but even smaller 0-4-0 No. 20 "tank" engine, without any tender, was added as a switch engine, but it never achieved the same popularity as the No. 4.

At the other end of the spectrum, Carlisle & Finch produced two other road locomotives that are much larger and handsomer, both quite accurate copies of common passenger locomotives of the era called "Atlantic" types, with 4-4-2 wheel arrangements. These were the No. 45 of 1903, mentioned previously, and the No. 34 of 1908. Except for the small mining engines discussed in Chapter Three, these four locomotives constituted the entire roster of Carlisle & Finch passenger and freight motive power. Fairly extensive variations occurred from time to time in all of these engines, and these are detailed in the sections that follow.

CARLISLE & FINCH HEADLIGHTS

All Carlisle & Finch steam outline locomotives are equipped with dummy headlights, the most common of which is a nicely detailed cast-iron oil-type headlight, found on the Nos. 4, 20, and 45 locomotives from 1903 through 1908, and, in some cases, including the 1911 or 1912 models of No. 34. Although dummy electric-type headlights were generally substituted in later years, no working electric headlight was provided on any production locomotive.

This is particularly surprising in view of the fact that Carlisle & Finch's first extant catalogue in 1897 and every subsequent catalogue through 1915 listed one or more miniature incandescent light bulbs for 10 or 12 volts. In addition, in the 1906–1908 period three principal competitors — Howard and Voltamp in 2-inch gauge and Lionel in three-rail Standard Gauge — provided electric headlights on locomotives and on some trolleys.

That customers wanted working headlights is indicated by the fact that several No. 4 Carlisle & Finch locomotives have been found with their oil-type dummy headlights altered by customers to contain miniature light bulbs. The only engine with electric headlights believed to have been made by Carlisle & Finch, however, was a preproduction enlarged and modified 0-4-0 locomotive that appears to have been made at some unknown time after 1906 — possibly an early design of what later became the No. 34. The late Don McClain discovered this engine in Cincinnati in the 1950s and sent a photograph to George Hopkins, whose son Dick made it available to us. It appears on page 64.

DETAILED LISTINGS FOR NO. 4 AND NO. 20

> **Side-of-car numbers:** 131, 171, 683

No. 4 STEAM OUTLINE LOCOMOTIVE, 1899-1915: Five groups of significant variations occurred in this little engine in this seventeen-year period, and each will be separately detailed below. In the interest of avoiding duplication, however, the common characteristics of all these models will first be described.

These 0-4-0 engines are all 12" long, 4" wide, and 5½" high, with eight-wheel two-truck tenders that are 6" long, 3" wide, and 3½" high. Boilers and cabs are of sheet metal with a wooden frame and red cast-iron pilots on a wooden pilot beam. A reversing three-pole motor is geared to one pair of 2" driving wheels on split insulated axles. Brass side rods provide power to all four driving wheels and simulated brass driving rods connect to the two cyclinders. A reverse lever is usually located under the right side of the cab.

(A) 1898-1902. This earliest version has a tinplate body almost entirely covered by printed labeled paper. Rectangular side windows and smaller front windows on the cab are not cut out but their outline is printed in gold on the covering paper label, as is the gold number "683" below the side windows and four gold boiler bands. The 2" driving wheels have seven spokes. Finally, the smokebox front or door and center button, as well as the headlight, bell, and steam dome are all wooden trimmings. The tender body is tinplate with a wooden base, and is also covered with labeled paper which is lettered in gold on each side "L.S. & M.S.R.R.", for the Lake Shore and Michigan Southern Railroad, then a subsidiary of the New York Central system. The tender's letters are framed by narrow gold stripes. The number "683" in gold is on the tender's rear panel. Eight red-painted cast-iron wheels, 1" in diameter, use nails driven into the

Gd   Exc

two-truck bolsters as axles. A link and pin coupler is on the back of the tender. There is no coupler on the locomotive's pilot.

Note: Carlisle & Finch files examined by Frank Loveland indicate that two hundred of these engines were made in the first run in 1899. This version is extremely rare today.

650 – 1000

(B) 1903-04. The models in this series were the same size and configuration with wooden frame, smokebox front, gold-painted wooden smokebox button, and red-painted pilot beam, but the boiler and cab are formed of sheet zinc, with a nickel finish between the smokebox and cab. The smokebox, cylinders, and the cast-iron oil-type headlight on top of the smokebox are painted with black enamel. A brass bell, cast-iron nickeled steam dome, and embossed boiler bands complete the boiler details. The number "171" is embossed under stamped arched cab windows. In catalogue illustrations, the cab sides and roof are black and the embossed number "171" is painted gold, with gold horizontal lines above and below the numerals, but examples examined have had unpainted nickel finish on cab roof, sides, and "171". Round portholes are stamped out on each side of front of cab. This version retains the red-painted driving wheels with seven flat spokes; brass drive and side rods. Both locomotive and tender have bumper band couplers; bottom of coupler is 1¼" above rail. Tender is unchanged, with wooden frame and same "L.S. & M.S.R.R." printed wrapper markings framed by gold lines.

650 – 1000

(C) 1904-07. This series continues with embossed "171" on cab sides and sheet-zinc boiler and cab with nickel finish, but there are now twelve-spoked driving wheels and tinplate sheet-steel wooden frame tenders marked "B. & O." in painted gold letters with two gold stripes on sides and one on back. Earlier models in this group have sheet-zinc boilers and cabs, with plain portholes on the front of the cab. Later models have nickeled tinplate boilers, usually with sheet-zinc cabs and embossed porthole edges. Many of the engines in the entire 1903-07 period have all-black-painted cabs with embossed "171" in gold and with gold stripes above and below these numerals on the cab sides. Many are found, however, with nickel-finished cabs, with black cab sides and nickeled roof, or with nickel cab sides and black roof. Some also have vertical gold stripes on the headlight. Most of these combinations are so common that it is believed that they are production variations, but some may have resulted from subsequent changes by owners.

500 – 900

(D) 1908-11. In this middle or transition version, the locomotive is all-black-painted tinplate, with two nickeled boiler bands. The number "131" is embossed on cab panel and painted gold between two embossed but unpainted horizontal stripes under similar arched cab windows with embossed edges, and with embossed portholes. Locomotives in this series have metal smokebox fronts, gold-painted smokebox buttons and pilot beam, and red-painted pilot deck braces. The cylinders, each of which was formerly attached separately to the boiler, have now been made up into a proper steam chest assembly with the cylinders mounted into a saddle. This assembly is painted black and is decorated with gold lining on the embossed detail. Tender body with wooden frame is unchanged from earlier version, but has ⅞" brass

Closeup of a 1899 paper label locomotive, the first steam-type toy electric locomotive made in America and the first use of spur gear drive by C & F. Note the hand-painted rivets on the side of the smokestack. George Hopkins Collection; photo by Dick Hopkins.

Gd   Exc

wheels mounted in trucks with black steel side-frame trucks. Instead of "B. & O.", the letters "N. & M." (of a fictitious railroad apparently invented by Carlisle & Finch) are embossed but usually unpainted on tender sides, with gold stripes above and below the letters and on rear of tender.

500 – 900

(E) 1912-15. In this last version of the No. 4, the locomotive body is modernized with an electric-type "drum"-shaped headlight and a lower "derby hat"-shaped steam dome. Handrails now appear along the boiler. The cab windows are now square and do not have embossed frames; the portholes on cab front are now embossed. Bumper band couplers are used to connect locomotive and tender. The tender is now an all-metal box type with embossed circles on sheet-metal frame around bolster fastenings. The same embossed and unpainted "N. & M." lettering is now framed by orange stripes on sides and back. Engine and cab trim, handrails, and lettering are all picked out in orange, including embossed number "131" and the embossed stripes below cab windows. Orange lines on roof probably simulate a vent hatch. Some of the locomotives in this series have slightly higher stacks and domes. Some of the tenders have a single row of rivets embossed on top and down front on each side, and others have a double row of rivets. In addition, some tenders are "empty" and some are filled with a simulated coal pile of stamped sheet steel. The chronology of these variations is uncertain.

700 – 1100

No. 20 TANK-TYPE SWITCH ENGINE, 1904-07: This little 0-4-0 engine, designed for switching rather than road service, is a tank engine with a coal bunker behind the cab instead of a tender. The reverse lever is located on the right side of this bunker. In place of the pilot or "cowcatcher" found on road engines this switch engine has two steps for the switchmen fastened to the wooden pilot beam on the front of the engine. The distance from front of cab to back of smokebox is 5", compared to 7" on the No. 4, making total length 10". Except for its length and the above details, it is very similar to the No. 4 locomotive without its tender.

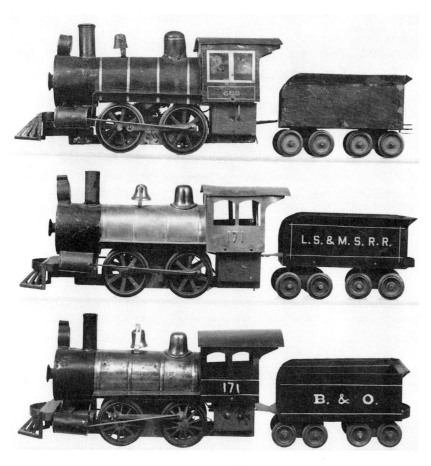

Three early No. 4s. Top: A partially reconstructed No. 4 engine as it was likely made from 1899 through 1902 with link and pin couplers on the rear, paper label-covered boiler, and uncutout cab windows; accompanied by an LS & MSRR tender. Center: No. 4, 1903, with nickel boiler, brass bell, and nickel steam dome; tender similar to example above but with bumper band couplers on both front and rear. Bottom: Most common version of the No. 4, here with tender marked "B. & O.". This model is found with variations in cab finishing — sometimes all-black cab and roof, sometimes black cab sides with nickel roof, sometimes nickel cab sides and black roof, and sometimes nickel sides and roof.

Top and middle: Additional versions of the 1904–1907 No. 4, with variations in the cab painting. The top engine has a black cab with nickel roof, while the middle engine has nickel sides and black roof. Bottom: No. 20 switch engine, 1904–1907, with a coal bunker at the rear of the cab instead of a tender. Also has steps on the front for the switchman instead of a pilot. Except for its length and the other features noted it is the same as No. 4 of the same period.

Later versions of the Nos. 4 and 20. Top: No. 4, 1908–1911, changed to all black with two nickel boiler bands and the tender lettered for the fictitious railroad N & M, 1908–1911. The trucks have steel side frames and brass wheels; the cab is numbered 131 rather than 171. Middle: Further modernization of No. 4, 1912–1915: main changes are new electric-type, round, dummy headlight; a smaller steam dome; and square instead of rounded cab windows. The tender was totally redesigned to form a box-type tender with the same brass wheels and black side-frame trucks used on earlier models. Bottom: No. 20, 1912–1915: this 0-4-0 is not a switch engine but a suburban, with pilots on both ends for running in both directions; round headlight, small steam dome, small square cab windows, all-black boiler. Another version, 1908–1911, had pilots on both ends but otherwise was more like the early switch engine.

| | Gd | Exc |

Note: The 1904 and 1905 catalogue illustration is inaccurate in several details, including the length of the boiler, but later catalogues included accurate illustrations of this switch engine.

(A) 1904. In this year the No. 20 had the same seven-spoked driving wheels, the nickeled boiler, and black-painted smokebox and cab, with embossed gold numerals "171" below the cab windows and the horizontal line trim as described for the No. 4 in this period. The coal bunker, of course, is also painted black.   **550 – 800**

(B) 1905-07. Same as (A) above, but in this period, like the No. 4, the driving wheels had twelve spokes and the composition and surface finishing of boiler and cab had variations similar to those reported in this period for No. 4.   **700 – 1000**

No. 20 DOUBLE-ENDED "SUBURBAN" LOCOMOTIVE, 1908-15:
In 1908 the switch engine was changed to become a road engine designed to run equally well in either direction. This type of engine was frequently used in the early 1900s on suburban commuter trains so that it would be unnecessary to provide a turntable or wye on which to turn the engine. With a red cast-iron pilot substituted for a pair of steps on the front of the engine, and a second pilot behind the coal bunker, the length was increased from 10" to 13". The locomotive's characteristics are otherwise generally similar to those of the 1904 No. 20.   **900 – 1300**

(A) 1908-11. The changes listed for No. 4(D) are applicable here, although at the outset in 1908 the number "171" may still have been used for a short time until "131" was substituted for it.

(B) 1912-15. The changes listed for No. 4(E) are applicable here, except that no handrails are provided along the sides of the shorter boiler.

THE FAMOUS NO. 45

This large Atlantic-type express passenger locomotive and tender was at the top of the Carlisle & Finch line. Production spanned from 1903 to 1915. While the catalogues listed and illustrated this 4-4-2 engine without substantial change throughout the whole period, in fact two quite different locomotives were assigned the same catalogue number. These two versions will accordingly be described separately as the 1903 No. 45 and the 1909 No. 45, these being the years in which these two different models were first listed.

| **Side-of-car number:** 82 |

1903 No. 45 EARLY 4-4-2 ROAD LOCOMOTIVE, 1903-08: This engine is almost a scale model of the New York Central and Hudson River Railroad's fast passenger locomotive that was then hauling the new 20th Century Limited between New York and Albany. While not a true scale model, the No. 45 was an exceptionally good toy representation of this high-stepping Atlantic locomotive.

Overall length is 27½" long including tender. The locomotive is 5½" wide at the cylinders, and 6¼" high at the cab. The red-painted spoked driving wheels are 2 9/16" in diameter and are set onto the usual split insulated axles.

Unlike all other Carlisle & Finch locomotives, this engine does not have a wooden frame, but instead has a two-piece cast-bronze frame. The boiler, cab roof, and front ends of cylinders and valve chests are finished in polished nickel. The smokebox is painted black with a thin gold stripe between it and the boiler. The steam chest and cab sides are painted black, with gold-painted number "82" framed by two unpainted embossed lines below the two arched cab windows. Small rectangular windows are on cab front. Cast-brass crossheads and brass drive and side rods are all nickel plated, but there is no representation of valve gear. Black-painted cylindrical air tanks are under each side of the cab. In some examples the boiler is nickel-plated sheet brass; other examples have been found of both sheet zinc and tinplated sheet steel with a similar nickeled finish, as noted below. The brass or cast-iron pilot and pilot beam are painted gold and are fixed to the pony truck, so that pilot and truck swivel independently of the locomotive frame and body. Brass flag staffs on the pilot beam have a polished nickel finish. Red-painted pilot wheels are 1⅛"-diameter pressed brass with inside bearings, while similar brass trailing wheels have outside bearings and are 1¼" in diameter. All of these are on split insulated axles. A cast-iron oil-type headlight projects forward from the smokebox top, behind which is a black-painted stack, a brass bell, large cast-iron nickel-plated sand and steam domes, and whistle. Nickeled handrails run along boiler sides. A curved handrail runs around the button on the smokebox front. (This was the handgrab used by the fireman when he serviced or lit the headlamp.) Feedwater piping and check valves are on both sides of boiler and are similar to those on the prototype locomotive. The reversing switch is located under the right-hand side of the cab.

The all-metal tinplate tender is 8¼" long, not including couplers, 4" wide, and 4⅝" high above rail. Circles embossed

An illustration of this prototype of the No. 45 appeared in Carlisle & Finch catalogues in 1903 and 1904 (see back cover of this book).

in the metal frame served both to reinforce the point at which the king pins passed through and to steady the bolsters. "N.Y.C. & H.R." appears in large gold lettering on each side, with gold handrails and striping above and below lettering and on back of tender. The tops of the tender sides are flared out all around. The two four-wheel tender trucks have wooden bolsters and all but the earliest models had handsome cast-brass freight-type side frames. The pressed-brass 1¼"-diameter wheels are on the usual split insulated axles.

The most important feature of the No. 45 locomotive is its powerful and unusual motor. It has a six-segment commutator and six-pole "Gramme ring" armature. The large-diameter armature acts as a flywheel. This feature, together with an unusually direct gear ratio, enables the engine to make very smooth starts and stops. The brass motor casting on each individual engine carries a different

Last model of No. 45, showing pinned domes and round electric-type headlight. Carlisle & Finch never made any "working" headlights as did Lionel or Voltamp. G. Hopkins Collection; photo by Dick Hopkins

Three versions of the No. 45. Top and middle: This 1903 early form is practically a scale model of the New York Central and Hudson River Railroad locomotive that pulled the 20th Century Limited in 1902 from New York to Albany. It has a six-segment commutator and a six-pole armature that was so large it acted as a fly wheel. There are link and pin couplers on both the pilot and the rear of the tender. The top engine, 1903–1904, has link and pin couplers on both pilot and rear of tender. The middle engine, generally 1904–1908, has bumper band-type couplers on the tender and no pilot coupler. Bottom: The late version, 1909–1915, is in almost all respects an entirely different engine. It has a standard three-pole motor, the pilot is rigidly fixed to a wooden frame, instead of swiveling with the pilot truck, and the body has been modernized with rectangular cab windows, cab roof ventilator, and a simulated electric-type headlight. In this photo, the headlight is still the cast-iron, oil-type headlight — a substitution made for the missing original headlight.

Gd   Exc

serial number, the significance of which has not been determined.

A number of minor variations took place between 1903 and 1908, as listed below.   **1600 – 2700**

(A) 1903-04. At the outset in 1903, this engine had brass drive wheels and pilot and pilot beam, nickel-plated tinplate steel boiler, and link and pin couplers. Some of the very earliest link and pin tenders had the older 1"-diameter cast-iron wheels on box-type trucks with solid side frames.[1] Tender trucks of this type can been seen on the illustration of the prototype engine, and careful examination shows them also on the No. 45 tender that is illustrated as part of outfit No. 67 in the 1904 catalogue, page 34.

An early No. 45 that precisely resembles the illustration used in the 1905 and later catalogues has also been found with a nickel-plated boiler made of tinplate steel and with brass driving wheels and a brass pilot and link and pin coupler soldered to it. When found, the pilot beam was missing and the pilot itself was not properly attached, but that it is authentic Carlisle & Finch is indicated by the letters "C & F"

and a stock number that are stamped on it. The link and pin tender that came with this locomotive had the cast-brass truck side frames and 1¼" pressed-brass wheels, rather than the earlier box trucks and iron wheels. An example has also been found of an early No. 45 locomotive with this type of link and pin coupler on the tender but no coupler on the pilot, as shown in some of the catalogue illustrations of assembled train sets with No. 45 locomotives.

Carlisle & Finch factory drawings found by Frank Loveland from the 1904-05 period indicate that mass production of the No. 45 locomotive probably did not begin until late 1904, which probably explains why the very early 1903 versions of this engine described above are so rare.

(B) 1904-06. Same as above, with no coupler of any type on the cast-iron pilot, and a boiler of nickel-plated sheet brass. A bumper band coupler is on rear of tender, with bottom of bumper band 1¾" above rail to match those on passenger cars Nos. 51 and 52 first listed in 1904. At some point, believed to be in late 1904 or early 1905, bumper band couplers were also added between engine and tender.

(C) 1907-08. Same, but driving wheels are now described in catalogue as iron instead of brass. Although there is no indication in the catalogues of any other change, a No. 45 has been found with a nickel-plated boiler made of sheet zinc instead of brass. Since the bodies of several passenger cars and the No. 2 interurban were made of sheet zinc in this period, the same material seems to have been used for at least some of the No. 45 boilers at this time.

1909 No. 45 LATE 4-4-2 LOCOMOTIVE, 1909-15: In 1909 the locomotive and tender were entirely redesigned. That 1909 was the date of this change is corroborated by a significant change in the description of the locomotive's electric motor that first appeared in the 1909 catalogue, although there was no change in the catalogue illustration.

The new model, however, does not have many of the features that made the 1903 model so memorable. Instead of the two-part insulated cast-bronze frame and six-pole motor with Gramme ring armature, a much smaller standard three-pole motor is mounted on a wooden block frame, as is the case with all other Carlisle & Finch engines. The smaller motor requires double-reduction spur gearing, giving less smooth starts and stops. In addition, the red cast-iron pilot and pilot beam are no longer integral with the swiveling pilot truck, but are fastened rigidly to the wooden frame.

In external appearance this No. 45 is somewhat modernized from the 1903 model, but it is still more handsome and well-proportioned than almost any other known toy electric locomotive. The fixed pilot allows the addition of the usual pilot deck braces to the boiler. Red-painted pressed-brass 1¼" pilot wheels and similar-sized brass trailing wheels all have inside bearings and split insulated axles. A dummy iron or steel headlight is located on top of the black smokebox forward of the stack, not on brackets on the top of the smokebox door as in the earlier model. A brass bell and two large domes painted black are on the nickel-plated boiler, which is now "decorated" by three copper boiler bands, mounted between embossed lines around the boiler. A heavy

brass handrail and a brass feedwater pipe run along on each side. A double row of rivets runs between the black smokebox front and the nickeled boiler; the smokebox front and gold-painted round button are now metal; a slim brass handrail runs below the button. The steam chest has been redesigned so that the front of the cylinders are painted gold with vertical stripes on the sides. The crossheads have been simplified, and the drive and side rods are brass.

The cab is painted black, with an actual ventilation hatch and a square painted in orange around it on the roof. The two cab windows on each side are rectangular and lack embossed frames, but there are round embossed portholes on the cab front. An orange stripe is applied above the windows and the same number "82" and two corrugated lines painted orange are in the panel below the windows. A cylindrical air tank with its strap picked out in orange is below the cab on each side.

Bumper band couplers are on rear of tender and between tender and engine, but there is no pilot coupler. The bottom of the bumper coupler on the rear of the tender is 1¼" above rail to match the bumper couplers of Nos. 4, 20, and 34 engines and their cars. The earlier No. 45 had its bumper band coupler mounted 1¾" above the rail to match the larger passenger and freight cars intended for its consist. The all-metal tender has been redesigned, with top of sides flared out only along coal bunker. Tender trucks have wooden bolsters, with the same cast-brass freight-type side frames, but with 1¼" insulated late-style pressed-brass wheels on solid steel axles. Double rows of rivets and painted orange stripes are above and below the orange-painted letters "N.Y.C. & H.R." on tender sides, and extend around the tender back. There are black handrails on both ends of tender and on locomotive cab.   **1800 – 2800**

(A) 1909-12(?). Most examples from this period have round electric-type dummy headlights mounted on top of the black smokebox, but an example has been found with the earlier oil-type headlight and with a fixed brass bell without bell bracket.

(B) 1912(?)-15. The last version of this model has the round electric-type headlight and lower "derby hat"-pinned black domes. It has been suggested that boilers on some of these last models may have been painted black, and that the tender may have had black steel side frames similar to those on freight and passenger cars of this period, but this has not been verified.

THE WELL-KNOWN NO. 34

Side-of-car number: 131 (on tender; "P.R.R." on locomotive)

No. 34 MEDIUM-SIZED 4-4-2 LOCOMOTIVE, 1908-15: Introduced in the 1908 catalogue but listed as a 1909 model, this engine has the same driving wheels (2⁹⁄₁₆" diameter) as the No. 45 but is significantly smaller — 4¾" wide, 6½" high, and 23" long, including tender. Boiler top has dummy headlight, stack, bell, and two full-size domes with brass piping on each side of boiler. The smokebox is black, with black metal smokebox front and gold-painted metal numberboard. The

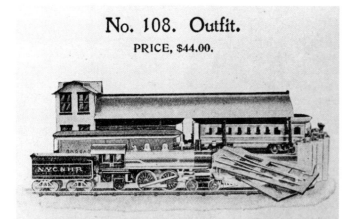

No. 108. Outfit.
PRICE, $44.00.

This railway is very complete and will afford amusement and instruction to more advanced students. It consists of:

No. 45 Locomotive and tender.   1 No. 10 -R Switch.
No. 51 Baggage car.   1 No. 10 -L Switch.
No. 52 Passenger cars.   5 Lengths of track and ties (45 Ft.)
No. 97 Passenger station.   12 "Special" Dry Batteries.
No. 45 Locomotive and tender.
Weight, boxed, 80 lbs

Catalogue illustration of outfit featuring the No. 45.

Top: In 1911 the No. 34 engine finish was changed to all black with three nickel boiler bands and a cast-iron, oil-type headlight and yellow trim. Bottom: Between 1911 and 1915 the trim changed to orange.

Gd   Exc

round cylinders and pilot deck braces are black. Rudimentary brass crossheads similar to those on the 1909 model of No. 45 connect with brass drive rods and brass side rods. Engine has four small inside bearing red pressed-brass pilot wheels ⅞" in diameter, each wheel insulated from the solid steel axles, and two inside bearing 1¼" trailing wheels set on a split insulated axle. The cab has two rectangular windows on each side with one embossed line above the windows and two below them, with no number but the embossed letters "P.R.R." in the space between the two lines. The cast-iron pilot and pilot beam and pilot deck braces are painted red. The three-pole motor and double reduction spur gearing are similar to those of the 1909 model of No. 45.

The black all-metal two-truck eight-wheel tender is similar in design, but it is smaller than the tender furnished with the 1909 model of the No. 45. It is 8" long, 4" wide, and 4" high, with "131" embossed on each side and painted stripes across top and bottom of sides and back. The edge of each side along the coal bunker is flared. Black bumper band couplers are between engine and tender, on the pilot beam of the engine, and on the rear of the tender, with bottom edge 1¼" above the rail. This height matches the couplers on the No. 4 and the 1909 model of No. 45. The tender trucks have small insulated brass wheels, solid axles, and black-painted steel side frames, similar to the side frames used on the small freight and passenger cars of this period, as detailed in Chapters Five and Six.   **1400 – 2200**

(A) 1908-09. The initial No. 34, as accurately illustrated in catalogues, has all of the characteristics described above, but has nickeled boiler, four simulated boiler bands, brass bell and nickeled bell bracket, large nickeled sand and steam domes, nickeled cab, brass handrails along sides, and curved brass handrail on smokebox front. In addition, a unique cup or dish-type brass or copper-plated electric-type dummy

headlight is shown. Small vertically aligned rectangular windows without embossed frame detail are on front panels of cab. The tender number "131" and striping are in gold.

Several later variations of No. 34 are listed below in what is believed to be the order in which they were produced, but no information is available as to the precise year in which the various changes were made. Except for the first variation listed, the changes are relatively minor.

(B) 1911. Same as above, but both engine and tender are all black with three nickel boiler bands with gold-painted trim and lettering, including the embossed "P.R.R." and three embossed lines on each side of cab, and the simulated cab roof hatch. There is brass piping on each side of boiler, but no handrails along black-painted tinplate boiler or on smokebox front. Cast-iron oil-type headlight is mounted on top of smokebox forward of the smokestack, and brass bell and large black-painted domes are on boiler. Front ends of cylinders are painted gold.

(C) 1911-12. This version is identical to (B) above, but locomotive and tender have orange instead of gold-painted trim and lettering, and small windows on front panels of cab are no longer rectangular but are round portholes with embossed frames.

(D) 1912-14(?). Same as above, but dummy headlight is round electric type instead of oil type.

(E) 1914-15. In this final version the steam and sand domes are believed to be the smaller "derby hat" type pinned to boiler top.

NOTE

1. The late Burt Logan, a founding member and first president of the Train Collectors Association, had one of these tenders that he describes in the January 1956 issue of the TCA *Quarterly* (Vol. 2, no.1, p. 9). He called the trucks "Fox designed."

CHAPTER FIVE

★

PASSENGER AND BAGGAGE CARS

Carlisle & Finch made three sizes of passenger coaches and baggage cars. The smallest cars, 12 inches long, were first listed in 1899 and 1900 and the line expanded in

No. 32. Electric Locomotive and Passenger Train.

PRICE, $12.85.

8 to 10 VOLTS. ¾ **AMPERE.**

This is the modern express train, and consists of locomotive, tender, baggage car and two coaches.

The locomotive is the same as that furnished with our No. 4 equipment.

The speed of the train is from 150 to 200 feet per minute.

The complete equipment consists of locomotive tender, baggage car, two passenger cars, 18 feet of 2-inch gauge strip steel track, and 6 dry batteries. These dry batteries are connected together and mounted in the packing box with terminals wires ready for use.

Price of extra track, locomotive, etc. same as with the No. 4 train.

Length of train, 4 feet 9 inches.

Weight, boxed, 23 lbs.

———

New York, N. Y.

Gentlemen:

A few days ago I purchased from J. H. Bunnell & Co., your New York agents, one No. 20 switch engine, one No. 18 motor car, a No. 43 loop, six cars and some extra track, switches, etc. The engine is better and runs better than I expected and will pull a number of cars at a good speed. I expect to get for Christmas a No. 4 electric locomotive and some more cars and track. I run my train by electric light current, which enables it to run constantly and at a very high speed.

Yours truly,
LOUIS HENRY FROHMAN,
117 W. 58th St.,
New York, N. Y.

———

Pawtucket, R. I.

Dear Sirs:

I received your latest catalogue and am very thankful for same. I hope you will mail me every new one as they are distributed. My father gave me one of your coal mining outfits and 36 feet of track. I have a regular railway system with stations, tunnels, grades and all. It climbs grades and runs at high speed on five cells dry battery. Every night after school I have a troop of boys admiring it. I am willing that you should use this letter as a testimonial, as I am pleased with your fair ways of dealing.

Yours truly,
ELMER ROBINSON,
3 Victoria Street,
Cambridge, Eng.

A page from the 1911 catalogue, selling set No. 32, featuring Nos. 13 and 13B passenger and baggage cars with the No. 4 — and including letters from satisfied customers. The illustration of 1900 equipment ran in every catalogue from 1900 to 1915.

1904. In addition, for a short time (1905–1906) a vestibuled Pullman parlor car 18 inches long was also included in the passenger car roster to go with these smaller cars. The largest cars, 19 inches long, were introduced in 1904 to go with the 1903 No. 45 locomotive. Finally medium-sized 15½-inch-long cars were listed in 1909 to go with the No. 34 locomotive that had been offered the previous year. Each of these and their significant variations will be described below, in the order of their development.

SMALL CARS (and the No. 87)

In 1899 Carlisle & Finch offered its first passenger car, No. 13. In the next year a companion baggage car, No. 13B, was added. Both of these cars are the smallest and most commonly found of the Carlisle & Finch passenger train cars. They were designed for the ubiquitous No. 4 locomotive, but they were also appropriate for operation behind later engines Nos. 20 and 34. In every catalogue from 1900 through 1915 train sets consisting of a No. 13B baggage car and two No. 13 passenger coaches behind a No. 4 locomotive were listed as Outfit No. 32. In 1905 No. 87, a long, vestibuled Pullman parlor car to go with these earlier cars, was added, pulled by a No. 4 locomotive.

Side-of-car number: 26

Gd Exc

No. 13 SMALL COACH, 1899-1915: This car, first listed in 1899, was described as "same size as our No. 2 Motor Car but without motors." It has two four-wheel trucks and is 12" long, 5" high, and 3½" wide, with a wooden frame,[1] seven arched windows on each side, arched door openings at the ends, open platforms with steps having two treads on each side, and without any platform to roof braces. The various versions are described below.

(A) 1899-1901(?). Polished sheet-brass smooth-side body, roof, platforms, and platform ends, and rounded-end clerestory roof. Brass platforms are soldered to body at each end; wooden frame does not extend under platforms. Trucks consist of swiveling wooden blocks or bolsters, each with four 1"-diameter cast-iron wheels nailed into them, the nails serving as axles. Car has link and pin couplers and small black-printed yellow paper label "ELECTRIC RAILWAY" below windows. **300 – 450**

(B) 1902(?). Same as above, but clerestory roof is squared off and three corrugations are added along sides and on ends. Exact date of this change is uncertain, but is believed to have been late 1901 or early 1902, when the same change was made in the No. 2 trolley described in Chapter Two.

Gd   Exc

(C) 1903. Same as above, but bumper band couplers are substituted for the link and pin couplers. The bottoms of the bumper bands are 1¼" above the rail. The brass platforms are no longer soldered to the body of the car, but are instead supported by a thin block of wood which extends under the platforms and then is nailed to the wooden frame.

(D) 1904-06. Same as above, but at some point during this period the yellow and black paper labels were replaced by the words "ELECTRIC RAILWAY" placed below the windows in embossed letters. The platforms and platform ends are now tinplated sheet steel painted black.

(E) 1907-08. Same as above, but the body and roof are now made from nickeled sheet zinc instead of brass. The wooden frame now extends under the end platforms.   **200 – 375**

(F) 1909-10. Same as above, but metal trucks now appear with black steel side frames and ⅞"-diameter insulated brass wheels on solid steel axles.

(G) 1911-15. Same as above, but the body is now fabricated of enameled tinplate, usually painted orange, with black-painted roof, platforms, and platform ends. The windows now have embossed frames. There are now only two instead of three corrugations along the sides and on the ends of the body, one above the windows and one below the embossed lettering.   **200 – 375**

No. 13B SMALL BAGGAGE CAR, 1900-15: Two four-wheel trucks with tinplated sheet-steel body, roof, and platforms, and a wooden floor. It has the same dimensions as passenger car No. 13 — 12" long, 5" high, 3½" wide — and was made in several variations as described below. This car and No. 13 were intended for use with locomotives Nos. 4, 20, and 34.

(A) 1900-01. Tinplated sheet-steel body, black clerestory roof with rounded roof ends and black platforms and platform ends; body covered with printed paper label reading "Union Pacific RR", "The Overland Route", "BAGGAGE", and "EXPRESS", with "U.S. MAIL" in small letters on sliding baggage doors. As with passenger car No. 13, the wooden floor extends only under the car body, and the end platforms are soldered to this body. The trucks consist of swiveling wooden blocks or bolsters, each with four 1"-diameter cast-iron wheels nailed to them. Link and pin couplers are fitted.   **275 – 450**

(B) 1902(?). Same as above, but with squared-off clerestory roof as with car No. 13. Exact date of this change is uncertain, as with the No. 13 coach and the No. 2 trolley, but it was probably 1901 or 1902.

(C) 1903-06. Same as above, but with bumper band couplers 1¼" above rail, instead of link and pin couplers. A piece of wood, nailed to the floor of the car body, is used to support the end platforms which are no longer soldered to the car body.

(D) 1907-08. Same as above, but instead of having paper labeling the body is painted orange. "BAGGAGE" and "EXPRESS" are embossed near ends on each side, and "26" is embossed on the sliding baggage doors. These letters and numbers are sometimes painted black. The wooden frame is extended in one piece under the end platforms. Wooden truck bolsters and iron wheels on nails as axles remain unchanged.   **200 – 425**

(E) 1909-15. Same as above, but with metal trucks with black steel side frames and insulated ⅞"-diameter pressed-brass wheels on steel axles.

Note: Catalogue indicates brass wheels were 1" diameter, but actual measurement is closer to ⅞".

No. 87 VESTIBULED PULLMAN PARLOR CAR, 1905-06: 18" long, 5" high above rail, and 3½" wide. The usual three embossed lines run along the sides and around the ends. Two small square windows and a door are stamped into each body end. Metal seats are provided for the passengers. The unique trucks used on this model have a wooden bolster and black-painted cast-iron side frames. Each truck has six 1"-diameter cast-iron wheels and the usual split insulated axles. The name "PULLMAN" is rubber stamped in black below the windows, but this lettering has often been rubbed off most specimens.   **350 – 700**

LARGER CARS

Two larger cars were intended for running with No. 45 locomotive. Each has metal body and roof with wooden floor, and is 19 inches long, 6 inches high above rail, and 3¾ inches wide. Each car also has bumper band couplers; some cars are found equipped with emergency coupling chains. The bottom of the bumper couplers is 1¾ inches above rail, to match the 1904–1908 No. 45 locomotive; it is not certain whether these cars in 1909 — the last year in which they were listed — continued their bumper band couplers at 1¾ inches above the rail, or whether they were changed to the 1¼-inch height to match the 1909 version of the No. 45 engine — a coupler height that thereafter was uniform for all new equipment. The trucks have wooden bolsters and handsome cast-bronze passenger-type side frames. Four 1¼-inch-diameter pressed-brass wheels are fitted onto split insulated axles. Both cars have open platforms with steel corner braces to the roofs and steps. There was no change after 1904 in the baggage car (No. 51) and both cars were discontinued after 1909.[2] The 51 and 52 are two of the largest and most handsome cars made by Carlisle & Finch. They are quite rare.

Side-of-car number: 3, 111; possibly 29

No. 51 LARGE BAGGAGE CAR, 1904-09: Enameled orange tinplated sheet-steel body and platforms, with black roof and black detail stripes. A large sliding door is centrally located. "BAGGAGE" is stenciled in black letters near the left end of each side, and "EXPRESS" near the right end. All cars inspected have the number "111" stenciled on the baggage door, but the catalogue illustration shows "29". No subsequent variations have been found.   **300 – 600**

No. 52 LARGE COACH, 1904-09: The passenger car has ten arched windows on each side. Roof, platforms, and platform ends are painted black. There are three corrugations, two beneath the windows and one above them, which continue around the body ends to the edges of the door. The catalogue illustration shows the lettering "N.Y.C. & H.R." stamped above the windows and the number "3" below them, but these markings have rarely survived. Full train sets catalogued from time to time as Outfit No. 88 included a No. 51 baggage car and two No. 52 coaches behind the No. 45 locomotive.

(A) 1904-06, polished brass body with metal interior seats, one by each window.   **350 – 700**

Top left: No. 13 coach, 1899–1901, with smooth sides, cast-iron wheels, link and pin couplers, rounded roof ends, and "ELECTRIC RAILWAY" paper label. Top right: Brass car, 1903, with squared-off roof ends with black platform and bumper band couplers 1¼ inches; "ELECTRIC RAILWAY" label missing from this model. The same car, 1904–1906, had "ELECTRIC RAILWAY" embossed below windows in place of label. Middle left: 1907–1908, same as above, with embossed lettering, except body is nickel-plated. Middle right: Enameled orange body with black roof, embossed "ELECTRIC RAILWAY" and similar black platform ends and bumper couplers. Windows now have embossed edges and new trucks with black steel side frames and brass wheels. Bottom left: No. 13B baggage car, 1903–1906, with smooth sheet-steel body, black squared-off clerestory roof, and bumper band couplers. Note pieces of wood nailed to car body floor that support the end platforms. Bottom right: A late 13B, 1909–1915, with embossed lettering on sides and "26" on sliding doors.

Gd   Exc

(B) 1907-09. The catalogue descriptions for these three years indicate that seats were omitted from the No. 52 coach, and state that the car was "made of polished metal" instead of brass. No examples have been identified, but a number of the quite similar No. 2 interurban and also the small No. 13 passenger cars, both described as "nickel plated" in this period, have been found. The bodies of these cars are made of nickeled sheet zinc, and it seems likely that the No. 52 cars from this period were similarly constructed. It is also likely that the 1907 cars had unembossed windows like the earlier brass cars, but that the 1908 and 1909 cars had embossed windows, as was the case with the No. 2 interurban in 1907 and 1908.   **350 – 700**

MEDIUM-SIZED CARS

The No. 59 and the 60 were introduced in 1909, intended for the consist of the new locomotive No. 34, but were likewise suitable for use with the later model No. 45

locomotive. Both of these new cars have metal bodies and roofs with wooden floors and are 15½ inches long, 6 inches high above rail, and 3½ inches wide. The Nos. 59 and 60 were 3½ inches shorter than the Nos. 90 and 91, which they replaced after 1909.

Both of these new cars have open platforms without corner roof braces. The bottom of their bumper band couplers is 1¼ inches above the rail, the same measurement as for couplers on the Nos. 4, 20, and 34 locomotives. The Nos. 59 and 60 will couple to the 1909–1915 model of No. 45, but their coupler heights are incompatible with the earlier No. 45 and with the larger cars Nos. 51 and 52. The 59 and 60 have late-model metal trucks with black-painted steel side frames, with 1¼-inch insulated pressed-brass wheels and solid steel axles.

| Side-of-car numbers: | 171; possibly 68 |

No. 59 MEDIUM-SIZED BAGGAGE CAR, 1909-15: Painted tinplated sheet steel, with black roof and platforms

Top: No. 87 vestibuled Pullman car with five large windows, closed-end vestibules, six-wheel trucks with iron wheels; it was produced only for years 1905 and 1906. Middle left: No. 60 medium-sized passenger coach, 1909–1915, designed for No. 34 locomotive, 15½ inches long, late-type steel side frames on trucks, brass wheels. Middle right: No. 59 baggage car with similar characteristics. Bottom left: No. 52 passenger car, 1904–1906, for No. 45 locomotive, with ten arched windows, 19 inches long, brass body, black roof and platforms. Cast-brass side frames with spring detail and brass wheels (1907–1909 cars were made with nickel plate, not brass). Bottom right: No. 51 baggage car, 1904–1909, also for No. 45 locomotive, with stenciled lettering on sides and "111" on doors (catalogue illustration shows "29").

Gd   Exc

and orange body. "BAGGAGE" and "EXPRESS" respectively are embossed near the end of each side, with embossed lines above and below the lettering. The baggage door in one version is unnumbered and in another version has the number "171". Catalogue illustrations show "68". **275 – 450**

No. 60 MEDIUM-SIZED COACH, 1909-15: Polished sheet brass with black-painted tinplated sheet steel roof and platforms. Nine arched windows have embossed frames, and the usual three corrugations run along sides and ends. The No. 87 Pullman parlor car has similar couplers and can be operated in a single train with these cars, but its body is only 5" instead of 6" high.   **350 – 700**

NOTES

1. This "composite" type of construction is typical of early United States–made large-gauge toy trains. The wood frame provided the necessary stiffness before the period where advanced stamping equipment made the all-steel body possible.

2. It should be noted that the 1903–1908 models of the No. 2 interurban are very similar to and the same size as the No. 52 passenger car described above, except that there are no roof braces on the corners of the open platforms, and no bumper or other couplers.

CHAPTER SIX

★

FREIGHT AND WRECK CARS

U nlike the situation on most prototype railroads, the toy passenger train tends to be given more emphasis than freights. Nevertheless, Carlisle & Finch and most other toy train makers produced a variety of freight equipment. As with its passenger cars, Carlisle & Finch over the years included small, large, and finally medium-sized freight cars of assorted types. These will be described in some detail below, but a unique Carlisle & Finch derrick or wrecking crane car will first be considered. This car, the No. 53, is among Carlisle & Finch's most unusual innovations. It is believed to be the only electrically operated wrecking crane made by any company for toy train operation.[1]

A three-pole reversing motor is mounted on the wooden car floor and connected through a reduction gearbox to a drum. A linen "cable" is coiled on the drum, passes over a pulley at the top of the derrick, and is attached to a "big hook" with a spherical iron weight. The motor is powered from the track through the wheels and brass-bound wooden bolsters of the car. A reversing lever controls the direction of the rotation of the drum, raising, lowering, or stopping the hook. Its speed is controlled by the voltage fed to the track. The derrick itself can be swiveled manually as required.

The car itself is not self-propelled but must be pulled by a locomotive. In 1906 and 1907, Carlisle & Finch listed as Outfit No. 70 a "wrecking train" that included appropriate freight equipment and the derrick car pulled by a No. 4 locomotive. The derrick car has been successfully used on an operating Carlisle & Finch layout to lift and re-rail overturned cars.

No. 53 derrick, 1905–1907, the only motorized wrecking derrick, or crane, mounted on trucks built by an American toy train company

Gd   Exc

No. 53 OPERATING DERRICK, 1904-07: Electrically powered derrick on car is 10½" long and 3" wide, and it is 9½" from the top of the rail to the top of the derrick. The derrick is mounted on a wooden flatcar with standard bumper band couplers, the bottoms of which are 1¼" above the rail. The trucks have wooden bolsters to which are fastened brass plates which support split insulated axles and 1" cast-iron wheels. The wooden bolsters have sheet-brass edgings which support the axles of both trucks. **1200 – 2000**

SMALL FREIGHT CARS, 1899–1915

The smallest and most popular freight cars, as with the passenger cars, are the seven 10-inch cars designed primarily for the Nos. 4, 20, and 34 locomotives. Two cars, the No. 11 gondola (called "flat" in the catalogue) and the No. 12 boxcar, were introduced with the No. 4 locomotive in 1899. The caboose (No. 46) appeared in 1903, and the remaining four small freight cars in 1904. All of them are described as 10 inches long over couplers and 3 inches wide, varying in height with the particular type. It should be noted, however, that these dimensions vary somewhat from one production lot to another. For example, both early and late gondolas have been found with lengths over couplers varying from 9⅝ inches to a full 10 inches.

Side-of-car numbers: 26, 131, 171, 1141, 8681; possibly 868

Early Cars

No. 11 SMALL GONDOLA (or FLAT), 1899-1915: This car is 2⅝" above the rails. All versions found have an all-tinplate body and are labeled on each side "131 P.R.R. 131". **125 – 200**
(A) 1899-1902. Sides are covered inside and out by red paper label with black letters and numbers. An early version is

Opposite: three small freight cars. Top left: No. 48 cattle car, 190. 1908, bumper couplers, steel wheels, wood bolsters. Top right: Simil. car, 1909–1913, with steel trucks and brass wheels. Middle left: No. B & O orange hopper car, 1904–1908, iron wheels. Middle rig. Same car with "N. & M." embossed on the sides and steel trucks w. brass wheels. Car on left of middle shelf has a ratchet that opens t. hopper by a chain inside the car; the one on the right has a handle th. directly opens the hopper from underneath. Bottom left: No. 49 ta. car, unmarked, with bumper couplers, iron wheels, hand brakewhee. side railings, and "171" embossed on the frame. Bottom right: La. model, with slightly lower dome, no railing, no brakewheel, handr. attached to tank, no tank markings, steel trucks, and brass wheels.

Top left: CB & Q No. 12 boxcar, 1899–1902, with paper label, link and pin coupler, cast-iron wheels. Top right: PRR red label No. 11 gondola, which should have link and pin couplers (this is the 1903 version with bumper band couplers). Middle left: 1903–1909, same as car above but with tin floor and bumper couplers. Middle right: Blue No. 11 gondola, 1904–1909, with bumper couplers. Bottom left: Last version of boxcar, en-ameled orange with steel side-frame trucks and brass wheels, em-bossed letters "H.V." (Hocking Valley), with "26" on the sliding door. Bottom right: Last gon-dola, em-bossed blue "P.R.R." letters, brass wheels, steel trucks.

No. 4. Electric
Locomotive and Freight Train.

PRICE, $10.00.

8 to 10 VOLTS.   ¾ AMPERE.

A complete and perfect model of a modern freight train. The locomotive has headlight, cylinders, connecting rods, pilot, bell, steam dome, etc. The locomotive is operated by an electric motor concealed in the boiler. The power is transmitted to the wheels by means of double reduction spur gearing with accurately cut teeth.

The locomotive runs at a high speed, about 150 to 200 feet per minute, and is of such power that it will haul ten or twelve freight cars.

The locomotive will haul the two cars up considerable grades, but it is best to have the track as nearly level as possible. Wheels of locomotive are of iron, 2 inches in diameter, while those of the tender and cars are 1 inch diameter.

In the cab of the locomotive is placed a reversing switch, and a lever projects outside of the cab, by means of which the locomotive may be started, stopped and reversed.

The motor is a self-starting one, and has no dead center.

The complete equipment consists of Locomotive, Tender, Flat Car and Box Car; 18 feet of 2-inch gauge steel track; a battery of five zinc-carbon elements, and two 20-oz. jars of Chromite.

We do not furnish battery jars, on account of the extra weight and the danger of breakage in shipment. Use ordinary tumblers or jelly glasses.

When it is desired to run the locomotive by means of 110-volt direct electric light current, refer to page 13 for diagram of connections, etc.

Length of complete Train, 39 inches.
Length of Locomotive and Tender, 18 inches.
Weight of complete outfit, boxed, 16 pounds.

LOCOMOTIVE with TENDER, $6.50.
Flat Cars, 55 cents each. By mail, 75 cents.
Box Cars, $1.20 each. By mail, $1.55.
Price of Chromite, zincs, track, etc., same as for the No. 2 Railway.

This page from the 1901 catalogue features a set with the two early freights. Later catalogues showed the No. 4 with three freights and the No. 45 with three large freight cars and three large passenger cars.

Opposite page, top: Top left: No. 50 flatcar, 1904–1909, iron wheels. Top right: 1911–1915 flatcar, steel trucks and brass wheels. Middle: No. 46 caboose, 1903, paper label "L.S. & M.S. RY." above windows. Bottom left: Red-enameled caboose with black roof, "N & M" embossed. Bottom right: Steel trucks, brass wheels, "N. & M." embossed.

Opposite page, below: Medium and large freight cars. Top: No. 90 large gondola, 1905–1909, 15 inches long, brass side-frame trucks, large brass wheels. Later there was also a medium-sized No. 90 gondola. Middle left: No. 91 15-inch-long NYC & HR boxcar. Middle right: Later No. 91, 13½ inches long, black steel side-frame trucks, brass wheels. Bottom left: No. 92 15-inch-long NYC & HR caboose. Bottom right: Medium-sized No. 92 caboose, 1909–1915, black side-frame steel trucks, brass wheels.

Gd   Exc

reported to have had heavy cardboard sides and a wooden floor, but the catalogue describes the car as made of "heavy tin." Its two trucks have wooden bolsters to which are nailed 1"-diameter cast-iron wheels, the nails serving as axles. The car has link and pin couplers on both ends.

(B) 1903. Same as above, but car now has bumper band couplers, the bottoms of which are 1¼" above rail.

(C) 1904-05(?). Same as above, but instead of paper label covering, the sides are now painted dark red and the "131 P.R.R. 131" lettering is embossed. In some examples embossed letters and numbers are painted gold, but originality of this gold paint is uncertain.

(D) 1906(?)-09. Same as above, but sides and embossed lettering are painted blue.

(E) 1911-15. Same as above, but car has metal trucks with black steel side frames and ⅞"-diameter insulated brass wheels on solid steel axles.

No. 12 SMALL BOXCAR, 1899-1915: The car is 4¾" high above rails with tinplate sides and black tinplate roof.

125 – 200

(A) 1899-1902. This car has a wooden floor. Body sides and ends are covered by light yellow paper label with black lettering and trim. "1141" and "C.B. & Q. / R.R" printed near each end of both sides, and the same legend plus "Fast Freight" is in smaller letters on center sliding doors. It has two wooden bolster trucks, 1"-diameter iron wheels on nails as axles, and link and pin couplers.

(B) 1903-09. Same as above, but floor is tinplate instead of wood, and bumper band couplers 1¼" above rail are substituted for link and pin couplers.

(C) 1911-15. Same as above, but instead of having labeled paper the body is painted orange, with "H.V. 26 H.V." in embossed letters on sides and door. (H.V. stands for "Hocking Valley," a railroad in southern Ohio that became a part of Chesapeake & Ohio Railway, now CSX.) Trucks are metal with black steel side frames, insulated brass wheels ⅞" diameter, and solid steel axles.

Note: Professor Franklin Loveland, in the course of his examination of Carlisle & Finch experimental models of the early 1930s (detailed in Chapter Ten), located an orange boxcar of the 1911-15 vintage with the lettering "Prince Majestic Flour" hand-painted across the entire side of the car in black enamel. Inside was a letterhead telling which mill made this kind of flour. If — as seems likely — this was a factory original, it is the only known example of a product promotional car by Carlisle & Finch.

No. 46 SMALL CABOOSE, 1903-15: This car is 5½" high above the rails and is made entirely of tinplate (including floor), with black roof and single steps on each side. Bumper band couplers 1¼" above rail are on both ends of the car.

175 – 275

(A) 1903-04(?). Body is completely wrapped by red paper on which are printed black vertical lines to simulate board siding. High cupola has vertical rectangular windows. Black-lettered "L.S. & M.S.RY" above three arched windows on each side, and very large black numbers "8681" are below the windows. Car has two four-wheel wooden bolster trucks to which are nailed 1" iron wheels, turning on the nails as axles. The roof, cupola sides, and open caboose platforms are painted black and have no roof braces on the corners. No examples of the "Chicago and Northwestern" lettering or the number "868", shown in the catalogue illustration, have been found.

(B) 1905(?)-07. Same as above, but caboose now has wire braces from the four corners of the platforms to the roof. Exact date of this change is uncertain.

(C) 1908-11. Same as above, but paper label on body is replaced by red enamel on sides and ends, with embossed letters "N. & M." in black below windows on each side. The cupola sides and the end platforms are not also enameled red.

(D) 1911-12. Same as above, but trucks are metal with black steel side frames and ⅞"-diameter insulated brass wheels on solid steel axles. The caboose "N. & M." letters are not separately painted.

(E) 1912-15. Same as above, but with a slightly lower cupola with square instead of rectangular cupola windows, and no platform to roof braces.

Four Small Freights, 1904–1915

No. 47 COAL (HOPPER) CAR	175 – 275
No. 48 CATTLE CAR	125 – 200
No. 49 OIL (TANK) CAR	125 – 200
No. 50 FLATCAR	75 – 150

(A) 1904-09. These cars, first listed in 1904, like all of the other small freight cars, are 10" long, 3" wide, with individually varying heights. They have the usual wooden bolster trucks, iron wheels 1" in diameter turning on nails as axles, and bumper band couplers 1¼" above rail.

The coal or hopper car (No. 47) is 4" high and is painted orange with black trim and "B. & O." in black. It has a crank and ratchet on the top of one side that opens or closes the bottom hopper doors by a short chain. It has a tinplate floor.

The cattle car (No. 48) is 4¾" high, and is painted yellow with sliding center doors and a wooden floor. It is unmarked, and has cross-bracing on the doors and on the slats at each end, as well as a diagonal brace at the ends of both sides.

The oil car (No. 49) is 4¾" high, and is painted yellow. It has brakewheels on each end and a railing fastened to the frame along each side. The number "171" is embossed on each side of the frame, which is all metal.

The flatcar (No. 50) is yellow with "171" embossed on sides of frame, and a very low raised edge around the deck. It is all metal.

(B) 1911-15. All of these cars now have metal trucks with black steel side frames, insulated ⅞"-diameter brass wheels, and solid axles. The cars remain otherwise unchanged except as follows:

The coal or hopper car (No. 47) has a handle at the bottom of one side that directly opens or closes the hopper doors. Instead of "B. & O." it is labeled "N. & M." in embossed letters on each side

The cattle car (No. 48) still retains its wooden floor, but the car ends are now solid instead of having slats, the spaces between the slats on the sides are rounded at the ends, and there are no diagonal braces on the sides. The sliding doors remain the same, with cross-bracing.

The oil car (No. 49) has a handrail along the tank on each side instead of a railing fastened to the frame and no brakewheels.

The tank dome is also lower and there is no number embossed on side of frame.

The flatcar (No. 50) is unchanged.

LARGE FREIGHT CARS, 1905–1909

The following three 15-inch tinplate freight cars were brought out in 1905 to accompany the early No. 45 locomotive. They are of all-metal construction and have bumper band couplers with their bottoms 1¾ inches above the rail, which makes them compatible with the No. 45 locomotive and the large baggage and passenger cars Nos. 50 and 51; it is not certain, however, whether this coupler height was continued in 1909 (the last year in which these 15-inch-long cars were listed) or whether the coupler height in this year was changed to the 1¼-inch height that became standard thereafter. The trucks of these cars have wood bolsters and cast-bronze freight-type side frames with 1¼-inch pressed-brass wheels on split insulated axles.

No. 90 LARGE GONDOLA, 1905-09: 15" long, 4" wide, and 3" high, painted dark yellow and lettered "N.Y.C. & H.R." in gold. Black-painted brakewheels are at each end. **300 – 500**

No. 91 LARGE BOXCAR, 1905-09: 15" long, 4" wide, and 5¼" high, painted orange with a black roof; lettered "N.Y.C & H.R." in gold on both ends of each side. Black-painted brakewheels are mounted on roof at each end, and a sliding loading door is in the center of each side. **400 – 600**

No. 92 LARGE CABOOSE, 1905-09: 15" long, 4" wide, and 6¾" high. Six arched windows on each side, with two arched windows and a door on each end to open platforms with braces from platform corners to roof, and two small rectangular windows on the sides and ends of the cupola. Body, cupola sides, and platforms are reddish brown with black roof, with "N.Y.C. & H.R." in gold letters below windows on each side. **400 – 600**

MEDIUM-SIZED FREIGHT CARS, 1911–1915

Between 1909 and 1911 (no catalogue was issued in 1910), the large freight cars described above were discontinued and smaller cars of the same type were produced, as described below. The catalogues continued the same illustrations and the same catalogue numbers, but the new series of cars are 1½ inches shorter than the earlier cars. They are referred to here as medium-sized freight cars.

These cars are of all-metal construction, are 13½ inches long, and all have bumper band couplers with their bottoms 1¼ inches above the rail. These cars are intended for use with the late (1909–1915) locomotive No. 45, and their couplers match those also of Nos. 4, 20, and 34 and associated cars. The trucks are all metal in one piece, with black steel side frames and 1¼-inch insulated pressed-brass wheels on solid steel axles.

Side-of-car number: 171

No. 90 MEDIUM GONDOLA, 1911-15: 13½" long, 4" wide, and 3½" high, painted dark yellow or orange and lettered

Gd   Exc

"N.Y.C. & H.R." in black. Like the earlier and longer No. 90, it has black metal brakewheels on each end.   **300 – 500**

No. 91 MEDIUM BOXCAR, 1911-15: 13½" long, 4" wide, and 5¼" high, painted orange with a black roof and black-painted embossed letters "N. & M." on ends of each side, with an embossed but unpainted "171" on the center of the sliding doors. This car also has black brakewheels on roof at each end.   **300 – 500**

No. 92 MEDIUM CABOOSE, 1911-15: 13½" long, 4" wide, and 6¾" high. Five arched windows on each side with only a

Gd   Exc

door (no windows) at ends to open platforms, with braces from platform corners to roof. It also has two rectangular windows on sides and ends of cupola. Body, cupola sides, and platforms are painted orange with black roof, with "N.Y.C. & H.R." stenciled in black on each side, below windows.   **300 – 500**

NOTE
1. Lionel made an O Gauge powered crane but not a wrecking derrick.

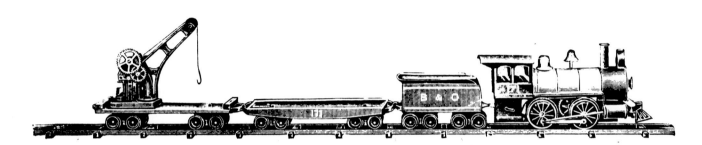

No. 70 Electric Locomotive and Wrecking Train set included No. 4 locomotive and tender, No. 50 flatcar, No. 53 derrick, eighteen feet of strip-steel track and ties, and six dry batteries.

CHAPTER SEVEN

★

TRACK, SWITCHES, BRIDGES, AND STATIONS

From the beginning of the Carlisle & Finch production of 2-inch-gauge two-rail trolleys (1897), the company offered track, switches, bridges, and stations to go with its rolling stock. This section of the book will be a description of this range of trackage and accessories. Carlisle & Finch advertising followed that of the other toy train companies in encouraging customers to purchase accessories so as to turn a train set into a complete model railway system.

TRACK

By way of reminder, in nineteen of the twenty years in which Carlisle & Finch produced toy electric trains and trolleys, the track was 2-inch gauge and two-rail. Only during the first year of toy train production — late 1896 — was 2-inch-gauge trackage offered of the inside third-rail type. As already noted, however, no examples have been found of this three-rail track or of the trolley car designed to use it.

The 2-inch-gauge two-rail track exclusively used from 1897 on was made up from "strip-steel" track pressed into slots cut in wooden ties. In later years, however, brass

No. 14. Rail Connector.
PRICE, 3c. Each.   By Mail, 4c. Each.
For Strip Steel Track.

In order to make electrical connection between the ends of the rails when two or more sections of track are used, it is necessary to either solder wires to the rails and twist these wires together or to solder the rails themselves together, or what is probably the best way is to use these rail connectors. They are applied instantly, or removed with equal ease. The two rails are placed with their ends abutting and one of these connectors slipped up from beneath.

The piece of thin brass set into the wood block serves to make electrical connections between the two rails and also to hold them firmly in position. The small screw and washer should be placed on the outer side of the track so as to allow the battery wires to be attached.

— — —

Tracks and Ties (Strip Steel). •
PRICE, 35c. One Set.   By Mail, 50c.

tubular rail (called "Tee Rail") with wooden ties was also available, both in pieces and in prefabricated sections.

Track connectors and bumper posts were available, but these were designed for use with the strip-steel rail only.

UNNUMBERED STRIP-STEEL TRACK, 1897-1915: Strip-steel rails with ⅜" profile and slotted wooden ties 3" long were listed in all Carlisle & Finch catalogues. Slots exactly 2" apart were cut in each tie. Strip rail was available from 1897 in 9′ lengths, two pieces of which, with the prerequisite ties, would form a circle of about 3′ in diameter. The customer himself would have to bend the rail to the appropriate radius while assembling the track. Train sets were described as including varying amounts of track materials, but in most cases additional rail in 9′ lengths was also mentioned at the end of the descriptive material; with this extra rail, the customer could vary the configuration to be oval or circular, with such radius as he chose. Beginning in 1907, the lengths of this rail with thirty-three ties were separately listed and were illustrated in the annual catalogues, but the trackage was never assigned a separate catalogue number.

From 1897 through 1901, the wooden ties were ⅞" wide by ⅜" thick, and examples found from this period are stained a dark purple color. Beginning in 1902, however, the ties were smaller, with a cross-section of about ¾" by ⅜", and the usual color was dark green.

No. 14 TRACK CONNECTOR, 1899-1915:
(A) 1899-1904. A track connector was needed to couple adjacent sections of strip-steel rail, and this was made available in the 1899 catalogue. This consisted of a U-shaped clamp to be inserted under the rail ends of the connection rails. Set screws were used to make the connection tight on each rail end.
(B) 1905-15. In 1905 a new design of rail connector for strip-steel track was adopted. The new connector consisted of a green wooden block about 1½" square with a slot cut across it. A very thin brass sheet covered the top of the block and also was bent so as to fit down into the slot. A small screw served both to fasten the brass sheet to the block and as an electrical terminal for a feed wire.

No. 85 BUMPER POST, 1904-15: In 1904 a track bumper post was offered. This item consists of a short wooden base with slots cut into it to hold the rail. A wooden block firmly attached to this base served to protect against siding end derailment.

No. 93 TEE RAIL TRACK, 1905-15: Rolled sheet-brass rail (called Tee Rail in the catalogue) with a tubular bull head and realistic profile was introduced in 1905. As with the strip-steel track, the brass rail and wooden ties were sold as separate components. The rail came in 24" lengths with a steel pin in one end, and the ties came in boxes of one hundred. The customer constructed the track himself, carefully bending the rail to the desired radius for curves and using small nails as spikes to hold the foot of the rail in the ties. The ties were recessed so as to make the system "self-gauging."

UNNUMBERED SECTIONAL TEE RAIL TRACK, 1908-15: Factory built-up brass Tee Rail sections were first offered in 1908. This may have been done in response to the all-metal built-up sectional track then being offered by competition such as Lionel, Knapp, and the German makers. No catalogue number was assigned to this track either. The rails are similar to those listed above as No. 93. They are nailed to wooden crossties, but are without a rigid sub-base. Each standard straight section was 15" long, and curved sections were made to an 18" radius, eight sections forming a full circle of about 3'. Half-sections of both straight and curved track were also offered. Wider radius curves were not listed, and that meant that this rather flimsy sectional track could not accommodate the large No. 45 locomotive.

SWITCHES AND CROSSINGS

The listings here are not given in catalogue number sequence but in a progressive order to chronicle development of items.

No. 6 STRIP-STEEL TRACK CROSSING, 1897-1915: In its first extant catalogue (#2, 1897), Carlisle & Finch listed a 90-degree crossing for strip-steel rail. It consists of short pieces of strip-steel rail driven into a slotted wooden base, measuring 6" square. This crossing continued substantially unchanged through 1915.

No. T-6 TEE RAIL TRACK CROSSING, 1908-15: This is a similar 90-degree crossing and was introduced to the line in 1908 to match the Tee Rail track being offered at that time. The Tee Rail is nailed to a wooden base that is 6" square.

No. 10 "Y" SWITCH, 1897-1905: The first Carlisle & Finch switch or turnout[1] was listed in a supplement to the 1897 catalogue, and was a "Y"-type switch, curving both to the left and to the right. It was made entirely of standard ⅜" strip-steel rails. The fixed or "stock" rails are pressed into appropriately cut slots in a base made up of three lateral ⅜" boards 5¾" long and of varying widths. These, in turn, are fastened together at their ends by similar longitudinal strips of wood to form a rectangular base 12½" long and 7½" wide. This results in an "open frog" type of switch, with guardrails positioned so as to prevent wheels from derailing at the gaps in the "frog" necessary where two rails necessarily cross. The moving points are controlled by a small lever and are held in position for either route by a light coil spring. This was a very simple but ingenious arrangement and worked well.

Nos. 10-R and 10-L SWITCHES (early), 1900-05: These right-turning (10-R) and left-turning (10-L) switches were introduced in 1900 and discontinued in this form after 1905. There were two version of these switches.

(A) 1900-02(?). As introduced in 1900, these switches were identical in all respects including size to the early No. 10 "Y" switch. The curved portions of these switches have a radius of 18".

No. 85. Track Bumper.

PRICE, 20c.   By Mail, 27c.

For Strip Steel Track.

No. 93. Brass Tee Rail.

PRICE of each single rail, per 24 inch length, 10 cents.
Postage, on one rail 8 cents additional.   On two rails, 12 cents additional.
Cross Ties for Tee Rails 75 cents per 100.
Postage on 100 ties, 23 cents additional.

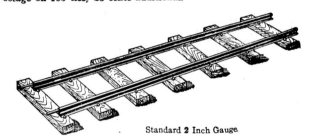

Standard 2 Inch Gauge.

This rail is made of sheet brass stamped and rolled into "T" section. It is $\frac{5}{16}$ inch high. Each length has a steel pin in one end and the other end is hollow so that the rails can be attached together in long lengths. The rails are fastened to the ties by nailing them down with small flat-head brads or tacks. The track can be laid out straight or curved easily between the fingers and will stay in any position when fastened to the crossties.

No. 94-RT. Right-Hand Switch.

PRICE, $1.00.   By Mail, $1.25.

Gauge, 2 Inches.

This switch is made of "T" rail and can be used only with our "T" rail track. It is of suitable curvature for the No. 45 locomotive. The rails are made of tin.
Length, 15 inches. Width, 7½ inches.

No. 95-LT. Left-Hand Switch.

PRICE, $1.00.   By Mail, $1.25.

(B) 1903-05. Probably about 1903, the throw mechanism of these "late" switches was changed and the coil spring pressure-locking arrangement was eliminated. Instead, a bent rod with a handle on one end could be turned so as to lock the movable points into the straight or curved position.

Nos. 58-R and 58-L SWITCHES, 1904-05: In 1904 this pair of switches was listed with a curvature radius of 30" (5'-diameter circle) to accommodate the large No. 45 locomotive that had been introduced the previous year, 1903. In all other respects (including the throw mechanism), these switches were identical with the 1903 version of the earlier No. 10 switches, as described in (B) above. These switches were made in this form for only two years, and were replaced in 1906 by the late model Nos. 10-R and 10-L described below.

Nos. 10-R and 10-L SWITCHES (late), 1906-15: In 1906 the earlier small radius No. 10 switches, as well as the similar wide radius No. 58 switches, were replaced by a new pair of switches given the same catalogue numbers, 10-R and 10-L. These new switches, however, are of entirely different design and construction. Their curvature is the same as that for the No. 58 switches described above — a 30" radius for a circle of track with an inside diameter of 5'. The metal rails are not set in slots but are fastened directly to a solid wooden base board, measuring 15" x 6½". Short slots are cut in the base board at each rail end to receive the ends of standard ⅜" strip-steel rails from connecting tracks. The rail-holding slots are lined with sheet metal as were the second series of rail connectors. More importantly the movable point rails are integral to a stamped-metal plate that is pivoted on the base board and turns when the switch is thrown. This results in a "closed frog" switch.[2] The bent rod throw mechanism is

similar to that of the No. 58 switches and of the 1903 version of the earlier No. 10 switches. See illustration.

No. 94-RT and No. 95-LT SWITCHES, 1905-15: These right- and left-hand switches were introduced in 1905, to be used with the brass Tee Rail that was first offered in that year. As in the wide-radius "late" No. 10 strip rail switches described above, the Tee Rail of these new switches was fastened directly to a 14½" x 6¾" base board, and the movable point rails were similarly attached to a pivoting metal plate. The curves are fixed to a radius of 30", which makes these switches able to accommodate all Carlisle & Finch equipment including the larger No. 45 locomotive. See catalogue illustration.

"Compromise Joints"

This is the term used by prototype railroads to connect together two pieces of rail of different sizes or weights. Although Carlisle & Finch never made or referred to such joints, they are needed wherever strip steel and tubular track is to be joined. To make these for an operating layout, it is only necessary to solder a short piece of strip-steel rail to the inside web of a piece of tubular track. With a bit of filing, cars will pass over such a joint without derailing or jolting.

BRIDGES

All bridges were designed for strip-steel track and are so designated in the catalogues. An ingenious customer, however, could of course rearrange the bridge ties to accommodate Tee Rail track or even sectional track.

No. 5 BRIDGE, 1897-1915: At the same time that Carlisle & Finch listed its first two-rail trolley, No. 1, it also listed its first bridge, No. 5. Over the years, however, this No. 5 bridge came in two quite different versions as described below.

(A) 1897-98. This early bridge is described as "an ornamental brass bridge . . . made of yellow brass, dipped and lacquered." Purple-stained wooden piers about 3" high by 4¾" wide, as well as a middle bridge tie, are slotted to receive strip-steel rails. The bridge is 10" long, with 4⅝" clearance between the cast-brass sides. The sides themselves have brackets cast into them at each end and in the middle for attachment to the end piers and to the intermediate tie.

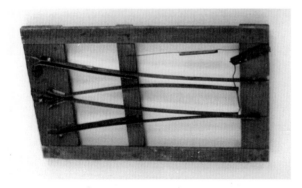

No. 10 "Y" Switch from 1897–1905 and No. 10-L wide-radius switch for strip-steel track, 1906–1915

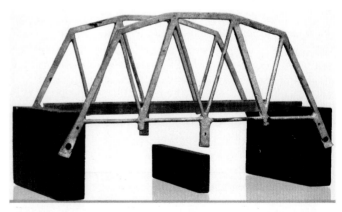

No. 5(A) bridge from 1897, the version illustrating "No. 5 Ornamental Railway Bridge" in all catalogues. The center wooden block would have been suspended from the bridge.

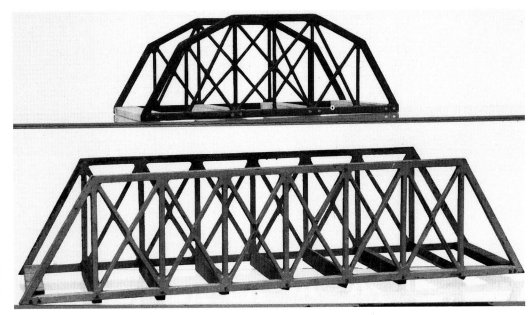

Top, No. 5(B); bottom, the No. 56 truss type. These bridges could have wooden abuttments raise them above the table or floor but would also work placed directly on the layout surface.

This bridge could not be used without ramps to raise the connecting tracks to the bridge level.

(B) 1899-1915. In 1899 the early yellow brass bridge described in (A) above was replaced by a generally similar but longer and heavier bridge of cast iron. While intended for use with similar 3"-high wooden piers at each end, this bridge has no cast brackets extending below the track level, so that it can be placed at grade level. This iron bridge is 12½" long, and it was continued in the catalogue through 1915, although the catalogue illustration was never changed from the one used in 1897 to illustrate the yellow brass bridge. The iron sides are painted, usually a dark red, and clearance between sides is about 5". This bridge accordingly could not be used by No. 45 locomotives unless assembled with longer ties to provide at least 6" clearance between sides.

No. 56 TRUSS BRIDGE, 1904-15: This large overhead-type truss bridge, 23" long, was first listed in 1904 and continued without change through 1915. Its cast-iron sides are usually painted orange or yellow. Again it is intended to be used with wooden piers at the ends about 3" high, but without the piers it can be assembled at ground level. As designed this bridge is also too narrow for the No. 45 locomotive, but could be assembled with 6" clearance between the sides by using longer ties between the cast-iron sides.

No. 57 SUSPENSION BRIDGE, 1904-15: This very large suspension-type bridge has its cast-iron sides in four separate

pieces, and is 36" long when assembled. It was designed to be used by any Carlisle & Finch equipment, having the 6" clearance between sides necessary for the large No. 45 locomotive. Unlike the late Nos. 5 and 56 bridges, which could be placed at ground level, this bridge has cast-iron piers that lift the rails about 3" above the surrounding ground or floor. The bridge is usually painted a dark yellow or brass color. Probably because of its size, its relatively high cost, and its limited usefulness in most layouts, it is quite rare. See catalogue illustration.

STATIONS

Over the years, Carlisle & Finch listed a number of passenger and freight stations. Accessory platforms and loading derricks were often included with the larger stations.

No. 9 PASSENGER STATION, 1897-1915: In a supplement to its 1897 catalogue Carlisle & Finch listed a passenger station that was continued with some variations throughout its whole period of production. These variations are listed below.

(A) 1897-1901. The first station was a peaked-roof rectangular structure with a gable over the telegrapher's bay. It is 12" long and 6" high, and its four walls are covered with brightly lithographed paper on which are printed rectangular windows, doors, and red brick detail. The name "BUFFALO" is printed above the doors in large letters.

This earliest station included a pair of electromagnetically activated train order semaphore signals. Each signal was wired in series between the power supply and a control section of one of the rails, so that the semaphore arm is raised whenever a locomotive or motor car enters that section of track and draws current through the solenoid coil, and it falls when the engine has passed off of the control rail. This is certainly the first electrically operated signal for any toy train — more than a quarter of a century before Lionel offered its first working semaphore.

No example of this earliest model has been examined, but company records examined by Frank Loveland show that

No. 57. Suspension Bridge.

PRICE, $3.00.

The semaphore solenoid for the late (1909) No. 9 station has two wires — one wired to an insulated rail, the other connected directly to the current source. Earlier stations had two semaphores, each activated by a separate control track. When a locomotive passes over the control track with its insulated rail, it draws its current through the solenoid and the increased current flowing through the solenoid is sufficient to raise the signal without appreciably slowing the locomotive. Lionel developed a special track section some years later to activate trackside accessories. The Lionel version utilized its three-rail configuration and passed power from one outside rail to the insulated other outside rail through the rolling stock wheels and axles. Hence in the Carlisle & Finch system, only a locomotive or powered trolley activates the accessory, whereas in the Lionel system, every car in the train activates the signal.

some two hundred of these stations were made in September 1897 at a cost of 69 cents each, 112 more were made in September 1898 — when the cost soared to 86 cents.

(B) 1901-02. About 1901 the No. 9 station was changed by eliminating the single gable and substituting a clerestory roof for the peaked roof of the earlier model. While neither the catalogue illustration nor the description in 1901 showed this change, it is indicated by a drawing of the electrical connections for the two signals on page 18 of the 1901 catalogue, reproduced on page 58.

(C) 1903-07. The 1903 model of the No. 9 station was still covered in a gaily printed red brick detail paper, but was otherwise changed significantly. A rain-diverting "gable" protected each of the two passenger doors, and these gables were repeated on both sides of the station. The clerestory roof was continued, thus allowing better light to enter the waiting rooms. The two operating train order signals were now placed together between the two gables. "DEPOT" on a signboard was substituted for the earlier "BUFFALO". The new station was larger — 7" wide, 13" long, and 7" high. This station was described in the 1903 catalogue as "our new 1903 model," and a new illustration conformed to the above description.

(D) 1909-15. No No. 9 station at all was listed in the 1908 catalogue, but in 1909 a No. 9 station, with no change in the 1903 illustration, was said to be "our 1909 design." It is described as having only a single automatic signal and is slightly smaller than the previous model, with stated dimensions of 12" long, 7½" wide, and 7" high. An example of this station has been found in excellent condition, covered with red brick paper on which architectural details are printed. It has a clerestory roof without gables and a single automatic signal, as described above. Again, the windows and doors are rectangular and the name is "BUFFALO"; in fact, the building appears very similar to the 1901 station described in (B) above.

No. 55 LOADING PLATFORM AND DERRICK, 1904: This freight-loading platform is made of wood and was 12" long, 5" wide, and 2¾" high. An electrically operated derrick was described in the catalogue as being located at one end of the platform. This item was listed only in the 1904 catalogue. Accordingly, it is extremely rare and none is known to have survived.

No. 96 FREIGHT DEPOT WITH DERRICK, 1905-08. This large "freight depot" is described in the catalogue as being 29" long, 14" wide, and 11½" high. It consists of a raised loading platform protected by a barrel roof which is supported by six columns. A loading derrick, this time hand-operated, was placed at the opened end of the platform. This depot is very rare, and no specimens were available for examination (page from 1908 catalogue reproduced here).

No. 97 PASSENGER TERMINAL, 1905-08: This was the largest passenger station offered by Carlisle & Finch — 36" long, 14" wide, and 12" high. It was described as made of cast iron with sheet-iron roof. It consisted of two stub-end tracks with passenger platforms covered by a wide barrel roof with a station building and two-story "head house" at end. Although listed for four years, because of its size and complexity it is a very rare item, and one was not available for examination for this book. See catalogue illustration.

No. 96. Freight Depot, with Loading Derrick.

PRICE, $3.00.

This Depot has wood base, cast iron columns and sheet iron roof, neatly painted. The derrick operates by hand windlass and swings around on a pivot. No track is furnished at above price. This depot is large and elaborately finished and will be found indispensable in making up railway systems.

Length, 29 inches. Width, 14 inches. Height, 11½ inches. Weight, crated, 21¾ lbs.

No. 97. Passenger Station.

PRICE, $5.00.

A double track station. Made of cast iron with sheet iron roof and wooden floor. Has two tracks and platforms. Nicely painted and decorated.

Can be used in connection with any of our railways.

    Length....................................36 inches.
    Width......................................14   "
    Height.....................................12   "
Weight, crated, 30 lbs.

Two rare items, from a 1908 catalogue, which carried prices lower than those of earlier years — a Carlisle & Finch response to market pressure

NOTES

1. A "turnout" is the entire arrangement by which a train can be turned out to the side of a rail line. The "switch" is the arrangement by which the movable "points" of rail can be set to accomplish this turning. Turnout is the preferred term.

2. While open frogs are normally used by prototype railroads, they also use closed frogs for high speed or heavy freight service. These closed frogs, however, are quite different in design from those used on toy railroads Turnouts are often "bench-built" by prototype railroads and then transported to the site for installation.

3. Although Carlisle & Finch never made "compromise joints" to permit connection of strip-steel track to tubular track, these are relatively easy to effect. It is necessary simply to solder a short piece of strip-steel rail to the inside web of a similar piece of tubular rail. A bit of filing might be necessary to avoid the trains jolting as they pass through the conversion joint.

CHAPTER EIGHT

★

POWER SOURCES

In the early days, one of the great impediments to sales of electrically operated toy trains was the difficulty of providing a satisfactory low voltage/high amperage sustainable power source. Many homes did not have electric lighting at all, and even those which had been electrified had no safe or convenient method of reducing the rather high main direct or alternating current to the low voltage required for toy train operation. The various devices offered and the methods suggested by Carlisle & Finch in this period provide an interesting sidelight on the condition of early domestic electrification.

BATTERIES

1897–1902:   Chromite Batteries

The primary source of power suggested by Carlisle & Finch in the early days was the Chromite wet battery.[1] A Chromite battery was furnished as part of the sets offered from 1897 through 1902. The following explanation from the catalogue is enlightening:

The battery consists of three zinc-carbon elements (electrodes) and one ten-ounce can of chromite.... The use of chromite does away with all acids. To operate the battery, dissolve the ten ounces of chromite in one quart of water. This makes enough solution for two charges.

The customer was to furnish his own glass jar, presumably a large Mason or pickling jar, pour in half of the chromite solution, insert the zinc carbon electrodes, and connect these with wires to the two rails. There was apparently no way to vary the voltage or speed except by partially withdrawing the electrodes from the solution. The car would simply run when the wires were connected, and it would stop when they were disconnected.

After 1902 the chromite battery was no longer sold or recommended.

1903–1915:   Dry Batteries

Beginning with the 1903 catalogue, the only type of battery suggested or included as part of train sets was the dry cell battery. The introduction to this catalogue stated:

Dry batteries are used exclusively.... They are absolutely safe and may be handled by a small child. Cannot spill if upset.

This statement was repeated in every subsequent catalogue through 1915, even though a transformer for household alternating current and a direct current reducer for household direct current were first listed in 1908 and thereafter. That the use of dry cell batteries was considered adequate to the end of Carlisle & Finch production is justified by statements in the later catalogues that Carlisle & Finch equipment drew less current than did competing makes and so could be operated better and more cheaply on dry batteries. What was not pointed out was the very limited life and the replacement expense of these batteries. For example, when the large No. 45 locomotive was introduced in 1903, it was suggested that eight dry batteries would be required to operate it; this number was increased to ten in later catalogues.

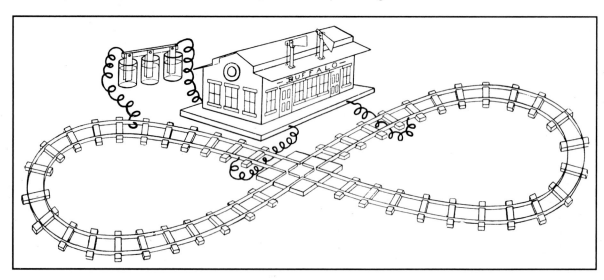

The 1901 catalogue demonstrated how to connect battery, station, and a figure 8 track.

The hand-powered dynamo, first offered in 1897

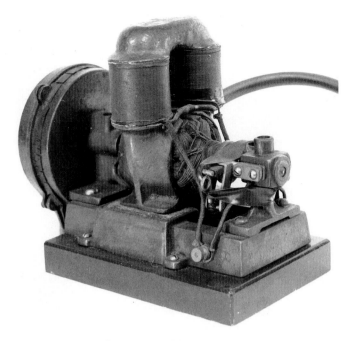

The water-powered generator, 1897–1915

Again, a rheostat for varying the battery voltage was never mentioned nor listed in the catalogues, although it was badly needed — if not essential — for most operating layouts.

DYNAMOS

The need for sustainable power sources was recognized from the beginning of Carlisle & Finch production, when two dynamos were listed along with the earliest motorized cars.

No. 7 HAND-POWERED DYNAMO, 1897-1915: This device consisted of a flywheel, to which is attached a crank handle which, when turned, drives a direct current generator through spur gears. Sufficient voltage was provided with which to operate the smaller locomotives and motor cars, and this could be varied by varying the speed of the hand-wheel and its generator.

No. 7-S LARGER DYNAMO, 1899-1915: This larger and more powerful hand-operated dynamo was introduced in 1899. It generated 10-20 volts DC at up to two amperes. A surviving example has been used to operate the large No. 45 locomotive with a three-car train. The height of the dynamo is 7" and the height over the hand-wheel is 11½".

No. 8 WATER POWER PLANT, 1897-1915: To avoid the need for muscle power, this hydroelectric generator was listed from the beginning. It was designed to be attached by means of a hose to a water faucet. A water pressure of 40 to 50 pounds per square inch gives 8 to 10 volts DC at 1 to 2 amperes. This was sufficient power to operate any Carlisle & Finch engine or car. Speed could be varied by varying the water flow through the faucet. In the early days of production, a dynamo such as this was the only thoroughly satisfactory way to power an electric

toy, if it could be located in a sink, basin, or tub within which the water-powered generator could be placed and through which the waste water could drain.

No. 16 LARGER WATER GENERATOR, 1899-1915: This "hydro-electric dynamo," introduced in 1899, was much larger and heavier than No. 7 above, and produced about three times as much electricity as No. 7 for the same amount of water. The No. 16 generator operated on water pressures of from 40 to 90 pounds per square inch, and produced a maximum current of from 2 amperes at 15 volts DC to 3½ amperes at 25 volts DC, depending on the water pressure. A surviving specimen able simultaneously to power several large Carlisle & Finch locomotives has proved a very satisfactory power source for operating a Carlisle & Finch layout.

Note: Included in various Carlisle & Finch catalogues from 1899 to 1915 are several even larger dynamos designed to be belt-driven by small horsepower internal combustion engines also offered by Carlisle & Finch as "prime movers." These items are outside the subject of Carlisle & Finch's train production, however, and will not be individually described.

TRANSFORMERS AND DC REDUCERS

No. 58 TRANSFORMER, 1908-15: Carlisle & Finch first listed its only transformer in 1908 and continued it without change through 1915. It was designed for either 110 or 220 volts of alternating current input. The transformer was in the shape of an upright cylinder 5¼" in diameter and 7½" high, with small cast-iron brackets at the base which could be used to fasten the device to a table or the floor. A wooden handle on top could be adjusted from "off" to five different voltage steps between 10 and 15 volts. While Carlisle & Finch never indicated amperage, a surviving specimen has successfully powered large Carlisle & Finch and Voltamp locomotives.

Carlisle & Finch
transformer

No. 58 DIRECT CURRENT REDUCER, 1908-15: Under the same catalogue section each year from 1908 through 1915, reference is also made to a direct current reducer which would provide 10 to 15 volts DC from either 110 volts or 220 volts of direct current. In some areas of New York and other cities, the household power in this period was direct rather than alternating current, and in these cases, a DC reducer had to be used instead of a transformer. Today, few if any households served by commercial power companies have direct current. Although all the power sources described above were available for the last eight years of Carlisle & Finch's toy train production, the catalogues consistently listed dry batteries as preferred.

OTHER POWER SOURCES

As noted in Chapter Two, in 1897 and 1898 the No. 2-S eight-wheel trolley, designed for show window use, had its motors especially wound so that they could be run on household current in series with a light bulb. Warnings were given not to use in this way directly connected household lighting for operation of other trolleys or trains.

Nevertheless, from 1899 through 1901 the catalogues included instructions and a diagram for operating trains or trolleys from household direct current by connecting an electric light bulb in series with a homemade lead-acid storage battery, with this in turn connected parallel with the tracks. Apparently, the double danger provided by a glass jar full of sulfuric acid and one of the track rails directly connected to a high voltage line caused this scheme to be deleted from later catalogues.

In this connection, it should be noted that it was customary during this period for European electric train manufacturers to provide a somewhat similar arrangement as a power source. This device consisted of a wooden box on which was mounted a socket for an electric light bulb that was wired in series with a variable resistance contained in the box. Such an arrangement could use household 110-volt or 220-volt direct or alternating current. This avoided the danger from the sulfuric acid of a battery, but the risk of electric shock from the simultaneous touching of a grounded water pipe or radiator and a rail directly connected to a 110-volt line made this arrangement too dangerous for use by children. One of these devices by an unknown manufacturer has been successfully used experimentally on 110-volt alternating current to operate Carlisle & Finch and Voltamp trains.

NOTE
1. Chromite, $FeCr_2O_4$, an oxide of iron and chromium, is a naturally occurring mineral.

CHAPTER NINE

★

RELATED CARLISLE & FINCH
ELECTRICAL TOYS

Included in the various Carlisle & Finch catalogues are a few other electrically operated toys that would, if specimens were ever to surface, be prized collectors' items.

No. 4 INCLINED PLANE RAILWAY, 1897: This is described in the 1897 catalogue as follows:

> Reproduction in miniature of the inclined plane railways used in cities having high hills and of coal industries on banks of rivers. It is entirely automatic, one car going up while the other descends. Motor is reversed when each car reaches the top of plane.

Frank Loveland believes these toys were most likely models of the Price Hill Incline in Cincinnati, which was located close to Carlisle & Finch's factory on West Sixth Street, and photographs of this incline appearing in the second volume of *Cincinnati Street Cars*, by Wagner and Wright, seem to support this conclusion.

The plane is 28" long and its height is 20"; the motor can be stopped and started at any point. This device was particularly recommended for show window display, and was probably sold primarily for this use. Frank Loveland's search of the Carlisle & Finch files reveals that one hundred of these inclines were made in November 1897, and some twenty additional ones appeared later. Thanks to his research, we are able to reproduce a page from the production records to document the planning of incline manufacture. Collectors are still looking for a surviving incline toy, but none has yet turned up. The No. 4 incline was not listed in any catalogue later than 1897.

No. 4. Inclined Plane Railway.

Price, $4.00.

The only published description of the incline railway, in the 1897 Carlisle & Finch catalogue

No. 19 ELECTRIC AUTOMOBILE, 1899-1900: This little electric car is similar to the buggylike full-sized electric automobiles of this era. It is 10" long, 7" wide, and 7½" high. An electric motor under the car is attached to the rear wheels by spur gears. A wet chromite battery placed in a compartment under the seat was said to provide enough current to run the car "from one half to one hour."

This car was discontinued after two years, possibly because of the rather short running time provided by this type of battery. This automobile is extremely rare, but an example was examined for this book.

No. 20 ELECTRIC TORPEDO BOAT, 1899-1900: Carlisle & Finch responded to the contemporary excitement over the torpedo boat by listing this little electric boat for two years, 1899 and 1900 (catalogue drawing below). It was quite large and had a copper hull with a length of 24", a beam of 5½", and a depth of 4". The hull was divided into watertight compartments. A small motor inside the hull drove the

Compare this Carlisle & Finch catalogue illustration of a toy car with the Roundabout produced by Hafner (see page 77 of this book).

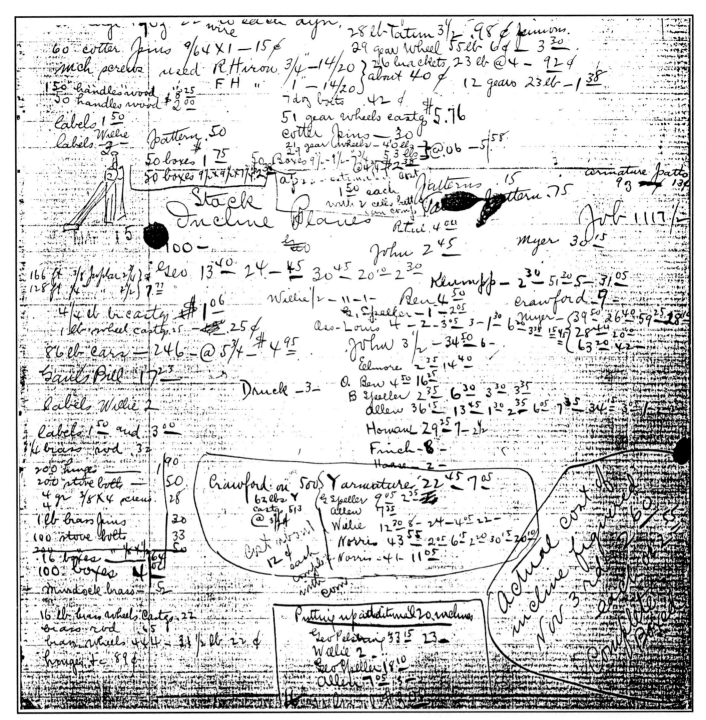

Copy of an excerpt from the Job Order Book for first one hundred No. 4 Inclined Plane Railways. Note the calculated cost of $2.60 in lower right-hand corner; today it is impossible to put a value on these toys. Courtesy Franklin O. Loveland

propeller at the stern. The rudder could be set for straight or for circular sailing.

A small chromite wet battery in the hull was said to provide power for a two-hour run. So far as is known, none has been found.

No. 109 ELECTRIC TELEGRAPH SET, 1905: In 1905 what is called "a complete telegraph system in miniature" was listed. It consisted of two telegraph keys with sounders and a battery, connected by wires to be strung on twelve wooden poles, each with an appropriate crossarm. As the catalogue put it: "This apparatus is designed for use in connection with any of our electrical railway systems, having a key and sounder at each end of track." It was offered for one year only.

No complete telegraph set is known to have been found, but telegraph poles made out of a dowel and a block of wood stained green appear to be parts of this set; they are said by Frank Loveland to be in the H. P. Albrecht and Morley Collections. See (*TCQ*, Vol. 13, no. 1, p. 12.)

CHAPTER TEN

★

1934 PREPRODUCTION SAMPLES

by Franklin O. Loveland

The following discussion deals with the special samples made by the Carlisle & Finch Company in the 1930s, when they were reconsidering entering the electric toy train business. This chapter consists of a summary of some of the research which was published in the *Train Collectors Quarterly* (Vol. 37, no. 4, Summer 1991),* which was a followup on my previous article in the *Quarterly* (Vol. 26, no. 5, pp. 28–29). It includes findings from a subsequent visit to the Carlisle & Finch archives in Cincinnati, Ohio, which I reported in *TCQ* (Vol. 38, no. 2 (Spring 1992), pp. 20–22). Other citations of my findings are found in previous chapters of this book. The illustrations in this chapter have been gathered by me in the course of my research.

A number of experimental or special items which were not available for sale to the general public have turned up in the hands of collectors, thanks to the efforts of the late Don McClain, who owned a train store in Cincinnati and purchased some of these samples from Carlisle & Finch employees. According to McClain (*TCQ*, Vol. 5, no. 2, p. 11), he purchased one of these handmade samples of a locomotive that was never put into production from the daughter-in-law of the chief designer.

McClain explains the emergence of these experimental models:

Carlisle & Finch. . . . planned to reenter the electric train field in the mid-1930s when the streamline train was the newest thing and remote control was considered standard equipment. Their sample cars are cast aluminum and hand-painted. A new and different remote control device was engineered, and a new track using rolled rail was designed. Evidence that new and longer locos were planned can be seen in the mockups of them. (*TCQ*, Vol. 2, no. 1, p. 8)

Hertz and his classic *Collecting Model Trains* (page 223) makes clear the importance of handmade samples:

Probably no items are more eagerly sought by collectors than handmade samples or experimental models. Unfortunately the very nature of these items makes them extremely difficult to obtain. Such samples have three purposes in the tinplate train manufacturing process: to test a new design for possible faults in design that are unsuspected in the drawing board stage, or to test market reactions before going to the tremendous expense of tooling up for a new model; as aids to the tool and diemakers in the actual tooling up process; and, finally, to illustrate in catalogs and to display to the trade before the production models (usually not ready until the fall) are actually available.

LOCATING AND COLLECTING SAMPLES

Hertz's ideas about their special nature — and of course their limited quantities — would explain why they are hard to find. This certainly holds true in the case of Carlisle & Finch. The fact that McClain sold many of the experimental models he got from Carlisle & Finch employees to collectors like Herb Morley, as well as the fact that some of the other samples were lost or stolen, makes the search for them even more difficult. But there are clues. The first is in Figure 119 on page 222 of Hertz's *Collecting Model Trains*, where some of what I believe are McClain's Carlisle & Finch samples are shown.

As I followed up my interest in these samples and experimental models, I began to poke around beyond the published materials. The search began with my own piece, "More on Carlisle & Finch," (*TCQ* Vol. 26, no. 5, pp. 28–29). In response to that piece, I received a phone call from a collector who told me that the 1934 Carlisle & Finch experimental models in the Morley Collection were in good hands and could be seen if I could get to the West Coast. My first search of the records, which include scrapbooks containing documentary photographs, at the present-day factory in the Cincinnati area turned up photos of the No. 383 streamliner with three 171 cars as well as set No. 75, with a 7000 Atlantic-type locomotive and tender and Ohio passenger car (see the two historical photographs, Figures 1 and 2, we are pleased to reproduce here). In a conversation Brent Finch, the current president of Carlisle & Finch, told me that the streamliner had disappeared some time ago and that they believed an employee had stolen it. This was all I was able to learn about these samples, and so I still felt the need to go and see the Morley Collection for myself.

In January of 1983, when I went to visit a fellow collector on the West Coast, I had an opportunity to see the samples. They were crude, but very, very interesting. The yellows and reds were very bright. I believe these are the cars (Ohio) pictured in the book at the factory and similar to those that Don McClain had. They are cast aluminum (and sheet metal) and fit together — in the case of the passenger car, in three pieces — two sides and a floor. The caboose has just two sides of cast aluminum and a tin floor and roof. The boxcar is similar to the caboose. Colors are bright. The switch unit is massive and the motor is also large with unusual features. It is obvious they were quite serious and saw trains as a way out of the Depression.

*Portions of this chapter are copyright (c) Franklin O. Loveland, 1991

Figure 1. Courtesy Brent Finch

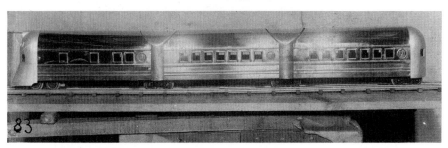

Figure 2. Courtesy Brent Finch

DETAILED DESCRIPTIONS

What follows is a listing of experimental models made by Carlisle & Finch. All of these items are one of a kind, and the last reported sale of any of them was some years ago. I would rate them all in excellent condition. Examination of Carlisle & Finch records make it clear that they were all made at some time during 1934. Since there was no Carlisle & Finch catalogue listing these experimental models, I will use the numbers on the pieces and the Carlisle & Finch sample numbers and lettering, all of which are deeply embossed and stand out from the castings when they are present.

Sets

No. 75 SET: Includes the 7000 locomotive and tender and Ohio passenger car as described below. All pieces are made of cast aluminum and sheet metal and are pictured as Figure 2 and in the Hertz book (page 222, Figure 119).

No. 83 BURLINGTON ZEPHYR SET: Three-piece cast-aluminum streamliner with the number 171 and Carlisle & Finch logos on the side of the casting — similar to the American Flyer Zephyr concept. Looks like it has sheet-metal ends, but not certain (has not been located as yet for observation; pictured as Figure 1).

Locomotives

No. 7000 ATLANTIC-TYPE: This is a steam Atlantic-type locomotive shown in Figure 2, with a 2-4-2 wheel arrangement and an eight-wheel tender with the C & F RR logo on the tender. The version shown in Figure 2 appears to be black, while the one shown in the Hertz book appears to be black with a gray or nickel boiler and brass or copper trim.

Note: Neither of the samples was actually found and therefore I cannot give any additional information about their construction. McClain did tell Morley that it was longer than previous Carlisle & Finch engines. Figure 1 appears to be black with a gray or nickel boiler and brass or copper trim.[1]

A second, earlier locomotive was in McClain's collection. Dick Hopkins informs me that his father George corresponded with Don McClain about this "special" locomotive (shown in Figure 3), back in the late 1950s. According to Dick, this loco appears to have a very high smokestack, two domes, piping along the sides like a No. 34, and a sheet-metal backing behind the cowcatcher. The light-colored boiler front and headlights are unlike typical Carlisle & Finch locos. Dick believes this locomotive (Figure 3) is not the same as the one shown in Figure 2 and in the Hertz book. In a letter dated November 27, 1991, Dick writes:

As you can see the special C & F loco doesn't look like the #7000. In fact, it's a rather ugly 0-4-0. Looks like they used the 12-spoke #4 wheels. The working

Figure 3. Courtesy Dick Hopkins

headlight would be the only example of a C & F loco like this. [This raises the interesting question of whether C & F was trying to emulate Howard in building this loco with a working headlight.] The cowcatcher appears to be sheet metal with "spokes" soldered to it. I really can't tell. The two domes are very oversized. This loco just doesn't make it when compared to a #34, or even a humble #4.

Although I prefer not to make value judgments, I will say that this loco seems like a cross between a No. 4 and a No. 34, like a small steam engine yet oversized, designed to compete with some of the Howard locos of that period. To my knowledge, this engine has no specific number.

Rolling Stock

No. 273 C & NW BOXCAR: C & NW logo with "273" below on one end of the side and a spiral logo on the other, as shown in Figure 4. Bright yellow; two pieces of cast aluminum with a sheet-metal roof and floor. At one time it had a brakewheel, apparently lost, as the illustration in the Hertz book reveals a brakewheel but the sample (Figure 4) which we saw does not. The boxcar is 12⅛" long, 3³⁄₁₆" wide, and 3¾" high or 5³⁄₁₆" to the table. The roof is 12⁹⁄₁₆" long with a ³⁄₁₆" overhang on each end. The doors, roof, and frame are made of sheet metal while the sides are cast aluminum. It has bumper band couplers and late black four-wheel Carlisle & Finch trucks. The black ladder is found only on one side of the car and is 1¹⁄₁₆" wide and 2¹¹⁄₁₆" high.

ERIE GONDOLA (no discernible number): This car is shown in the Hertz book and appears to have cast-aluminum sides lettered "ERIE", with possibly a number or logo in lower left of car. Mounted on late Carlisle & Finch trucks. Would assume frame is sheet metal and possibly ends, but not sure.

OHIO PASSENGER CAR (no number): Shown in Figure 5. The Ohio passenger car is one of those special kinds of prototypes. Decked out in a colorful yellow, the body is made of cast aluminum with two pieces. It has hinged brass stock doors and two beautiful blue air tanks cast into the frame. It

Figure 4. Photo by Dick Hopkins

Figure 5. Photo by Dick Hopkins

Figure 6. Photo by Dick Hopkins

Date	Dr. No.	Name of Plate	Symbol	Remarks
July 11 '04	314	Contact Rings	SL 32	
" 13 '04	315	4-Pole Alternator	T	
" 14 '04	316	Jump Sp. Con't Maker	ME 6	
" 14 '04	317	Intake Elbo	ME 6	
" 14 '04	318	Elevated R.R. Pole	T	
" 19 '04	319	Feed Scr. & Cur. Bon Hldrs	SL 32	
" 20 '04	320	Search Light Case	SL 32	
" 22 '04	321	Track Switch No. 10L	T	
" 22 '04	322	" " No. 46L	T	
" 22 '04	323	" " No. 46R	T	
" 22 '04	324	" " No. 10R	T	
" 22 '04	325	" " No. 10	T	
" 26 '04	326	800 Watt - Yoke & Bearings	T	
" 28 '04	327	" " Comm. Shaft Arm	T	
Aug 4 '04	328	⅛ H.P. Engine Details	T	
" 7 '04	329	Case	SL 24	Dispersion Lens.
" 8 '04	330	Armature & Shaft	T	800 Watt Dynamo.
" 13 '04	331	Reverse Gear & Clutch	ME 6	
" 22 '04	332	Contact Maker	ME 4	

Excerpt from the Carlisle & Finch drawings book

is mounted on distinctive six-wheel passenger trucks. These trucks have copper journal boxes. The car has silver steps with brass door handles. The wheels are painted red and the window trim appears silver. According to Dick Hopkins, the window plate is cast aluminum, also set inside the body. The car is 13⅝" long, 3⁷⁄₁₆" wide, and 3⅚" high or 5" high from table. It appears to have something like a diaphragm attached onto the end of the car. As pictured on page 222 of the Hertz book, it appears darker than in Figure 5.

PENNSYLVANIA RAILROAD CABOOSE (no number): This is shown in the Hertz book without trucks or wheels and with a set of late Carlisle & Finch trucks in Figure 6. The aluminum casting on this lovely red caboose is much thinner than on the other pieces. This piece has aluminum sides and ends, a sheet-metal frame, roof, and cupola. It has been put on standard late four-wheel Carlisle & Finch trucks, as shown in Figure 6. This is the only piece of C & F freight rolling stock that Carlisle & Finch identified with their own mark. The round logo between the windows on the side of the caboose has "CF" in the center. This same logo is also found on the individual units of the streamliner. The body is 7½" long, 10" with roof, ladder, and rails. It is about 5⅜" high and 3½" wide. The cupola is situated 2⁷⁄₁₆" from short end of the roof and is about 3½" long, 2½" wide, and ½" high. The black ladders are ¾" wide and 2⅞" high/long on the caboose. It is assumed that someone (probably McClain or Morley) put late C & F trucks under the caboose pictured in the Hertz book to create the caboose shown in Figure 6. All of these cars have cast numbers and letters in silver, which created a contrast with the bright colored paint.

A NOTE ON RESEARCHING AND DATING THE SAMPLES

Some detective work is of course required. For example, Regarding the actual dates of manufacture of the handmade C & F items shown in the photograph book and here as Figures 1 and 2, this probably occurred between February 1 and November 1, 1934. According to the *List of Drawings* record book (an excerpt is reproduced above), Drawing #1815 was made on February 1, 1934, and showed "1934 Locomotive Rail" and conductor, while Drawing #1822 depicts "Locomotive Drive Wheels" and was done on May 18, 1934. The photograph of the locomotive and the car is #75 (see Figure 2), and we know from the sample album that photo #74 was made in February of 1934, so we may assume it was made around then. Examining the order books for this period (an excerpt appears in Chapter Nine, and a summary of my examinations of Job Order Book One is provided on pages 68 and 69), we find an order #7374 was placed on February 2, 1934, for the special item pictured in photograph #74, while an order #7376 was placed for a special item pictured in photograph #77 on March 7, 1934; therefore, the locomotive and tender pictured in photograph #75 must have been completed between February 2 and May 7, 1934.

Regarding the drive wheels and the May 28th date given for them, I have no explanation for why they were drawn up so much later unless Mr. Finch planned to change them or mass produce them and needed a separate drawing — which was not done until after the handmade sample was completed.

As for the streamliner, photograph #83 (Figure 2) and a transformer which came to light (#84), I believe these were built in late September and early October of 1934. The reason I believe this is that the date for photograph #82 is found to be September 18, 1934, by the record for order #7438 in the order book and a September 1934 date in the photo book. Unfortunately there are no dates in the photo book for any picture until #90, which is shown as February 11, 1935, with no further conclusive evidence in the order book to date them more accurately. To sum up succinctly, the locomotive and car were probably produced in February 1934, while the streamliner and transformer were probably produced in late 1934 between mid-September and the end of October.

In all research, serendipity works its magic and some surprises turn up. Shown is a list of drawings from the first Carlisle & Finch drawings list book, which I came across quite by accident. Although the drawings, or more correctly, tracings, no longer exist, we know from these lists that they were made in the 1904–1905 period.

By inference, we can assume that Carlisle & Finch did not really go into mass production of the large No. 45 until November of 1904 and that the new line did not emerge fully until Christmas of 1904, with all the new versions of the freight and passenger cars of the middle period, including the revised Nos. 3, 4, and 42. The big Nos. 52 and 53 baggage and passenger cars as well as the new trolleys, the Nos. 18 and 19, appear for the first time in 1904. Even the trolley poles are traced, as are the rare Terminal Depot and Elevated Railway Pole. The Depot drawings must have been either the No. 96, the Freight Depot with Derrick, or the No. 97 Passenger "Terminal" Station first pictured in the 1905 catalogue.

It is to be hoped that this new evidence will prove useful to tinplate historians and will shed light on the development of the Carlisle & Finch line. It may also help to explain why Howard developed a broad line in 1905 and why Lionel Standard Gauge emerged in 1906 in competition with the diverse Carlisle & Finch and Howard electric toy train lines.

NOTE

1. Herb Morley observed that a motor and reversing unit, pictured here, are different from earlier ones from Carlisle & Finch. The motor is about the size of a Lionel Super motor and the reversing unit is also fairly large.

Both are too large to go into an engine. Just what they intended with these we do not know. Morley also said that McClain had a small experimental loco minus the tender that was different from any of the 7000s I have described, but there is no information available about it, as Morley never saw it (*TCQ*, Vol. 26, no. 5, p. 29). This is possibly the mystery engine in Figure 3, which appears to be different from the 7000.

ACKNOWLEDGMENTS

Special thanks to Bruce Greenberg for including publication of this material in the Carlisle & Finch section of this book.

My sincere thanks for helping provide information and support are extended to C. H. Buckley, who with Dick Hopkins and Chuck Schaffer made the special arrangements for me to see the handmade samples; W. Graham Claytor, Jr.; Brent Finch, who made photographs and archival materials available to me; Richard Hopkins, incomparable in sleuthing out photographs, who supplied many of the photos used in this article; and Bruce and Anna Manson, who along with Anthony Annese and Dick Hopkins read drafts of this manuscript and encouraged me in my research. Chuck Canestro and Elsa van Bergen helped edit and proofread several versions of this material. The *Train Collectors Quarterly* is published by the Train Collectors Association, P.O. Box 248, Strasburg, Pennsylvania 17579, a Non-profit 501 C3 Corporation, and material used in this book has been reprinted with permission.

My gratitude is especially extended posthumously to Herb Morley for pointing me in the right direction.

CARLISLE AND FINCH PRODUCTION RECORDS 1896–1900
Compiled by F. O. Loveland from C & F Job Order Book One

Cat. No.	Description of Item	Run	Order No.	No. Produced	Date	Prod. Cost/ Unit	Wholesale Price	Notes
#1	Streetcar	1st	1003	500	Sept. 15, 1896	.94	Not given	This was the first electric three-rail trolley car made in mass production.
#1	Streetcar	2nd & 3rd	1057	1000	Nov. 13, 1896	.95	Not given	Second and third runs. Advertising cost on these runs was $149. Believe these were two-rail trolleys. Price $3.50.
#1	Motor cars (sketch included)	4th	1116	3000	Feb. 29, 1897			Fordization arrives at C & F.
#1	Trolley cars (sketch included)	4th	1169	1750, may be part of order #1116	July 28, 1897	None given	None	This is a bit confusing, and I can't decide if this goes with job #1116 or is a separate run.
#1	Streetcar tops (sketch included)	4th	1194	1700, part of orders #1116 and #1169	Nov. 24, 1897	None given	Not given	This is to complete other jobs.
None	Big electric cars (#2?)	1st	1052	7	Nov. 11, 1896	None shown	Not given	This car is an anomaly — no number, no early production figures available had poles. None ever found. Was it an early #2?
#2	Big cars #2	1st	1156	150 followed by 350, then 300 more	July 1897	None	None	Early models have no wooden base. Retail price $6.50.
#2	Trail cars	1st	1125	50	None given, probably Mar. 30, 1897	.50	None	Gives data on regular #2 outfits, not on trail cars.
#2	Large cars — just tops	2nd	1398	100	Began Jan. 1899 Finished Apr. 1, 1899	.30(?)	Not given	First job of 1899 — power or trail cars? Possibly #13 coach.
#3	Coal cars and coal locomotives (sketch included)	1st	1127	500 (250 and 250) plus another 150 later. 500 coal cars bases and 2000 wheels made	Apr. 28, 1897 Oct. 5, 1897	1.60	2.75	Retail at $5 per set — outfit included: 1 loco, 3 cars, 3 battery cells, 1 can of chromite, 20 feet of track, and 90 ties — all manufactured, first gates of wheels and tops cast.
#3	Coal car buckets	2nd	1194	733 tops, 1300 bases	Nov. 25, 1897	None given	Not given	To complete job #1127.
#3	Mining locos (sketch included)	2nd	1145	300	Mid–June 1899	None	None	This is the second version of #3 mining loco, paper label on tin body.
#3	Mining locos	2nd	1500 goes with #1445	200	Oct. 30, 1899	None	None	This was the last run of pre-1900 mining locos.
#4	Incline toys (sketch included)	1st / 2nd	1117 / —	100 / 20	Mar. 15, 1897 / No date	2.60 / Same	None / None	This is the rare incline toy. Retail price $4. / —
#4	Locomotive (sketch included)	1st	1445	200	Sept. 21, 1899 (completed)	2.10	4.60	Retails at $6.50. This is the beginning — first steam locomotive train ($3.42, $6.75, $10).
#5	Bridges (sketch included)	1st	1124	50	Mar. 30, 1897	.249	.40	Early brass bridge. No actual stock no. given.
#5	Red Iron Bridge	1st	1490	150	Sept. 30, 1899	None	None	This is the second run of #5 bridges but the first of the Red Iron Bridges — different from the brass. Price $.75.
#6	Crossover (w/picture)	1st	1157	50	July 1897	.176 ea.	None	None.
#7	Hand Dynamos (sketch included)	1st	1117	51	Mar. 15, 1897	2.50 ea.	None	Provided electricity to run the trains. $2.70 for the water dynamo #8.
#8	Water wheel outfit	1st	1126	None given (100 boxes ordered)	None given, probably Mar. 30, 1897	2.70	None	Think they produced less than 100 in first run.
#8	Water dynamo	2nd	1172	#7 & #8, 427	Aug. 24, 1897	2.94	None	This is confusing — combines 1st and 2nd runs total 427, including #7 and #8.

Cat. No.	Description of Item	Run	Order No.	No. Produced	Date	Prod. Cost/ Unit	Wholesale Price	Notes
#9	Stations	2nd	1375	112	Sept. 27, 1898	.86	Not given	This is the only toy job done in 1898. Spanish-American War? 1899 retail price $1.50. Shift of production to wartime?
#9	Station tops — just tops	3rd	1400	100	Jan. 30, 1899	.698	Not given	No indication as to when these were finished.
#10	Wye switch (sketch included)	1st	1157	787	July 1897	.19 or .20	None	None.
#11	Flatcar	1st	1468	150	Aug. 18, 1899	.188	None	Probably made more flatcars (gondolas) than boxcars because more play value and orders separate. Retail price $.55.
#11	Flatcars	2nd	1502	100	Oct. 30, 1899	None	None	Needed to complete the sets for Christmas of 1899 as 200 locos had already been made.
#12	Boxcar	1st	1468	100	Aug. 18, 1899 or later	.454	None	Boxcar is very hard to find today.
#12	Boxcars	2nd	1502	100	Oct. 30, 1899	None	None	Needed to complete sets. Retail price on sets $10. Boxcar alone $1.20.
#19	Automobiles (toy)	1st	1483	100	Sept. 20, 1899	3.70 to 3.75	5.75	Retail $8.50. This car was a wonderful model of our early auto. Under carriage similar to the one Mr. Finch built in 1901.
#20	Toy boats	1st	1436	12	May 3, 1899	5.81	8.50	None of these has been found. Sold for $12 retail.
#20	Toy boats (sketch included)	2nd	1494	35-13 and then 22	Oct. 16, 1899	4.90	None	This was the last run of the boat.

Paul A. Doyle

CONTENTS

★

PREFACE 75

ACKNOWLEDGMENTS 76

ONE ★ THE HISTORY OF THE HAFNER MANUFACTURING COMPANY 77

TWO ★ LOCOMOTIVES 84

THREE ★ TENDERS 95

FOUR ★ COUPLERS AND FRAMES: An Overview of Those Used with
Passenger, Baggage, and Freight Cars 100

FIVE ★ EARLY PASSENGER AND BAGGAGE CARS (Pre-1938) 104

SIX ★ ONE-PIECE COACHES, INCLUDING THE SUNSHINE SPECIAL CARS . . . 117

SEVEN ★ EARLY FREIGHT CARS (1920s–1936) 121

EIGHT ★ THE STREAMLINER ERA 127

NINE ★ LATER PASSENGER CARS 131

TEN ★ LATER FREIGHT CARS (1937–1951) 136

ELEVEN ★ ACCESSORIES 144

TWELVE ★ THE WYANDOTTE TRAIN STORY 151

GLOSSARY, SUMMARY OF TYPES, and INDEX appear at the end of this volume

PREFACE

★

A few specific points must preface this book. First, it is surprising that many collectors and train meet-goers do not realize that Overland Flyer trains were made by Hafner. Currently, two major mail-order lists of toy trains for sale invariably place Overland Flyer items under the heading of American Flyer. Even at train meets, a Hafner tender occasionally turns up with a seemingly well-matched American Flyer locomotive or vice versa. Inquiry reveals that the seller conceived of the whole unit as American Flyer. Similarly, Hafner engines have often been paired with Joy Line tenders.

The Hafner Manufacturing Company is in great part to blame for this mix-up, since for almost twenty years it put its name on only a few products it produced. Except for the eight-wheel cars and the Toy Manufacturers' Pullman, it was not until the 1930s that Hafner began to place its name on many of its trains. Consequently, for more than half of the thirty-seven years of the company's existence, Overland Flyer was the name the public would see when it viewed tenders, coaches, and similar cars. I hope this book will remedy the confusion of denomination, so that collectors and others involved with toy trains will have the basic information to differentiate between Hafner and American Flyer, Joy Line, and other makes.

DATING AND DESCRIBING HAFNER TRAINS

Unlike Lionel, Ives, Carlisle & Finch, and some other companies, Hafner neglected to issue yearly catalogues. When it did produce a folder or catalogue, there was, until after World War II, no issuing date indicated. As a result, the dating of Hafner trains becomes a very hazardous and uncertain endeavor. Some collectors boldly assign a specific date, even if it is questionable; others feel the question of dating should remain more or less untouched. I have tried to take a middle position by giving a spread of years for approximate dating. I feel this is the most sensible approach because it gives collectors and newcomers to the hobby a helpful, general time frame in which the various puzzle pieces fit. Whenever specific dating can be verified, that information has been recorded; otherwise, I have used liberal guidelines for chronology.

The dating problem for Hafner items is additionally perplexing because we know certain cars and engines were carried in the line during years in which they were not listed in the few catalogues or folders available. For example, Hafner produced low-priced one-piece cars, although they are often not listed in Hafner catalogues for some of the years during which these cars were sold.

Not only are relatively few catalogues or descriptive folders available from year to year, but frequently the Hafner Company did not put identifying numbers on the sides of many of its locomotives, tenders, passenger, and freight cars. This identification by item number — customary with Lionel and Ives, for example — becomes uncommon with Hafner products.

Listings of Hafner items are here entered primarily by the number on the side of the car, whenever this number exists; items are entered by car type or road name if no car number is available. Where catalogue numbers are available, I have indicated them within the listing's description. The index covering Hafner, found in the back of this volume, lists all numbers,

catalogue and side-of-car. Note that in some cases *only* a catalogue number can be cited, and in other instances, *only* a side-of-car number. On occasion we have *neither* a catalogue nor a side-of-the-car number and the listing is indexed under the road name, alphabetically unless otherwise noted. "Unnumbered" means that there is no number on the side of a specific car; if an entire group of cars is unnumbered, that fact is pointed out in the text that introduces the group of listings.

CHALLENGES FOR HAFNER COLLECTORS

John Hafner, who succeeded his father as president of the company, observed that Hafner sent a sales representative to the yearly New York Toy Fair. There, jobbers were persuaded to buy Hafner trains. At that point, John Hafner told me, the trains "could be sold anywhere the jobbers wished." Usually the trains were distributed mainly to department stores and mail-order houses. Such a form of distribution, while successful for Hafner, did not have the immediate public, universal impact of, say, advertising catalogues in the Sunday newspaper comic sections. Hafner limited its advertising principally to the trade magazines — *Playthings* and *Toys and Novelties*. Hafner rarely sold through the five and dime stores as, for instance, Marx did. In a sense, then, Hafner's distribution was not as widespread as it could have been. The jobbers also seemingly made distribution eclectic, since some Hafner items were sold in certain outlets, while during the same year other items were sold at different stores.

The Hafner chronicle was further complicated by the rush of Christmas season orders, which meant that sometimes parts were assembled in great haste by busy workers. For instance, one can find a 1010 oil tanker with one end white and the other end gray. Because of production expediency, it appears that roofs, end pieces, doors, drive rods, couplers, etc., were often interchanged without particular logic or color consistency. The rush to get trains out of the factory to fill orders sometimes led to a frantic pace. Chester Holley, one of the pioneer train collectors and the owner of a toy train hobby shop, relates how he once visited a Marx factory during the rush production season, and saw workers grabbing whatever parts were available without always following a definite pattern. The same situation can be visualized in the Hafner shops, thereby offering one explanation of the inconsistencies in Hafner train production. Reusing sheet metal may be a further cause of some of the variables found in Hafner products.

As a matter of economy, Hafner thoroughly depleted its inventory. Nothing was wasted. Consequently, a certain car could be made with a new type of coupler, but many of these same cars could also be found with couplers from leftover inventory. I stress this point over and over in my study of Hafner trains. I have never seen an Overland Flyer Chicago and Northwestern coach with Type IV couplers, but that does not mean this version does not exist. And the Hafner student should not be surprised at any such overlap. The vagaries of Hafner production strongly indicate that, in some cases, train parts were lying about the factory and used at a later date.

I should pause here to explain that all of the various Type designations for Hafner items have been devised by me. Although several magazine articles have previously been written by others on various aspects of Hafner trains, they make no attempt to categorize, outline, or establish Type designations. I first distinguished the various locomotive Types in an article in the *Train Historians Hotline* in 1984. From that point, I developed Type designations for the other Hafner products including couplers and frames.

The situation caused by the vagaries of Hafner production can cause another problem — unregulated tampering. Roofs and doors, for example, can be easily switched. At this point, a new type of rare variation may be erroneously claimed. Therefore, collectors should look for Hafner boxed sets. When those are not available, the buyer should carefully examine the condition of individual items. Note scuffs, scratches, or the like which might indicate that the roof, or frame, or door, or end piece in question did not originate with that particular car.

In this book, I have attempted to include items I have actually seen or have observed in photographs from reputable sources. Several variations of color combinations have doubtless been omitted because, in addition to aspects of production expediency, much of Hafner's marketing strategy was built on using eye-catching colors of many different types and hues.

Finally, none of the above comments should deter anyone from collecting Overland Flyer and Hafner trains. On the contrary, this information can be useful in spurring collectors on investigative journeys, for new discoveries are constantly made. And the products of which we have knowledge are unquestionably worth the pleasure of ownership.

Acknowledgments

Many collectors and train enthusiasts aided in my Hafner research. First, I must thank **John Hafner** himself, who many years ago answered my first inquiring letter. Since then, he has always been gracious and willing to respond via letter, or more recently, by telephone.

Dan Mordell and I have corresponded on Hafner matters for over fourteen years, and he and his wife **Mary** extended superb hospitality during my visits to their home to discuss his fine collection. He has given generously of his considerable knowledge of our favorite train subject, and has loaned trains for photographing at York, Pennsylvania. I thank him here most appreciatively.

Bill Sanchez loaned his splendid eight-wheel early Overland Flyer set, headed by the incredibly rare No. 127 locomotive, for photographing at York, Pennsylvania. Throughout the years, he answered my questions when I sought him out at train meets.

Jerry Cirinelli lent me trains for photographing, and also showed me several interesting boxed sets. **Alan Littlejohn** called my attention to some unusual variations, and **Arno Uhlhorn** has always been willing to help research the subject of early lithography.

Bill Braem chatted about his Hafner collection before its dispersal, and also loaned me his correspondence. **George Foss** expanded my knowledge of his eight-wheel Illinois Central car, and **Gordon Blickle** wrote about some interesting Hafner pieces in his collection. **Bruce Garver** aided by describing his rare Canadian Flyer tender.

Roger Arcara, one of the first collectors to actively collect Hafner trains, gave the manuscript a thorough reading and added much useful information. He wants it noted that he disclaims any knowledge of prices. **Frank Merrell** and **Chris Rohlfing** supplied some significant data.

Phil Timpone brought his unusual Century of Progress boxed set to a New Jersey train meet for me to study, and **Phil Giles** allowed me the use of his old Standard Gauge Association newsletters. **Harry Osisek, Jr.**, whose knowledge of trains extended far beyond his fine Ives reproduction circus set, kindly supplied Hafner data. **Mike Vargas** not only sought out early Overland Flyer, but graciously photographed Hafner pieces to accompany the articles I have written over the years.

Lou Redman assisted by helping to analyze the "Pittsburg Flyer" situation. **Al McDuffie** added details about the uncommon yellow and red Burlington Zephyr and supplied several other pieces of interesting information.

Bill Becker and **David Gast** responded to my inquiries about Bing trains. **Debby** and **Jim Flynn** sent me photos of their Hafner collection. **Ray Jorgensen**, **Thomas Mackowiak**, **Al McCollough**, **Dick Sappelli**, and supplied important data. **Ron Morris** and the staff of the TCA Museum Library were always extremely helpful. **Gary Anderson** and **John Rosser** furnished me details about trains that had crossed the border to Mexico. **Ken Cook** wrote about Wyandotte motors and the Piqua, Ohio, factory. **Tony Hay** willingly shared data about Hafner variations and knowledgeably answered my questions about early trains. **Karl A. Harbeck**, the archivist of the Wyandotte, Michigan, Historical Society, was exceedingly helpful in assisting me locate fresh material on the history of the All Metal Products Co., which took over the Hafner line in 1951. **Charles Thorne** of Montgomery Ward cooperated in my search for catalogues of his firm's products. I thank most appreciatively **Alan Schuweiler** for allowing me to use information that he gathered from his studies of Chicago newspaper files and from G. Sommers Wholesale Catalogues. Mr. Schuweiler's research was helpful in dating some early Hafner train production.

Other collectors who aided this study are **Bob Lakemacher**, **Bob Lindsey**, **Jim Lynch**, **Joe Ranker**, **Dave Schnakenberg**, **Dick Stafford**, and **Bob Stekl**.

I extend my deepest gratitude and appreciation to all of the above-named Hafner enthusiasts.

The phrase "last, but not least" has become a cliché, but in this case it is incredibly accurate. My son, **Robert Doyle**, holds a deep appreciation for the beauty of lithography, and he also is a collector of prewar trains. Together, we have collected, discussed, and researched Hafner for over fifteen years, and enjoyed other trains long before that. He has discovered many rare and unusual pieces at train meets, and he has corrected several points I made in the first draft of this manuscript and added details that I had overlooked. He even typed part of the manuscript. My greatest debt is due to him — Robert's help and interest trimmed years off the duration of this study, thereby enabling me to complete this book in a more timely manner.

Paul A. Doyle

CHAPTER ONE

★

THE HISTORY OF THE HAFNER MANUFACTURING COMPANY

EARLY PRODUCTION

William F. Hafner, who was born in Chicago, Illinois, on February 19, 1870, and who married Addie Skinner in 1892, was the creative originator of American Flyer and Overland Flyer trains. When his involvement in the secondhand wooden packing-crate business did not satisfy his inventive mind and dynamic personality, he followed his natural mechanical bent and developed in his spare time a reliable clockwork motor. He quickly realized the potential of uniting his motor with toys. Acting on this idea, William launched his lifelong career.

The Hafner Company was formed in 1901 as the Toy Auto Co. From 1902 to 1907, it was designated as the William F. Hafner Company. (A notice in the September 1938 issue of the toy trade manufacturers' magazine, *Playthings*, supports this dating.) His earliest toys in 1901–1902 were automobiles, trucks, and miniature swings on which small dolls or figures could be placed. One toy that proved to be an especially popular seller was a roofless car that could seat two people. This was a common style of automobile in the early 1900s and the general term "runabout" was used to describe such a vehicle.

Called the Roundabout by Hafner because the car could turn in a circle, it had one cloth seat for a driver and a passenger, and a wooden tiller bar which turned the front wheels. The steering rod went down under the floorboards and could be moved into different grooves impressed into the metal under the floor. Positioning the steering rod in these various grooves would achieve turns of different circumferences. The standard Hafner toy Roundabout had nineteen grooves into which the wheels could be turned.

No name or lettering was used on the Hafner Roundabout. The sides and front, however, had a circular entwined tendril decoration that was colored in gold. The windup motor came completely encased (rather than the open frame type) with an almost two-inch-long rod leading to a thin key handle. The key hole and the key were threaded. When these old toy cars are found today, the motor usually still works effectively, attesting to the dependability of Hafner's motor.

An illustration of the Hafner Roundabout in a 1902 issue of *The Youth's Companion* describes the vehicle in the following manner: " . . . made of sheet steel, richly ornamented in colors and gold. The wheels, which are of cast metal, have rubber tires. The spring motor is strongly made, and when wound will carry the Roundabout over one hundred feet. By means of the steering handle the Roundabout will run in a large or small circle, or in a straight line. It is seven inches long and proportionately wide."

Hafner devised variations on the Roundabout. For example, he produced a police patrol wagon — in effect an open paddy wagon which could be used to transport several policemen to an emergency or a group of prisoners to the local jail. (Viewers of Mack Sennett's old Keystone Kops films may recognize this type of vehicle.) Hafner's police wagon used a bare metal four-spoke steering wheel, instead of the wooden tiller bar found on the more sedate Roundabout.

William Hafner developed a number of interesting windup toy variations. He manufactured a very realistic small toy swing, two styles of four-seater touring cars, a baggage truck, an auto truck (which today would be called a stake truck), and a dump wagon. The dump wagon could be filled with sand or dirt. It operated by means of a long metal lever that held the floor of the wagon closed until moved backward, thereby dumping the load. Hafner's early mechanical toys appear to have sold reasonably well, although the sales did not achieve financially secure levels. These early Hafner toys survived the strenuous play of youngsters, and many remain in prized toy auto collections today.

One of the first toys designed by William F. Hafner, dating from as early as 1901–1902. The steering handle of this "Roundabout" (as Hafner called it) automobile could be set in various grooves and run in small or large circles, or straight ahead. The windup motor used to power the car was essentially the same type used in later Hafner locomotives.

Top: Early Edmonds-Metzel production of an American Flyer (the predecessor of Hafner) locomotive with red stripe and companion 328 tender. Bottom: "Chicago" coaches which accompanied the engine and tender in this ca. 1907–1910 boxed set. R. Doyle Collection.

EDMONDS-METZEL/ AMERICAN FLYER PERIOD

In 1905 William Hafner adapted his proven clockwork motor to a cast-iron locomotive shell of his own design. At this moment, American Flyer and Overland Flyer were unofficially born. William also produced a lithographed passenger coach. William's sons, John and Robert, both recall this train running down the hallway of their childhood home. Both brothers independently remember that a few of the trains were sold in very limited production in the Chicago area. Alan Schuweiler, however, has reviewed the November and December 1905 and 1906 issues of the *Chicago Tribune*, the *Chicago Daily News*, and the *Chicago Record Herald* and found no advertisements for Hafner trains. Some toy train historians have speculated that the earliest Hafner trains were floor or pull toys, but John Hafner is certain that the first trains his father made ran on O Gauge track.

In the post-1905 era, further development of William Hafner's train line was hampered because he suffered for a time with typhoid fever, and he also lacked adequate financing to tool and gear up a facility capable of mass producing engines, tenders, and coaches.

Entering the scene at this point was William Ogden Coleman, Sr., owner of Burley and Company, a china store whose old china warehouse later became the American Flyer factory. Contrary to some reports, Coleman did not run Pitkin and Brookes, which sold hotel and dining car china to Burley and Company. Coleman was, however, involved in the operation of a company named Edmonds-Metzel, which made farmers' hardware.

William Hafner, eager to develop and expand his clockwork train line, sought Coleman for the necessary financial backing to do so. Coleman, needless to say, wanted assurance that a toy train venture would be profitable. So in 1907, according to John Hafner, his father took trains and track he had made to Steinfeld Brothers, a major New York City toy distributor and jobber. The Steinfeld firm, impressed with the quality of the trains and their sales prospects, gave William Hafner a $15,000 order. John reminds us that this was a very large order for that particular time. A facsimile of this order is printed in the January 1969 issue of the *Train Collectors Quarterly*.

When Coleman learned of this encouraging financial beginning, he decided to finance William Hafner's train production. Hafner joined the Edmonds-Metzel Manufacturing Company, and train production there commenced in 1907.

Train sales proved so successful that Coleman decided to devote all Edmonds-Metzel production to the manufacture of mechanical trains. Consequently, in 1910 the firm's name was changed to the American Flyer Manufacturing Company. John Hafner recalls that his father ran the train business, while Coleman continued as the firm's financial pillar and focused on the other business activities in which he was involved.

Before continuing, let us address the confusion that exists as to the actual lettering on the 1905–1906 pre–Edmonds-Metzel Hafner passenger coaches. In the late 1970s John Hafner told more than one collector that the coaches were lettered with the name "HAFNER" on the sides. Some train enthusiasts have been searching unsuccessfully for this type of car ever since. However, when Lou Redman, who is known as "Mr. TCA #3" — and who is in fact the third founding member of the Train Collectors Association — visited John in June 1990, contradictory information was given. Redman showed John Hafner an Edmonds-Metzel set, and John not only said that the early 1905–1906 trains had "CHICAGO" lettered on the side, but that the 1907 Edmonds-Metzel trains were the same as the Hafner 1905–1906 trains. When I eventually learned indirectly of this new development, I telephoned John Hafner on April 5, 1991, and inquired if this discrepancy between the Hafner and Chicago names could be resolved. John Hafner replied that he was "now unable to clarify this discrepancy. It was just too long ago."

Closeup of the beautifully colored paper label on the top of a Edmonds-Metzel American Flyer boxed set. William Hafner created the trains for Edmonds-Metzel and American Flyer. R. Doyle Collection.

OVERLAND FLYER/HAFNER ERA

According to John Hafner, Coleman and William Hafner made a verbal agreement that if the company profits reached a certain point, William was to receive a significant share of the business. However, when the profits reached the designated point, Coleman reneged on the agreement. As a

result, William left American Flyer in 1914 and founded his own toy train firm in Chicago — the Hafner Manufacturing Company. The new business moved to a three-story building at 648-50 North Robey Street, and production of Overland Flyer trains began.

John Hafner reports that as a result of his father's failure to receive his rightful share of the American Flyer business, unpleasant feelings arose between the Coleman and Hafner families. But John's brother, Robert, tells a different story. In an interview conducted by Chris Rohlfing and printed in the *Train Collectors Quarterly* (October 1984), Robert Hafner maintained that despite his father's formation of a rival train company, the two families remained friendly. Robert Hafner cited several examples of subsequent amicable relationships between the Coleman and Hafner families, including gifts sent for Robert's own wedding in 1917. He maintained that his "father would not have countenanced any hard feelings between our families. The break (the forming of Overland Flyer) was simply for business reasons."

There has been speculation, of course, among some train historians about the reason for the business separation between Coleman and Hafner. Some theories suggest that Coleman wanted to give his own son more power in the company. What does appear evident is that William Hafner recognized his own creativity and potential and felt he should be doing much better financially. He knew he could best accomplish this goal by forming his own company. John recalls that his grandfather, also named William Hafner,

Close affinities between early American Flyer and Hafner. Top: American Flyer 1107 coach; Overland Flyer unnumbered Erie herald coach. Middle: American Flyer 120 tender; Overland Flyer 1180 tender. Bottom: American Flyer 6¼-inch 1106 Union Pacific coach; matching Overland Flyer Union Pacific coach. William Hafner was the creator of both styles.

Closeup of the Overland Flyer Toy Manufacturers car

gave monetary support in the new business venture and became the firm's vice-president. Grandfather Hafner had earlier been a partner in a successful soda fountain manufacturing business.

Because the American Flyer name had become so well known in toy trains, William sought for his company a name which would retain a similar identification. The word "Flyer," which connoted speed, was frequently used to designate real passenger trains. Couple "Flyer" with "Overland," and the famous Union Pacific comes to the minds of many people. The Union Pacific ran the "Overland Limited," a crack passenger train which had established speed records between the Midwest and California. The Union Pacific had earlier gained favorable publicity as one of the railroads involved in the famous Golden Spike wedding on May 10, 1869 at Promontory, Utah. Here, locomotives and cars from the Union Pacific and the Central Pacific (later the Southern Pacific) met, and the last spike was driven to create the first transcontinental railroad. A further connection with the new toy train line would be recognized in the Union Pacific's advertisement of itself as "The Overland Route." William Hafner could not have chosen a name more rich in railroad history and fame than "Overland Flyer."[1]

WORLD WAR I

The Hafner train line proved financially rewarding — much more so than Hafner's earlier mechanical toys. The success of these trains was aided considerably by the outbreak of World War I. Up to this time, German toy trains had been a dominant force in the American toy market. A news item in the August 1915 issue of *Playthings* pointed out that almost half of the toys sold in America at Christmas were made in Germany. With the war restrictions placed on German imports, American manufacturers now had an opportunity to secure the majority share of the toy train business.

On June 9, 1916, the Toy Manufacturers Association of the United States of America was formed to take advantage of the war situation by boosting American toy sales. It was hoped that during the war American toy companies would strengthen their market position against European

competitors, so that when the war ended the U.S. firms would be in the forefront. A. C. Gilbert was elected the first president of the Toy Manufacturers Association, and Harry Ives the first vice-president of the group. Both William O. Coleman, Sr., and William F. Hafner were members of the organization.

The Toy Manufacturers Association adopted a colorful logo featuring Uncle Sam's hat turned upside-down, as a cornucopia of various toys flowed from the brim, as shown in the photograph of the logo commemorated by Hafner on a delightful lightographed red, white, and blue passenger car. Thus, Hafner made more than a token effort to advance the selling goals of the American companies. (Lionel used the same association logo on many of its boxes as recently as the 1950s.)

The World War I years proved extremely prosperous for Hafner trains and consequently helped to firmly establish the company's name and reputation. The Overland Flyer line was assured a significant share of the toy train market. Butler Brothers, George Borgfeldt, and Sears Roebuck were among the largest buyers and sellers of Hafner trains during this period.

Economical pricing constituted one of the major selling appeals of Hafner trains. They also sold well because of their "pleasing colors" and "durable brass gears," as noted in advertisements. Although low-priced, the trains were very well made. Hafner trains were advertised "for boys and girls" (*Playthings*, September 1920). And a later advertisement stated, probably with more truth than realized, "Dads like to play with them too" (*Playthings*, November 1920). The readers of the trade journals *Toys and Novelties* and *Playthings* were told that Hafner trains "go fast — look like . . . the speedy expresses in real life . . . have handsome appearance and durability."

These trade journal advertisements cause much frustration for the researchers of toy train history. Other manufacturers — Lionel, Ives, American Flyer — often showed pictures of their trains in their advertisements. The majority of the Hafner ads simply contained short word statements; consequently, the historian cannot get the visualization or dating specifics significant for research. And the Hafner Company rarely advertised elsewhere. Hafner ads were invariably teasing. Year after year, they noted that Hafner had new trains or that changes were made. But in order to see the trains, one had to come to the New York Toy Fair, where attendance was restricted to toy manufacturers and wholesale buyers. Hafner rarely deviated from this type of frugal advertising approach. The researcher's frustration with repeated notices like "Come over — see us! Mr. W. F. Hafner has something new to show you" is very real.

After serving in the Navy in World War I, John Hafner joined his father's firm in 1918. John had been born in 1897 in River Forest, Illinois, and married Catherine Patch in 1923. He settled into the company as his father's right-hand man. When William Hafner retired during World War II, John succeeded his father as president of the firm. Robert, John's brother, also worked for the company for several years as a salesman. An announcement in the January 1927 issue of *Playthings* reported that Robert Hafner left the company to pursue his own business, "handling a limited number of representative toy lines in Chicago and adjacent territory."

Hafner's third plant, No. 1010, after which a locomotive was named, on North Kolmar Avenue, Chicago; its 50,000 square feet was quite an advancement from the first factory, where they paid $50 rent.

Hafner motors being assembled from clockwork parts

Locomotive bodies were stamped from flat lithographed sheets and then curved over the tool shown between this worker's hands. Photos courtesy John Hafner.

In addition to its line of toy trains, the Hafner Manufacturing Company eventually made other products: automobile accessories, tools, lawn chairs, and Christmas tree holders. In 1919 it even produced a toy submarine which was personally demonstrated by William Hafner at the New York Toy Fair. According to the account in *Playthings*, this toy "submerged to the bottom of a large plain tank and rose to the water surface at regular intervals, keeping up this action for hours." Based on various ads in *Playthings*, it was evident that submarines, which had achieved considerable attention during the war, attracted toymakers during the postwar years. In addition to Hafner's endeavor, Ives, the Wilkins Toy Co., and the American Toyland Creators of Brooklyn also offered working submarines. The February 1925 issue of *Toys and Novelties* reported yet another out-of-the-ordinary product for Hafner: "A departure from the train field is a dump truck that is absolutely true to scale, with workable tailgate, made of heavy sheet steel, furnished with a variety of combinations of colors. Balloon shaped metal tires."

Every once in a while, a comment appeared in print to the effect that Hafner had joined forces with Lionel and American Flyer to rescue financially troubled Ives in the late 1920s. John Hafner has emphasized that this statement was not accurate. Although William Hafner was approached to join in the Ives bailout negotiations, he did not wish to involve his company in what he considered a risky financial venture. Roger Arcara reports that some late Ives locomotives have Hafner punched-out steel wheels which he believes were purchased from the Hafner Company.

HAFNER LITHOGRAPHY

The Hafner Company's lithography rivaled that of all other toy train companies. Although Hafner produced a line of trains aimed at thrifty buyers, the lithography applied to the models used from 1914 to the early 1930s never suffered in quality.

The four-wheel, 5½-inch passenger cars, for example, were produced in several colorful versions and featured authentic railroad heralds. In addition to the heralds of United States railroads, Hafner also issued the eye-catching beaver logo of the Canadian Pacific Railway. Such cars as the previously mentioned Toy Manufacturers' commemorative and the New York Flyer Pullman, with its pleasing stars and stripes shield, are still sought eagerly by collectors today. The eight-wheel coaches remain especially impressive and desirable. Perhaps the most attractive of these coaches is the Southern Pacific Pullman, with gold, red, green, white, black, and tan lithographic ink. Unfortunately, some hobbyists approach Hafner trains by way of the later cheapened production items and remain unaware of the early glory years of this manufacturer.

After World War I Hafner trains continued to sell quite well. In 1920 Hafner moved from its original Robey Street plant to 3128-3140 Carroll Avenue. And early in 1930 a further move was made to a large one-story plant at 1010 North Kolmar Avenue adjoining a Chicago and NorthWestern railroad siding. The Depression saw the end of some of the great toy train manufacturers — such as Ives, Dorfan, and Boucher — but Hafner responded to it by expanding into a new plant. Henry Katz became a representative for Hafner in the 1930s and was very successful in increasing sales. He continued in this capacity until the beginning of World War II.

Some cheapening of the line occurred during the Depression, and again later during the immediate pre– and post–World War II years. During these times, certain materials were expensive and difficult to acquire. The lithography became much less complex and the color combinations less varied. Further surprises are often found on the inside surfaces of the sheet-metal car bodies.

The Hafner Company sometimes resorted to creative means to save money or to acquire the tinned sheet steel necessary for production. It often purchased, from various companies, sheets of tinned stock earmarked for the production of bottle caps or containers. Hafner simply printed on the underside of this irregular or overstock tin to make its tinplate engines and cars. Looking on the underside of some cars and engines, one notes that even Hafner's own lithography was used on occasion. This happened when Hafner discontinued a car, and leftover tin (known as "reused tin" in the industry) from that car was turned over and reused. This can be a very frustrating experience for collectors, because lithography pieces from what are today some of Hafner's rarest cars can be seen on the underside of common coaches and engines!

This practice saved the company a considerable amount of money and added an intriguing aspect for collectors. It would be nearly impossible to enumerate the myriad of non-train products advertised underneath certain Hafner items. The products range from such well-known companies as Coca-Cola and Kraft, to "Lash's Real Orange Carbonated Drink with Sugar, Water, Juice Pulp, and ⅟₂₀th of 1% of Benzoate Soda" and "Jumbo / A Super Cola / Cash Value ½ Cent — Gastonia, N.C."

Not all of the various product names are clearly in view. Some are under the cross braces which hold the middle of the car together, or under the upper cab parts of streamliner engines. Sometimes the lithography is on the back of a wheel or a coupler. Designs are also imprinted over each other or overlapped in such a way as to make both examples undecipherable. Several of the designs simply reveal an array of different colors. A small dental mirror is helpful for reading some of the writing.

A most interesting incident involving product lithography occurred several years ago at a York, Pennsylvania, Train Collectors Association meet. A bright yellow Hafner No. 1010 locomotive materialized, with about ten lithographed chickens on it located an inch or two apart. The chickens wore American Revolutionary War soldiers' hats and played fifes. The word "Pfeiffer" was written near each chicken. In many ways the locomotive resembled the Marx Mickey Mouse locomotive, except the chickens appeared much more frequently than did the Disney figures on the Marx locomotive. To some collectors, this seemed to be a special promotional edition to advertise a Chicago beer.

I wrote to John Hafner, who assured me that his company never produced this promotional item. Further investigation revealed that the lithography had been accidentally reversed — the bright yellow chickens and "Pfeiffer" should have been on the underside of the locomotive. How many of these fife-playing chicken locomotives escaped quality control at the Hafner plant is unknown. Perhaps it was a one-time lark produced by a factory employee. At any rate, the colorful and attractive look of this locomotive suggests that both the Hafner and Pfeiffer companies missed a fascinating opportunity for a memorable promotional model.[2]

When the streamliner era arrived in 1934, the various toy train companies offered their versions. Hafner produced its own model of the Union Pacific M-10000 in 1935, and a few years later brought out a replica of the Burlington Zephyr. Although the most common color used was the prototypical brown and yellow, Hafner produced streamliners in a wide variety of colors. Chrome and copper were also used. Hafner was one of the pioneer users among toy train manufacturers of both copper and chromium plate. The Hafner streamliners were immensely popular with train buyers. The more common color versions of these trains appear with regularity at large train meets today. The later Zephyr models, however, are uncommon.

THE OVERSEAS MARKET

From the late 1930s until the advent of World War II, the Lionel Corporation distributed Hafner trains overseas. Because Lionel had stopped manufacturing its own line of clockwork trains, it was eager to capitalize on the great overseas demand for mechanical engines and cars, since many countries had areas without electricity. Lionel and Hafner worked out an agreement whereby they joined in a common bond for a few years. It would be interesting to know the precise financial details of this arrangement. Although the pact is confirmed by John Hafner and is supported by Hafner advertising, the specifics of the agreements appear to have been lost.[3]

The Hafner Company never made electric trains. Robert Hafner observed that when the topic was raised in conversation with his father, William Hafner responded that such trains were not really toys. He said electric trains were "too big and too expensive." Collector and train historian Al McDuffie said that he once wrote to the Hafner Company suggesting it put an electric motor in its engines and add a third rail. In response, the company said it had an arrangement with Lionel for selling Hafner mechanical trains overseas and it did not want to do anything which might endanger this agreement.

WORLD WAR II

Toy train production was severely interrupted and restricted by World War II. The American government, understandably focusing its attention on the war effort, prohibited the use of metal for toy making. Several Hafner trains which were already completed before the war restrictions went into effect received government approval for sale. These sets display the following designation on their boxes: "Permission granted by WLB to resell tin without further permission H-43-18204." A letter to Hafner employees noted that the War Production Board restrictions mandated that all metal toy production be stopped by June 30, 1942. A limited number of leftover and already completed sets were sold during the 1942 Christmas season.

John Hafner has confirmed that no train sets were manufactured during the war. The lightweight 30-gauge tinplate that the Hafner Company had in stock to make trains was not of a heavy enough gauge to produce military equipment. So Hafner stayed in business mainly by turning out bottle caps for the Fox Brewing Company. The Hafner Company did make some war equipment when the company subcontracting the work to Hafner furnished materials, but Hafner's lightweight stock was used only for bottle caps.

William Hafner chafed under the wartime production restraints, which directly led to his decision to retire as president and turn control of the company to his son John. Bill Hafner moved to Hendersonville, North Carolina, where he died after a long illness on December 29, 1944.

Robert McCready, publisher of *Playthings,* had known William Hafner since his early years in the toy industry and wrote a glowing obituary notice in his trade journal. McCready said, in part, that he honored and respected William Hafner "as a man and a friend, as well as for his energy and capacity as a manufacturer. He had a simple code: shoot straight, keep your word, pay your debts, and speak ill of no man."

At the end of the war, Hafner train production resumed. For toy train sales, the immediate postwar years were boom years. Lionel, American Flyer, and Marx, as well as Hafner, found the demand for toy locomotives and cars had increased dramatically after the austerity and deprivations of the war years.

A June 1950 news story in *Playthings* announced that the Hafner Company merged with the Wallace A. Erickson Co., a Chicago plastics manufacturer. The announcement stated that this union would give Hafner expanded facilities for faster delivery of orders. Both companies were to retain their own plants and personnel. John Hafner said that nothing really developed from this merger, pointing out that

he sold his company less than a year later. The major goal of the merger had been to save production costs by exploring the feasibility of using plastic parts for trains, such as wheels. (It should be observed that Wyandotte was to add this type of wheel to its train line a few years later.)

THE WYANDOTTE YEARS

In 1951 John Hafner decided on early retirement and sold the company. Louis Marx's brother David went to Chicago to tour the plant and examine the inventory, but he made no offer. The last day of production was March 8, 1951, and the company was advertised for auction the same month. The All Metal Products Company of Wyandotte, Michigan, however, did buy all the tools, dies, and inventory. The Hafner building was sold separately to a plastics manufacturer — not the Erickson Company, but another firm located nearby. The All Metal Company, maker of Wyandotte Toys, had been in the toy business since the early 1920s and was elated to add such a reputable line of trains to its products. According to John Hafner, the final production day for his company was March 8, 1951.

Wyandotte Toys continued the Hafner line, changing very little. In 1956, however, Wyandotte filed for bankruptcy, the details of which are revealed in Chapter Twelve. The Louis Marx Company eventually bought all the Hafner-Wyandotte tools and dies in order to eliminate possible future train competition. Most of this material was then shipped to Mexico and used by Marx to produce trains there.

This completes our brief history of the Hafner Manufacturing Company, which encompassed over half a century — if one combines the early production, the Edmonds-Metzel/American Flyer period, the main Overland Flyer/Hafner era, and the last Wyandotte years. As the years go by, the details become sketchier. Conflicting information may never be resolved, as memories dim and records are lost. This historical account supplies the student of Hafner with the solid groundwork necessary for future research.

NOTES
1. Mike Vargas writes that "modern day movie fans should well remember the scene from the film *Butch Cassidy and the Sundance Kid,* when the 'hole in the wall' gang robs 'the Flyer.' The artwork on the tender proudly proclaims 'Overland Flyer' in beautiful living color."

2. Pfeiffer was a brewery founded by Conrad Pfeiffer in Detroit, Michigan, in 1890. The company's logo was a Revolutionary War figure caricature. The company brewed "Pfeiffer's Famous Beer" until 1962, when it merged with E and B Brewing Co., and became part of the Associated Brewing Co. complex.

3. Ron Hollander, in his excellent survey of Lionel, *All Aboard,* did not come upon any material relative to this agreement when he researched Lionel files (phone conversation, March 7, 1988).

CHAPTER TWO

★

LOCOMOTIVES

This chapter begins by surveying the complicated story of the development of the Hafner windup locomotive. Note that the chapter ends with a summary chart of all the types.

The earliest Hafner locomotive shells were made of cast iron. According to the earliest known catalogue — theorized as dated either 1914 or 1915 — the engines varied in length from 6½ inches to 7½ inches and came with either one or two boiler bands. A red stripe was painted under the cab. The earliest 6½-inch locomotives came in two versions — an inexpensive model without brake or drive rods and a slightly higher-priced engine that had both brake and drive rods. All Hafner locomotives had a 0-4-0 wheel arrangement.

The motor was a well-constructed and reliable clockwork mechanism that had an S-shaped ratchet. The motor was always (except in the case of the No. 127 locomotive) wound from the left side. This mechanism, with very minor changes, was used throughout the over fifty years of the company's production. The use of brass gears was frequently stressed in mail-order advertisements, and John Hafner has reported that the gears were made by the Western Clock Company of Lasalle, Illinois. The key could be threaded in or out, and since it could be left in its socket at all times there was less likelihood that it would be misplaced or lost.

The earliest clockwork mechanisms utilized rectangular side plates and had cast-iron open-spoked wheels. For a short time (ca. 1918) Hafner was forced, presumably because of World War I shortages, to substitute a stamped sheet-metal drive wheel with convex cross-section punched-out spokes.[1] For a period following World War I the convex-spoked drivers were continued on most locomotives. Flat cross-section spoked wheels were later used.

The Hafner Company decided in 1925 to follow the practice — used widely by Ives in particular — of stamping the patent date on the motor. Thus for several years we find the lettering "PAT. Dec. 1. '25" on the back end of the motor casing.

At some point in the 1930s Hafner began to employ unpunched, embossed spoke wheels, which were more economical, and they continued this practice until the firm was sold in 1951. Knowing the vagaries of Hafner's manufacturing inventory arrangements and the rush of production expediency, it is quite possible that there were overlaps and even deviations from the progression related above, but at least it establishes a general, useful pattern.

Over the years, the brake controller arm underwent different changes. In the first-produced locomotives, the brake control lever protruded toward the end of the cab but turned left at a right angle for a half inch. When the lever was pushed in, the brake was released. Later a horizontally pivoted brake lever was used. This was moved to the left to

stop the motor. Eventually a vertical brake lever was adopted for the steam outline locomotives. A short vertical brake lever protruding from the top of the engine was used for the Nos. M-10000 and 1010 engines, while still later the Nos. 2000 and the 115041 engines had a longer vertical actuator end.

As an aid for those workers assembling the locomotives, as well as for inventory purposes, most Hafner cast-iron locomotives had the number of the engine embossed inside the shell with the location of the left and right sections designated "L" and "R". Thus the No. 109 engine, for example, has "109L" and "109R" cast inside the shell.

The back of the early Hafner motor side plates had two notches that clasped the boiler/cab casting, and the front of the motor was attached to the casting by a screw inserted in the left side of the motor. In the early 1930s the screw was replaced on some of the engines, and the front of the motor was equipped with a knob which slipped into a frame piece designed to hold it. With the advent of the City of Salina streamlined engine in the mid-1930s, the screw was returned but was inserted through the engine roof and fastened to the top of the motor. The later Nos. 1010, 2000, and 115041 locomotives were all attached by a screw to the top of the boiler shell.

THE NEED FOR GREATER MOTIVE POWER

Early in its production, Hafner decided to produce eight-wheel passenger cars, and it was determined that a larger motor was required in order to furnish more pulling power. The boiler/cab casting was lengthened to 7½ inches and was modeled closely on the Ives two-dome No. 17 locomotive of the 1912–1914 period. The Ansonia Clock Company of Connecticut was contacted and produced a large windup mechanism that had many similarities to the Ives No. 17 motor (see the photos on page 87 that compare the Ives No. 17 and the Hafner No. 127). Unlike all other Hafner engines before and after, this motor was wound from the right side. Instead of using the Ives square knob key insert style, this motor had a threaded boss into which the key was screwed.

This locomotive was advertised in several Sears catalogues through 1919. Robert Hafner, who worked for the company at that time, recalls that the No. 127 locomotive was produced for approximately five years and estimates that about five hundred sets were made each year. This estimate may be much too high because very few of these engines appear to have survived. Very few collectors have ever seen this locomotive; in fact, some train historians have even

doubted its existence, believing that Hafner simply used the Ives No. 17 engine. The No. 127 is the rarest locomotive Hafner ever manufactured and one of the most difficult locomotives — of any toy train manufacturer — to locate today.

In the tentatively dated 1914–1915 Hafner catalogue, the No. 127 appears with an 1180 tender (see reproduction of catalogue page, above). On a later page it is shown pulling a set of three 6-inch four-wheel passenger cars. The colorful Hafner Manufacturing Company stationery (an example was donated by Robert Hafner to the TCA Museum) pictures the No. 127 locomotive pulling three eight-wheel cars — the Wells Fargo baggage, a Union Pacific coach, and a Southern Pacific coach. The letter written on this stationery was dated 1922, but Robert Hafner feels the stationery may have been printed about 1920 and was used in later years by the company even after the production of the No. 127 locomotive ceased.

Certainly the eight-wheel car set led by the No. 127 is a very impressive train outfit, and it is understandable why the company would wish to publicize such a consist even if the locomotive was no longer in production. It is interesting to note that a full-page ad in the January 1922 issue of *Playthings* (and duplicated the same month in *Toys and Novelties*), emphasizing that Hafner train prices had been lowered, displays a rough artist's illustration featuring the No. 127 engine and two eight-wheel passenger cars. The question then arises: was the No. 127 locomotive produced at least until 1922, or was Hafner simply publicizing its trains with what was its finest and most imposing locomotive?

At some time in the 1920s (probably 1929), Hafner brought out a new line of locomotives, and the company did its best to confuse future collectors by listing three of the engines with the same numbers used for the first three earliest engines: Nos. 109, 110, and 112. As a consequence, the terms "early" and "late" must accompany these numbers in order to designate the precise locomotive to which one is referring. These engines are described in a Sears catalogue as "mogul types," but the term is not used accurately since a real-life mogul locomotive means that the engine would have a 2-6-0 wheel arrangement. The late Nos. 109 and 110 engines had boiler castings which were much more detailed than those of their earlier counterparts.

An especially interesting feature of the early 1930s period was the introduction of an 8-inch-long locomotive whose body was made of cast aluminum. This late No. 112 engine was an early experiment in lightweight construction in order to reduce shipping costs. In a 1930 Hafner catalogue it is pictured pulling a large tender and three 6½-inch cars. This locomotive was made for only a short time and was terminated because of high production costs. This aluminum shell had, of course, the regular Hafner motor. Although this aluminum locomotive is not nearly as rare as the No. 127, it

is uncommon today and seldom appears for sale at train meets.

For years the Hafner Company had a standard policy of repairing without charge broken motors or springs. Only return postage was requested. John Hafner has stated that this policy created much goodwill among customers. A slight unsuccessful motor change about 1933 was discussed in a letter to Hafner train purchasers:

> For twenty years our percentage of "returns" and replacement on train motors never exceeded 2 percent of the number of sets produced in the current year, and this 2 percent of returns included hundreds of motors that had been in use from one to five years.
>
> Hoping to better this record last season, we made a change in the hook on the main wheel which engages and holds the spring. This hope of improvement did not materialize, although our usual test of 100 feet of running on track of each engine showed the engine met all requirements. The springs do not break, but a greater percentage become unhooked from the main wheel. We will change back to the former construction of our motor in our 1934 production.

THE INTRODUCTION OF COLOR

The early 1930s constituted the most varied period in the history of Hafner locomotives. The company turned to producing stamped-steel engines with colorful lithographed designs such as blue, red, and green with gold trim. Many of the new locomotives were equipped with flashlight batteries that were used to illuminate a bulb in the boiler front. This feature was patented. A bell was also introduced. For a very short time a tender may have been produced to mount the bell, but normally the bell was attached under the engineer's cab, and upturned track tie tabs caused the bell to ring as the locomotive proceeded around the track.

The new colorfully lithographed engines were matched with cars of similar or mixed colors and are today among the most sought after Hafner sets by collectors. The lithographed locomotive also came in a copper-plated version best remembered for its appearance in a 1937 freight set, although Hafner had earlier made a copper-plated engine.

In the midst of this medley Hafner turned to the production of streamliner imitations of the M-10000 and later of the Burlington Zephyr. Although the streamliners will be discussed in a separate chapter, they are mentioned here because of the frequently changing and varied Hafner locomotive styles of this period.

In 1938 Hafner manufactured a No. 1010 engine (numbered after their 1010 Kolmar plant address) in considerable numbers and in a countless array of colors. It was modeled on the design of the Southern Pacific Daylight locomotives, which appeared that year. Although ultimately this engine was made in a version that exposed the dome and all the boiler top features, it usually appeared with a "shroud," or cowl, covering the boiler top and with streamlined side plates or fairings. Dan Mordell recalls photos of prototype locomotives of this period with captions referring to the "skyline shroud." The shroud and side plate styling were replicas of many real railroad streamline steam types which were very popular in the 1930s. The Pacific No.

2906 of the Union Pacific Railroad, for example, with its streamline shroud and side plates has many similarities to the Hafner No. 1010 engine. Hafner No. 1010 locomotives appear very frequently at train meets and flea markets today, so it is apparent that this engine was produced in large numbers and sold exceedingly well.

Immediately after the end of World War II, which had terminated train production, Hafner manufactured another streamlined steamer, which came in unnumbered form, as well as with the Nos. 2000 and 115041. This style was also modeled on several real-life locomotives of the 1930s. Various prototypes have been suggested as the model for this engine. Dan Mordell suggests the Milwaukee Road's Class "F-7" 4-6-4 as the likely source, although, of course, the Hafner wheel configuration was 0-4-0. Whatever particular engine Hafner designers had in mind, several steamers of this type appeared during the streamliner years, and Hafner was carrying on this tradition in their toy train replicas.

The unnumbered engine as well as the Nos. 2000 and the 115041 were almost the same except for the lithography. The unnumbered engine appeared in black and had cutout doors and windows; the 2000 was lithographed either in black, red, and silver, or in blue, red, and silver, while the 115041 came in a combination of yellow, blue, silver, and orange.

It is disappointing that after the considerable variety of locomotives produced in the late 1920s and early 1930s Hafner essentially produced only one style of engine (excluding differences in lithography) during the 1940s and until the company's sale to All Metal Products in 1951. John Hafner comments that economy was the reason for this lack of locomotive variety. Hafner trains were selling very well, and new engines would require greatly increased production costs, so why tamper with a good thing?

THE LISTINGS

The locomotives described in the ensuing lists are treated in **approximate chronological order**. Remember, however, that several were issued at the same time, and bear in mind the usual Hafner caveat that the dates of production are never to be considered definitive. They are approximate dates, but certainly the best that can be determined unless new and more precisely dated Hafner research materials turn up. John Hafner reports that company records and files were discarded. Some locomotives do not have their numbers cast into the inner side of the shell casing. Wherever certainty is possible, the tender that came with a particular locomotive is also indicated, but in many instances, especially in the 1930s, tenders were mixed and matched with various locomotives; and, hence, different tenders would be sold with the same engine. Tenders could also be purchased separately. Production expediency and inventory availability were dominant facts in Hafner's history.

Note: Prices listed are for locomotives only. Prices for tenders are given in the next chapter. The "M-10000" and "Burlington Zephyr" motor units will be discussed in the chapter on streamliners.

No. 109 LOCOMOTIVE (EARLY): Ca. 1914-20s. Cast iron. Number taken from shell casting and from catalogue.

(A) Rectangular window; one silver boiler band; red window stripe; ten open-spoke cast drivers; three vertical rows of boiler rivets. Boiler top order: headlamp projecting over boiler, rivets, stack, rivets, bell, band, rivets, steam dome; no drive rods; no brake. Catalogued as 6½" long. Came with "1181" early version tender. (See Chapter Four.)   30   60

(B) Same as (A), but with red boiler band.   30   60

(C) Same as (A), but with yellow boiler band.   30   60

(D) Also later came with eight open-spoke stamped-steel drivers and silver boiler band.   30   60

(E) Same as (D), but with gold boiler band.   30   60

No. 110 LOCOMOTIVE (EARLY): Ca. 1914-20s. Cast iron. Number taken from shell casting and from catalogue.

(A) Rectangular window; red window stripe; ten open-spoke cast drivers; three vertical rows of boiler rivets. Boiler top order: headlamp projecting over boiler, rivets, stack, rivets, bell, band, rivets, dome; drive rods; brake. Catalogued as 6½" long. Came with "1180" (Large) tender.   35   70

(B) Same as (A), but without drive rods.   35   70

No. 112 LOCOMOTIVE (EARLY): Ca. 1914-20s. Cast iron. Number taken from shell casting and from catalogue. (Note: There was no No. 111 ever produced.)

(A) Rectangular window; two silver boiler bands; ten open-spoke cast drivers; three vertical columns of boiler rivets. Boiler top order: headlamp projecting over boiler front, rivets, stack, rivets, bell, band, rivets, dome; drive rods; brake. Catalogued as 7" long. Came with "1180" (Large) tender.   45   90

(B) Also later came with open-spoke stamped-metal drivers.   45   90

(C) Also came with one boiler band.   45   90

No. 127 LOCOMOTIVE: Ca. 1914-19, but even approximate dating is in question. (A Butler Bros. 1914 catalogue indistinctly shows this engine.) Cast iron. Number taken from shell casting and from catalogue. Rectangular two-part window; one silver boiler band; ten open-spoke cast drivers; key on right; seven vertical rows of boiler rivets. Boiler top order: headlamp projecting over boiler front, rivets, rivets, stack, rivets, bell, rivets, rivets, smaller dome, rivets, larger dome, rivets; drive rods; brake. Catalogued as 7½" long. Came with "1180" (Large) tender.   NRS

Note: This is the locomotive that is modeled on the Ives No. 17 of the 1912-14 period. Both engines are the same length and — seen in a picture or from a distance — both look the same, although the 127 has a red stripe under each window. The Ives No. 17 motor fits in the Hafner No. 127 shell. The key of the No. 127 is on the right-hand side, the only Hafner locomotive ever made that does not have the winding key on the left side. The differences on closer inspection become more apparent. The Ives No. 17 has red wheels, two metal bands, and nine horizontal boiler rivets near the engineer's cab. The Hafner No. 127 has black wheels, one metal band, ten horizontal boiler rivets on one side and eleven on the other side (apparently resulting from imperfect casting). The Hafner casting in general is much rougher than the Ives, in some places having jagged or uneven edges. Ives uses a square key insert, while the Hafner model has a threaded key. The Hafner brake lever in the cab has a longer loop, and the Hafner motor has a wider spring and a smaller size front gear.

Top: No. 109 locomotive (Early); 110 (Early) with brake and drive rods. Middle: No. 112 (Early); 127 — probably the rarest locomotive of any manufacturer today. The top unit of the 127 is Hafner, but the motor shown is from an Ives No. 17 engine. Hafner produced the 127 by copying the Ives 17 of the 1912–1914 era (see the separate photo below of the Ives No. 17 from 1912–1914, shown with "IVES/N.Y.C. & H.R." tender). Bottom: Stamped-steel locomotive produced near the end of World War I because of a shortage of cast iron; No. 100 locomotive used to pull many bottom-of-the-line sets.

Gd   Exc

UNNUMBERED STAMPED-STEEL LOCOMOTIVE:
Ca. 1917-20. A 1920 Hafner jobber advertisement appears to picture this engine, but the artist may have been using an illustration from the previous year. Rectangular window; one silver boiler band; engine shell entirely in black with no stripe; eight open-spoke stamped-steel drivers; no rivets. Boiler top order: rectangular piece attached to boiler top used to simulate a headlight, stack, bell on top of boiler band, dome; no drive rods; no brake. 6" long. Usually came with early version "1181" tender.   **75   150**

Note 1: This stamped-steel unnumbered locomotive is a particularly uncommon engine since it had a limited production run during the late World War I period. John Hafner reports that on account of material shortages the company had to turn to stamped steel to supplement their cast-iron locomotive line.

Note 2: Dan Mordell has in his collection a most unusual variation of this locomotive. Red lithographed boiler; brass-plated boiler band and stack; no rectangular simulated headlight; dummy hooded brass-plated headlight on boiler

Top: No. 109 locomotive (Late) (A); 110 (Late) with brake and drive rods. Bottom: No. 110 (Late) with extra-long brake activator; 112 (Late) aluminum shell locomotive produced mainly to reduce the cost of shipping cast-iron engines — offered for sale only in 1930 and 1931.

	Gd	Exc

front; cab sides are rubber stamped "48-103"; 6½" long. Probably a preproduction model. **NRS**

No. 100 LOCOMOTIVE: Ca. 1920s-early 1930s. Cast iron. Number taken from shell casing and from catalogue.

(A) Rectangular window; one boiler band; red window stripe; eight open-spoke stamped-steel drivers; three rows of boiler rivets. Boiler top order: headlamp projecting over boiler front, rivets, stack, rivets, bell, band, rivets, dome; no drive rods; no brake. Catalogued as 6" long. Came with early version of "1181" tender and with "1180" (Small) tender.

25 50

(B) Same as (A), but with gold boiler band. **25 50**

No. 109 LOCOMOTIVE (LATE): Late 1920s-early 1930s. Cast iron. Rectangular two-part window; no boiler bands; red window stripe; eight open-spoke stamped-steel drivers; four rows of boiler rivets.

(A) Number taken from catalogue. Boiler top order: rivets, stack, bell, rivets, rivets, dome, dome, rivets, smaller dome; no drive rods; no brake. Catalogued as 6½" long.

30 60

(B) Early 1930s. Same as (A) but number taken from shell casting; two domes instead of three; catalogued as 6" long.

30 60

Note: (B) was probably produced, as Dan Mordell suggests, to save on shipping costs.

No. 110 LOCOMOTIVE (LATE): Late 1920s-early 1930s. Cast iron. Number taken from shell casting and from catalogue. Rectangular two-part window; no boiler bands; red window stripe; eight open-spoke stamped-steel drivers; four rows of boiler rivets. Boiler top order: rivets, stack, bell, rivets, rivets, dome, dome, rivets, smaller dome; drive rods; brake. Some of these engines have an unusually long brake

	Gd	Exc

lever. See Note at end of listing for No. 112 locomotive (Late). Catalogued as 6½" long. **35 70**

No. 112 LOCOMOTIVE (LATE): 1930-31. Number taken from catalogue. This is the cast-aluminum shell engine. Rectangular two-part window; no boiler bands; no window stripe; eight open-spoke stamped-steel drivers; two rows of boiler rivets. Boiler top order: rivets, stack, bell, dome, smaller dome, rivets; drive rods; brake. Catalogued as 8" long. Came with "1180" tender. **90 180**

Note: In order that the operator need not reach so far under the long cab roof to use the horizontal brake lever, a 1¾" piece of metal has been riveted to the lever on *some* of these No. 127 (Late) locomotives. These extended brake lever pieces are sometimes found on smaller Hafner engines so that leftover stock would not be wasted.

Stamped-Steel Locomotives

The following listing describes a series of locomotives which have similar styling. Most of these engines are unnumbered, but some bear the lettering "1110" under the cab window. The motor casing in this type of locomotive is equipped with a knob which slips into a circular frame piece which holds the knob tightly. These engines come in three frame styles.

CHICAGO "CENTURY OF PROGRESS SPECIAL" UNNUMBERED LOCOMOTIVE: Ca. 1933-35. Stamped steel. Rectangular window arched at top corners; no boiler bands; eight open-spoke stamped-steel drivers; no boiler rivets. Boiler top order: stack, dome, bell, larger dome; battery holder inside boiler shell; drive rods; brake; 7" long; Type I frame. Usually came with Type Id No. "1190" tender

Frames for No. 1110-Style Locomotives

Type I A raised platform rests on the top of the frame shelf. The platform runs the length of the frame as well as the front and back of the engine. It is designed to elevate the shell to make room for the battery holder which was inserted over the top of the motor.

Type II Does not have the platform. Since there are no batteries in this type of engine, extra room at the top of the casing is not needed. The frame shelf is bent downward so that a side strip runs the entire length below the frame shelf. The section of the frame under the cab representing firebox sides is slightly shorter in Type II.

Type III Similar to Type II, but the frame shelf is not bent downward on the sides so there is no side strip running the entire length.

                                     Gd   **Exc**

(see Chapter Three). This engine was designed for use with sets called the "Century of Progress Special" produced to coincide with Chicago's Century of Progress Exposition (*Playthings*, July 1933). This black-enameled engine has a red boiler front and a bell under the cab which is activated by a crosstie-tripped clapper. The engine's white electric bulb protruded from the boiler front, and the illuminated feature was a very important selling attraction. Bulbs used in Hafner locomotives were the standard 2½-volt flashlight type, and batteries were two-cell "penlight" types. This locomotive usually has a stationary drawbar, but a few came with a swiveling drawbar. Because the engine was a big seller, it turns up at train meets quite frequently which decreases its price value. **20** **40**

Note: Some of these "Chicago Special" locomotives also came with a black boiler front.

No. 1110 LITHOGRAPHED LOCOMOTIVE: Ca. early 1930s, first produced in 1931, according to Hafner "Descriptive Sheet." Stamped steel. Number lettered on locomotive; rectangular window curved at top corners; three lithographed gold boiler bands; window stripe numbered "1110" in gold on lithographed red background; eight open-spoke stamped-steel drivers. Boiler top order: stack, dome, two sanding pipes simulated in gold lithography commencing at dome and running down sides in triangular form, bell, large dome has gold lithographed pipe running down sides and curving toward the middle of the boiler; drive rods; brake; 7" long; Type II frame.

(A) Boiler and cab lithographed in bright red with gold details; red boiler front has hooded copper-plated simulated headlight; black frame; handrails; bell; drawbar has slight curved offset at rear. **75** **150**

(B) Same as (A), but with blue boiler shell, cab, and front; handrails curve down and around part of the boiler front; straight drawbar. **75** **150**

(C) Same as (B), but with red boiler front. **75** **150**

(D) Same as (A), but with green boiler, cab, and front; handrails curve down and around part of boiler front; straight drawbar. **75** **150**

                                     Gd   **Exc**

(E) Same as (B), but with Type I frame and light; boiler bands do not curve down and around the boiler front; boiler front has circular hole in center for headlight bulb to protrude. **90** **180**

(F) Same as (A), but with Type III frame. **75** **150**

(G) Same as (D), but with red boiler front and Type I frame for battery headlight. Boiler band does not curve down and around the boiler front; drawbar slightly curved inward. R. Sappelli Collection. **90** **180**

Note: Dan Mordell reports a No. 1110 engine with a wire protruding from rear of cab which would indicate the use of a battery tender in the manner of American Flyer. Further data at present not available.

UNNUMBERED 1110-STYLE LOCOMOTIVE: Ca. early 1930s; one engine issued in 1937. Rectangular window curved at top corners; no boiler bands; eight closed-spoke stamped-steel drivers; no boiler rivets. Boiler top order: stack, dome, bell, larger dome; driving rods; brake; 7" long; Type II frame.

Note: This locomotive is unnumbered but is in the style of the Chicago Special and No. 1110 engines.

(A) All-copper boiler; has drive rods, brake, and bell; green boiler front with circular hole in the center; no headlight hood; stationary drawbar with slightly offset rising curve. **90** **180**

(B) All black with separate orange metal plates attached under cab windows; no drive rods, brake, or bell; open-spoke drivers; stationary straight drawbar; no handrails; gold hooded headlight piece on boiler front to simulate headlight; gold hardware on top of boiler. **60** **120**

(C) Same as (B), but has no metal plates under cab windows. The two punched-out holes on each side to mount the metal plates remain. **45** **90**

(D) Same as (A), but all black with gold hardware; open-spoked drivers; gold simulated headlight hooded piece; stationary drawbar. **40** **80**

(E) Same as (A), but boiler cab, front, and top hardware all in red; boiler front has circular hole punched out in center; stationary drawbar slightly offset upward. **NRS**

(F) Same as (A), but all-copper boiler and boiler front; copper hooded headlight piece on boiler front to simulate light; swivel drawbar. Type III frame. This was the last engine made in the 1110 styling. It is pictured with a freight set in a 1937 Granger's catalogue. Louis Hertz writing in *The Model Craftsman* (June 1938, p. 43) seems to suggest this engine was made in 1938, but in the June 1939 issue (p. 41) it is clear that he is referring to the No. 1010 copper variant. **NRS**

No. 1010 LOCOMOTIVE: First produced in 1938; late 1930s, 1940s — pre- and postwar. The date of the first production of the "1010" engine has been estimated by Hafner collectors anywhere from 1934 to 1938. John Hafner says "about 1934" and at least two collectors "recall" the engine from the 1934-35 period. Louis Hertz writing in the June 1938 issue of *The Model Craftsman* (p. 43), reports the appearance of this engine. The following year in the June 1939 issue (p. 41) Hertz notes that this locomotive was sold in some stores in 1938 but now is available for quantity distribution.[2] Material at the TCA Library confirms that the No. 1010 locomotive was sold in 1938.

Top: Unnumbered locomotive which pulled the popular Chicago "Century of Progress Special" set; unnumbered 1110-type locomotive with orange metal plates under the engineer's cab. This locomotive was also sold with the plates removed though the plate holes remained. Middle: No. 1110 locomotive with all-red boiler shell; copper shell 1110-type engine. Bottom: Blue 1110 and green 1110 locomotives, beautifully lithographed and uncommon.

                                                                    Gd   Exc

Stamped steel. Number embossed on locomotive. This engine comes in four different forms, with the distinguishing characteristics summarized in the box.

No. 1010 Types

Type I Steamlined cowl on roof; sideboards run the length of the engine.

Type II Streamlined cowl discarded; smokestack, bell, and two domes now visible.

Type III Similar to I, but has embossed ridge on sideboards.

Type IV Similar to I, but sideboards extend only 2½ inches from the front; "HAFNER" stamped on sideboards.

Type I Two-part window with forward side of first window slanted; no boiler bands; window stripe embossed with "1010" on side plates under windows; eight closed-spoke stamped-metal drivers; no boiler rivets. Boiler top order: shroud runs from the boiler top to the cab and has open stack hole, embossed sand dome, punched hole and slot for motor mounting screw and brake lever, embossed steam dome; drive rods; brake; 7" long.

Note 1: On the 1010 engines the rivet arrangement to hold end of sideboard under engineer's cab varies. Some engines have the rivet located before the "1010" lettering; others have a tab after the "1010" mating with a hole under the cab windows.

Note 2: The reverse side lettering with the Pfeiffer beer figures has already been mentioned. Another factory error 1010 locomotive has turned up with the Pfeiffer lithography on the boiler front and right sideboard and a large circled "R" and "M & S" in small letters forming the left sideboard and cowl pieces.

(A) The Type I 1010 engine, seemingly the most common locomotive Hafner ever produced, came in a great variety of colors. It is frequently seen in red with silver boiler front, a silver shroud, and silver sideplates which are stamped "HAFNER" near the front and "1010" under the cab; circular hole in center of boiler front; not illuminated; has track-actuated bell. Some collectors feel the color should be designated as aluminum rather than silver.   **15   30**

(B) Same as (A), but black instead of red. Just as frequently appearing as the red and silver version.   **15   30**

(C) Same as (A), but with dark gray boiler front, shroud, and side plates.   **15   30**

(D) Same as (C), but with silver boiler front.   **15   30**

(E) Same as (B), but with gray shroud, side plates, and boiler front.   **15   30**

Top: Chicago "Century of Progress Special" set locomotive missing drive rods; cheaper version with simulated headlight on boiler front. Bottom: Especially rare unnumbered all-red boiler variation.

	Gd	Exc

(F) Same as (B), but the number "1010" does not appear on the right (that is, facing toward the engine front) side of the cab. **15 30**

(G) Same as (A), but with copper side plates and shroud; silver boiler front. **15 30**

(H) Same as (G), but with copper boiler front. **15 30**

(I) Same as (A), but in yellow with red side plates and shroud and red boiler front. **25 50**

(J) Same as (A), but with gold side plates. **20 40**

(K) Same as (A), but with metallic red boiler front, black shroud, and red side plates. **25 50**

(L) Same as (K), but with red shroud. **25 50**

(M) Same as (A), but green with copper boiler front, shroud, and side plates. **25 50**

(N) Same as (A), but with silver boiler front, shroud, and side plates. **25 50**

(O) Same as (C), but with whitish-gray boiler front, shroud, and side plates. **15 30**

(P) Same as (K), but with red boiler front. **25 50**

(Q) Same as (B), but has six rivets on each of the two cowl domes; "1010" does not appear on the right side under the cab window. **15 30**

(R) Same as (E), but one sideboard is off-white. **NRS**

(S) Same as (A), but with nonlithographed tinplate shrouds and side plates. **12 25**

(T) Same as (B), but with nonlithographed tinplate shrouds and side plates. **12 25**

(U) Same as (A), but with chrome boiler front, shroud, and side plates. **20 40**

(V) Same as (A), but with gold boiler front, shroud, and side plates. **20 40**

Type II

(A) Same as Type I No. 1010 engine, but the streamlined shroud has been replaced with a smokestack, bell, and two domes have been added on the top of the boiler. Green boiler and cab; copper side plates and boiler front. **35 70**

	Gd	Exc

(B) Same as (A), but with blue boiler and cab; chrome side plates and boiler front. **35 70**

(C) Same as (B), but with gray boiler front. **35 70**

(D) Same as (A), but with red boiler and cab; chrome sideplates and boiler front. **35 70**

(E) Same as (D), but with gold boiler front. **35 70**

(F) Same as (B), but ivory sideplates. **35 70**

(G) Same as (D), buth with copper side plates and boiler front. **35 70**

Type III

(A) Same as Type I No. 1010 engine, but has additional embossed ridge running along the top of the side plates and no lettering or numbering. Beige boiler and cab with chrome shroud, side plates, and boiler front. **25 50**

(B) Same as (A), but with red boiler and cab, chrome shroud, side plates, and boiler front. **25 50**

(C) Green boiler and cab, copper shroud, side plates, and boiler front. Has "HAFNER" and "1010" lettered on side plates. **35 70**

(D) Same as (A), but has lettering on side plates.

25 50

Type IV

(A) Same as Type I No. 1010 engine, but side plates extend from the front bottom of the pilot up and back along the boiler only 2½" in contrast to the typical 1010 where the side plates extend from the pilot all the way back to the engineer's cab. "HAFNER" stamped on side plates but no embossed "1010." Red with gray shroud and side plates; chrome boiler front. Came with and without handrails. **35 70**

(B) Same as (A), but with gilt boiler front. **35 70**

UNNUMBERED BLACK 2000- and 115041-STYLE LOCOMOTIVE: Postwar 1940s-1951. Stamped steel. Two punched-out cab windows; lower section of the door is also punched out; eight closed-spoke stamped-steel drivers; no

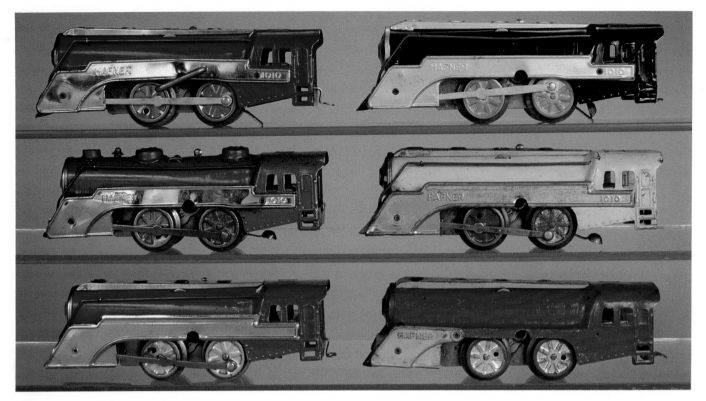

Some variations of the No. 1010 locomotive. Top: Red and gold; black and silver. Middle: 1010 Type II, blue and chrome, without the top shroud — sometimes called Hafner's Girls' Train engine; 1010 Type III beige and chrome with embossed ridge along sideboards; 1010 Type III, red and chrome. Bottom: 1010 Type IV, short sideboard model usually found in poor condition because of excessive wear. Engine should have driving rods.

	Gd	Exc

boiler details; drive rods; brake. 8½" long. Comes with Type Va tender with either silver or black frame.

Lithographed solid black; hooded bulb cover at the top of the boiler front over socket for bulb — same as No. 115041. On-and-off lever is at the bottom of the boiler front — same as 115041 — but no lettering. Has light, bell, and clapper.

30   60

Note: The motor that accommodated the M-10000 body now required a stamped sheet-metal spacer to support this higher body. This is also true of the Nos. 2000 and 115041 locomotives.

No. 2000 LOCOMOTIVE: Postwar 1940s-1951. Stamped steel. Number lettered on locomotive. Three-part lithographed window; third window is part of the cab door; eight closed-spoke stamped-steel drivers; four vertical rows of lithographed boiler rivets. Boiler top order: plain black lithographed integral shroud with embossed detail. Only brake lever and motor mounting screw protrude; drive rods; brake; 8½" long. Comes with Type Va tender.

(A) Black, silver, and red lithography. "HAFNER TRAINS" lettered in silver on sides on a red background, part of which forms a star. "HAFNER TRAINS" lettered in black and enclosed in a circle on boiler front. "2000" lettered in silver under the cab. Came with a battery holder inside the boiler front; bulb at the top of the boiler front. On and off switch for the battery protruding through pilot with lettering "ON" and "OFF" in black. Silhouette of an engineer lithographed in black in cab window; bell and clapper under cab. **15   30**

	Gd	Exc

(B) Same as (A), but no lettering on boiler front; has no battery holder or light. Boiler front has punched-out hole in which an eyelet serves to simulate headlight. Eyelet secures a weight inside boiler front to compensate for omitted battery and holder. **15   30**

(C) Same as (A), but no battery holder or light. Has punched-out hole in boiler front bordered by a lithographed silver bezel to simulate headlight. **15   30**

(D) Same as (A), but no lettering on boiler front; silver bezel lithographed on boiler front under headlight socket.

15   30

(E) Same as (A), but in blue, red, and silver lithography. "HAFNER TRAINS" lettered in silver; engineer is lithographed in blue; no battery or light; punched-out hole in boiler front bordered by lithographed silver bezel to simulate headlight. No weight. **20   40**

(F) Same as (E), but punched hole in boiler front in which an eyelet is inserted to simulate headlight. Eyelet secures a weight inside boiler front. **20   40**

(G) Chris Rohlfing reports a very unusual 2000-style engine in his collection. It is all black with no cut-out windows; has no battery light but contains the opening for the light near the top of the boiler front. Chris writes that if one examines the engine closely "you can see lithographed detail under the black paint and the number 2000 under the paint." It is in original "set box 902F from 1951. The tender has a chrome frame and black body with embossed rivet detail and embossed 'HAFNER' on the side. The set also included 14825

Top: Extremely colorful yellow and red No. 1010 locomotive; black 2000 engine, unlighted version.   Middle: Blue 2000 engine; black 2000 locomotive, lighted version. Bottom: Unnumbered all-black engine with cut-out cab windows and doorway; colorful 115041 locomotive with headlight and bell.

	Gd	Exc

brown ATST boxcar, 91876 green and brown Hafner gondola, 614333 red C & NW caboose, and a figure 8 track layout."

NRS

No. 115041 LOCOMOTIVE: Postwar 1940s-1951. Three-part lithographed window; third window is part of the door; eight closed-spoke stamped-steel drivers; six rows of boiler and cab roof rivets lithographed vertically plus rectangular rivets lithographed over cab roof on both sides. Boiler top order: lithographed striped integral shroud with no separate stacks, domes, etc. Has top-located brake lever and motor- mounting screw; drive rods; brake; 8½" long. Comes with Type Vb tender.

(A) Yellow, blue, orange, and silver lithography. "HAFNER / TRAINS" lettered in white on sides. "115041" lettered in white near the boiler front and again at rear of the cab roof. Has "HAFNER TRAINS" lettered in black and enclosed in a circle both on the boiler front and under the cab. Came with a battery holder located vertically inside the boiler front; headlight at the top of the boiler front. On and off switch for the headlight protruding through the lithographed pilot with lettering "ON" and "OFF" in black. Silhouette of an engineer lithographed in cab window; bell and clapper under cab.

	Gd	Exc

Lettered "BUILT BY / HAFNER TRAINS / CHICAGO, ILL. / U.S.A." near the bottom under the cab. Lettering "KEEP OUT" at bottom of cab door. | **15** | **30** |

(B) Same as (A), but with darker blue lithography.

15   **30**

Note: This locomotive was carried over by the All Metal Products Company in their Wyandotte toy line when they purchased Hafner. They first used up Hafner inventory, then put the Wyandotte herald on the front and removed the Chicago lettering. The motor was also eventually changed. Consult the chapter on Wyandotte trains.

NOTES

1. The July 1968 issue of the TCA *Quarterly* reports that castings during World War I came from the Susquehanna Castings Company of Wrightsville, Pennsylvania.

2. An article in *Railroad Model Craftsman* (October 1951) claims Hafner dropped all steam engines from its line for three years after 1934, but Hafner price sheets and catalogues show that steam engines were sold in 1935 and 1936, and a jobber's advertisement lists one steam engine set in 1937.

SUMMARY OF LOCOMOTIVE TYPES

I 109 (Early)
Lowest-priced engine in Hafner's first line
Cast iron
No brake or drive roads
6½ inches long

II 110 (Early)
Similar to the 109, but equipped with brake and drive
rods

III 112 (Early)
Larger than 109 and 110 (7 inches long)
Usually has two silver boiler bands
Has brake and drive rods
Used with higher-priced sets

IV 127
Most impressive Hafner engine
Copied from Ives No. 17 engine of the 1912–1914
period
8 inches long with impressive detailing, including
horizontal rivets
Powerful motor, used to pull eight-wheel cars
Only Hafner engine with winding key on right side
Very rare

V
Unnumbered stamped steel
World War I production
Antiquated nineteenth-century styling
Small (6 inches long)
No drive rods or brake

VI 100
Used with lower-priced sets
6 inches
No brake or drive rods

VII 109 (Late)
a: Very detailed cast iron
6 inches long
Three domes
No brake or drive rods
b: Identical to VIIa, but has two domes and is ½ inch
shorter
Probably devised to save on shipping costs

VIII 110 (Late)
Similar to VIIa, but came with driving rods and brake

IX 112 (Late)
Cast-aluminum shell
Rectangular two-part window
No window stripe
Later models had extra-long brake lever
8 inches long

X Century of Progress Special Unnumbered Locomotive
Stamped steel
Red boiler front
Battery-operated headlight bulb
Bell under cab
7 inches long

XI 1110 Lithographed Locomotive
Stamped steel
Number lettered under cab windows
Usually came with No. 1110 Type II frame, although
can have Type I frame with headlight, or Type III
Came in red, blue, or green with gold piping
7 inches long

XII Unnumbered 1110-style Locomotive
Similar to IX
Usually came with black boiler, although also
produced with copper or red boiler
No battery headlight; usually has simulated headlight
hooded cover

XIII 1010 Locomotive
Stamped steel
7 inches long
"1010" usually embossed on engine
Came in four distinct types (see text)

XIV Unnumbered 2000, 115041-style Locomotive
Stamped steel
Punched-out cab windows
Punched-out lower section of door
All black
No lettering
Battery-operated headlight and bell
8½ inches long

XV 2000 Locomotive
Stamped steel
Colorfully lithographed in either black, silver, and red,
or in blue, red, and silver
"2000" lettered under cab
Came with and without battery-operated headlight
8½ inches long

XVI 115041
Stamped steel
Yellow, blue, orange, and silver lithography
"115041" lettered on boiler front and at rear of cab roof
Came with battery-operated headlight and bell
8½ inches long

CHAPTER THREE

★

TENDERS

In its very earliest production, Hafner made two tender styles — the large 1180 and the smaller 1181. Both tenders continued in the Hafner line from 1914 until the early 1930s. The 1180 tender had disappearing couplers on both front and back. The 1181 tender, on the other hand, used this coupler only on the rear. The front floor of the 1181 extended out and included a large-sized hole into which dropped the locomotive drawbar. Couplers (and frames for rolling stock) are fully described and illustrated in Chapter Four. Refer to the boxed summary in that chapter for clarification of the coupler types found on various tenders.

It is evident that Hafner styled the 1180 tender after the early American Flyer Type 2 tender (for explanation of that typology, see *Greenberg's Guide to American Flyer Prewar O Gauge*, pp. 23-24 in the 1987 edition; note that a new edition of this book is expected to be published in 1993), which in the 1916 American Flyer catalogue was numbered 120. The small 1181 tender is very similar to the American Flyer Type 1 tender numbered "328" on its sides. We can classify Hafner tenders into five main categories, as summarized in the boxed list to the right.

TYPE I TENDER

In the first known Hafner catalogue, this tender was designated as "1180". It is the larger of the early tenders and usually came with the higher-priced sets. The sides of the frame are particularly elaborate with clearly delineated lines of the springs and the journal boxes. This style tender usually came with an embossed stamped-metal coal load.

Gd   Exc

1180 (Early Large)
(A) "OVERLAND FLYER" lettered in white on sides; "1180" lettered in white on back; the lettered number and words are enclosed within white-outlined panels which are in turn enclosed by red lines; black sides and frame.   **25   50**
(B) Same as (A) but "OVERLAND FLYER" and "1180" are enclosed in yellow-outlined panels which are in turn enclosed within red lines.   **25   50**
(C) "OVERLAND FLYER" lettered in green on sides; "1180" lettered in green on back; the lettered number and words are enclosed within green-outlined panels which are in turn enclosed within red lines.   **30   60**
(D) "CANADIAN FLYER" lettered in white on sides; "1180" lettered in white on back; the lettered number and words are enclosed within white-outlined panels which are in turn enclosed by red lines. Bruce Garver Collection.   **NRS**
(E) Same as (A), but "NEW YORK FLYER" lettering. James K. Lynch Collection.   **NRS**

In the late 1920s and into the early 1930s, Hafner took this same large style and length 1180 tender and changed the

---

Tender Types

Type Ia 1180 (Large) Larger of the two earliest tenders; usually lettered "OVERLAND FLYER" but has been found with "CANADIAN FLYER" and "NEW YORK FLYER" lettering

Note: Numbering changed from "1180" to "1190" in the late 1920s for the following four subtypes:

Type Ib Red sides, black frame; lithographed with iridescent gold heralds of various railroads

Type Ic Black sides and frame; various railroad heralds on sides

Type Id Green or red sides, black frames; "HAFNER'S / OVERLAND FLYER / RAILWAYS" bar and circle herald on sides

Type Ie Green, red, or blue sides, red or black frame; has extended front floor piece with hole rather than usual sliding coupler

Type IIa 1181 Smaller size of earliest tenders; "OVERLAND FLYER" lettered on sides, "1181" lettered in black; also came in no lettering and no number versions

Type IIb 1180 (Small) Lettering changed from "1181" to 1180 in the late 1920s; usually has railroad herald on sides; "HAFNER'S / OVERLAND FLYER / RAILWAYS" bar and circle herald on some tenders; also came with no lettering

Type III Copper-plated body with green rounded end pieces; no lettering; high triangular pedestal trucks

Type IVa Center body unit with rounded end pieces; various colors; coffin-style without high pedestal trucks; "HAFNER" is embossed on sides

Type IVb Similar to IVa, but "HAFNER TRAINS" lettering centered on sides; center body unit comes in gray, gold, or cream; "1010" lithographed to the left of center on both sides; "Made in U.S.A." lettered on bottom at right

Type Va Square shape without separate end pieces; winglike top sides curving inward; black or blue sides; unnumbered; "HAFNER" embossed on center of both sides

Type Vb Similar to Va, but yellow, blue, orange, and gray lithography on sides or plain black sides; usually numbered either "90131" or "78100" on top front of sides

Top: Three variations of the 1180 tender — red with Hafner logo but without coal load, red showing coal load, and rare bell tender. Middle: 1181 tender with Overland Flyer lettering and unusual mahogany frame and plain black styles. Bottom: Late versions of 1180 Type II tenders — Illinois Central and Southern Pacific heralds.

Top: 1190 iridescent gold herald Santa Fe tender; 1190 Type Ic black Santa Fe herald tender. Middle: 1190 iridescent gold Southern Pacific herald; 1190 Type Ic black Pennsylvania herald. Bottom: 1190 Id Hafner herald tender; 1190 Ie Hafner herald with unusual red frame.

Gd Exc

number to "1190". 1190 tenders came with either Type II or Type III couplers (more frequently with Type II) and usually had coal loads. These large tenders came in the following four distinct forms, which we have designated as Ib, Ic, Id, and Ie.

1190 (Type Ib): Red sides and black frame; iridescent gold herald on sides lettered in gold; herald enclosed by iridescent gold lines. No number on end.

	Gd	Exc
(A) "Santa Fe" herald.	35	70
(B) "ILLINOIS CENTRAL" herald.	35	70
(C) "SOUTHERN / PACIFIC" herald.	35	70
(D) "CHICAGO / NORTH WESTERN / LINE" herald.	35	70
(E) "PENNSYLVANIA / LINES" herald.	35	70
(F) "NEW YORK / CENTRAL / LINES" herald.	35	70

1190 (Type Ic): Black sides and frame. Both herald and number are enclosed in white-outlined panels on all three sides of tender. Except where noted, "1190" is lettered in white on back of tender.

	Gd	Exc
(A) "Santa Fe" herald.	30	60
(B) "ILLINOIS CENTRAL / RAILROAD" herald.	30	60
(C) "SOUTHERN/ PACIFIC" herald.	30	60
(D) "CHICAGO / NORTH WESTERN / LINE" herald on sides. No white-outlined panel on back of tender and does not have "1190" lettering.		NRS
(E) "PENNSYLVANIA / LINES" herald on sides.	30	60
(F) Same as (E), but no white-outlined panel on back of tender and does not have "1190" lettering.		NRS
(G) "New York / Central / Lines" herald on sides.	30	60
(H) Same as (B), but no white panel on back and does not have "1190" lettering.	30	60

1190 (Type Id): Usually manufactured with Type II couplers and coal loads.

(A) "HAFNER'S / OVERLAND FLYER / RAILWAYS" bar and circle herald lettered on sides; "1190" lettered in white on back; white-outlined panels enclose the herald and number and occur on all three sides; green sides; black frame.
25 50
(B) Same as (A), but with red sides. **25 50**

1190 (Type Ie): Came with a front extended floor piece frame with hole to fit the locomotive drawbar as opposed to the other types of 1190 tenders which have disappearing couplers. This style of tender usually has Type II couplers and comes with and without coal load.

(A) "HAFNER'S / OVERLAND FLYER / RAILWAYS" bar and circle herald on sides; "1190" lettered in white on back; herald and number are enclosed in white-outlined panels on all three sides; red sides and darker red frame. **25 50**
(B) Same as (A), but with green sides. **25 50**
(C) Same as (B), but has a box ¾ length in inside area; like a battery box but no evidence of wires or contacts. No coal load. **NRS**
(D) Same as (A), but with blue sides and black frame. **25 50**
(E) Same as (A), but with no lettering or outlined panels. This tender is usually found with the Chicago Century of Progress set. Usually has coal load. **15 35**
(F) Same as (A), but with blue sides and red frame. **30 60**

Gd Exc

(G) Same as (E), but with black frame. **20 40**

TYPE II TENDER

This is the smallest of the Hafner tenders and came in the most economically priced sets. In the early catalogue it is numbered "1181"; a late 1920s–early 1930s catalogue, however, designates this tender as "No. 1180". This renumbering has caused considerable confusion because although at some point in the 1920s the early small 1181 tender becomes 1180, it retains the same size and shape.

In the meantime the large-sized tender listed as No. 1180 (a Type I tender) in the early catalogue is renumbered "1190" in the late 1920s–early 1930s listing. It is evident that Hafner was not thinking of collectors or even a logical numbering sequence as, for example, Lionel used. This is pertinent because tenders were catalogued as separate items. This same confusion is similar in some ways to Hafner calling three of its early locomotives No. 109, No. 110, and No. 112, and then later producing three completely different-styled engines using the same numbers. With the early 1181 tender, however, there is at least the consistency that when it was renumbered it continued to have the same size and styling, although, of course, there were coloring and lettering variations. Choosing to change the No. 1181 to No. 1180 when the larger and more impressive early 1180 tender had been sold for many years appears unduly arbitrary and even confusing from a marketing product point of view since potential buyers would possibly be perplexed.

Most 1181 tenders came without coal loads.

1181
(A) "OVERLAND FLYER" lettered in white on sides; "1181" lettered in white on back; the lettered number and words are enclosed within white-outlined panels which are in turn enclosed by red lines; black sides and frame. Type I or Type II couplers. **25 50**
(B) Same as (A), but no lettering or outlined panels. Type I or Type II couplers. **20 40**
(C) Same as (A), but with lithographed wood-grained frame. Type I or Type II couplers. **NRS**
(D) Same as (A), but with lithographed wood-grained sides and frame. Type I or Type II couplers. **NRS**

1180 (Later Small): I have designated the later version of this type tender (that is, the earlier 1181, as listed above) as "1180 (Small)" in order to differentiate it from the early large-sized Hafner 1180 tender.

No. 1180 (Small) tenders usually came without coal loads. This later version is usually identified by having a railroad herald on its side. Usually, this tender came with Type II couplers and "1180" may or may not be lettered on the back of the tender.

(A) "SOUTHERN / PACIFIC" herald on sides. Yellow-outlined panels enclose herald and run the three sides of the tender. No number on back; black sides and frame. **25 50**
(B) Same as (A), but with "ILLINOIS CENTRAL / RAILROAD" herald on sides. White-outlined panels enclose herald and run the three sides of the tender. "1180" lettered on back. **25 50**

Top: A variety of 1010 tenders: gold, chrome, and gray with lithographed letter. Middle: Rare unnumbered high-pedestal gold and green style. Bottom: Type Va blue tender which accompanied the blue 2000 locomotive; 78100 yellow, blue, orange, and gray tender, which matched the 115041 engine.

	Gd	Exc

(C) Same as (A), but with "CHICAGO / NORTH WESTERN" herald on sides. White-outlined panels enclose herald and run the three sides of the tender. "1180" lettered on back. **25 50**

(D) Same as (A), but with "Santa Fe" herald on sides. White-outlined panels enclose herald and run the three sides of the tender. "1180" lettered on back. **25 50**

(E) "HAFNER'S / OVERLAND FLYER / RAILWAYS" bar and circle herald lettered on sides. "1180" lettered on back; red sides; black frame. Came with and without coal loads. **20 40**

(F) No lettering. Tender has bell and track-activated clapper. Has been observed only with No. 110 (Late) locomotive; red sides, black frame. Type II coupler. **NRS**

(G) All red with no lettering or bell. Type II coupler. **20 40**

(H) Same as (A), but "1180" on back of tender. **20 40**

(I) Same as (B), but with "PENNSYLVANIA / LINES" herald on sides. No number on back. **25 50**

Note: Readers should be reminded that the designated tender coupler types are ones that have actually been verified. All of the 1180 (Small) tenders probably came in some instances with Type III couplers.

TYPE III TENDER

This tender is probably the rarest of all the tenders in the Hafner line. It was produced for only a short time and may have possibly come only with one freight set. There is a picture of this tender in a 1937 Grainger's catalogue, and it is shown in a 1938 Hafner folder.

The concept of the two separate rounded endpieces attached to a body stamping unit was employed. A long piece of sheet metal was folded into a U shape and held together by an underframe cross brace. The steps and pedestals are an integral part of the main piece. The pedestals are cut high in triangular form and have the "high frame transitional" styling similar to the Sunshine Special and 919 passenger car series.

UNNUMBERED TENDER: Copper-plated body; green end pieces; thirty rivets on the top as decoration; forty-eight rivets on each side. No lettering. 5½" long. Type IV coupler. **NRS**

TYPE IV TENDER

This tender, in some instances lettered "1010", is a very common, coffin-style tender. Like the Type III tender, it is composed of a body stamping and two stamped and formed end pieces. The body stamping top and sides are usually the same color, but some tenders have a stripe at the bottom of the sides that is colored differently. As with Type III, a cross brace between the wheels holds the body stamping together with a tab-and-slot arrangement.

Most of these tenders are unnumbered, but the word "HAFNER" is embossed and centered on the sides of the majority of them. "1010" is a convenient and logical designation because these tenders in a wide variety of colors

Gd Exc

came with the No. 1010 locomotive. There are two basic styles.

UNNUMBERED TENDER (Type IVa)

(A) Unnumbered coffin tender. Black body stamping and end pieces. Forty-eight rivets on each side; seventeen rivets on each end piece; "HAFNER" embossed in the center on both sides. Type V coupler. **4 8**
(B) Same as (A), but lower part of the body stamping in white on both sides. **4 8**
(C) Same as (A), but copper-plated body stamping and green end pieces. **7 15**
(D) Same as (A), but red body stamping and darker red end pieces. **4 8**
(E) Same as (A), but silver body stamping and end pieces. **4 8**
(F) Same as (A), but gold body stamping and end pieces. **10 20**
(G) Same as (A), but red body stamping and gold end pieces. **5 10**
(H) Same as (G), but dark copper end pieces. **5 10**
(I) Same as (A), but gray body stamping and red end pieces. **4 8**
(J) Same as (A), but chrome body stamping and red end pieces. **15 30**
(K) Same as (J), but green end pieces. **15 30**
(L) Same as (G), but copper end pieces. **15 30**
(M) Same as (A), but red end pieces. **5 10**
(N) Same as (C), but "HAFNER" name omitted. **10 20**
(O) Same as (J), but "HAFNER" name omitted. **10 20**
(P) Same as (I), but off-white body stamping. **5 10**
(Q) Same as (D), but with silver end pieces. **5 10**
(R) Same as (E), but with black end pieces. **5 10**
(S) Same as (K), but "HAFNER" name omitted. **15 30**
(T) Same as (A), but black body stamping and red end pieces. **10 20**
(U) Same as (A), but blue body stamping and silver end pieces. **10 20**
(V) Same as (J), but blue end pieces. **15 30**
(W) Same as (A), but all aluminum lithography. **12 25**

1010 (Type IVb): All have Type V couplers.
(A) Gold body stamping with green trim on the bottom of each side. "1010" in green lithographed to the left of center on both sides. "Made in U.S.A." lettered in green on bottom right. "HAFNER / TRAINS" lettered in green within a green-outlined panel; ladder steps and rivets also lithographed on sides. Green end pieces. **20 40**
(B) Gray body stamping with red trim on the bottom of each side. "1010" in red lithographed to the left of center on both sides. "Made in U.S.A." lettered in red on bottom right. "HAFNER / TRAINS" lettered in red within a red-outlined panel; ladder steps and rivets also lithographed on sides. Red end pieces. **20 40**

(C) Off-white body stamping with blue trim on the bottom of each side. "1010" in blue lithographed to the left of center on both sides. "Made in U.S.A." lettered in blue on bottom right. "HAFNER / TRAINS" lettered in blue within a blue-outlined panel; ladder steps and rivets also lithographed on sides. Blue end pieces. **20 40**
(D) Same as (C), but with green end pieces. **20 40**
(E) Same as (C), but with gray end pieces. **20 40**

TYPE V TENDER

This type of tender comes unnumbered, and also numbered as 90131, or as 78100. Despite these number differences they are all essentially the same style although there are variations in the frame and in the coal load. This tender has winglike top sides ("coal boards") which curve inward on both sides to increase the coal load capacity of the tender.

This is the last type of tender manufactured by Hafner and was carried over into the Wyandotte Toys line when Hafner sold out to the All Metal Products Co. in 1951. See Chapter Twelve on Wyandotte trains.

UNNUMBERED TENDER (Type Va)
(A) Black sides, end, and frame. Sides decorated by fifty-eight rivets; end has twenty-two rivets. "HAFNER" embossed on each side and enclosed in rectangle. Coal pile is level for approximately 1", then slopes chutelike toward the front; frame is slightly lower than on Type Vb tender. Type V couplers. Some of these couplers come with a smaller hole opening — see the next chapter. **5 10**
(B) Same as (A), but has metallic dark blue sides. Coal pile level for almost 1½" before it slopes to the front. **8 16**
(C) Same as (A), but has metallic light blue sides. **8 16**

90131 (Type Vb): Yellow, blue, orange, and gray lithography. Silver frame. "HAFNER" lithographed on white background enclosed in a gray-outlined panel; gray-lithographed steps and handrails; sides decorated by fifty-eight rivets; end has twenty-two rivets; "90131" in orange on top front of both sides. Coal pile level for 2½", then slopes slightly near the front. Frame slightly higher than that found on Type Va tenders. Type VI couplers. **4 8**
78100 (Type Vb): Same as No. 90131, but with black frame. "HAFNER" embossed on sides within embossed panel; "78100" in orange on top front of both sides. **4 8**

UNNUMBERED TENDER (Type Vb)
Same as No. 90131, but unnumbered; all black except for the bottom of the sides which has a silver stripe. The name "HAFNER" is omitted. Has slightly higher frame than found in Type Va. **5 10**
(A) "HAFNER" embossed on each side and enclosed in a rectangle. Coal pile level for approximately 1", then slopes chutelike toward the front. **5 10**

(See Chapter Twelve for the continuation of the Hafner tender in the Wyandotte line.)

CHAPTER FOUR

★

COUPLERS AND FRAMES:
AN OVERVIEW OF THOSE USED WITH
PASSENGER, BAGGAGE, AND FREIGHT CARS

COUPLERS

One can find six different types of couplers on Hafner passenger, baggage, and freight cars. These are summarized in the box and described in the text following.

Coupler Types I, II, and III are shown from right to left.

Coupler Types

Type I Hook with straight shank and tab end

Type II Hook end is inverted T-shape; banjo-shaped hole

Type III Similar to Type II, but with notch at front of banjo-shaped hole

Type IV T-shaped hook turned upward; banjo-shaped hole without notch

Type V Upturned hook coupler; small hole and thin hook

Type VI Upturned hook coupler; similar to Type V, but longer; fits into floor frame rather than end piece

---

Coupler Type IV is shown front left; V is front right; VI is back left.

Type I Coupler

The earliest Hafner coupler is very similar to the Type 4 coupler used by American Flyer (again, see *Greenberg's Guide to American Prewar O Gauge*). This is understandable since William Hafner left that firm to establish his own company. The coupler is made of sheet metal with a straight shank and tab end. The tab is inserted into a slot on the frame floor and twisted so that the coupler is held firmly yet given the freedom to slide inward and outward easily and also to swivel at the end sufficiently to handle track curves. Close examination reveals that the Hafner hook is slightly longer and the coupler hole smaller than the Type 4 American Flyer coupler.

Type II Coupler

Because of the dating difficulty associated with Hafner items, it is uncertain when the Type II coupler was adopted. A probable date would be about 1916. This coupler was banjo shaped with a round hole. The hook end of the coupler was

an inverted T shape. Joy Line was later to copy this style, but their coupler used a heavier-gauge metal and had a slightly wider and shorter shank.

The material for this Hafner coupler comes in both heavy and light thicknesses. It was believed that the lighter, very thin coupler came only on some of the later cars, but even some early cars use this thin coupler.

Type III Coupler

The Type III coupler was similar to the previous form except for a notch at the front of the hole — that is the hole area closest to the inverted T-shaped hook. Some approximate dating can now be determined. The first three Hafner freight cars — the 31400 New York Central sand and gravel car, the 31320 Santa Fe boxcar, and the Overland Flyer caboose (Hafner catalogue No. 83) were first manufactured in or about 1929. These cars all came with the notched Type III coupler. Some passenger cars that can be dated 1928 use this coupler, so at least we have a more precise approximate date than is usual with Hafner products (cf. *The Collector*, Spring 1989).

In 1933 Hafner released one of its most popular selling sets — the "Century of Progress Special" — which came with three narrow-bodied cream and red cars, baggage, Pullman, and illuminated observation. This set often appears at train meets and seems always to have Type II couplers. Knowing Hafner's use of overlapping inventory, I cannot claim that all of these cars had unnotched couplers, but it can be theorized with considerable certainty that 1933 was a definite cut-off date. As a consequence, 1932 was likely the last year the notched Type III coupler was used, except possibly for leftover inventory. About 1933, then, Hafner returned to the Type II coupler.

The Hafner freight cars of the 1933–1934 era — for example, the 62425 boxcar and such bar and circle Hafner herald freights as the sand and gravel car and the illuminated caboose — usually have Type II couplers.

Type IV Coupler

At some time between 1934 and 1937, the Type II unnotched banjo coupler had its T-shaped hook turned upward. This was probably done to make it more difficult for the cars to become unhooked from one another. When many years later the Unique Art Company turned to making trains, they adopted a similar upturned coupler, probably borrowing the concept from Hafner.

Type V Coupler

In 1938 Hafner began to produce long 6¾-inch freights, the most prominent of these being the 13789 boxcar, the 1350141 cattle car, and the long 3057 caboose. These cars appear with new type couplers — a smaller hole, thinner hook version. These freights will occasionally turn up with unnotched banjo Type IV couplers, but this is uncommon. The author has such a 1350141 stock car in his collection and once saw the 13789 boxcar with the same coupler. While cars with this type of coupler are unusual, they suggest that the unnotched banjo couplers were terminated about this time (approximately 1938) and that Hafner in typical fashion was using up leftover inventory.

This Type V upturned hook coupler came with a small hole and also with a larger hole. The hook also appears in a thinner as well as in a somewhat thicker form, but the coupler is essentially the same whether its tab turns downward on end piece cars or turns upward to attach to the frame as it does on the unnumbered tender that usually comes with the No. 2000 locomotive. The Type V coupler continued to be used as long as Hafner remained in business and was carried over by Wyandotte on the 91746 sand and gravel car.

Type VI Coupler

Hafner manufactured square-corner frame freights in the 1940s and until 1951. Since these cars were not using the separate end piece type of construction, they needed a longer drawbar end to fit into the floor frame. These couplers were still upturned and are very similar to the Type V coupler, but longer. These Type VI couplers were used on such cars as the Bx 32 and the 14825 Santa Fe boxcars, the X1357-90 cattle car, and the two late cabooses — the 41021 Hafner (and later Wyandotte) and the 614333 Chicago & North Western. This Type VI coupler was also used for the colorful yellow, blue, and silver 90131 tender which accompanied the similarly colored No. 115041 locomotive. Thus Hafner used both Type V and Type VI couplers at the same time for as long as they continued in operation — the Type V for usually the separate end piece cars and the Type VI usually for the square-corner frame cars.

Note 1: In a separate category, of course, are the one-piece cars which have an integral prong coupler at one end pointing upwards and an integral loop coupler at the other end, similar to American Flyer's "Hummer" cars.

Note 2: Upturned Type IV, V, and VI couplers are sometimes turned downward. This was done by individual "runners" who wanted a more realistic looking coupler and a coupler that would match more closely trains of other manufacturers.

FRAMES

For ready reference, we include a boxed summary of the nine frame types described below.

Frame Types

Type I Length, journal box configuration, air tank style, and frame notches similar to AF's Type 3 frame

Type II Length and high journal box styling followed the arrangement used by AF for its early 6⅜-inch herald cars

Type III Integral bottom for one-piece cars

Type IV Eight-wheel frame with truss rod, vertical post, and open space on both sides of post

Type V Low-slung frame used on only a few of the 5⅞-inch passenger cars

Type VI High triangular axle supports; come in short and long versions

Type VII Streamliner frame for cars pulled by the M-10000 and Zephyr power units; comes in articulated and nonarticulated versions

Type VIII Used with streamliner-style post-1938 freight and passenger cars

Type IX Square corner frame used on several late-production freight cars

---

Type I Frame

The first frame used by Hafner was very similar to American Flyer's Type 3 frame. In fact it is difficult to detect differences if one studies the journal box configurations, the air tank design, and the body-mounting slot locations. (See comparison photos of early Hafner and American Flyer coaches earlier in the book.)

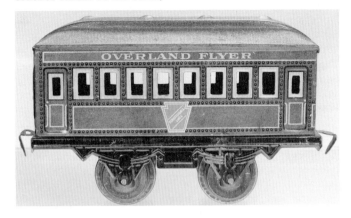

Type II Frame

This frame, similar to that used on the early American Flyer 6¼-inch cars, was used for the early large 6¼-inch herald passenger cars, as well as for the Union Pacific herald version of these cars produced into the 1930s.

Type III Frame

Used for the low-priced passenger cars, this frame came with the one-piece coaches and is, of course, an integral part of the whole car.

Type IV Frame

The Type IV frame was used exclusively for the highlight cars of the Hafner line — the eight-wheel herald baggage and passenger cars. The under-the-frame truss rod arrangement with the vertical post and the two open spaces on either side is in general reminiscent of the truss rod styling found on both Ives and Bing eight-wheel cars.

Type V Frame

Found on some of the later four-wheel 6¼-inch herald cars, this is a low-slung frame which represents a transitional phase in Hafner's production.

Type VI Frame

This also is a transitional frame, but instead of being low slung it has high triangular axle supports and comes in a Type VIa short form (see photo below) on the 4⅞-inch "Sunshine Special" cars and the 1937 unnumbered copper tender, Overland Stock car, and Overland Freight caboose. It is found in the longer VIb form (see top left photo, next page) in the 5⅞-inch 919 passenger set.

Type VII Frame

This frame is used with the M-10000 and Burlington Zephyr streamliner cars. It is bent inward in two different ways depending on whether the car is an articulated Type VIIa (see first photo below) or nonarticulated Type VIIb (see second photo below).

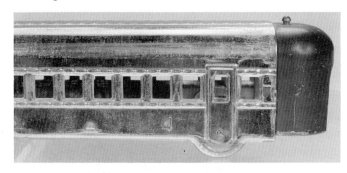

Type VIII Frame

Type VIIIa (see first photo below) was especially used with the long streamline freight cars and passenger cars. Came in Type VIIIb form (see second photo below) with the same styling but with a shorter length as, for example, on the short 3057 caboose.

Type IX Frame

This is found with the late-production square-corner cars such as the 14825 Santa Fe boxcar, and the 614333 Chicago & North Western caboose. Designed for use with the square-corner cars, this frame curved slightly on both sides of the axle.

CHAPTER FIVE

EARLY PASSENGER AND BAGGAGE CARS:
(PRE-1938)

Hafner did not have any freight cars in its train line until the mid-1920s, so the very earliest Hafner cars were all passenger coaches or baggage units.

The majority of these cars were four-wheelers with bright, colorful lithography. Heralds of actual railroads were placed on the sides of the cars, and the logos of the following railroads were represented: Chicago & North Western, Santa Fe, Baltimore & Ohio, Pennsylvania, Erie, New York Central, Union Pacific, Southern Pacific, Northern Pacific, Illinois Central, and Canadian Pacific. Although Hafner was in business for almost forty years, no other prototype railroads — except for those on the sides of the Bing freight cars once sold to supplement the Hafner line — were ever listed in its production. Some collectors have faulted the company for this limitation. It is true that this situation does not provide the train collector as broad a challenge as, for example, the numerous actual railroads mentioned on Marx cars. Hafner was, of course, making toys and not thinking of the collecting interests of future train hobbyists. John Hafner reported that initially Hafner received payments from the railroads whose heralds were lithographed, but during the Depression this practice ended.

In addition to the passenger coaches, Hafner produced four differently lettered baggage cars: Adams, Wells Fargo, American Express, and Union Pacific.

The earliest passenger and baggage cars were catalogued in two lengths: 5½ inches and 6¼ inches. What is regarded as the first Hafner catalogue pictures the 5½-inch-long coaches with the following road names: Chicago & North Western, Pennsylvania, Santa Fe, and New York Central. The longer cars represent Illinois Central, Southern Pacific, Northern Pacific, and Union Pacific. It is interesting to note that the heralds of these last four railroads appear never to have been used on the shorter cars, and, except for the Union Pacific, these railroad names were dropped from the Hafner line in 1929. The bodies for the 6¼-inch cars were used for the eight-wheel cars.

EARLY CATALOGUING

Incidentally, the date of the alleged first Hafner catalogue has been called into question. The catalogue cover illustrates a 4-6-2 steamer pulling a passenger consist. The lettering "1612" is on the boiler front, on one of the domes, and on the sides of the tender. Written in the cloud of steam billowing from the smokestack is the word "Overland". Although there is no designation as to what actual railroad was represented by the "1612", I corresponded with Thomas Mackowiak, of the Chicago and North Western Historical Society, who revealed that the "1612" was indeed an actual C & NW steamer built by the Schenectady Locomotive Works in 1916–1917.[1] The "left-hand running" evident on the double-track in the illustration was English practice and unique with C & NW in the United States.

Ray Jorgensen, the secretary of the Chicago and Northwestern Historical Society, reveals in a letter to the author, further research on the C & NW class E Pacifics. He asserts that the Hafner catalogue cover is not a drawing of C & NW 1612, but "is a very good illustration of the C & NW 4-6-2's 1500–1539, built in 1909–1910 (1512 would have been a better choice of number by the artist). The identification clues are the rectangular value gear hanger, the inside steam pipes, and the single level walkway.... The engine in the illustration has an oil headlight. C & NW locomotives did not have electrical headlights until 1913; therefore the era of this illustration would be constrained to 1909–1913."

In March 1965 the Train Collectors Association printed a page from this catalogue and dated it "ca. 1915". Some other collectors have suggested 1914 or 1919 as the possible dates. If the catalogue was published in 1916 or later, it would most likely show the impressive eight-wheel passenger cars which were seemingly first made in 1916. As a consequence, the author is inclined to date the catalogue as either 1914 or 1915. Nevertheless, it should be noted that John Hafner reports 1919 as the correct date (*TCQ*, July 1968, p. 13), and a note in a Hafner "Scrapbook" at the TCA Museum Library marks the date as 1919, probably on the basis of John's comment since the note appears an afterthought.

The No. 1612 locomotive photo also appears on the box cover of the earliest Hafner sets that have yet been discovered. This fact would tend to support the 1914 or 1915 dating.

The dates of the eight-wheel passenger cars are also a puzzle. The eight-wheel baggage and passenger cars are shown in the 1916 Sears catalogue but do not appear in Sears catalogues after 1919. However, a Hafner catalogue, usually dated ca. 1924–1926 (but it could be a year or two earlier), pictures one set with two eight-wheel cars (one with a Union Pacific herald, the other with a Southern Pacific herald). A 1925 advertisement in the *Chicago Daily News* shows a set with two eight-wheel cars. Several years ago, Robert Hafner showed Arno Uhlhorn a letter on Hafner Manufacturing Company stationery picturing a set of eight-wheel cars. Arno managed to have this stationery reproduced and enabled it to be widely distributed among interested Hafner and lithography collectors. (The original has now been donated to the TCA Museum Library in Strasburg, Pennsylvania.) The text in the stationery indicates that this particular sheet was used in 1922. Together with the 1925 advertisement in the *Chicago Daily News*, this letterhead indicates that Hafner did manufacture some eight-wheel cars beyond 1919 and into the mid-1920s even if they were not sold by Sears after 1919.

In addition to the eight-wheel coaches and an eight-wheel Wells Fargo baggage car, the colorful sheet of Hafner Company stationery preserved by Robert Hafner pictures four-wheel Adams and American Express baggage cars as well as four-wheel coaches representing the following railroads: Baltimore & Ohio, Santa Fe, Pennsylvania, Chicago & North Western, New York Central, and Canadian Pacific. Since William Hafner left the American Flyer Manufacturing Company in 1914 to form his own business, it is not surprising to note the close similarity between American Flyer and Hafner passenger cars of this early period. Even underframes and bodies were interchangeable! The dimensions of the early American Flyer station and Hafner's No. 400 station are obviously related.

SIMILARITIES WITH AMERICAN FLYER

Taking an American Flyer 1107 coach, for example, and comparing it with Hafner passenger cars of this period, one cannot help but be struck by the close resemblance. Both the American Flyer 1107 and the Hafner Overland Flyer herald coaches are 5½ inches in length; both have eight punched-out windows on each side and two additional windows punched out over the two doors on each side. The roofs are very similar — the four knobs on the top of each roof being slightly larger in the Hafner version. The roofs, incidentally, fit interchangeably. Collectors will find at train meets some of these early American Flyer cars with Hafner roofs and vice versa. The frame of the Hafner car is very much like that designated as the American Flyer Type 3 frame in *Greenberg's Guide to American Flyer Prewar O Gauge*. Like the first Type 3 American Flyer frames, the Hafner frames had plain slots for the couplers.

Each car end has three punched-out windows, one being the door window. Black rivet lithographic details on both the ends and the sides are again almost exact with the American Flyer rivet detail being almost imperceptibly larger.

The most obvious difference apart from the "American Flyer Line" lettering as opposed to the "Overland Flyer" lettering is the under-the-windows designation. American Flyer put the car number "1107" twice on each side — near each door. The Hafner Company did not usually number its cars but centered the particular railroad herald on the sides of the car. When American Flyer did use a particular herald they centered it on the sides as did Hafner but continued using the "1107" numbering to the left and right on each side.

Another noticeable difference between the two cars is the coupler. The American Flyer coupler of this period (Type 4 per the *Greenberg's Guide to American Flyer Prewar O Gauge*, p. 174) has a straight shank and tab end. The coupler opening to hold another coupler hook is a small rectangular hole slightly curved at each end. The Hafner coupler has a slightly wider shank and has a larger hole to hold a mating coupler. For many years Hafner cars had black-lacquered

(japanned) wheels while American Flyer used plain tinplate wheels. The japan was a very thin black coating. John Hafner reports that after the japan-coated wheels were in use for some time, the japanning wore off, and the wheels did not look as attractive as they should. It was then decided to discontinue the black-coating process, and additional production cost was saved.

As time progressed, American Flyer was to change its car frame styles and coupler forms much more frequently than Hafner, so eventually the differences between the passenger cars were to become immediately apparent, but in the period from 1914 to about 1920 the Hafner and American Flyer similarities are fascinating.

HAFNER AND AMERICAN FLYER EIGHT-WHEEL CARS

The differences between the American Flyer and Hafner eight-wheel passenger cars were, on the other hand, much more pronounced. While it is true that the cars of both manufacturers were of the same length, and if necessary the roof from an American Flyer eight-wheeler can easily be interchanged with the roof from a Hafner coach (even though a close examination shows that the American Flyer roof has a wider monitor and larger "ventilator" knobs than the Hafner), the difference in the trucks is immediately noticeable. The American Flyer Type 2 truck of this period (as designated in the Greenberg book on Flyer O Gauge) had realistic embossed details over each journal box and had a firm, solid construction which gave a reliably reassuring massive appearance that the truck and the wheels were united in a permanent, unbreakable bond. Except for the fact that there was no aperture in the unit, the American Flyer truck reminds some collectors of what is called in Ives parlance the "hM" or high Märklin-type truck.

On the other hand, the Hafner eight-wheel truck is cut inward on both sides and then is bent outward to enclose both wheels. This truck does not have the same appearance of strength and solidity as does the American Flyer version, yet it is attractive and most serviceable. This Hafner truck closely resembles the Bing inverted "T"-type eight-wheel truck, and some collectors have even suggested that Hafner bought these trucks from Bing. On closer inspection, however, differences can be observed. While it is probable that Hafner copied the style of their eight-wheel truck from Bing, the following dissimilarities can be noted: the Hafner truck is wider at the top and bottom and at the embossed journal box, the Hafner journal box is shorter, and the Hafner coupler openings are slightly less circular than those used by Bing. It is true, however, that from a distance, say on a collector's shelf, the trucks would appear to be the same.

EARLY HAFNER LITHOGRAPHY

The herald cars of this first period are the most sought-after cars in the whole line of Hafner production. These cars are pursued not just by Hafner collectors, but by those who delight in the particular glow and charm of exquisite lithography. Indeed many of the searchers for these cars are primarily American Flyer or Ives collectors.

Two of the heralds found on Hafner passenger cars: the New York Flyer thirteen-star "MADE IN AMERICA" shield and the Canadian Flyer coach's beaver logo of the Canadian Pacific Railroad. The toy manufacturers' logo appears in Chapter One.

This Hafner lithography is particularly exquisite and detailed. Several colors are used, and the lithography precisely outlines such details as the door panels, doorknobs, grab irons, and window inserts. Black rivet details are stressed to add realism, and the colorful heralds of the different railroads add a further touch of nostalgia for the old days before flags had fallen. When the railroad is still in existence, the delight in continuity exists as one views the alert beaver crouching over the Canadian Pacific Railway herald or recalls the famous Shasta engines when the Shasta Route is mentioned on the Southern Pacific herald.

Even when a particular type of car never existed, much appeal stems from the delightful lithography. Certainly one of the most attractive toy railroad coaches ever lithographed is Hafner's red, white, and blue coach honoring American toys. Uncle Sam's top hat with stars is filled to overflowing. "TOY MFRS U.S.A." lettered on its bright red banner that is unfurled at the top of the herald is not only exceedingly

The eight-wheel Overland Flyer Southern Pacific coach and its herald represent a masterful example of the art of lithography: seven different-colored inks were used here.

attractive in its own right but further offers a reminder of a time when the American toy market was shaking off European domination and just commencing to come into its own. This particular car was for about twenty years the only four-wheeler that the Hafner Company actually put its name on. This early rare lettering proudly proclaims "HAFNER-CHICAGO" on a striking blue background at the car ends, indicating that the Hafner Company was extremely pleased to be a part of this new American unified movement.

The window inserts of the earliest four-wheel cars are lithographed in two colors, while the later cars used only one color for the window inserts. The earliest four-wheel cars apparently did not have a middle cross piece under the roof in order to give firm support to the sides. Some early cars, however, have square unpunched marks where a cross piece could be inserted.

While collectors' demands for the four-wheel Hafner herald cars are especially persistent, the desire for the eight-wheel herald is even more intense but frustrating. Very few of these beauties seem to have survived since they were made only for a relatively short period and in limited numbers. They came with the highest-priced sets in the Hafner line, and were the most costly to manufacture, so these factors probably contributed to their relatively short production run. Another factor, which has been stressed by John Hafner, was that small children had difficulty placing cars with eight wheels on the track.

Again the lithography is exquisite and unusually colorful. Small oval windows on each side of the four large windows are especially decorative intermingling four different colors. The small gold and white arches decorating each window top also add to the visual pleasure, and the 6⅜-inch length with double trucks gives the cars an ideal symmetry.

Each of the eight-wheel cars has the word "HAFNER" embossed on the middle of the base. This is a distinctive identification mark since a car mounted on a Bing frame would appear to look like a Hafner car. Actually, it would be possible to attach the car sides to an Ives or an American Flyer eight-wheel frame.

The sides of the earliest eight-wheel cars were held together primarily by a cross brace centered under the roof. If more than a slight squeeze is exerted while hand-holding the car by its sides, the sides tend to buckle inward. To

Top: Two color variations of Overland Flyer Pennsylvania herald coaches. Middle: Chicago & North Western herald coach; Baltimore & Ohio version. Bottom: New York Central and Santa Fe herald coaches.

Top: Two color variations of New York Flyer coach. Middle: Canadian Flyer coach; another color version of the New York Flyer Pullman. Bottom: Two variations of the Toy Manufacturers herald coach, mahogany frame and black frame. These three different herald cars are the crème de la crème of Hafner four-wheel cars.

overcome this fragility, the company at some point in the production added two additional cross braces nearer the ends, and the three-cross brace support solved the problem. This arrangement was retained until the cars were discontinued from the line.

LESSENING OF REALISM

In 1929, except for some leftover inventory, Hafner eliminated all railroad heralds — other than Union Pacific — from the sides of its passenger cars and began to emphasize a wide variety of colors; e.g., all-red cars, all-green cars, or combinations of colors where the sides were principally of one color and the roofs of another color. Most sets came with cars of different colors; thus, for example, a set might consist of a cream-colored baggage with green roof, an all-red Pullman, and a blue observation with darker blue roof. Usually the colors were bright and even at times flashy, thus rendering the cars more toylike than replicas of actual railroad stock. Quite a few collectors regret this change, although it is obvious that the Hafner Company felt less realism and more showy and eye-catching colors created additional sales appeal. It must be admitted that many enthusiasts of toy train lithography find these cars in their seemingly endless color varieties most collectible.

The two cars primarily involved in these "mix and match" color patterns are the catalogue-numbered 86 passenger coach (5½ inches long) and the number 88 observation (same length). The number 87 baggage car did, fortunately for realism at least, usually retain the American Express herald.

The larger-sized (6¼-inch) cars — number 96 coach, number 97 baggage, and the number 98 observation — did continue the Union Pacific herald and combined this logo with the new emphasis on a variety of colors. In this case even when the color variations appear at times too flashy, the retention of the Union Pacific herald (always lithographed in gold) gave these cars an element of realism that has made them very attractive and acceptable to collectors.

OTHER PASSENGER SETS

This early 1930s period also gave rise to the Hafner "Sunshine Special" passenger cars. Using the name of the famous Texas and Pacific passenger train, Hafner lettered over the windows of several of its cars the word "SUNSHINE SPECIAL". These cars will be discussed in the next chapter.

Two additional passenger sets of the early period which are especially notable are the Chicago "Century of Progress" set and the 919 Transitional set. The "Century of Progress" unit, timed to coincide with the 1933–1934 Chicago World's Fair, was apparently Hafner's all-time best seller. It featured a battery-powered headlight on the locomotive and a rear headlight on the observation car. Appropriately, the engine had a white headlight, the observation car a red taillight. In producing the 919 Transition set, Hafner for the first time put numbers on the sides of its passenger cars.

The first period of Hafner passenger cars thus ended in the early 1930s with (except for the baggage cars and 96, 97, and 98 Union Pacific series) the emphasis mainly on using a considerable variety of colors designed to catch the customer's eye. These colors would certainly appeal to a child or to an adult more interested in attention-grabbing appearance than in realism. From this point Hafner was now ready to begin its streamliner phase, which will be discussed in a subsequent chapter.

5½-INCH-LONG PASSENGER CARS

Type I Frame, May Come with
Type I, II, or III Couplers

All the 5½-inch-long passenger cars are numbered 102 in the earliest catalogue. **Note:** No numbers appear on any of these cars. Also: the early four-wheel herald cars have two colors for the window trim.

BALTIMORE & OHIO (PASSENGER): Ca. 1914-28.

	Gd	Exc
(A) Blue with gold trim; black roof and frame; "OVERLAND FLYER" on letterboard in gold on blue background; "BALTIMORE & OHIO R.R." herald lettered in white and blue on blue and white background centered on sides; herald has lettering "LIBERAL STOP-OVER" at the top, "PRIVILEGES" at the bottom, and pictures the Capitol dome; windows trimmed in gold and brown; windows and door windows punched out and embossed inward.	50	100
(B) Same as (A), but with darker blue sides and windows trimmed in gold.	50	100
(C) Same as (B), but with royal blue roof.	50	100
(D) Same as (A), but with light blue sides.	60	125

CANADIAN FLYER (PASSENGER): 1915-early 1920s. Red and tan with gold and green trim and black detailing; black frame and roof; "CANADIAN FLYER" on letterboard in gold on tan background; "CANADIAN / PACIFIC / RAILWAY" herald lettered in red on white background with figure of crouching beaver on top, centered on sides; windows trimmed in gold and green; windows and door windows punched out and embossed inward. **200 400**

CHICAGO & NORTH WESTERN (PASSENGER): Ca. 1914-28.

(A) Tan with green and gold trim and black detailing; black frame and roof; "OVERLAND FLYER" on letterboard in gold on green background; "CHICAGO / NORTH WESTERN / LINE" herald lettered in white, on red and black background centered on sides; windows trimmed in gold and red; windows and door windows punched out and embossed inward.

	Gd	Exc
	40	80
(B) Same as (A), but in darker green lithography.	40	80
(C) Same as (A), but windows trimmed in gold.	40	80
(D) Same as (C), but with tan roof.	40	80
(E) Same as (C), but with orange roof.	45	90
(F) Same as (C), but with robin's-egg blue roof.	45	90

ERIE (PASSENGER): Ca. 1914-28. Red with gold and brown trim and black detailing; black frame and roof; "OVERLAND FLYER" on letterboard in gold on red background; "ERIE" herald lettered in white on black background centered on sides; windows trimmed in gold and brown; windows and door windows punched out and embossed inward. **70 140**

NEW YORK CENTRAL (OBSERVATION): A Bing car used by Hafner in the 1920s, ca. 1922-26. (A Hafner catalogue numbers this car 310; in actuality, this is the Bing

Gd Exc

number 529 observation car with, of course, Bing couplers; 5⁷⁄₁₆" long. Hafner at this time had no observation of its own so it advertised this car, which could be used with Hafner passenger coaches. Just as the first freight cars Hafner used were purchased from Bing, so too was this observation. Hafner's own first observation cars, catalogue numbers 88 and 98, appeared in the late 1920s.) Green wood-grained lithography with orange trim; "NEW YORK CENTRAL LINES" is lettered in orange; "529" is also lettered in orange near the left and right ends on both sides of the car; windows trimmed in orange, punched out and embossed inward; brown roof; brown standard Bing frame; gold observation fence; punched-out door on the left side of the observation deck; awning in gray with two circular orange simulated taillights. **18 35**

NEW YORK CENTRAL (PASSENGER): Ca. 1914-28.

(A) Green with gold trim and black detailing; black frame and roof; "OVERLAND FLYER" on letterboard in gold on green background; "NEW YORK / CENTRAL / LINES" herald lettered in white on red background centered on sides; windows trimmed in gold and brown; windows and door windows punched out and embossed inward. **50 100**

(B) Same as (A), but in darker green and windows trimmed in gold. **50 100**

(C) Same as (A), but with light green roof. **60 120**

(D) Same as (B), but windows trimmed in brown. **50 100**

NEW YORK FLYER (PASSENGER): Ca. 1917-28.

(A) Orange and red body with gold and green window trim; black detailing; black frame and roof; "NEW YORK FLYER" on letterboard in gold; "MADE IN AMERICA" on shield herald (with thirteen stars — lettering in white and red on blue and white background) centered on sides; windows and door windows punched out and embossed inward; red on letterboard and on stripe beneath windows. **125 250**

(B) Same as (A), but with green and orange body; gold and red window trim; orange on letterboard and on stripe beneath windows. **125 250**

(C) Same as (A), but with green and red body; gold and white window trim; red on letterboard and on stripe beneath windows. **125 250**

(D) Same as (A), but with orange and white body; gold and green window trim; white on letterboard and on stripe beneath windows. **150 300**

PENNSYLVANIA (PASSENGER): Ca. 1914-28.

(A) Maroon with gold and brown trim and black detailing; black frame and roof; "OVERLAND FLYER" on letterboard in gold on maroon background; "PENNSYLVANIA / LINES" herald lettered in white on red background centered on sides; windows trimmed in gold and brown; windows and door windows punched out and embossed inward. **75 150**

(B) Same as (A), but with maroon roof. **75 150**

(C) Same as (A), but frame has mahogany lithography. **80 160**

(D) Same as (A), but with cream roof. **75 150**

(E) Same as (A), but frame has wood-grained lithography. **80 160**

(F) Same as (A), but with windows trimmed in gold. **75 150**

(G) Same as (A), but with yellowish-orange roof. **75 150**

Gd Exc

(H) Same as (A), but in dark brown instead of maroon. **75 150**

PITTSBURG FLYER (PASSENGER): 1920s. Red with gold and brown trim and black detailing; black frame and roof; "PITTSBURG FLYER" on letterboard in gold on red background; "ERIE" herald lettered in white on black background, centered on sides; windows trimmed in gold and brown; windows and door windows punched out and embossed inward. **NRS**

Note: This coach, with the misspelling of Pittsburg,[2] is believed to have been a promotional model — a department store special, probably for Gimbel's (as John Hafner has suggested) or possibly for the Kaufman and Baer store in Pittsburgh. Efforts to obtain further information about the date this car was sold and what engine and tender it came with have so far been unsuccessful. The car is the same as the Erie herald coach, but "PITTSBURG" has been substituted for "OVERLAND". The famous American Flyer specialist, the late Bill Clapper, acquired this car from Harry Osisek, Jr., in a trade for Lionel Mickey Mouse items. It passed from Bill Clapper's hands into the collection of Lou Redman. A second car appeared at the TCA York, Pennsylvania, meet of Spring 1992.

SANTA FE (PASSENGER): Ca. 1914-28.

(A) Red and green with gold trim and black detailing; black frame and roof; "OVERLAND FLYER" on letterboard in gold on green background; "Santa Fe" herald lettered in white on blue and white background centered on sides; windows trimmed in gold and brown; windows and door windows punched out and embossed inward. **50 100**

(B) Same as (A), but with tan roof. **50 100**

(C) Same as (A), but darker green and windows trimmed in gold. **50 100**

(D) Same as (A), but with orange roof. **50 100**

TOY MANUFACTURERS (PASSENGER): Ca. 1918-early 1920s.

(A) Red with blue and white trim; black frame and roof; "OVERLAND FLYER" on letterboard in white on blue background; Toy Manufacturers logo centered on sides; "TOY MFGS U.S.A." lettered in white on red background. Uncle Sam's inverted hat holding overflowing toys lithographed in blue and white, and "AMERICAN / TOYS" lettered in red on bottom of the hat; "HAFNER — CHICAGO" lettered in white on both ends of the car; windows trimmed in white and blue; windows and door windows punched out and embossed inward. **200 400**

(B) Same as (A), but frame has wood-grained lithography. **250 500**

Type I Frame, May Have Type II or Type III Couplers (unless a different frame or coupler type is specified)

PASSENGER: (Numbered 86 in a Hafner catalogue, however no number appears on these cars; the 86 and 88 cars are first listed in the 1929 Hafner "Descriptive Sheet"); 1929-early 1930s; gold trim; black frame; "OVERLAND FLYER" on letterboard in gold on black background; windows and doors punched out and embossed inward. (The "Descriptive Sheet"

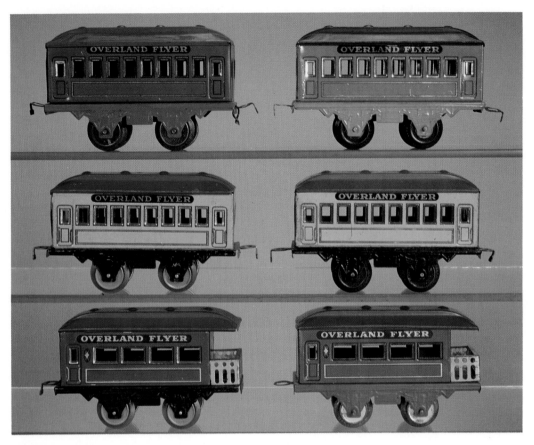

A variety of the colorful 80-series cars. Top: Catalogue number 86 all-green coach; orange-and-blue variation. Middle: Coach of the "Century of Progress" set; 919 Transitional set Pullman — one of the few Hafner coaches that has a number on the side. Bottom: Observation car of the "Century of Progress" set; observation car of the 919 Transitional set — both observation units in these sets contained battery holders and had red bulbs in the drumhead.

	Gd	Exc
is erroneously marked 1928 in the TCA Library Hafner Scrapbook.)		
(A) Tan body; burnt orange roof.	35	80
(B) Green body and roof.	35	80
(C) Same as (B), but with green frame.	40	90
(D) Red body; green roof.	50	100
(E) Same as (D), but with burnt orange roof.	50	100
(F) Same as (D), but with red roof and frame.	55	110
(G) Same as (A), but with green roof.	35	80
(H) Same as (A), but with blue roof.	35	80
(I) Yellow body with bright yellow roof and frame.	55	110
(J) Orange body and frame; royal blue roof.	55	110
(K) Same as (A), but with black roof.	30	60
(L) Same as (C), but with black roof.	30	60
(M) Orange body with black frame and roof.	50	100
(N) Tan body with orange roof.	35	80
(O) Cream body with light blue roof.	35	80
(P) Blue body with light blue roof.	50	100
(Q) Same as (B), but with black roof and green frame.	35	80
(R) Same as (P), but with yellow roof.	50	100
(S) Same as (P), but with blue frame.		NRS
(T) Same as (P), but with royal blue roof.	55	110
(U) Same as (A), but with yellow frame and black roof.	35	80
(V) Same as (A), but with red roof.	35	80
(W) Same as (J), but with orange roof.		NRS
(X) Same as (B), but with black roof.	30	60
(Y) Same as (J), but with orange roof.	50	100

	Gd	Exc
(Z) Same as (B), but with black roof and frame.	30	60
(AA) Same as (P), but with blue frame and yellow roof.	55	110
(BB) Same as (B), but with blue roof.	35	80

OBSERVATION: (Number 88 in a Hafner catalogue; no number appears on these cars); 1929-early 1930s; gold trim; black frame; "OVERLAND FLYER" on letterboard in gold on black background; windows trimmed in gold; small oval window between side rectangular windows and side door window; side windows and doors punched out and embossed inward; gold observation fence.

Note: The location of the observation door varies. On some cars it is on the right side of the platform; on other cars the door is on the left side.

	Gd	Exc
(A) Tan body; burnt orange roof.	35	80
(B) Green body; green roof.	35	80
(C) Same as (B), but with green frame.	40	90
(D) Same as (B), but this car has notch into which the roof fits to hold the non-observation deck end. Since the observation end roof lacks strong support because it hangs over the deck, this notch arrangement on the front end effectively helps to keep the roof in place. This special feature appears on some (C) variant cars and also on some cars with green sides but with black roofs and frames. Other differently colored observation cars may also have this feature, but no additional ones have been verified at present.	75	150
(E) Blue body with light blue roof.	50	100
(F) Red body with dark red roof.	55	110
(G) Same as (B), but with red observation fence.	40	90

Top: Rare 5½-inch Adams baggage car; American Express baggage unit. Bottom: 80-series Overland Flyer baggage car; unusual and very rare baggage car using the body and roof style of the 31320 Santa Fe boxcar and Peerless stock car but relithographed with baggage car lettering.

	Gd	Exc
(H) Same as (B), but with black roof.	30	60
(I) Same as (A), but with light blue roof.	35	80
(J) Same as (B), but with light blue roof.	35	80
(K) Cream body with light blue roof.	35	80
(L) Same as (E), but with royal blue roof.	50	100

(M) Same as (E), but with red frame and with battery holder for lighted red bulb protruding through observation fence.

	60	120
(N) Same as (A), but with blue roof.	35	80
(O) Same as (A), but with maroon roof.	35	80

(P) Same as (B), but with yellow observation fence. Color of roof needs verification.

		NRS
(Q) Same as (A), but with red roof	50	100
(R) Same as (B), but with red roof.	35	80

(S) Green body with the common black frame, but with reddish-maroon roof.

	35	80

Note: A set with 86, 88 cars has been found with turned-up air tanks to represent steps. Although the set was found in excellent condition in the original box, we do not know if this feature was sold by Hafner or changed by a "runner."

5½-INCH-LONG BAGGAGE CARS

The following three cars are identical in size and style, but the lithography differs considerably. Again, no numbers appear on sides of cars. An American Express (A) variant baggage has been found with turned-up air tanks to represent steps. It is unknown whether or not this was done by Hafner or by a "runner."

ADAMS EXPRESS COMPANY BAGGAGE: Ca. 1915-1920s. Yellow with black and red detailing; black roof and frame; Type I, Type II, or Type III couplers; "OVERLAND FLYER" on letterboard in gold; "EXPRESS / BAGGAGE" lettered in black to the left of the door; "UNITED STATES / MAIL" lettered in black to the right of the door; "ADAMS / EXPRESS / COMPANY" herald in white lettering on red background to the left of the door above "EXPRESS / BAGGAGE"; five-panel non-punched-out door; 5½" long.

	150	300

Note: A photo of an eight-wheel Adams Express baggage car has been circulated, but the body has been attached to a Bing eight-wheel frame.

AMERICAN EXPRESS CO. BAGGAGE: 1929-early 1930s.

(A) Green with black and red detailing; black roof and frame; "OVERLAND FLYER" on letterboard in gold; "EXPRESS BAGGAGE" lettered in white to the left of the door; "UNITED STATES / MAIL" lettered in white to the right of the door; "AMERICAN / EXPRESS CO." herald with red, white, and blue shield lettered to the left of the door above "EXPRESS BAGGAGE"; five-panel lithographed non-punched-out doors.

	35	70
(B) Same as (A), but with punched-out doors.	60	120

(C) Same as (B), but "OVERLAND FLYER" lettered in silver; orange roof.

	45	90

(D) Same as (A), but with wood-grained lithographed frame.

		NRS

(E) Same as (A), but four-panel sliding doors; the two top panels punched out.

	75	150
(F) Same as (B), but with green roof.	60	120

BAGGAGE: Early 1930s. (Numbered 87 in a Hafner catalogue; no number appears on car); black frame; "OVERLAND FLYER" on letterboard in gold; "EXPRESS BAGGAGE" lettered in black to the left of the door; "UNITED STATES / MAIL" lettered in black to the right of the door; 5½" long.

(A) Green body with gold trim; green roof; four-panel green sliding doors — two top panels punched out.

	60	120

(B) Red body with gold trim; four-panel orange sliding doors — two top panels punched out. Need verification for color of roof.

	60	120

(C) Same as (B), but with burnt orange roof; doors punched out.

	45	90

	Gd	**Exc**

(D) Same as (C), but with red frame and green roof; body and roof is that of the Santa Fe 31320 boxcar and 31280 Peerless stock car; dates ca. 1934. **NRS**

6¼-6⅜-INCH-LONG CARS — FOUR AND EIGHT WHEELS

The longer (6¼- and 6⅜-inch passenger cars are characterized by the same body and roof length, but the frames of the four-wheel cars are 6¼ inches long while the eight-wheel cars measure 6⅜ inches. (All the early larger passenger cars are numbered 103 in the earliest catalogue, but no numbers appear on the cars.) Large four-wheel cars have Type III frame; large eight-wheel cars have Type IV frame.

ILLINOIS CENTRAL (PASSENGER): Four wheels and eight wheels (ca. 1916 to early 1920s). Green with gold trim and black detailing; black roof and frame; "OVERLAND FLYER" on letterboard in gold on green background; "ILLINOIS CENTRAL" herald centered on sides; "ILLINOIS CENTRAL / RAILROAD" lettered in black on white background; "CENTRAL & ROUTE" lettered in white on black background; "MISSISSIPPI VALLEY" lettered in white on red background; windows trimmed in red; small oval non-punched-out windows in gold and red trim flanking five rectangular windows on each side; windows and door windows on sides punched out and embossed inward; windows and doors in gold and red trim on car ends punched out but not embossed inwards. Identical lithography on both four- and eight-wheel versions.

(A) Four-wheel car — Type I or II couplers. **250** **500**
(B) Eight-wheel car — Type I or II couplers. **550** **1100**

NORTHERN PACIFIC (PASSENGER): Four wheels and eight wheels (ca. 1916 to early 1920s). Green with gold trim and black detailing; black roof and frame; "OVERLAND FLYER" on letterboard in gold on green background; "NORTHERN / PACIFIC" herald lettered in black and white on white and black background, centered on sides; windows trimmed in brown; small oval non-punched-out windows flanking five rectangular windows on each side; windows and door windows on sides punched out and embossed inward; windows and doors on car ends punched out and not embossed inward. Identical lithography on both four- and eight-wheel versions.

(A) Four-wheel car — Type I or II couplers. **225** **450**
(B) Eight-wheel car — Type I or II couplers. **475** **950**

SOUTHERN PACIFIC (PASSENGER): Four wheels (1914-late 1920s); eight wheels (ca. 1916 to mid-1920s). Red with green and gold trim and black detailing; black frame and roof; "OVERLAND FLYER" on letterboard in gold on red background; "SOUTHERN / PACIFIC" herald lettered in white on blue and red background, centered on sides; windows trimmed in orange-brown; small oval non-punched windows flanking five rectangular windows on each side; windows and door windows on sides punched out and embossed inward; windows and doors on car ends punched out but not embossed inward.

Note: This car came with identical lithography in both four- and eight-wheel versions.

	Gd	**Exc**

(A) Four-wheel car — Type I, II, or III couplers. **200** **400**
(B) Eight-wheel car — Type I or II couplers. **450** **900**

Note: The word "HAFNER" is embossed on the bottom of the frame on the eight-wheel cars.

UNION PACIFIC (PASSENGER): Four wheels (1914 to early 1930s); eight wheels (ca. 1916 to mid-1920s). Dark blue with gold trim and black detailing; black frame and roof; "OVERLAND FLYER" on letterboard in gold; "UNION / PACIFIC" herald lettered in white on blue background, alternating red and white stripes, centered on sides; windows trimmed in brown; small oval non-punched-out windows in gold and brown trim flanking five rectangular windows on each side; windows and door windows in gold and brown trim on sides punched out and embossed inward; windows and doors on car ends punched out but not embossed inward. Identical lithography on both four- and eight-wheel **early versions** of these large Union Pacific cars.

(A) Four-wheel dark blue car (early) — Type I or II couplers. **200** **450**

(B) Eight-wheel dark blue car — Type I or II couplers. **450** **900**

Note: The early eight-wheel very dark blue version of the Union Pacific passenger car was discontinued in the mid-1920s. It is very rare. At some point in the late 1920s and continuing into the 1930s the Union Pacific four-wheel passenger cars were made in many different colors and in large numbers. Consequently, the very early dark blue four- and eight-wheel version would command considerably more in price than the later and rather common Union Pacific four-wheelers.

Later Variations of the Four-wheel 6¼-inch Union Pacific Coach: (Numbered 96 in a Hafner catalogue; no number appears on the car.) Gold trim and black detailing, black frame; "OVERLAND FLYER" on letterboard in gold; "UNION / PACIFIC" herald lettered in gold on black background, alternating gold and black stripes, centered on sides; window and door details similar to the early version. Four-wheel cars have Type I, II, or III couplers.

(A) Tan body; green roof. **40** **80**
(B) Same as (B), but with blue roof. **40** **80**
(C) Dark peacock blue body; black roof. **40** **80**
(D) Dark green body; black roof. **40** **80**
(E) Blue body with black roof. **40** **80**
(F) Red body with dark red roof. **50** **100**
(G) Same as (F), but with dark red Type V frame. This is the low-slung transition frame with attached steps. **125** **250**
(H) Same as (E), but with blue roof. **45** **90**
(I) Same as (C), but with blue roof. **45** **90**

6¼-INCH-LONG OBSERVATION CARS

UNION PACIFIC OBSERVATION: (Number 98 in a Hafner catalogue; no number appears on the cars.) 1929 to early 1930s. Gold and black trim; black frame; "OVERLAND FLYER" on letterboard in gold; "UNION / PACIFIC" herald lettered in gold on black background, centered on sides. Windows and door windows punched out and embossed inward; windows and door windows on car ends punched out but not embossed inward. Four wheels only.

Class-of-the-line eight-wheel herald cars. Top: Southern Pacific and Union Pacific herald coaches. Bottom: Northern Pacific and Illinois Central herald coaches. All Hafner eight-wheel cars are rare, but the Illinois Central is the most difficult to find. Hafner copied its eight-wheel truck style from Bing.

	Gd	Exc

(A) Tan body; blue roof; observation door, window, and overhead observation awning in light blue; yellow observation fence.   40   80

(B) Same as (A), but with gold observation fence.   40   80

(C) Same as (A), but with dark blue sides; black roof; gold observation fence.   40   80

(D) Dark peacock blue body; black roof; observation door and window in yellow; observation awning in reddish maroon; gold observation fence.   40   80

(E) Same as (B), but with lighter peacock blue body.   40   80

(F) Same as (B), but with blue roof.   40   80

(G) Same as (B), but with blue sides and roof; observation awning in gold.   40   80

(H) Same as (B), but in cream with blue roof.   40   80

(I) Same as (E), but with blue roof; gold awning and observation fence.   40   80

(J) Red body with darker red roof; observation window piece in dark red; gold awning and observation fence; black frame.   40   80

(K) Same as (J), but with dark red low-slung Type V frame.   125   250

Note 1: Regular observations of this size have one punched-out door and window at the end. This car has a battery holder for the end light; as a consequence, the observation deck area has two cut-out windows and a circular opening to allow the battery casing to reach the observation platform.

Note 2: Usually, but not always, the piece containing the observation window and door on the No. 98 6¼-inch cars is the same color as the roof.

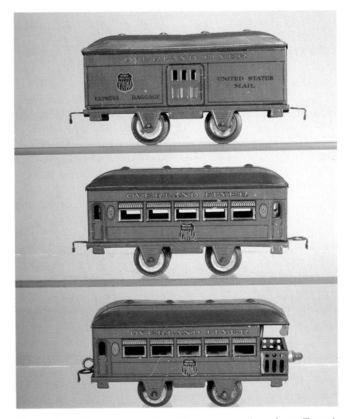

Unnumbered baggage car from the very rare low-slung Transitional set, matching Pullman, and observation car with illuminated end.

Complete catalogued Hafner eight-wheel set with the incredibly rare No. 127 locomotive. Top: No. 127 locomotive and 1180 tender; Wells Fargo baggage car. Bottom: Union Pacific and Illinois Central coaches. W. Sanchez Collection.

	Gd	Exc

6¼–6⅜-INCH-LONG BAGGAGE CARS

ADAMS EXPRESS COMPANY BAGGAGE: (Numbered 97 in a Hafner catalogue); ca. 1915-1920s. Gold and black trim; black roof and frame; "OVERLAND FLYER" on letterboard in gold; "ADAMS / EXPRESS / COMPANY" herald in white lettering on red background to the left of doors; "EXPRESS BAGGAGE" lettered in black under herald; "UNITED STATES / MAIL" lettered in black to the right of doors; Type II or III couplers. Four wheels only.

(A) Orange body with punched-out doors. **90 180**

(B) Dark green body with "ADAMS / EXPRESS / COMPANY" herald lettered in gold on black background with punched-out doors. **95 190**

(C) Same as (B), but with "ADAMS / EXPRESS / COMPANY" herald lettered in white on gold background "OVERLAND FLYER" on letterboard in white. **100 200**

UNION PACIFIC BAGGAGE: (Numbered 97 in a Hafner catalogue; no number appears on the cars.) Ca. 1929-early 1930s. Gold and black trim; black frame; "OVERLAND FLYER" on letterboard in gold; "UNION / PACIFIC" herald lettered in gold on black background to the left of doors. "EXPRESS BAGGAGE" lettered in black to left of doors; "UNITED STATES / MAIL" lettered in black to right of doors; four wheels only.

(A) Tan body; green roof; green sliding door with six panels; three top panels punched out. **40 80**

(B) Dark peacock blue body; black roof; punched-out doors. Also came with blue sliding doors with six panels; three top panels punched out. **40 80**

(C) Lighter peacock blue body; blue roof; blue sliding door with six panels; three top panels punched out. **40 80**

(D) Same as (C), but with blue body and black roof. **40 80**

(E) Same as (C), but with punched-out doors. **40 80**

(F) Same as (C), but with royal blue roof. **40 . 80**

(G) Same as (A), but with cream body. **40 80**

(H) Red body with darker red roof; red sliding doors with six panels; three top panels punched out; black frame. **40 80**

(I) Red body with green roof and darker red frame. "UNION / PACIFIC" herald lettered in gold on black background to the left of doors; sliding door has six panels; three top panels punched out. Type V frame. **125 250**

WELLS FARGO: Baggage, four wheels (ca. 1915-20); eight wheels (ca. 1916-20). Yellow with black detailing; black frame and roof; "OVERLAND FLYER" on letterboard in gold; "Wells / Fargo & Co / Express" diamond herald lettered in white in blue circle within red diamond to the left of doors; "EXPRESS BAGGAGE" lettered in black under Wells Fargo herald; "UNITED STATES / MAIL" lettered in black to the right of doors; punched-out doors. Identical lithography on both four- and eight-wheel versions.

(A) Four-wheel car — Type I or II couplers; 6¼". **250 500**

Top: Two variations of the rare 6¼-inch Adams baggage car. Middle: Large 6¼-inch Southern Pacific herald coach; uncommon four-wheel Illinois Central herald Pullman. R. Doyle Collection. Bottom: Large observation car with Union Pacific herald catalogued as number 98; cream and blue Union Pacific coach, catalogued as number 96. Hafner passenger sets would often come in dissimilar colors.

Top: Baggage car of the Chicago "Century of Progress Special" set; 919 Transitional set baggage unit. Middle: Coach of the "Century of Progress" set; 919 Transitional set Pullman — one of the few Hafner coaches that had a number on the side. Bottom: Observation car of the "Century of Progress" set; observation car of the 919 Transitional set — both observation units in these sets contained battery holders and had red bulbs in the drumhead.

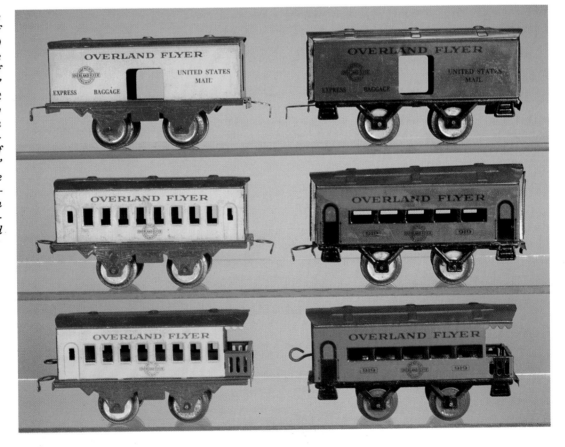

Gd Exc

(B) Eight-wheel car — Type I or II couplers; 6⅜".

550 1100

Note: Verification needed as to whether this car came without punched-out doors.

"CENTURY OF PROGRESS SPECIAL" PASSENGER CARS

One of the most famous and most popular Hafner sets was produced to coincide with Chicago's 1933–1934 "Century of Progress Exposition". All cars are 5⁷⁄₁₆ inches long, with narrow 1⁹⁄₁₆-inch-wide bodies with Type I frames and Type II couplers. There was also a "Century of Progress Special" freight set with the No. 82 (31400) New York Central sand and gravel car, the No. 62425 boxcar, and the unnumbered caboose with four windows on each side and taillight on the end.

OVERLAND FLYER BAGGAGE: 1933-35
(A) Cream and red; red roof and red frame; "OVERLAND FLYER" lettered in red near the top of each side; bar and circle herald lettered "HAFNER'S / OVERLAND FLYER / RAILWAYS" in red and positioned to the left of the punched-out doors; "EXPRESS BAGGAGE" lettered in red under herald; "UNITED STATES / MAIL" lettered in red to the right of doors.   20   40
(B) Same as (A), but only "OVERLAND FLYER" lettered on sides.   30   60

OVERLAND FLYER COACH: 1933-35. Cream and red; red roof and red frame; "OVERLAND FLYER" lettered in red near the top of each side; bar and circle herald lettered "HAFNER'S / OVERLAND FLYER / RAILWAYS" in red and centered on sides; windows and door windows all punched out.   20   40

OVERLAND FLYER OBSERVATION: 1933-35. Cream and red body; red roof and red frame; "OVERLAND FLYER" lettered in red over windows; bar and circle herald lettered "HAFNER'S / OVERLAND FLYER / RAILWAYS" in red and centered on sides; windows and door windows all punched out; has battery casing and opening in observation fence for red bulb to protrude; battery regulator lever protrudes from hole at other end of car.   20   40

919 TRANSITION CARS

(While essentially a one-piece car, the larger size and use of floors and vestibules puts it in a higher category than the Overland Flyer "Hummer-style" one-piece cars — see Chap-

Gd Exc

ter Six.) Cars are 5⅞ inches long with Type VIb frame. Type II couplers.

UNNUMBERED OVERLAND FLYER BAGGAGE CAR: Mid-1930s. (Unnumbered but came with "919" set.)
(A) Dark red with black lithography trim. "OVERLAND FLYER" lettered in black over windows; bar and circle herald lettered "HAFNER'S / OVERLAND FLYER / RAILWAYS" in black and positioned to the left of the punched-out doors. "EXPRESS BAGGAGE" lettered in black under herald; "UNITED STATES / MAIL" lettered in black to the right of the doors; silver vestibules attached at each end; couplers attached to floor.   60   120
(B) Same as (A), but couplers part of vestibules.   70   140

919 OVERLAND FLYER COACH: Mid-1930s.
(A) Dark red with black lithography trim for doors, window inserts, and frame; "OVERLAND FLYER" lettered in black over windows; bar and circle herald lettered "HAFNER'S / OVERLAND FLYER / RAILWAYS" in black centered on sides; "919" in a black-lined rectangle lettered in black to the left and to the right of herald; windows punched out and embossed inward; door windows not punched out; silver vestibules attached at each end; couplers attached to floor.   60   120
(B) Same as (A), but couplers part of vestibules.   70   140

919 OVERLAND FLYER OBSERVATION: Mid-1930s.
(A) Dark red with black lithography trim for doors, window inserts, and frame. "OVERLAND FLYER" lettered in black over windows; bar and circle herald (lettered "HAFNER'S / OVERLAND FLYER / RAILWAYS" in black) centered on sides. "919" in a black-outlined rectangle lettered in black to the left and right of herald; windows punched out and embossed inward; door windows not punched out; has battery casing and opening in observation deck fence for bulb to protrude; battery regulator lever protrudes from hole at other end of car; couplers attached to floor.   60   120
(B) Same as (A), but couplers part of vestibules. No battery holder.   70   140

Note: Roger Arcara reports a No. 919 coach and a No. 919 observation in blue and black lithography. Further details needed on coupler attachment.

NOTES
1. Letter from Thomas Mackowiak, March 19, 1989.
2. One reviewer objects to the misspelling designation. He writes: "Between 1894 and 1911, Pittsburgh was spelled 'Pittsburg' without the 'H', by official decree of government. The 'H' was restored in June 1911, by the U.S. Geographic Board of Names under petition by U.S. Senator George Oliver. Naturally, there were many years after and before where it was spelled both ways."

CHAPTER SIX

★

ONE-PIECE COACHES, INCLUDING THE SUNSHINE SPECIAL CARS

Most toy train manufacturers produced at least one set and/or line of cars that could be sold at the cheapest possible price. Lionel Scout sets, for example, comprise one illustration of this practice since these sets are certainly among the most famous economically priced train items ever issued. In 1916, a date established by Alan Schuweiler, American Flyer produced a group of fragile one-piece cars priced to sell at bottom-of-the-line prices. Flyer called this series its "Hummer" line.

About the same time, the Hafner Company developed and marketed its own line of one-piece passenger cars to reach the lowest-priced market. The sides of the car were bent down from the roof and folded. Then the car ends were bent and joined to the sides by tabs so that two tabs from one side bent and folded over the end. At the same time two tabs from the car end bent over the side, and the four tabs held one end and one side together. The same tab and fold arrangement was used on the other side and end. The couplers were part of the one-piece ends, one end having a loop and the other end having a hook; hence, when the sides and ends were folded and tabbed, the car had ready-made couplers. Although American Flyer made some of its Hummer cars with floors, Hafner never added floors to its ordinary one-piece coaches. Sunshine Special cars did have floors.

That these low-priced, one-piece cars were popular is attested to by the fact that they appeared in the Hafner line even as late as 1929, and they turn up with reasonable regularity at the larger train meets today and, occasionally, at flea markets and antique stores.

Compared to the American Flyer Hummer cars, the lithography of the one-piece Hafner coaches was rather unimpressive. The Hummer cars usually had a number, such as "500" or "502" on the sides, and many of these small Pullmans, with or without the number, had a eye-catching lithographed winged "A.F.L." logo which made the cars appealing.

The name "Hafner" never appeared on any of these cars, and even today at train meets some people will inquire what company made these trains. These cars have even turned up on some mail-order lists advertised as being made by American Flyer.

A fascinating aspect of the one-piece passenger coaches is the fact that although most of them have the lettering "OVERLAND FLYER", these cars were also produced with the lettering "CANADIAN FLYER" as well as the designation "NEW YORK FLYER". Needless to say, the latter two cars turn up much less frequently than the one-piece cars lettered "OVERLAND FLYER".

The Hafner cars had seven square windows and two oval windows on each side. The car ends had one punched-out door and two unpunched lithographed windows at each end. Each car had three lithographed windows. Each car had three lithographed decorative panels on one side and two long decorative panels on the opposite side. The cars did come in a variety of colors, and some of the combinations are quite attractive. Perhaps the two most eye-catching are, first, a two-tone blue car which matches the color scheme of the Lionel "Blue Comet," and another which combines a most pleasing orange shade with a contrasting green. The cars were always coaches, which as Roger Arcara observed, appear European. A baggage car and an observation car were apparently never manufactured in this series.

ONE-PIECE COACHES

	Gd	Exc

CANADIAN FLYER: Ca. 1915-early 1920s. "CANADIAN FLYER" lettered in black over the windows; yellow sides with black detailing; black frame and roof; black window trim; doors at car ends trimmed in black.   **75**   **150**

NEW YORK FLYER: Ca. 1917-early 1920s. "NEW YORK FLYER" lettered in black over the windows; yellow sides with black detailing; black frame and roof; black window trim; doors at car ends trimmed in black.   **75**   **150**

OVERLAND FLYER: Ca. 1916-29.
(A) "OVERLAND FLYER" lettered in black over the windows; yellow sides and ends with black detailing; black frame and roof; red window trim; nine windows punched out on each side; one door punched out at each end.   **12**   **25**
(B) "OVERLAND FLYER" lettered in green over the windows; light green sides and ends with dark green detailing, dark green frame and roof.   **12**   **25**
(C) Same lettering as (B), but orange sides and ends with green detailing; dark green frame and roof.   **12**   **25**
(D) Same lettering as (B), except yellow sides and ends.   **12**   **25**
(E) "OVERLAND FLYER" lettered in red over the windows; yellow sides and ends with red detailing; bright red frame and roof.   **12**   **25**
(F) "OVERLAND FLYER" lettering in blue over the windows; light blue sides and ends with blue detailing; dark blue frame and roof.   **15**   **30**

Variations of the one-piece passenger cars similar to the American Flyer "Hummer" production. Top: Overland Flyer all-blue coach; yellow and black coach. Middle: Yellow and red coach; Canadian Flyer version. Bottom: New York Flyer coach; orange and green Overland Flyer coach.

	Gd	Exc

(G) "OVERLAND FLYER" lettered in black over the windows; dark red sides and ends with black detailing; black frame and roof.   **20   40**

(H) Same as (G) but lettered in gold over the windows.   **25   50**

Note: Only in (A) version are the door windows at the car ends lithographed in red. On the other cars the window color is the same as the color of the car sides.

SUNSHINE SPECIAL CARS

Probably developed from the one-piece-style passenger cars, but much more elaborate and attractive, are the "Sunshine Special" coaches and observation. These Sunshine Special cars came in two forms — the short 5-inch cars and longer 5½-inch Pullmans, the latter cars being the same size as the early herald coaches and the later 80-series passenger cars. The Sunshine Special title has proved to have considerable collecting charm and appeal even though few collectors today probably recall the famous Texas and Pacific Railroad passenger train with that designation.

The short Sunshine Special car had a one-piece body that consisted of a roof, sides, integral underframe, and partial end pieces. When the car was bent down from the roof, the sides were formed — similar to the early one-piece Hafner cars and the American Flyer Hummers. But now

forming the car became more intricate. The end pieces had four slots on the sides and two tabs on the bottom. A separate floor was inserted and held in place when the two tabs on each end were bent down and under, thus firmly gripping the floor piece. Two separate vestibule pieces were added. The tabs of the two separate vestibule pieces — one piece for each end — were then inserted in the car end slots and bent to hold the sides together. These vestibule pieces each contained combined loops and hooks for the couplers. The vestibule arrangement was ingenious, not only because of the saving in labor costs, and helping to hold the car together, but also because the vestibules on each end gave the cars a much more realistic appearance.

The Sunshine Special observation cars used the same technique on one end, but the observation deck area roof was punched out to the contour of an awning, the back of the car was completely open, and the end held together by a drumhead stamping whose tabs fitted into holes in the observation railings. It is, thus, the low railing and the small drumhead stamping that hold the car in place at the rear.

As mentioned earlier, the longer-type 5½-inch Sunshine Special cars fit the pattern of the regular Hafner herald coaches, although unfortunately an observation car appears never to have been made in the larger-size series.

As was the case with the Hafner one-piece cars, the Sunshine Special cars proved popular and appear with regularity at the larger train meets today. Aside from the

A variety of Sunshine Special cars. Top: Green and red coach; off-white and green observation car. Middle: Cream and red coach and matching observation. Bottom: Red and green variations; larger 5½-inch "Rainbow" coach.

quaint and nostalgic appeal of their title, the myriad colors in which these cars were produced render them very collectible.

Smaller Sunshine Special Cars

These cars actually measure 5½ inches from coupler end to coupler end, or 4¾ inches from vestibule face to vestibule face, but the Hafner catalogue lists them as "5 inches" long. The catalogue lists the small passenger car as number 90.

PASSENGER: ca. 1930-38.

(A) Cream body; red detailing, red frame and roof; "SUNSHINE SPECIAL" lettered in red over windows; four windows on each side punched out and embossed inward; doors and door windows not punched out; silver vestibules. Type VIa frame. **30 60**

(B) Same as (A), but with green sides; white and black detailing; black frame and red roof; "SUNSHINE SPECIAL" lettered in white over windows. **35 70**

(C) Same as (A), but with red sides; "SUNSHINE SPECIAL" lettered in white over windows; white window inserts; white and green detailing; green frame and roof. **35 70**

(D) Same as (C), but with gold and green detailing; "SUNSHINE SPECIAL" lettered in gold over windows; gold window inserts; white vestibules. **35 70**

(E) Same as (D), but with dark green vestibules. **35 70**

(F) Same as (D), but with light green vestibules. **35 70**

(G) Same as (D), but with silver vestibules. **35 70**

(H) Same as (D), but with gold vestibules. **35 70**

	Gd	Exc

(I) Same as (A), but with off-white sides; green frame and roof; "SUNSHINE SPECIAL" lettered in green over windows. **35 70**

(J) Same as (B), but with gold vestibules. **40 80**

(K) Same as (D), but with maroon vestibules. **35 70**

OBSERVATION CAR: Ca. 1930-38.

(A) Cream sides, red detailing; red frame and roof; "SUNSHINE SPECIAL" lettered in red over windows; four windows on each side punched out and embossed inward; door and door windows not punched out; silver vestibule; cream observation railing, red drumhead. Type VIa frame. **30 60**

(B) Same as (A), but with red sides; white and green detailing; green frame and roof; "SUNSHINE SPECIAL" lettered in white over windows; red observation railing. **35 70**

(C) Same as (A), but with off-white sides; green detailing; green frame and roof; "SUNSHINE SPECIAL" lettered in green over windows. **35 70**

(D) Same as (B), but with green and gold detailing; "SUNSHINE SPECIAL" lettered in gold over windows; gold window inserts. **35 70**

(E) Same as (D), but with white vestibules. **35 70**

Note: One Hafner folder lists a "SUNSHINE SPECIAL" observation car with battery holder and red taillight. Verification needed as to whether this car was actually produced.

Larger Sunshine Special Car

As with the herald coaches, these cars actually measure 5⁵⁄₁₆ inches long, but the catalogue lists them as 5½ inches.

The Sunshine Special car is particularly pleasing to the eye. It usually appears with yellow sides, green roof, and black frame with the words "SUNSHINE SPECIAL" lettered over the windows in a green-golden sheen. Underneath the windows is lettered the word "RAINBOW".

PASSENGER: Early 1930s.

(A) Red trim; black frame; green roof; "SUNSHINE SPE

CIAL" lettered in metallic green on red background over windows; "RAINBOW" lettered in red on yellow background centered on sides; metallic green window trim; all windows punched out and embossed inward; Type I frame; Type II or III couplers. **60   120**

(B) Same as (A), but with blue roof. **60   120**

(C) Same as (A), but with orange roof. **60   120**

CHAPTER SEVEN

★

EARLY FREIGHT CARS (1920s–1936)

Hafner did not have freight cars in its line until the early or mid-1920s when it chose a German company, Bing Brothers, to furnish this missing feature. Balancing the cost of manufacturing its own freight cars against purchasing cars from another firm, the Hafner Company decided on the second alternative by purchasing three boxcars, two reefers, a gondola, a hopper car, a tank car, and a caboose from Bing.

BING FREIGHT CARS

Founded in Nuremberg in 1863, the Bing Brothers firm first sold toys and hardware and soon concentrated heavily on train production. By 1908 it was the largest toy manufacturing company in the world. Although considerably hampered by strong competition from rival companies (most notably Märklin) and severely limited by the restrictions of World War I, Bing produced a seemingly endless series of locomotives, tenders, passenger, and freight cars, and railroad accessories for more than sixty years. One of the most significant aspects of Bing freight car production is the marvelous realism captured. Pierce Carlson in his *Toy Trains: A History* has pointed out that Bing used the American Car and Foundry Company catalogue as the basis for its freight car lithography. The real railroad rolling stock was portrayed in the catalogue, and Bing scaled down the size to miniature proportions, but kept the same lettering and even the exact car numbers used by A.C. and F.

To cite a few examples, the Old Dutch Cleanser car lithographed a detail such as "RETURN TO SO OMAHA", while the Jersey Central boxcar has the authentic sign: "POST NO BILLS". The Bing New York New Haven and Hartford boxcar not only carries the precise number of the actual car (32001), but also lists the car capacity, the weight, length, type of couplers, and indicates "AIR BRAKE". It is an authentic replica of the real boxcar. It is interesting, for

Top: Bing 528 NYC & HR caboose; Bing unnumbered crane. Middle: Bing 10205 Jersey Central boxcar; Bing 32001 NY, NH & H boxcar. Bottom: Bing Hocking Valley gondola; Bing Pennsylvania Coal & Coke Co. hopper. Although the crane could be bought separately from the Sears Roebuck catalogue that advertised other Bing-Hafner items, there is no evidence that it was ever sold in Hafner sets.

Top: Two color variations of the Bing 4226 Cudahy Old Dutch Cleanser refrigerator car. Middle: Bing 5933 Santa Fe reefer; Bing 7300 Swift's refrigerator car. Bottom: Bing 1000 Peerless tank car.

example, to look at the Bing catalogue for 1914 and see even at that date the freight cars (except the tanker) later used by Hafner.

Hafner turned to Bing not only to furnish its freight cars but also to supply its earliest accessories. Of course there is precedent, as for example American Flyer's purchase of its early accessories from Bing and the later purchase of its first standard gauge freights from Lionel. The precise dating of the Bing-Hafner arrangement is undetermined. There is a notation in a Hafner "Scrapbook" at the TCA Museum Library that the 1922 catalogue includes "import material," so the 1922–1928 period is a reasonable dating estimate. A Hafner "Retail Price List" for "Season 1924" advertises Bing cars and accessories. A Hafner folder ca. 1924–1926 depicts all the Bing cars and accessories, and the 1926 Sears Roebuck catalogue shows a Hafner set with Bing's Old Dutch Cleanser boxcar, Peerless 1000 tanker, and the 528 New York Central caboose. Some of the Bing stock was used by Hafner as late as 1929 since the 1929 Montgomery Ward catalogue displays the Bing 10205 Central Railroad of New Jersey boxcar as part of a Hafner freight car set. In its undated mid-1920s folder, Hafner renumbered the Bing cars in its listing; for example, the Bing tank car is numbered 307, but the Bing cars themselves were sold by Hafner exactly as Bing lettered and produced them for its own line. The cars were sold by Hafner with the Bing name on the car ends and the Bing logo stamped on the car bottoms, so in effect the cars were thoroughly of Bing production with Hafner acting as a distributor. All the Bing cars used by Hafner were four-wheelers.

Bing, of course, produced other freight cars; for instance, the gondola and the caboose were issued with Pennsylvania Railroad lettering, but there is no evidence that such cars were sold by Hafner. Bing also produced a realistic crane car that was advertised separately in several Sears Roebuck catalogues, but there is no evidence that it ever came in a Hafner boxed set. It is perhaps regrettable that Hafner did not sell the beautifully lithographed Bing Anheuser-Busch and Pabst refrigerator cars, but without a doubt the Prohibition Amendment prevented the sale of these cars.

The severe Wall Street crash of 1929 adversely affected Bing production and brought considerable financial debt. By 1932 the company was in receivership. Bing's plight in the late 1920s was undoubtedly one factor in Hafner's decision to commence producing its own freight cars.

Note: The following cars are listed in order of the Hafner catalogue number.

7300 SWIFT'S PREMIUM HAMS REFRIGERATOR CAR: (Numbered 301 in a Hafner catalogue.) This is the Bing No. 7300 Swift's Premium Hams car.

(A) Yellow sides; dark brown ends; gray roof; black frame; "SWIFT / REFRIGERATOR & LINE / 7300" lettered in black with red outline to the left of the door; "Swift's / Premium / Hams / Finest Quality" lettered in black to the right of the door, enclosed in a red rectangle outlined in black; double doors are hinged and handle turns to open and close doors;

	Gd	Exc

three hinges lithographed in black on each door; "The Bing's Miniature Railway System" lettered in white at the top of both ends. 5½". **80 160**

(B) Same as (A), but with white roof. **80 160**

4226 OLD DUTCH CLEANSER CAR: (Numbered 302 in a Hafner catalogue.) This is the Bing No. 4226 Old Dutch Cleanser car.

(A) Yellow sides; dark brown ends; white roof; black frame; blue-and-white-clad Dutch Cleanser lady brandishing a stick; "Chases / Dirt" and "Old / Dutch / Cleanser" lettered in black to the left of the doors; "CUDAHY / REFRIGERATOR / LINE / 4226" lettered in black to the right of the doors; double doors are hinged and handle turns to open and close doors; three hinges lithographed in black on each door; "Bing's Miniature Railway System" lettered in black at top of both ends. 5½". **90 180**

(B) Same as (A), but with white roof. **90 180**

(C) Same as (A), but with orange body and Dutch Cleanser lady in lighter blue and grayish white lithography. 5½". **90 180**

528 NEW YORK CENTRAL CABOOSE: (Numbered 303 in a Hafner catalogue.) This is the Bing 528 New York Central caboose. Dark brown sides, ends, and cupola sides; roof and cupola roof olive brown; black frame; "528 / N.Y.C. & H.R." lettered in white on sides; "NEW YORK / CENTRAL / LINES" lettered in white and enclosed in a black circle outlined in black and white; four windows punched out and embossed inward; light brown window trim; three windows embossed and punched out on each end, the center window serving as the door window, windows in orange trim; two cupola windows on each side; three cupola windows on each end, all embossed and punched out in orange trim; "The Bing Miniature Railroad System" lettered in white at the top of both ends. 5½". **25 50**

5933 SANTA FE BOXCAR: So listed in the Hafner catalogue (under number 304), but actually a reefer. This is the Bing No. 5933 Santa Fe refrigerator car.

(A) Dark brown sides and ends; gray roof, black frame; "VENTILATOR / AND / REFRIGERATOR" lettered in white to the left of the door; "Santa Fe" herald lettered in white on black and white background; "S.F.R.D. / 5933" lettered in white to the right of the door; sliding door with black handle; "S.F.R.D. / 5933" lettered in white on both ends; "The Bing Miniature Railway System" lettered in white at the top of both ends. 5½". **50 100**

(B) Also came with gold lettering on body. *Bing's* / MINIATURE RAILROAD SYSTEM" lettered in gold at ends. 5½". **50 100**

32001 NEW YORK NEW HAVEN AND HARTFORD BOXCAR: (Numbered 305 in a Hafner catalogue.) This is the Bing 32001 New York New Haven and Hartford car. Dark brown body, dark olive green roof, black frame; "New York / New Haven / and Hartford" lettered in white script to the left of the door; "32001" lettered in white to the right of the door; "N.Y.N.H. & H. / 32001" lettered in white on doors and on both ends; "Bing Miniature Railway System" lettered in white at the top of both ends. 5½". **45 90**

Note: This car was also produced by Bing with unlettered doors. The catalogue, however, indicates that Hafner sold the lettered door version.

10205 CENTRAL RAILROAD OF NEW JERSEY BOXCAR: (Numbered 306 in a Hafner catalogue.) This is the Bing No. 10205 Central Railroad of New Jersey car. Dark brown body and ends, gray roof, black frame. "CENTRAL RAILROAD / OF / NEW JERSEY" lettered in white to the left of the door; "10205" above a circle lettered in white to the right of the door; "C.R.R. of N.J. / 10205 / POST NO BILLS" lettered in white on doors; sliding door with black handle; "C.R. of N.Y. / 10205" above circle — lettered in white on both ends; "The Bings Miniature Railway System" lettered in white at the top of both ends. This car also came in a variation with the lettering "Bing Miniature Railway System" at the top of both ends. 5½". **50 100**

Note: Apparently previously unnoticed by collectors is the error "N.Y." instead of the proper "N.J." on the car ends. Whether this error was on all Bing Jersey Central boxcars is not known. The error was not made on Bing eight-wheel Jersey Central cars.

1000 PEERLESS TANK LINE OIL TANK CAR: (Numbered 307 in a Hafner catalogue.) This is the Bing No. 1000 Peerless Tank Line car. Gray domes and body; black frame; "PEERLESS TANK LINE / 1000" lettered in white on sides; all words and number underlined in white; "USE / NATIONAL / LIGHT / OIL" lettered in white to the left of center; "USE / WHITE / ROSE / GASOLINE" lettered in white to the right of center; "1000 PEERLESS TANK LINE 1000" lettered on bottom sides in white; "P.T.L. / 1000" lettered in white on both ends. 4½". **20 40**

1 PENNA COAL & COKE CO. CAR: (Numbered 308 in a Hafner catalogue.) This is the Bing Pennsylvania Coal & Coke Co. car. Gray body; black frame; "PENNA COAL & COKE CO" lettered in white to left of center; large number "1" and bar and circle herald lettered in white to the right of center; "The Bings Miniature Railway System" lettered in white at the top of both ends. 5½". **20 40**

4610 HOCKING VALLEY RY OPEN GONDOLA: (Numbered 309 in a Hafner catalogue.) This is the Bing Hocking Valley Railway car. Gray body; black frame; "HOCKING VALLEY / RY" lettered in white on sides of car; "H.V.R. / 4610" lettered in white on both ends. 4½". **40 80**

Hafner's Own Early Freight Cars

The Fall–Winter 1928–1929 Sears catalogue pictures several Hafner passenger sets, but the one mechanical freight set shown is Ives. The same Ives freight set is shown in the Fall–Winter 1927–1928 Sears catalogue. On the other hand, the Sears catalogue for Fall–Winter 1926–1927 features a set pulled by a Hafner locomotive and tender, but the three freight cars in the consist are Bing — the Peerless Tank car, the delightful 4226 Old Dutch Cleanser boxcar, and the New York Central caboose. In a taped interview John Hafner has noted that this and similar freight sets were put together in the Hafner factory using the Bing freights because at that time Hafner had no freight cars of its own.

Top: Overland Flyer boxcar and Chicago and North Western caboose. Middle: Two versions of Hafner's earliest sand and gravel car. Bottom: Another version of the New York Central sand and gravel car and the 31280 Peerless stock car.

Around 1929 Hafner decided to develop its own freight car line. Four cars make up the earliest Hafner-manufactured freights: the number 31400 New York Central sand and gravel car, which appears most frequently in red and blue; the 31280 Peerless stock car, which came in either yellow or blue; the 31320 Santa Fe boxcar, and the Overland Flyer caboose with the Chicago & North Western logo on the sides (Hafner catalogue number 83).

Since the Fall 1929–Winter 1930 Montgomery Ward catalogue pictures a Hafner freight set with the above mentioned sand car, stock car, and caboose, but includes a Bing Jersey Central boxcar as part of the set, it appears that Hafner's Santa Fe boxcar was made later than the other three early Hafner freights.

The Fall–Winter 1929–1930 Sears catalogue pictures a three-car Hafner freight set — the New York Central sand and gravel car, the Peerless stock, and the Chicago & North Western caboose. Unless further evidence is discovered, these data would indicate that Hafner's own freight cars first appeared ca. 1929–1930.

The new Hafner-made freights are very nicely lithographed, but except perhaps for the boxcar there is a distinctive toy look about them. The caboose, for example, has "CABOOSE" centered in large letters on the sides while the gondola does the same with the words "SAND AND GRAVEL". The very realistic replicas of real railroad freights which Bing had featured have been altered for the sake of a brightly colored, play-value toy look.

Note: The following cars are arranged according to their Hafner catalogue numbers whenever that number is available.

31320 SANTA FE OVERLAND FLYER BOXCAR: (Numbered 80 in a Hafner catalogue.) "OVERLAND FLYER" lettered in gold on the top of each side; "31320" lettered in black to the left of the door. "Santa Fe" herald lettered in gold with black and green background. "A.T.S.Fe. / 31320" lettered in black on both ends; black frame.

	Gd	Exc
(A) Green body; orange roof; no doors; Type I frame; Type II or III couplers.	45	90
(B) Same as (A), but with burnt orange roof.	45	90
(C) Same as (A), but with dark green four-panel sliding doors.	60	120
(D) Same as (C), but with orange-brown roof.	60	120
(E) Same as (A), but with green roof.	60	120
(F) Same as (A), but with red roof and red frame.	60	120

31280 PEERLESS STOCK CAR: (Numbered 81 in a Hafner catalogue.) "PEERLESS STOCK CAR" lettered in gold on the top of each side. "M.C.B. AIR BRAKE" lettered in black to the left of the doorway; "31280" lettered in black to the right of the doorway and on both ends; black frame.

	Gd	Exc
(A) Yellow body; burnt orange roof; no doors; Type I frame; Type II or III couplers.	45	90

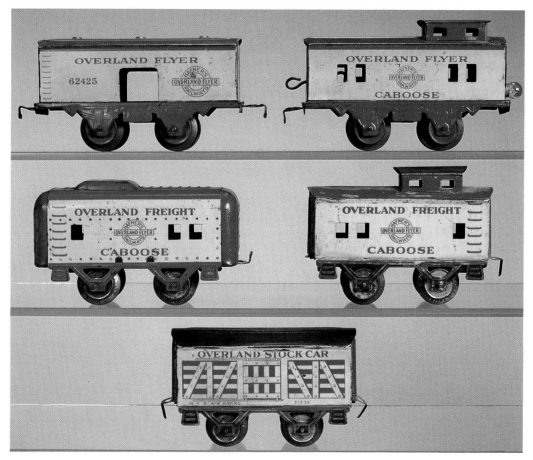

Top: Hafner 62425 boxcar, converted from the baggage car of the Chicago "Century of Progress Special" passenger set by merely changing the lettering; four-window unnumbered caboose containing battery holder and protruding knob to turn the battery on and off — the taillight was always appropriately red. Middle: Unusually lettered "OVERLAND FREIGHT / CABOOSE", sold only in 1937–1938; square-cornered version of the same caboose, which had a short production run. Bottom: Lithographed 31230 "OVERLAND STOCK CAR", sold in sets with the freight/caboose. All of these cars are uncommon and date from the 1934–1938 period.

	Gd	Exc
(B) Same as (A), but with light blue roof.	45	90
(C) Same as (A), but with dark green four-panel sliding doors with the top two panels punched out.	70	140
(D) Same as (A), but with dark brown roof; light brown four-panel sliding doors; panels not punched out.	60	120
(E) Dark blue body; orange roof; light blue four-panel sliding doors with the top two panels not punched out.	60	120
(F) Same as (E), but with royal blue roof; light blue four-panel sliding doors; panels not punched out.	60	120
(G) Same as (E), but orange four-panel sliding doors with the top two panels punched out.	70	140
(H) Same as (E), but with orangish-brown four-panel sliding doors; panels not punched out; maroon roof; Type III couplers.	60	120

31400 NEW YORK CENTRAL LINES SAND AND GRAVEL CAR: (Numbered 82 in a Hafner catalogue.) "SAND / AND / GRAVEL" lettered in gold at the center of each side. "M.C.B. COUPLERS" lettered in black at the bottom center. "NEW YORK / CENTRAL / LINES" herald lettered in gold on black to the left of center. "N.Y.C. Lines" lettered in black to the right of center. "31400" lettered in black at the right of bottom center; black frame.

	Gd	Exc
(A) Red body; Type I frame; Type II or III couplers.	40	80
(B) Same as (A), but with dark red frame; Type II couplers.	50	100
(C) Same as (A), but with blue body.	40	80
(D) Same as (A), but with cream body. Reported by Dick Stafford.		NRS
(E) Red body and frame; no lettering; Type I frame; Type II couplers. This car is part of the "Century of Progress Special" freight set but also came with at least one other Hafner set.		NRS

UNNUMBERED OVERLAND FLYER CABOOSE: (Numbered 83 in a Hafner catalogue.) "OVERLAND FLYER" lettered in gold on black background at the top of each side; "CHICAGO / NORTH WESTERN / LINE" herald lettered in gold on black background at the center of each side. "CABOOSE" lettered in gold underneath herald; no number on the car; four windows punched out and embossed inward on each side; gold window trim; three windows embossed and punched out on each end — the center window serving as the door window — windows in gold trim; four cupola windows on

Gd Exc

each side, two cupola windows on each end; no window trim; gold steps and railings on each end; black frame.

(A) Red body, burnt orange roof and cupola sides; dark red cupola roof; Type I frame; Type II or III couplers. **40 80**

(B) Same as (A), but with dark brown roof. **40 80**

(C) Same as (A), but with robin's-egg blue roof, dark blue cupola sides, and canary yellow cupola roof. **45 90**

(D) Same as (C), but with canary yellow cupola sides and robin's-egg blue cupola roof. **45 90**

(E) Same as (A), but with light red cupola roof. **40 80**

(F) Same as (A), but with light red cupola sides and roof. **40 80**

UNNUMBERED OVERLAND FLYER CABOOSE: Cream sides; red ends, cupola, and roof; red frame; "OVERLAND FLYER" lettered in red near the top of each side. "HAFNER'S / OVERLAND FLYER / RAILWAYS" lettered in red in bar and circle herald at the center of each side. "CABOOSE" lettered in red underneath the herald; four punched-out windows on each side; two punched-out windows on each cupola side; one punched-out window at each cupola side; one punched-out window at each cupola end. Car has a holder for flashlight batteries with red bulb protruding from the back end; wire to control the on-off status of the battery protrudes from the opposite end. Type I frame; Type II coupler. This caboose came with the Century of Progress

Gd Exc

Special freight set as well as with the No. 905 set which contained two sand cars, the lumber car, and the 62425 boxcar. **40 80**

62425 OVERLAND FLYER BOXCAR: (No catalogue number available.) Cream sides; red ends and roof; red frame; "OVERLAND FLYER" lettered in red near the top of each side. "62425" lettered in red to the left of the door; punched-out doors; "HAFNER'S / OVERLAND FLYER / RAILWAYS" lettered in red in bar and circle herald to the right of the door; red frame; Type I frame; Type II or III couplers. This car came in at least two Hafner sets including the "Century of Progress" freight set. **40 80**

UNNUMBERED OVERLAND FLYER SAND AND GRAVEL CAR: "HAFNER'S / OVERLAND FLYER / RAILWAYS" lettered in red in bar and circle herald centered on each side of the car; cream body; red frame; Type I frame; Type II couplers. **45 90**

UNNUMBERED AND UNLETTERED LUMBER CAR: No lettering; two black stakes; stakes were bent of short strip in one piece and eyeletted to floor of car on each side to hold lumber load; red frame; Type I frame; Type II couplers. **NRS** **Note:** In addition to the four standard freights just described, an unnumbered caboose appeared in this period, probably in 1933, with a narrow 1 9/16"-wide body.

CHAPTER EIGHT

★

THE STREAMLINER ERA

In the early 1930s the age of the streamliner passenger train arrived for America's railroads. Avant-garde, contoured engine styles that would decrease wind resistance and allow greater speeds captured the nation's fancy. In addition to the emphasis on speed which the new streamliners brought, there was the streamline look itself, whether in stainless steel or aluminum alloy, the look of sleek, graceful, gleaming glitter and glamour.

It was a thrill for the people in an era of Depression just to view these new vehicles of flashing allure. The glittering trains were a sign of hope, of better days, of forward and advanced thinking and doing.

The Union Pacific's M-10000 "City of Salina" was one of the first of these new streamliners to dazzle the public, and on May 26, 1934, the Burlington's "Pioneer Zephyr" set a new speed and endurance record as it ran nonstop 13 hours 5 minutes from Denver to the Chicago World's Fair at an average speed of 77.6 miles an hour. Other railroads joined the streamliner parade, and the resulting attention and publicity swept from coast to coast. It was not long before toy train manufacturers were caught up by the enthusiasm. Lionel produced its 752E "City of Portland" and its 616E "Flying Yankee." American Flyer issued its version of the "Burlington Zephyr," and Marx manufactured its own articulated Union Pacific M-10000 and the later M-10005. These models were among the first of what was to become several series of toy streamliners.

Hafner, like the other manufacturers, followed the vogue in 1935. Their first choice was reproducing a version of the Union Pacific M-10000 streamliner in prototype brown and yellow. The Hafner streamliner sets came with a varying number of cars — always according to the advertisements with at least three units (including the motor car) and with as many as seven units. Collector Jerry Cirinelli has an original boxed set with eight compartments, which has the engine and six additional units. The eighth compartment is empty, and since the track was placed in the bottom of the box it appears that an eighth car may have filled the empty spot. The Hafner motor unit was encased in a decorative lithographed shell, and the cast-iron nose piece was balanced at the rear by a punched-steel weight attached to the tin vestibule which itself was held to the body only by three tabs. That this three-tab arrangement was not very durable can be proved by the many power units that have survived but are missing this vestibule. The rear weight balanced the cast-iron nose and battery located in the front of the engine. If the vestibule on the back of the engine broke away, the front of the engine would drop to the track under the weight of the cast-iron nose and the battery. The wear and tear of running the train, especially on the curves, would often cause the rear vestibule containing the weight to snap off breaking the tabs.

Of all of the articulated connecting devices produced by the various toy train manufacturers, Lionel's was probably the most durable and sensible since the vestibules on its City of Portland and Flying Yankee were separate, sturdy four-wheel units. American Flyer's vestibules were part of the coaches and did not have their own trucks. The cars were joined by a strong wire clip which hooked on two partial vestibules which were attached to adjoining coaches. Marx handled the problem by extending a projecting horizontal piece into a slit in the car ahead and having a nail-like pin drop from the roof and bind two cars together. Other articulation techniques were developed so that, for example, the American Flyer Illinois Central streamliner and the tinplate Burlington Zephyr had extended roof pieces which hooked to a straight stud on the roof of the preceding car. It was this method of articulation which Hafner first employed. The first type Hafner vestibule had a stud at the top which served as a catch for the adjoining car which had an integral projecting hole tab on the roof.

The Hafner M-10000 bullet-nose engine was usually furnished not only with a bell but also with a headlight. In the earliest version the bulb was covered by a tab and slot mounted hood which could be opened only by prying off the hood with a screwdriver or similar tool, running the risk of breaking the holding tabs.

As mentioned, the coach unit of this train had an integral tab containing a hole which would engage the straight stud of the vestibule of the preceding car or motor unit. The other end of the coach had the sheet-metal vestibule with the straight stud attached so that the following coach or observation car could be joined in the same manner. It became apparent that this arrangement was not the most ideal. Fast-moving trains would often come apart on curves. Hafner later made the straight stud into a spike shape mushroom form which, of course, rendered the various train pieces less likely to separate. Seemingly, the mushroom-style stud did not last long since relatively few of these models turn up today. The mushroom stud would have proved too difficult for small children to detach if they wanted to separate the cars or locomotive unit. Hafner soon solved the coupling aspects of its streamliner units by producing a special floor piece or bracket containing a higher straight pin. This floor piece was riveted at the sides of the back of the motor unit. The coaches and observation units of this style had extensions of the existing floor pieces with holes which fit over the studs in the floor piece of the engine or car ahead.

Some Hafner streamliners can be found with both the roof connecting knob and the floor knob connector. This represents the changeover from roof to floor connection and demonstrates the Hafner Company's economy in using up leftover parts.

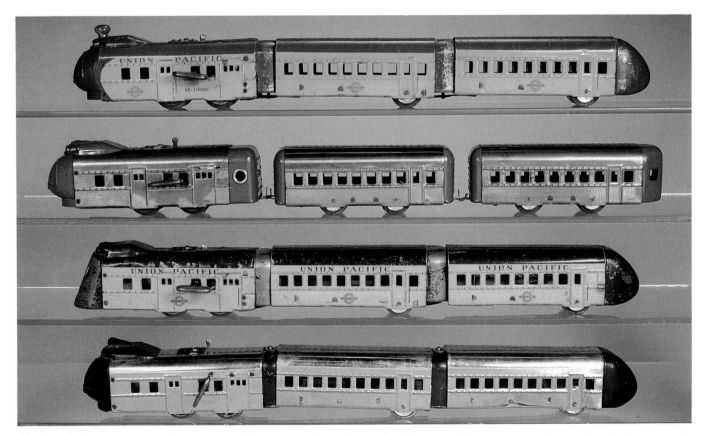

Top: Late production of the Union Pacific's M-10000 City of Portland streamliner with bulb protruding from the top of the motor unit. Second shelf: Nonarticulated green and gold M-10000 with cutout tail piece windows. Third shelf: Zephyr slant-nose streamliner. The Hafner Zephyrs are much more difficult to locate than the M-10000 bullet-nose style. Bottom: Chrome and blue M-10000 variation.

These were the two major vestibule-connecting types. Hafner did adopt a third form for joining its streamliners but this made the train nonarticulated. The motor unit had a formed sheet-metal end stamping with a weight inside, and an upturned regular Hafner passenger and freight coupler was inserted in the bottom of this end piece. Each of the passenger cars had rounded-edge tin pieces mounted at each end with the coupler at the bottom of each end. Thus, although such a set after a very quick look had the appearance of a streamliner, it was actually nonarticulated, and the cars were attached and pulled just as if they were coaches or freights being hauled by one of Hafner's steam locomotives.

In time, after doubtless hearing from many of its train purchasers, the Hafner company removed the casing holding the bulb. The bulb now protruded awkwardly from the top of the engine. Although realism was lost in this version of the streamliner, the bulb could be screwed in or out with ease, and perhaps this was also an economy measure.

The early nonarticulated Hafner streamliner coaches and observation cars and even some early freight cars have end pieces with a hole squarely in the middle. This hole serves no purpose in the finished product; it was simply left over from the tooling design process.

The power units of the nonarticulated sets came with one silver circular grommet on each side of the motor car's vestibule. Apparently the only articulated engine which has grommets on the body's sides is colored in copper and green.

Unlike the nonarticulated engines it did not have grommets embedded in the vestibule, but instead four silver grommets were placed in the windows of one side of the motor units and two grommets were used in the windows of the opposite side. These silver circular decorations gave the engine even more of a realistic streamline porthole appearance.

While prototype brown and yellow were the most common colors for the Hafner streamliners, the sets did come in a variety of shades. The most eye-catching were undoubtedly those which used chrome or copper plating. The sleek, shimmering glitter of the silver and gold had an immediately pleasing effect whether the train was racing around its track or simply gleaming from an original box or today on a collector's shelf.

Although made by Hafner a few years later than the M-10000, the slant- or shovel-nose Burlington Zephyr version was also produced starting in 1937. The engine's nose piece was made of stamped steel and riveted to the engine's body. The rear of the engine still featured a stamped-steel vestibule piece, but this version no longer coupled at the top. Instead the floor-type connection was used, the type developed on the later M-10000. Each unit had the extended floor piece with a hole on one end and the stud floor piece on the other end. Sheet-metal vestibules remained covering the floor piece connections so the train had a definitely articulated form. The Zephyr version was not illuminated and therefore did not have a battery unit in the nosepiece. This slant-nose style does not turn up too often at train meets today, which

Gd   Exc

probably indicates that not as many were produced and their manufacture came at the tail-end (no pun intended) of the streamliner boom period. It is curious, however, that for a time after World War II Hafner marketed a slant-nose streamliner set, obviously to use up prewar stock.

One of the most obvious aspects of Hafner articulated streamliners that have survived is the paint wear on the vestibules. As the trains were used and they sped quickly around the curves there was a heavy toll taken on the vestibule paint. Unless a set was rarely run and carefully boxed, the Hafner vestibules will show considerable wear, which in its own way is a tribute to their play value and the fact that Hafner trains were run and run and run to the joy and pleasure of countless children reared during the grand streamliner era of America's railroads.

STREAMLINER MOTOR UNITS

M-10000 BULLET NOSE POWER UNITS:
(A) Brown and yellow body; yellow vestibule with stud on top; battery holder; bulb encased in brown cover; "UNION PACIFIC" lettered in brown over the windows; bar and circle herald "HAFNER'S / OVERLAND FLYER / RAILWAYS" lettered in brown under front windows; "M-10000" lettered in brown under back side windows. Comes in two shades of yellow and the nose piece also can appear in two different shades of brown.   30   60
(B) Same as (A), but with brown vestibule and gold bulb cover.   30   60
(C) Same as (A), but with brown vestibule and silver bulb cover.   30   60
(D) Same as (A), but with brown vestibule and floor level coupler knob; no bulb cover.   30   60
(E) Same as (C), but without battery and bulb; open hole on top of cowl where bulb would protrude on a lighted model.
                                                        30   60
(F) Same as (E), but with yellow vestibule.   30   60
(G) Same as (A), but in red and white colors, red lettering, red vestibule, and with floor-level coupler knob. 30   60
(H) Same as (G), but "M-10000" lettering omitted.
                                                        60   120
(I) Same as (G), but in red and cream.   30   60
(J) Chrome and blue; blue vestibule with knob on top; bulb encased in blue cover, no lettering.   45   90
(K) Same as (J), but without battery or bulb; open hole on top of cowl where bulb would protrude on a lighted model.
                                                        35   70
(L) Copper and green coloring; green vestibule and floor-level coupler stud; did not come with battery or bulb; cowl enclosing bulb area has riveted detail; four silver circular grommets inserted in windows on left (key wind) side; two grommets in two windows on opposite side — only two windows on this right side, apart from door windows. 60   120
(M) Red and cream; no battery or light; cowl enclosing bulb area is riveted; vestibule is more squarish than customary and has two circular grommets on either side; upturned coupler attached to vestibule through slit at bottom. This vestibule and coupler style was used to pull the nonarticulated streamliner cars.   30   60

(N) Same as (M), but in red and white. This motor unit also pulled the nonarticulated cars.   30   60
(O) Chrome and red; no lettering; no battery or light; cowl enclosing bulb area is riveted; vestibule is more squarish than customary and has two circular grommets on either side; upturned coupler attached to vestibule through slit at bottom. This coupler form was used to pull the nonarticulated cars.   45   90
(P) Same as (O), but in copper and red, red vestibule and with floor-level coupler stud.   45   90
(Q) Same as (O), but brown and yellow; yellow vestibule; only lettering is bar and circle Hafner logo.   35   70
(R) Same as (M), but did not have the "M-10000" lettering.
                                                        50   100
(S) Same as (A), but with yellow bulb cover.   30   60
(T) Same as (M), but all red with no lettering.   60   120
(U) Same as (B), but with yellow window cowl piece under gold bulb cover.   30   60
(V) Same as (B), but chocolate brown nose and window cowl piece.   30   60
(W) Same as (A), but without battery holder and bulb.
                                                        30   60

ZEPHYR SLANT-NOSE POWER UNITS:
(A) Brown and yellow colors; brown front piece with three windows; brown vestibules and floor-level coupler knob; no battery or light; cowl encasing bulb area is riveted; "UNION PACIFIC" lettered in brown; bar and circle herald "HAFNER'S / OVERLAND FLYER / RAILWAYS" lettered in brown under front side windows; "M-10000" lettering in brown under back side windows.   40   80
(B) Same as (A), but in blue and yellow colors; blue front piece and vestibule; "UNION PACIFIC" lettered in blue; Hafner's bar and circle herald lettered in blue near front door; no other lettering.   50   100
(C) Same as (A), but in red and yellow colors; yellow front piece and vestibule. Hafner's bar and circle logo lettered in red near front door; no other lettering. 60   120
(D) Same as (B), but in blue and white; blue sides, white roof and vestibule; white front piece; pulled blue and white cars; other details not confirmed; reported by Alan Littlejohn.
                                                            NRS
(E) Same as (A), but with brown vestibules.   40   80
Note: A Zephyr set lettered "BURLINGTON NORTHERN" instead of the usual "UNION PACIFIC" has been reported, but no details have been forthcoming. Verification required.

STREAMLINER COACHES: The articulated coaches came with Type VIIa frames, while the nonarticulated cars had Type VIIb frames.
(A) Brown and yellow coloring, two wheels, yellow vestibule on back of car; stud on top; upturned tab roof coupler hole on other end of car; "UNION PACIFIC" lettering in brown over windows; bar and circle herald "HAFNER'S / OVERLAND FLYER / RAILWAYS" lettered in brown under windows. Comes in lighter and darker shades of yellow and brown.
                                                        15   30
(B) Same as (A), but with brown vestibule and floor-level coupler stud; extended floor-level coupler hole on other end of car.   15   30
(C) Same as (B), but no "UNION PACIFIC" lettering on the car.   40   80

	Gd	Exc

(D) Same as (B), but with yellow vestibules. **15 30**

(E) Chrome and blue; blue vestibule with stud on top; integral tab roof coupler hole on other end of car; no lettering. **20 40**

(F) Same as (E), but floor-level coupler stud under vestibule; extended floor-level coupler hole at other end of car. **20 40**

(G) Same as (F), but car is copper colored with green vestibule. **20 40**

(H) Red and white; red lettering; darker red vestibule and floor-level coupler stud; extended floor-level coupler hole on other end of car. **15 30**

(I) Yellow and blue; blue vestibule and floor-level coupler stud, extended floor-level coupler hole on other end of car; "UNION PACIFIC" and Hafner's bar and circle logo lettered in blue. This car appears to come mainly — if not always — with the shovel-nose Zephyr motor unit. **20 40**

(J) Red and white; has two darker red pieces with attached couplers; Type IV coupler; "UNION PACIFIC" and Hafner's bar and circle herald lettered in red; nine windows and one door window on each side. This car was used in nonarticulated streamliner sets. **20 40**

(K) Same as (J), but in red and cream; Type IV coupler. This car also used in nonarticulated streamliner sets. **20 40**

(L) Copper with green ends; Type IV coupler; couplers attached to end pieces; no lettering. This car was used in nonarticulated streamliner sets. **20 40**

(M) Yellow and red; yellow vestibule with extended floor-level coupler hole at other end of car; no lettering except for Hafner's bar and circle herald lettered in red. This is an uncommon car since the Zephyr set in this color is usually seen with just the motor unit and observation car. Al McDuffie has confirmed the existence of this coach. **NRS**

(N) Same as (B), but in copper and red; red vestibule and floor-level coupler knob; extended floor-level coupler hole and other end of car; no lettering. **30 60**

(O) Copper and red; red vestibule and floor-level coupler stud; extended floor-level coupler hole on other end of car; no lettering. **30 60**

(P) All red; couplers attached to end pieces; no lettering. Used in nonarticulated streamliner sets. **30 60**

STREAMLINER OBSERVATION CARS: The articulated observation cars came with Type VIIa frames, while the nonarticulated cars had Type VIIb frames.

(A) Brown and yellow; two wheels, darker brown bullet-nose tail piece; integral tab roof coupler hole on other end of car; "UNION PACIFIC" lettered in brown over windows; bar and circle herald "HAFNER'S / OVERLAND FLYER / RAILWAYS" lettered in brown under windows. Comes in lighter and darker shades of yellow and brown. **15 30**

(B) Same as (A), but with extended floor-level coupler hole on front end of car. **15 30**

(C) Same as (B), but with no "UNION PACIFIC" lettering. **40 80**

(D) Chrome and blue; blue bullet-nose tail piece; integral tab roof coupler hole on other end of car. **30 60**

(E) Same as (D), but floor-level coupler knob under vestibule. **30 60**

(F) Same as (D), but in copper with green bullet-nose tail piece. **30 60**

	Gd	Exc

(G) Red and white; red lettering; darker red bullet-nose tail piece; extended floor-level coupler hole on front end of car. **15 30**

(H) Same as (G), but nonarticulated; Type IV IV coupler in front end piece. **15 30**

(I) Same as (H), but in red and cream. **15 30**

(J) Yellow and blue; darker blue bullet-nose tail piece; extended floor-level coupler hole at other end of car; "UNION PACIFIC" and Hafner's bar and circle logo lettered in blue. This car appears to come mainly — if not always — with the shovel-nose Zephyr motor unit sets. **20 40**

(K) Yellow and red; pale yellow bullet-nose tail piece; extended floor-level coupler hole at other end of car; no lettering except for Hafner's bar and circle herald lettered in red. **30 60**

(L) Same as (K), but with dark yellow bullet-nose tail piece. **30 60**

(M) Copper and green; no lettering, green end piece with coupler in slot on bottom; other end has three punched-out windows in green circular observation tail piece. **30 60**

(N) Same as (M), but has green bullet-nose tail piece. **30 60**

(O) Copper and red with red bullet-nose tail piece; extended floor level coupler hole on front end of car; no lettering. **40 80**

(P) Same as (M), but no windows in tail piece. **30 60**

(Q) All red; no lettering; three punched-out windows in circular tail piece; used in nonarticulated streamliner sets.

Note: All observed Hafner streamliner coaches and observation cars have Type IV couplers. Given the vagaries of production expediency, this does not preclude some of these cars from having earlier or later style couplers.

Pricing Hafner streamliner sets is one of the most difficult areas of pricing due to the many combinations of variations possible, the varying numbers of cars per set, and the sets coming as both articulated (most desirable) and nonarticulated. Streamliner sets are often subject to inflated pricing; the following are guidelines for the most *typical* Hafner streamliner sets.

	Gd	Exc
M-10000, brown and yellow (including motorized units):		
three pieces	60	125
four pieces	75	150
five pieces	100	175
M-10000, chrome and blue:		
three pieces	85	170
four pieces	110	190
five pieces	130	220
Nonarticulated M-10000, red and cream:		
three pieces	60	125
four pieces	75	145
five pieces	100	165
Zephyr slant-nose, brown and yellow:		
three pieces	90	160
four pieces	110	190
five pieces	125	225
Zephyr slant-nose, blue and yellow:		
three pieces	100	180

CHAPTER NINE

★

LATER PASSENGER CARS

In William Hafner's opinion, the M-10000 and Zephyr streamliner diesel engine vogue was ending in 1938 (*Model Craftsman*, October 1951). He was talking only about the articulated power units and sets, however, because in 1938 his company began a whole line of nonarticulated streamline-style passenger cars. Again the precise year such cars appeared has been argued. At least one dedicated Hafner collector seems to remember these later cars appearing about 1935. John Hafner suggests 1934, but company advertisements presently available from that year do not picture any of the later passenger cars. The fact that such data are missing does not mean that such items were not sold since; for example, Hafner often omitted its one-piece cars from advertisements but sold them anyway. Material in the Hafner "Scrapbook" at the TCA Museum Library pinpoints 1938 as the date the long streamline passenger cars were first offered for sale.

When the late passenger coaches and observations were issued, they were not accompanied by baggage cars. Hafner apparently made no baggage cars after the early and mid-1930s. This is rather surprising since the play value of the train would be enhanced with a mail or baggage unit. Realism would be increased as well, but late Hafner production was not particularly concerned with true-to-life accuracy.

The later passenger cars continued the three-piece construction that had been derived from the company's articulated streamliner production. The long thin lithographed center piece was folded down and held together in the usual undercarriage manner. The two end pieces hooked into the center unit. Add wheels and couplers into the already precut holes and the complete car was formed. The same principle was applied to many of the late Hafner freight cars. Unlike the awkward appearance that some collectors feel occurs with the similarly constructed freights, the three-piece passenger cars seem better proportioned to the four-wheel arrangement.

The other feature that deserves to be emphasized is the considerable variety (one almost says "splash") of colors found on the late Pullmans and observations. John Hafner relates that in order to estimate the public's reactions to his company's product he used to take turns selling trains in various department stores when the regular employees would go off on their lunch hour. The major observation he made was that customers were attracted by the train colors, and so Hafner gave customers their color's worth. Of course this was not a new policy. It was a Hafner hallmark, products featuring a vast array of colors and mixtures of shades on its passenger cars.

In one of the merchandising news reports in an old issue of *Playthings*, a manager of Mandel Brothers Department

Store remarks that "bright colors have an irresistible appeal for the average child." He cited the example of a toy cannon the store was selling. One cannon was painted in realistic battleship gray, the other a flaming red. Mandel Brothers sold ten cannons in red for every one they sold in gray. The Hafner Company learned this lesson early, and as time progressed always embellished the concept of a variety of bright colors. In fact, Hafner was to produce some locomotives and sets with gold lacquer-coated wheels and track.

Undoubtedly the most attractive — and possibly the most popular selling passenger cars of the late period — were the colorful blue and cream Pullmans and observations. They were joined with a locomotive and tender in an extremely eye-pleasing set which Hafner specialist Dan Mordell has aptly described as "Hafner's Girls' Passenger Set." In his department store selling activity, John Hafner observed that many mothers bought trains for their daughters, and the blue/chrome scheme was the most appealing color to them.

The cars were headed by an attention-grabbing blue and chrome locomotive. Two parallel stripes ran the length of the passenger and observation cars' roofs so that the viewer's eye was immediately attracted whether he looked at the cars from above or from the sides. Furthermore, a decorative pattern of three blue stripes separated each of the six windows per car while uniting them in a blend of color harmony, seeming to give an illusion of speed, as well as the appearance of sleek, graceful streamlining. The chrome of the No. 1010 engine's sideboards added to this sense of speed and pleasing sight. The set spoke of grace, beauty, and rapidity.

Hafner added various other colors to similar passenger cars using, for example, red, green, and yellow. Hafner in typical economic fashion ingeniously used copper and chrome center pieces carried over from the M-10000 sets and matched them with colorful end pieces. When Hafner's No. 115041 yellow, blue, and silver locomotive appeared, it was joined with appropriately harmonious yellow and blue coaches. Even the No. 2000 engine was lithographed blue, red, and silver, given a metallic blue tender, and united with glittering blue and silver coaches. Whatever negative impression one might form because of a lack of realism, one could not but help be dazzled by the colors, and toy train buyers in considerable numbers could not resist.

By a somewhat strange irony, the Hafner Company — which began manufacturing trains in 1914, and had only passenger cars and sets in its line for approximately the first ten years of existence and then used the Bing Brothers Company's freight cars until it eventually created its own —

Gd Exc

ending thirty-seven years of producing trains with the emphasis on freights rather than passenger cars.

Freight units greatly outnumbered passenger sets in the last years of the company's existence. What is obviously the last catalogue the Hafner Company issued before its sale is a colorful four-page insert in the October 1950 *Playthings*. Four sets are advertised, and three of the four are combinations of freight cars. As John Hafner has noted, the last set the company made before it closed its doors was a freight consist. When Wyandotte took over the Hafner line, they produced freight sets exclusively.

MODIFICATIONS OF COACHES

In order to produce nonarticulated coaches and at the same time cut costs, the Hafner Company added two wheels to its streamliner coaches and changed the car ends by attaching two similar end pieces with couplers, thereby converting the cars into four-wheel Pullmans. These cars date from the late 1930s. Among these variants are the following:

PULLMAN: Late 1930s. Copper roof and sides; green end pieces; 6½" long; nine windows and one door window on each side punched out; two rows of rivets run parallel the length of the roof; Type IV couplers; Type VIIb frame. **20 40**
Note: This car was used with the copper-colored M-10000 nonarticulated streamliner sets and was later used in sets with the No. 1010 steam locomotive.

PULLMAN: Late 1930s. Chrome roof and sides; dark red end pieces; 6½" long; nine windows and one door window on each side punched out; two rows of rivets run parallel the length of the roof; Type IV couplers; Type VIIb frame.
20 40
Note: This car was used with the nonarticulated chrome M-10000 streamliner sets and was later used with the No. 1010 steam locomotive.

PULLMAN: Late 1930s. Red roof and cream sides; darker red end pieces; 6½" long; nine windows and one door window on each side punched out; two rows of rivets run parallel the length of the roof. "UNION PACIFIC" lettered in red over windows on each side; bar and circle "HAFNER'S / OVERLAND FLYER / RAILWAYS" herald lettered in red on sides; Type IV couplers; Type VIIb frame. **12 25**
Note: This car was used in nonarticulated sets with the M-10000 engine.

PULLMAN: Late 1930s. Red roof and white sides; darker red end pieces; 6½" long; nine windows and one door window on each side punched out; two rows of rivets run parallel the length of the roof. "UNION PACIFIC" lettered in red over windows on each side; bar and circle "HAFNER'S / OVERLAND FLYER / RAILWAYS" herald lettered in red on sides; Type IV couplers; Type VIIb frame. **12 25**
Note: This car was used in nonarticulated sets with the M-10000 engine.

PULLMAN: Late 1930s. Bright yellow sides and red roof; dark red end pieces; 6½" long; nine windows and one door window on each side punched out; two rows of rivets run parallel the length of the roof. "HAFNER STREAMLINERS" lettered in red over windows; bar and circle "HAFNER'S /

Gd Exc

STREAMLINER / RAILWAYS" herald lettered on sides; Type V couplers; Type VIIb frame. **20 40**
Note: This is a color variant that does not appear to have been issued in M-10000 or Zephyr streamliner sets but only with the No. 1010 locomotive.

NEW PASSENGER CARS

In addition to passenger cars converted from streamliner sets, Hafner developed longer (6⅞-inch), six-window coaches for use with its passenger trains. A Hafner folder lists the long streamline car as No. 405, but this number does not appear on the cars. These cars have Type VIIIa frames and usually come with Type V couplers. They are listed in roughly chronological order.
PULLMAN: 1938-1940s.
(A) Cream and dark blue; six windows and two door windows on each side; two white stripes and three blue stripes between each window; windows and door windows punched out; "PULLMAN" lettered in blue on white background over windows; "HAFNER'S / STREAMLINERS / RAILWAYS" bar and circle herald lettered in blue on white background and centered on sides; two white stripes dotted with upraised rivets run parallel the length of the roof; lighter blue end pieces. **12 25**
(B) Same as (A), but no rivet marks on roof. **12 25**
(C) Same as (B), but cream with light blue center piece and dark blue end pieces. **12 25**
PULLMAN: 1938-1940s. Cream and green; six windows and two door windows on each side; two cream stripes and three green stripes between each window; windows and door windows punched out; "PULLMAN" lettered in green on cream background over windows; "HAFNER'S / STREAMLINERS / RAILWAYS" bar and circle herald lettered in green on cream background and centered on sides; two cream stripes run parallel the length of the roof; darker green end pieces. **12 25**
PULLMAN: 1938-1940s.
(A) Cream and red; six windows and two door windows on each side; two cream stripes and three red stripes between each window; windows and door windows punched out; "PULLMAN" lettered in red over windows; "HAFNER'S / STREAMLINERS / RAILWAYS" bar and circle herald lettered in red and centered on sides; two cream stripes run parallel the length of the roof; darker red end pieces.
12 25
(B) Same as (A), but roof stripes are dotted with rivets. Although car says "PULLMAN" it has the circular three punched-out windows observation car tail piece. **15 30**
(C) Same as (A), but in red and gray. **12 25**
PULLMAN: 1938-1940s.
(A) Aluminum color; six windows and two door windows on each side; no lettering or herald on car; window and door windows punched out; two rows of rivets run parallel the length of the roof; slightly darker aluminum color end pieces.
25 50
(B) Same as (A), but all red with slightly darker red end pieces. **25 50**

Gd   Exc

PULLMAN: 1940s-1951.

(A) Silver with metallic blue; six windows and two door windows on each side; two metallic blue stripes and three silver stripes between each window; windows and door windows punched out; "PULLMAN" lettered in silver over windows; "HAFNER'S / STREAMLINER / RAILWAYS" bar and circle herald lettered in silver and centered on sides; two rows of upraised rivets run parallel the length of the roof; silver end pieces.   **12   25**

(B) Same as (A), but in dark blue.   **12   25**

Note: The earlier Hafner blue, red, and green No. 405 streamline coaches and the No. 406 observations contained the bar and circle herald lettered "HAFNER'S / STREAM- LINERS / RAILWAYS". At some point in the production, Hafner dropped the "S" in the herald, and "HAFNER'S / STREAMLINER / RAILWAYS" form was used. This change to the singular is particularly noticeable on the late produc- tion silver and metallic blue coaches and observation cars. However, the late 1930s bright yellow and red coach lettered "HAFNER STREAMLINERS" over the windows uses the sin- gular in the herald under the windows, demonstrating once again that consistency was not a Hafner characteristic.

2110471 PULLMAN: Late 1940s. Although essentially a No. 405-style car, the punched out windows are larger, and the car is numbered on each side. Like the No. 405 cars, it is 6⅞" long. Yellow and blue; yellow end pieces; six windows and two door windows on each side punched out; yellow window trim; "HAFNER TRAINS" lettered in yellow on blue background over windows; "PULLMAN" lettered in blue on yellow background and centered on sides; "2110471" lettered near the bottom of one door on each side; blue stripe with two rows of rivets runs the length of the roof. Type V couplers. Type VIIIa frame.   **30   60**

LATER OBSERVATION CARS

As was the case with the streamliner set coaches, Hafner took some of its streamliner observation cars and used them with its M-10000 nonarticulated sets. These cars date from the late 1930s, but were possibly at least in some color variations carried over in early 1940s production.

The length of the observation cars depends on the type of tail piece used. The windowless bullet-nose tail piece is ½ inch longer than the curved tail piece that has three punched-out windows. The overall length of the bullet-nose observation car is 7½ inches, while the curved tail piece-style measures 7 inches.

OBSERVATION: Late 1930s.

(A) Copper roof and sides; green end pieces; nine windows and one door window on each side punched out; no lettering on car; two rows of rivets run parallel the length of the roof; curved observation tail piece has two windows and one door window punched out; Type IV couplers; Type VIIb frame.   **20   40**

(B) Same as (A), but bullet-nose observation tail piece has no punched-out windows or door.   **20   40**

Note: In addition to its use in nonarticulated streamliner sets, this car appeared in some sets with the No. 1010 copper and green steam locomotive.

Gd   Exc

OBSERVATION: Late 1930s. Chrome roof and sides; dark red end pieces; nine windows and one door window on each side punched out; two rows of rivets run parallel the length of the roof; windowless bullet-nose observation piece; Type IV couplers; Type VIIb frame.   **20   40**

OBSERVATION: Late 1930s. Red roof and cream sides; darker red end pieces; nine windows and one door window on each side punched out; two rows of rivets run parallel the length of the roof; "UNION PACIFIC" lettered in red over windows on each side; bar and circle "HAFNER'S / OVERLAND FLYER / RAILWAYS" herald lettered in red under windows on each side; bullet-nose tail piece has no windows; Type IV couplers; Type VIIb frame.   **12   25**

OBSERVATION: Late 1930s.

(A) Red roof and white sides; darker red end pieces; nine windows and one door window punched out on each side; two rows of rivets run parallel the length of the roof; "UNION PACIFIC" lettered in red over windows on each side; "M-10000" and bar and circle "HAFNER'S / OVERLAND FLYER / RAILWAYS" herald lettered in red under windows on each side; bullet-nose tail piece has no window; Type IV couplers; Type VIIb frame.   **12   25**

(B) Same as (A), but "M-10000" lettering omitted on sides.   **18   35**

OBSERVATION: Late 1930s. Bright yellow sides and red roof; dark red end pieces; nine windows and one door window on each side punched out; two rows of rivets run parallel the length of the roof; "HAFNER STREAMLINERS" lettered in red over windows; bar and circle "HAFNER'S / STREAMLINER / RAILWAYS" herald lettered on sides; curved observation tail piece with two windows and one door window punched out; Type V couplers; Type VIIb frame.   **18   35**

Note: This color variant appears to have come only with No. 1010 steam locomotive sets.

Six-Window Observation Cars

These were six-window streamline observation cars, 6⅞ inches long, not used with the M-10000 or Zephyr streamliner sets. They were to accompany the catalogued No. 405 Pullmans. A Hafner folder lists this long streamline observation car as No. 406, but this number does not appear on the cars. These cars have Type VIIIa frames and usually come with Type V couplers.

OBSERVATION: 1938-1940s.

(A) Cream and dark blue; six windows and two door windows on each side; two white stripes and three blue stripes between each window; windows and door windows punched out; "OBSERVATION" lettered in blue on white background over windows; "HAFNER'S / STREAMLINERS / RAILWAYS" bar and circle herald lettered in blue on white background, centered on sides; two white stripes dotted with upraised rivets run parallel the length of the roof; lighter blue end pieces; curved observation tail piece with two windows and one door window punched out.   **12   25**

(B) Same as (A), but no rivet marks on roof.   **12   25**

(C) Same as (B), but cream with light blue center piece and dark blue end pieces.   **12   25**

Top: Chrome and red and cream and red coaches, which came originally with two wheels and one end cut off so they could be part of articulated M-10000 streamliner sets. Hafner later added ends and two additional wheels for use in nonarticulated passenger sets. Middle: Bright yellow and red coaches with "HAFNER STEAMLINERS" lettering over the windows. Bottom: All-aluminum lithographed coach; 102151 observation, one of the very few Hafner coaches actually numbered on the sides.

Top: Pullman and observation set in the long streamliner passenger car series. Middle: Cream and red Pullmans which came as a set. Note the second car has an observation car tail piece. Bottom: Silver and metallic blue set with the back of the observation constructed with a regular plain end piece without coupler hole.

Gd Exc

OBSERVATION: 1938-1940s. Cream and green; six windows and two door windows on each side; two cream stripes and three green stripes between each window; windows and door windows punched out; "OBSERVATION" lettered in green on cream background over windows; "HAFNER'S / STREAMLINERS / RAILWAYS" bar and circle herald lettered in green on cream background and centered on sides; two green stripes run parallel the length of the roof; darker green end pieces; curved observation tail piece with two windows and one door window punched out.   **12   25**

OBSERVATION: 1938-1940s.

(A) Cream and red; six windows and two door windows on each side; two cream stripes and three red stripes between each window; windows and door windows punched out; "OBSERVATION" lettered in red on cream background over windows; "HAFNER'S / STREAMLINERS / RAILWAYS" bar and circle herald lettered in red, centered on sides; two cream stripes run parallel the length of the roof; darker red ends; curved observation tail piece with two windows and one door window punched out.   **12   25**

(B) Same as (A), but roof stripes are dotted with rivets.   **12   25**

(C) Same as (A), but in red and gray.   **12   25**

OBSERVATION: 1938-1940s.

(A) All red with slightly darker red end pieces; no lettering or herald on car; six windows and two door windows on each side; windows and door windows punched out; two rows of rivets run parallel the length of the roof; three-window curved tail piece.   **25   50**

(B) Same as (A), but all-aluminum color; tail piece is the regular coach end piece without coupler hole.   **25   50**

OBSERVATION: 1940s-1951.

(A) Silver with metallic blue; six windows and two door windows on each side; two metallic blue stripes and three silver stripes between each window; windows and door windows punched out; "OBSERVATION" lettered in silver over windows; "HAFNER'S / STREAMLINER / RAILWAYS" bar and circle herald lettered in silver, centered on sides; two rows of upraised rivets run parallel the length of the roof; silver end piece with rivets; has regular coach end piece without rivets and without coupler hole rather than observation tail piece.   **15   30**

(B) Same as (A), but in dark blue; has coach rear end piece, but unlike (A) the end piece has coupler.   **15   30**

(C) Same as (B), but has rear regular coach end piece without rivets and without coupler hole.   **15   30**

102151 OBSERVATION: Late 1940s. Yellow and blue; yellow end pieces; six windows and two door windows on each side; windows and door windows punched out; yellow window trim; "HAFNER TRAINS" lettered in yellow on blue background over windows; "OBSERVATION" lettered in blue on yellow background, centered on sides; "102151" lettered near the bottom of the left door on each side; blue stripe with two rows of rivets runs the length of the roof; regular coach-type end piece — not observation tail piece. Verification needed on whether this car also came with three-window tail piece.   **30   60**

CHAPTER TEN

★

LATER FREIGHT CARS (1937–1951)

As did other toy producers, the Hafner Manufacturing Company plunged enthusiastically into the new age of the streamline train. From 1935 on Hafner produced streamline passenger sets by the thousands. In the excitement of this new development, it was only natural that the vogue would carry over to the freight car line. Consequently the ends of the cars were rounded and the roofs were curved in a very pronounced manner. Even the cupolas of some cabooses were given such streamlined styling that they could at first glance be mistaken for some other type car. In fact, Hafner went as far as placing the words "HAFNER STREAMLINERS" on the top of several of its freight cars.

Hafner constructed most of its late freights around a body stamping with integral unit of lithographed roof and sides. The body stamping was bent with a generous radius to form the sides and fastened at the bottom of the car center by a four-tab cross piece frequently embossed with the words "MADE BY / HAFNER / CHICAGO / U.S.A." Two separate curved-edge pieces were then attached at each end of the car. The couplers were connected to the end pieces while the axle holes were part of the body stamping.

Two Hafner freight cars — a stock car and a caboose — have high journal pedestals to hold the wheels. They are the same design of the pedestals found on the Sunshine Special passenger cars. These transitional freights illustrate a developmental move toward curved end piece construction which was to be a major feature of Hafner's late production.

31230 OVERLAND STOCK CAR: 1937-38. "OVERLAND STOCK CAR" lettered in red near the top of the car on each side; "M.C.B. AIR BRAKE" lettered in red to the left of the door at the bottom of the car; "31230" lettered in red to the right of the door at the bottom of the car; sides and non-punched-out doors lithographed to represent bars and slats for the cattle enclosure; red stripe at the bottom of the sides.
(A) Cream sides and red detailing; red roof; closed vestibule ends; 4⅞". (These attached vestibule pieces are similar to the "Sunshine Special" vestibules but have no opening for a door.)   **45   90**
(B) Same as (A), but dark red end pieces; no vestibules; 5¼"; has embossed rivets on sides of car and on roof; roof ends are curved as opposed to variation (A) because (A) has separate end pieces; Type IV couplers.   **45   90**

UNNUMBERED OVERLAND FREIGHT CABOOSE: 1937-38. "OVERLAND FREIGHT" lettered in red near the top of the car on each side; "HAFNER'S / OVERLAND FLYER / RAILWAYS" lettered in red in bar and circle herald at the center of each side; "CABOOSE" lettered in red underneath the herald; three punched-out windows on each side; low-slung cupola has no windows; red stripe at the bottom of the sides.

(A) Yellow sides and red detailing; red roof; closed vestibule ends; 4⅞"; square cupola sides with two punched-out windows on each side and one punched-out window on each cupola end; cupola roof curved; Type IV couplers.   **45   90**
(B) Same as (A), but dark red end pieces; 5¼"; no vestibules; streamlined cupola roof with no windows; Type IV couplers.   **45   90**

TYPE VIIIa FRAME FREIGHT CARS

Although Hafner's use of the high transitional pedestal was short-lived, the one-piece body stamping with the two separate rounded end pieces was continued and even expanded in 1938 to the 6¾-inch freights which bore the name "HAFNER STREAMLINERS" in large letters at the top of the sides. These cars, closely allied in appearance to the late streamline-style passenger cars, have aroused controversy because many collectors consider their structure awkward and unrealistic and too elongated in contrast to their short-spaced four-wheel separation. Dan Mordell notes that these cars are flimsy and are subject to tab loosening. Nevertheless, some collectors regard them as attractive freight car companions to the similarly constructed passenger car series.

It should be mentioned also that although these cars almost always come with Type V couplers, some have been found with Type IV couplers. The following listings follow the order of available Hafner *catalogue* numbers.

Stock Cars, Boxcars, and Cabooses

1350141 STOCK CAR: Listed in a Hafner folder as No. 401. "HAFNER STREAMLINERS" lettered in white on red background on the top of each side; "HAFNER'S / STREAMLINERS / RAILWAYS" lettered in white in bar and circle herald centered on the red lithographed doors; "1350141" lettered in red over the doors; doors not punched out; slats between sideboards are punched out; slots between sideboards are punched out; lithographed red ladders and rivet detail; three rows of red stripes run the length of the roof; two rows of rivets run the length of the roof.
(A) Off-white and red sides; dark red ends; Type IV couplers.   **20   40**
(B) Same as (A), but with Type V couplers.   **20   40**
(C) Yellow and red rivet detail; "HAFNER STREAMLINERS" lettered in yellow on red background on the top of each side; bar and circle Hafner herald lettering and "1350141" lettered in red on yellow background; dark red end pieces.   **23   45**

Gd Exc

(D) Same as (A), but cream and pinkish red color; dark red ends; no roof rivets.   **23 45**

Note: Although the parallel lines of rivets running in two rows the length of the roof of the 13789 boxcar and the 1350141 stock car have been listed, both cars came in some instances without these rivets. This same situation is evident with the long streamline Pullman and observation cars.

13789 BOXCAR: (A late 1930s-early 1940s Hafner folder lists this as No. 402.) "HAFNER STREAMLINERS" lettered in white on red background at the top of each side; "HAFNER'S / STREAMLINERS / RAILWAYS" lettered in red in a bar and circle herald to the left of the door; "AUTOMOBILES" lettered in red to the right of the herald; "13789" lettered in red to the right of the door; two rows of stamped rivets run parallel the length of the roof; six rows of red lithographed rivets run across the roof.

(A) White and red sides; dark red ends; white roof; red sliding doors; red door guides; Type IV couplers.   **9 18**

(B) Same as (A), but Type V couplers.   **9 18**

(C) Same as (B), but with green sliding doors and green door guides.   **9 18**

(D) Same as (B), but with silver sliding doors and green door guides. Punched-out door handles.   **12 24**

(E) Same as (B), but with copper-plated sliding doors. Dan Mordell Collection.   **12 24**

(F) Same as (B), but has no door guides; doors are merely punched out.   **15 30**

(G) Same as (B), but no doors or door guides.   **20 40**

(H) Same as (C), but with gray sliding doors.   **12 24**

(I) Same as (C), but with black sliding doors.   **12 24**

(J) Yellow and red with red rivet detail; "HAFNER STREAMLINERS" lettered in yellow on red background; bar and circle Hafner herald lettering, as well as "AUTOMOBILES" and "13789" in red on yellow background; dark red end pieces; green sliding door with red door guides; no rows of parallel stamped rivets on roof; six rows of lithographed rivets run across the roof.   **18 35**

(K) Same as (H), but with yellow sliding doors with red door guides.   **18 35**

3057 (LONG) CABOOSE: Hafner folder lists this as No. 404; there is a shorter caboose with the same 3057 number. "HAFNER STREAMLINERS" lettered in red on white background at the top of each side; "HAFNER'S / STREAMLINERS / RAILWAYS" lettered in white in bar and circle herald at the center of each side; four punched-out windows and two punched-out doors on each side; "3057" lettered in white both to the left and right of center on each side; "CABOOSE" lettered in white under the herald; red low-slung cupola has no window.

(A) Red and white sides and roof; dark red end pieces and cupola.   **10 20**

(B) Yellow and red; "HAFNER STREAMLINERS" lettered in red on yellow background; bar and circle Hafner herald as well as "CABOOSE" and "3057" lettered in yellow on red background; dark red end pieces and cupola.   **18 35**

Gondolas, Sand Cars, and Tankers

While the boxcar, stock car, and caboose fraternally and gaudily advertise their streamline status, the three freights associated with them — the gondola, sand car, and the tanker (all 6 inches) — are more conventional in design. The sand car, however, does have a pronounced V-shaped bottom rather than the typical square box railroad style. It should also be mentioned that some of the 91876 sand cars, some of the orange 1010 tankers, and some 3057 cabooses were produced with gold-colored wheels.

Hafner generally used the term "sand car" or "gravel car" for what would today be more commonly called a gondola. In an October 1950 Hafner advertisement in *Playthings*, the same car with different lithographed colors is called a sand car in one set and a gravel car in another set. Unlike the typical electric train set, windup sets could be taken outside and gondola-like cars could appropriately and easily be filled with sand or gravel. This feature enhanced play value as well as the year-round appeal of mechanical trains. This may be the reason that Hafner chose to emphasize sand and gravel terms rather than use the gondola designation; or perhaps Hafner was simply following the practice of American Flyer, which called their gondola-like freights sand cars, and Ives, which preferred the term gravel cars.

13788 GONDOLA: "13788" lettered in black to the left and to the right of center; "HAFNER'S / STREAMLINER / RAILWAYS" lettered in black in bar and circle herald at the center of each side; black rivet detail. (This car was apparently first produced in 1940, cf. *Model Craftsman*, May 1940.)

(A) Green sides with red ends and interior.   **12 25**

(B) Same as (A), but with red sides and "HAFNER TRAINS" lettered in black in a circle at the center of each side.   **15 30**

Note: From its slanted chute ends and general appearance, this car is referred to by Hafner collectors as a coal hopper. It certainly looks unlike a gondola, but an early 1940s Hafner folder refers to it as "No. 400 Gondola."

91876 SAND CAR: A Hafner folder lists this as "No. 407 Sand Car." "HAFNER / TRAINS" lettered in blue at the left end of each side; "HAFNER'S / STREAMLINER / RAILWAYS" lettered in blue in bar and circle herald at the center of each side.

(A) Gray and blue sides; blue lettering rivet detail; red end pieces.   **4 8**

(B) Same as (A), but with silver and black sides; black lettering and rivet detail; silver end pieces. Two of these same color cars often come in several freight sets. When the set is advertised, one car is called a sand car while the other is listed as a gravel car — but they are exactly the same.   **4 8**

(C) Same as (B), but with white end pieces.   **4 8**

(D) Same as (B), but with gray end pieces.   **4 8**

(E) Same as (A), but with silver end pieces.   **4 8**

(F) Same as (B), but with gold end pieces.   **6 12**

(G) Same as (A), but with green and dark brown sides; dark brown lettering and rivet detail; dark brown end pieces.   **4 8**

(H) Same as (F), but with chocolate brown end pieces.   **4 8**

(I) Same as (B), but with one white end piece and one gray end piece.   **6 12**

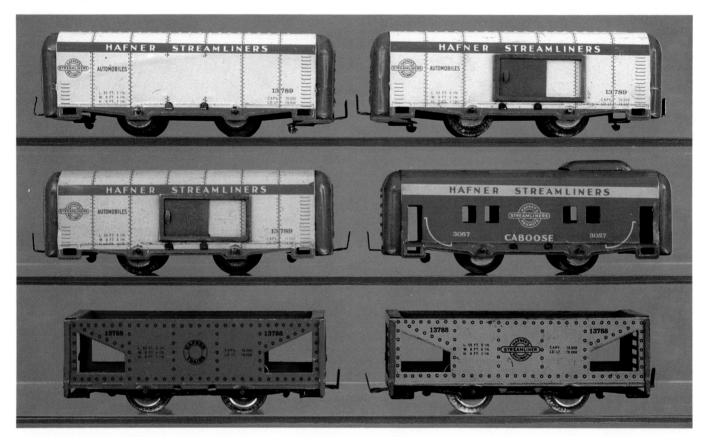

Top: Two versions of Hafner's 13789 streamlined automobile boxcar — rare doorless car; standard sliding door type. *Middle:* Yellow and red 13789 automobile car and accompanying yellow and red 3057 (long) caboose. *Bottom:* Two versions of what Hafner calls its 13788 gondola; collectors refer to these cars more appropriately, considering the shape, as coal hoppers.

Top: Orange BX 32 ATSF boxcar; brown 14825 ATSF boxcar. *Middle:* 3057 short streamlined caboose; 81932 Pennsylvania caboose. *Bottom:* 41021 colorfully lithographed caboose; 614333 Chicago & North Western caboose.

Top: White and chocolate brown 4825 ATSF refrigerator car; unnumbered yellow and red refrigerator car. Middle: Cream and brown 4825 reefer; unnumbered red, white, and blue refrigerator car. Bottom: X1357-90 cattle car.

	Gd	Exc
(J) Same as (B), but with off-white end pieces.	4	8
(K) Same as (B), but aluminum and black sides.	4	8
(L) Same as (G), but with gold end pieces.	5	10
(M) Same as (F), but with brass lithographed end pieces.	6	12

91746 SAND CAR: "HAFNER TRAINS" lettered in orange on each side; "HAFNER TRAINS" centered on each side in circular herald lettered in black on white background enclosing orange circle; "91746" lettered in orange to the left of center; black rivet detail.

(A) Yellow sides with orange and black trim; silver end pieces; silver inside. 4 8

(B) Same as (A), but with bright yellow ends. 4 8

(C) All-aluminum color without numbering or letters. 20 40

Note: For further, later variations of this sand car, see Chapter Twelve on Wyandotte trains. Wyandotte carried this car over into its line.

1010 OIL TANKER: A Hafner folder lists this as No. 403 tank car; "HAFNER" lettered in black to the left of the centered cut-out ladder; "NO. 1010" lettered in black to the right of the ladder; one center dome; cut-out railings extend along the sides from two holes (one on each side of the ladder) and attach to one hole at each end of the car.

(A) Silver with black detail; dark red dome and ladder; dark red end pieces. 6 12

	Gd	Exc
(B) Same as (A), but no railings.	6	12
(C) Same as (A), but with medium red end pieces.	6	12
(D) Gray with black dome; silver ladders; black end pieces; no railings.	9	18
(E) Same as (D), but with silver dome and gold end pieces.	9	18
(F) Same as (D), but with red dome, ladders, and end pieces.	9	18

(G) Orange with black detail; no railing; but two holes for railing remain on each side of red ladders; no holes in end pieces; red dome; silver end pieces. 6 12

| (H) Same as (G), but with white end pieces. | 6 | 12 |
| (I) Same as (G), but with silver dome. | 6 | 12 |

Post–World War II stock car. This is a very rare unnumbered and unlettered variant color version of the yellow-brown X1357-90 cattle car.

	Gd	Exc

(J) Same as (G), but with black dome and end pieces; black ladders. **6 12**

(K) Same as (G), but with silver dome; one white end piece and one gray end piece. **10 20**

(L) Same as (G), but with one white end piece and one silver end piece. **10 20**

(M) Same as (G), but with silver dome; gray end pieces. **6 12**

(N) Same as (G), but with gold dome; silver ladder. **6 12**

(O) Same as (N), but with white end pieces. **6 12**

(P) Same as (G), but with copper dome. **6 12**

(Q) Same as (G), but with pinkish red dome and silver end pieces. **6 12**

(R) Same as (G), but with copper dome; red ladders. **6 12**

(S) Same as (G), but with gray end pieces. **6 12**

(T) Same as (G), but with gold dome; gray end pieces; gray ladders. **6 12**

(U) Same as (G), but with silver dome; white end pieces. **6 12**

(V) Same as (G), but with white dome and white end pieces. **6 12**

(W) Same as (G), but with upturned notched Type III couplers. R. Lindsey Collection. **NRS**

(X) Same as (G), but with silver ladders and pinkish red dome and end pieces. **6 12**

(Y) Same as (G), but with silver ladders and gray end pieces. **6 12**

UNNUMBERED TANK CAR: Same shape and size as the No. 1010 tanker but has no lettering; silver with whitish-gray end pieces; red ladders; bronze dome; two holes on each side of cut-out ladders. **20 40**

PHILLIPS 66 TANK CAR: "Phillips / 66" herald lettered in orange and black to the left of the lithographed black ladder; "NO. 1010" lettered in black to the right of ladder.

(A) Orange and black; black dome; orange end pieces. **8 16**

(B) Same as (A), but has two holes on each side of the lithographed ladder. **8 16**

(C) Same as (A), but black end pieces. **8 16**

15731 TANK CAR: "Phillips/66" herald in black and silver centered on both sides of the car; "No 15731" lettered in silver to left of herald; two silver ladders lithographed on each side; two integral black domes at the top.

(A) Black and silver; black end pieces. **10 20**

(B) Same as (A), but with silver end pieces. **10 20**

TYPE VIIIb FRAME FREIGHT CARS

Although by virtue of their size and their overly evident streamliner lettering, the 6¾-inch freights are the most obvious of the later Hafner freight cars, several short freights were manufactured which are much more compact and realistic. These cars measuring 5⁵⁄₁₆ inches appeared both before and after World War II (although some were first produced after the war) and formed a better overall dimensional balance with the size of the engine and tender.

	Gd	Exc

With no catalogue numbers available, the following are listed by side-of-car number.

3057 (SHORT) CABOOSE: This is a scaled-down version of the 6¾" 3057 (Long) streamliner caboose which was produced to accompany the shorter freight cars. The bar and circle Hafner herald was reduced in size and the lettering at the top was altered from "HAFNER STREAMLINERS" to "HAFNER TRAINS". The use of the same number causes confusion; and, hence, the designations "Short" and "Long" have been selected to indicate the particular cars. "HAFNER TRAINS" lettered in red on white background near the top of both sides; "HAFNER / STREAMLINER / RAILWAYS" lettered in red in bar and circle herald at the center of each side; "3057" lettered in white to the left and right of the center; "CABOOSE" lettered in white in center under herald; three punched-out windows on each side; two lithographed solid doors on each side; low-profile cupola without windows; Type V coupler.

(A) Red sides and roof; dark red cupola and end pieces. **4 8**

(B) Same as (A), but aluminum end pieces. **4 8**

(C) Same as (A), but pinkish red end pieces. **4 8**

(D) Same as (A), but with brass lithographed end pieces. **6 12**

(E) Same as (A), but with gold lithographed end pieces. **6 12**

(F) Same as (A), but with pinkish red cupola. **4 8**

(G) No number and no lettering; completely red sides, roof, and end pieces. **10 20**

(H) Same as (G), but "HAFNER" embossed on both sides. **6 12**

(I) Same as (H), but one end piece has rivet decoration. **6 12**

(J) Same as (A), but black ends and pinkish red cupola. **7 14**

(K) Same as (A), but one red end piece and one black end piece. **10 20**

(L) Same as (G), but with dark red cupola. **10 20**

(M) Same as (A), but with pinkish red cupola and end pieces. **10 20**

4825 A.T.S.F. REFRIGERATOR CAR: "A.T.S.F. / 4825" lettered to the left of non-punched-out lithographed doors; unlettered Santa Fe-style herald lithographed to the right of the doors; "VENTILATED / REFRIGERATOR" lettered under herald; end pieces are lettered "A.T.S.F. / 4825" at the top and "HAFNER TRAINS" near the bottom; Type V couplers.

(A) Cream with light brown lithography. **6 12**

(B) Same as (A), but in dark brown lithography. **6 12**

(C) Same as (A), but with chocolate brown lithography. **6 12**

(D) Same as (A), but end pieces are lithographed in dark brown. **6 12**

(E) Same as (B), but end pieces are lithographed in chocolate brown. **6 12**

UNNUMBERED OVERLAND REFRIGERATOR CAR: "HAFNER TRAINS" lettered near the top of both sides; "VENTILATED / REFRIGERATOR" lettered to the left of the non-punched-out lithographed doors; shield herald to the right of doors; herald consists of three stars, six stripes, and

Gd Exc

the word "OVERLAND" slanted downward from left to right; no lettering on end pieces; Type V couplers.

(A) White, blue, and red with blue rivet details; white roof; dark red end pieces; "HAFNER TRAINS" lettered in white on blue background; "VENTILATED / REFRIGERATOR" lettered in blue on white background; shield herald has three blue stars, six red stripes, and "OVERLAND" lettered in white on blue background. **12 24**

(B) Yellow sides and roof with red trim and rivet detail; "HAFNER TRAINS" lettered in yellow on red background; "VENTILATED / REFRIGERATOR" lettered in red on yellow background; shield herald has three red stars, no stripes, and "OVERLAND" lettered in red on yellow background; mustard end pieces. **12 24**

(C) Same as (B), but with brass litho end pieces. **12 24**

(D) Same as (B), but with dark red end pieces. **12 24**

(E) Same as (B), but with yellow end pieces. **12 24**

81932 PENNSYLVANIA CABOOSE: "PENNSYLVANIA" lettered in black on both sides with black line over the word; "81932" lettered in black and underlined in black immediately below "PENNSYLVANIA"; three red and black lithographed windows on each side; black rivet details; one red and black lithographed door at each end with "81932" lettered in black over doors; black lithographed ladders and other details on each end; "HAFNER TRAINS" lettered in red on non-coupler end; low-slung streamlined cupola with two black and red lithographed windows on each side; Type V coupler.

(A) Dark red and black lithography. **8 16**

(B) Same as (A), but one end piece with rivets and coupler; other end piece plain red with no hole for coupler to protrude through. **10 20**

TYPE IX FRAME FREIGHT CARS

In the latter years of its existence the Hafner Company returned to the square-corner style for its boxcar, cattle car, and caboose. These cars are pictured in a Hafner freight set of 1949. Yet in the same circular issued by the Edward K. Tryon Company of Philadelphia, the short streamline refrigerator car and caboose were also shown in another freight set, so it is evident that the two different types of cars coexisted in the later years although in total numbers produced the square-cornered boxcars and cabooses predominated. Again, side-of-car numbers are used for the order of these listings.

BX 32 A.T.S.F. BOXCAR: "Santa Fe" herald in orange and white to the left of the doors; "A.T.S.F." lettered in white under the herald; "The / Grand Canyon / Line" lettered in white to the right of the doors; "BX 32" lettered in brown at the bottom to the left of the doors; sliding doors; brown rivet detail; "HAFNER TRAINS" circular herald lettered in black on white background enclosing an orange circle at each end; Type VI couplers.

(A) Orange sides; dark brown roof and frame; orange doors with fifteen lithographed horizontal lines to simulate door ribs. **6 12**

(B) Same as (A), but with plain dark brown doors and small "x" in "Bx 32" lettering; larger lettering for capacity, weight,

Gd Exc

etc., numbers; numbers to the right of the doors shift position — right column shifts to left column and left shifts to right; "cu. ft. 3826"; (on BX car "cu. ft." listed as "3926"); "HAFNER TRAINS" circular herald lettered in white on orange background enclosing a white circle at each end. **6 12**

(C) Same as (B), but with light orange sides. **6 12**

(D) Same as (B), but no doors. **4 8**

(E) Same as (A), but light orange sides and with fifteen lithographed horizontal lines on one door and thirteen lines on the other door, with ½" gap between four lines on top and nine lines on bottom. **6 12**

Note 1: The number of lines on the doors will change depending on the vagaries of factory lithography stamping.

Note 2: For further appearances of this car, see the chapter on Wyandotte trains.

X 1357-90 CATTLE CAR: "X 1357-90" lettered in brown near the bottom left end of each side; "HAFNER TRAINS" at each end in circular herald lettered in brown on yellow background enclosing a yellow circle; spaces between the slats are punched out horizontally; yellow sliding doors; Type VI couplers.

(A) Yellow sides with brown details; chocolate brown roof and frame. **12 25**

(B) Same as (A), but with white lithographed lines on doors to simulate door ridges. **12 25**

(C) Dark red sides and ends; no lettering; chocolate brown sliding doors; chocolate brown roof and frame. **18 35**

(D) Same as (C), but with white lithographed lines on doors to simulate door ridges. **18 35**

14825 A T S F BOXCAR: "Santa Fe" herald in white and chocolate brown to the left of the doors; "A T S F / 14825" lettered in white under the herald; "The / Grand Canyon / Line" lettered in white to the right of the doors; "Bx 32" lettered in white at the bottom to the left of the doors; sliding doors; white rivet detail; "HAFNER TRAINS" circular herald lettered in chocolate brown on white background enclosing a chocolate brown circle at each end; Type VI couplers.

(A) Chocolate brown sides, roof, doors, and frame. **6 12**

(B) Same as (A), but each door has nine horizontal lithographed lines to simulate door ridges. **6 12**

(C) Same as (B), but with black frame. **6 12**

(D) Same as (B), but with dark red frame. **6 12**

(E) Same as (B), but darker chocolate brown; one door has nine lithographed lines while the other door has eight lithographed lines. **8 16**

(F) Same as (B), but lighter chocolate brown; one door has nine lithographed lines while the other door has no lines. **8 16**

Note: The number of lines on the doors will change depending on the vagaries of factory lithography cutting. For further appearances of this car, see Chapter Twelve on Wyandotte trains.

41021 CABOOSE: "HAFNER TRAINS" lettered in white on each side; "HAFNER TRAINS" circular herald lettered in black on white background enclosing light red circle; "41021" lettered in white; four black lithographed windows on each side with lithographed figures of two trainmen in two windows; lithographed doors on each end; windows and doors not punched out; two lithographed windows on each side of

Two color variations of the 91876 sand car. Middle: 91746 yellow sand car; 91876 green sand car. Bottom: Orange and silver versions of the 1010 tank cars. The couplers on the silver tanker were turned down by a "runner" for more realism, an occurrence which occasionally is found with factory-issued upturned coupler cars.

Gd Exc

cupola; one lithographed window on ends of cupola; Type VI couplers.

(A) Light reddish sides and roof; dark red frame. 4 8

(B) Same as (A), but cupola has no windows. 4 8

(C) Same as (A), but dark red roof and cupola; cupola has two white and red lithographed shuttered cupola windows with three slanted lines on each side and no windows on ends; chocolate brown base. 4 8

(D) Same as (C), but with dark red frame. 4 8

Note: It seems probable that Hafner influenced Unique Art in the lithography form for the Unique Art Company's caboose. For further and later appearance of this caboose, see Chapter Twelve on Wyandotte trains. Wyandotte carried this caboose over into its line.

614333 CHICAGO AND NORTHWESTERN CABOOSE: "CHICAGO & NORTH WESTERN" lettered in white on the sides near the top; "CHCAGO / AND / NORTH / WESTERN /

Gd Exc

SYSTEM" herald lettered in white to the left of center; "614333" lettered in white at the center bottom of each side; four shuttered lithographed windows on each side; lithographed doors and end details on each end with "614333" in white over the doors; two lithographed windows on each cupola side; one lithographed window on each cupola end; Type VI coupler.

(A) Dark red sides and roof; medium red frame. 5 10

(B) Same as (A), but chocolate brown frame. 5 10

(C) Same as (A), but dark red frame; cupola has no windows. 5 10

(D) Same as (A), but with white and black stripes lithographed on roof and white rivet details on roof; plain black lithographed windows on cupola. (This type of lithographed roof usually comes with the "41021" caboose.) 10 20

(E) Same as (B), but no windows on cupola ends. 5 10

Top: Uncommon all-silver tank car with red ladder; orange 1010 Phillips 66 tanker. Middle: Black 15731 Phillips 66 tanker. Bottom: 1021 colorfully lithographed caboose; 614333 Chicago & North Western caboose.

CHAPTER ELEVEN

★

ACCESSORIES

Definitive information about some of the earliest accessories used with Hafner Manufacturing Company's trains is extremely difficult to obtain. Certain facts, however, do emerge.

The very first accessories that came with Hafner trains were pictured with train sets in the catalogues of mail order houses and were produced by a variety of firms. The 1916 Sears catalogue, for example, displays a Hafner passenger set with a bridge, a signal bridge with double arms, and what is called an "iron tunnel" — although more likely stamped steel is what is meant. On first glance the bridge and the semaphore appear to be made with Erector pieces. Closer examination indicates that the bridge and the semaphore are "made up of pieces from the American Model Builders Outfits." American Model Builder kits are listed for sale on a later page in this Sears catalogue. Such Erector-like sets were manufactured by the American Mechanical Toy Co. of Dayton, Ohio, whose kits were popular sellers in this period. In one year alone (1913) they advertised thirteen different sets of varying complexity. It is assumed that Hafner purchased these accessories from American Model Builder and supplied them with their train sets. Some collectors, however, suggest that the mail-order companies could have added these accessories.

In the Fall 1925–Winter 1926 Sears catalogue, a "complete railroad system," as it is designated, features a Hafner locomotive and tender with three passenger cars. In addition to the train and track, the following accessories are pictured: a passenger station, a tunnel, a double-arm semaphore, a clock attached to a pole, a crossing signal, a crossing gate, a whistle sign, and six telegraph poles.

The manufacturer of the tunnel appears to be the Kramer Firm of Chicago, and collectors of early toy railroad accessories will recognize that the passenger station was made by the J. B. Chein Company of Brooklyn, New York, and later of Harrison, New Jersey. All the other accessories (except the tunnel) have G-shaped bases and were produced by the Fergusson Company of Buffalo, New York. Dan Mordell calls these bases "pig-tail" because of their shape and the fact that they are formed integral with the heavy wire masts.

The six Fergusson accessories could be purchased from Sears separately — they were advertised in the previous year's (1924–1925) Fall–Winter catalogue. In the same year the tunnel, too, could be purchased by itself as could a passenger and a freight station. The stations were both produced by Bing, so the appearance of the Chein station is a surprise.

In the Fall 1926–Winter 1927 Sears catalogue, the "complete railway system" is again offered with the Chein station, the same Fergusson accessories, and the tunnel.

The same group of accessories is shown in the 1927–1928 Sears catalogue, but the appearance of the tunnel has changed, the six basic accessories appear as before but now with round solid bases, and what looks like a Hafner Glen Ellyn passenger station has replaced the Chein. The same group of accessories is pictured the following year, but a "9¼- inch metal water tower, with movable spout, finished in natural colors," has been added to the "whole railroad system." Ironically, the Chein station appears in both the 1928 and the 1929 Hafner catalogue sheets.

Given the embellishments and distortions that catalogue illustrators were, on occasion, prone to, it could be argued that the basic accessories shown were still made by Fergusson. It certainly would be much quicker for an illustrator to draw round bases than the curved G-shaped base that was always the Fergusson trademark. On the other hand, we know that Hafner (as John Hafner has psitively confirmed) produced, starting about this time, common railroad accessories with a round base and, shortly thereafter, with a square base, so apparently Fergusson was not involved at this juncture.

Besides the puzzle of what accessories were made *by* Hafner and what accessories were made *for* Hafner, the scenario just related becomes more complicated when we remember that a Hafner catalogue (usually dated about 1924 to 1926) features all Bing-made accessories. Hafner at this time made no freight cars of its own, so it purchased Bing cars as well as a considerable number of standard Bing accessories. How long Hafner used Bing accessories cannot be definitely established; some were sold at least until 1930.

There is no question that the first complete group of accessories Hafner used were German-made. What may have happened is that Hafner soon switched to accessories that were more prototypical of American railroads. For example, the Hafner catalogue featuring all Bing accessories advertised no crossing gate or double-arm semaphore. Both of these features would be basic to any American railroad layout.

The water tower is particularly puzzling. The ca. 1924–1926 Hafner catalogue pictures a Bing water tower which is described as "11 inches high." The actual measurement of the Bing tower is 9¼ inches, so the catalogue's accuracy must be questioned. The water tower used with the Hafner set in the Fall 1928–Winter 1929 Sears catalogue is listed as 9¼ inches high. Catalogue errors were not uncommon so it is likely the Bing tower was used in the earlier mid-1920s period.

The tower produced by Bing has the name of its manufacturer inscribed near the top in large letters. Was this lettering removed from the water towers that were sold by Hafner? The name Bing and its logo were not removed

Some of the Bing accessories sold with Hafner trains in the 1920s. Left to right, rear: 192 water tower, 619 larger single-arm semaphore, 62 single-arm semaphore, 29 crossing bell. Foreground: 621 freight station.

from the ends or bottom of the freight cars that Hafner sold. Did this situation also prevail with the tower, or was plain unlettered possibly orange lithography used for the Hafner tank?

The overall accessory situation is further complicated by an examination of the Fall 1929–Winter 1930 Montgomery Ward catalogue. This volume displays two Hafner trains — a passenger set and a freight outfit — with four accessories: a two-storied signal tower, a bridge, a semaphore, and a turntable. The signal tower is obviously Bing — the very same unit pictured in the mid-1920s Hafner catalogue featuring Bing accessories. The other three items are not shown in the Hafner catalogue, and although they are believed to be Bing, their appearance at this late date further complicates the issue. It is possible, of course, that Hafner used American- and German-made accessories at the same time, or perhaps mail-order houses used this mixture depending on economics and ready availability.

Some time between 1927 and 1930 Hafner began to produce its own accessories. The Glen Ellyn passenger station was advertised, and the five basic accessories (crossing gate, whistle sign, the clock, danger warning sign, and the double-arm semaphore) which had been sold in early years with Fergusson bases now appeared with circular bases and later with square bases. To these five are added telegraph poles which were first shown and advertised separately with G-shaped bases in the Sears 1924–1925 catalogue. Now they are pictured with circular bases similar to the other accessories.

Preserved in the TCA Museum Library is an undated Hafner sheet which advertises and pictures a box of ten accessories — five telegraph poles and the other five basic accessories mentioned above. The sheet notes that Hafner also makes accessories "like depots, tunnels, bridges, switches, extra track, freight cars, etc." On the same sheet, Hafner advertises a hydrometer to test automobile batteries.

Gd Exc

The clearest way to classify the various railroad accessories used by Hafner is to provide a three-fold division, first listing the Bing-made items used by Hafner; then itemizing unnumbered products with manufacturers in some cases unknown; and, finally, recording other accessories definitely made by Hafner.

EARLY ACCESSORIES USED WITH HAFNER TRAINS

These are Bing-produced items except where indicated otherwise. The numbers of all these accessories are taken from the *catalogue*.

St. 10 STRAIGHT TRACK: Each piece is designated with this number. Track, crossover, and the switches were made by Hafner. **.10 .20**

X 12 CROSSOVER UNIT: Consists of two straight pieces mounted on a metal platform. **.25 .50**

SW 16 SWITCHES: Consists of a left and right switch and listed as sold only in pairs. **1.50 3.00**

C 20 CURVES: Designation for each piece of curved track. **.10 .20**

24 ONE-ARM SEMAPHORE: Black base; black and white pole; red arm with white stripe. Not illuminated but has light housing behind the two celluloid windows; 15" high. Presumably this is the "No. 4514 Giant Lattice Girder Semaphore Tower" listed in a 1931 Hafner folder. **15 30**

29 CROSSING BELL: Bell is attached on the back of a railroad crossing warning pole; base lithographed in green and brown; bell has clockwork mechanism and tripper unit which attaches to track. When train passes over the tripper the bell rings. 7½" high. **25 50**

49 STREET LAMP: 6¾" high. **NRS**

62 SINGLE-ARM SEMAPHORE: Black circular base; black and white pole; red, black, and white arm that is shaped like a sideways V at the end. Arm may be raised and lowered by adjusting handle near base. 9½" high. **15 30**

70 DOUBLE-ARM CROSSING WARNING POLE: Both arms lettered "RAILROAD CROSSING" in black on white background; black square base; black and white pole; 7" high. **10 20**

192 WATER TOWER: Four gray legs and cross braces; black ladder and spout; red tank with stationary knob on top; 1½"-long lithographed gauge on side of tank; "Bing" lettered in white. A Hafner catalogue (ca. 1924-26) describes this accessory as "11" high"; all Bing water towers actually measure 9¼" high. A 1931 Hafner advertisement lists this as No. 3259 water tower, "over 9" tall," and "painted red and black." **20 40**

506 TUNNEL: 8" long; 7" high. **NRS**

508 TUNNEL: 13" long; 9" high. **NRS**

619 LARGER SINGLE-ARM SEMAPHORE: Black circular base; black and white pole; red arm with white stripe; two celluloid reflectors. Arm may be raised and lowered by adjusting handle near the base. 11" high. Listed in a 1931 Hafner folder as "No. 3115 Lattice Girder Semaphore Tower." **15 30**

Gd Exc

621 FREIGHT STATION: Freight platform has two steps on the left side of the building; sliding door has handle on left side; one lithographed window to the left of door and lithographed crane to right of door; "1000K" lettered in black over the crane; three lithographed windows on rear of building. The catalogue lists this station as 10" long and 3" high. Actual measurement is 10½" by 3½".

(A) Dark brown and tan lithography; dark gray base and platform. Maroon roof tiles with black detail. **25 50**

(B) Same as (A), but brown, red, and gray lithography; light brown base and brown platform. **25 50**

(C) Same as (A), but dark bluish gray roof tiles with black detail; handle on the right side of door. **25 50**

644 FREIGHT STATION: Listed in the catalogue as "larger size station"; has words "Freight / Station" lettered in white on dark background to the left of sliding door; crane lithographed to right of door; sloping runway leads to platform; 10½" long and 6" high. **45 90**

654 PASSENGER STATION:

(A) Dark green base; brown, green, and tan detailing; reddish brown tiled roof; green post; gray chimney; one hinged door in front; two hinged doors on side; one hinged door opening on a second-storied porch; 8¼" high by 6". **60 120**

(B) Same as (A), but came with light green base; light orange-brown tiled roof; tan post; greenish chimney. **60 120**

655 BRIDGE: Truss bridge with center piece and two sloped approach sections; 31" long. Appears in a later Hafner catalogue as Bridge No. 900. **NRS**

673 SIGNAL TOWER: Green and orange-brown base; green, brown, yellow, tan, and blue details; maroon roof; black chimney; outside stairs lead to second story; has a semaphore attached to base; semaphore arm can be raised or lowered by adjusting handle at the base of the pole; 7½" long. **60 120**

UNNUMBERED SCENIC BRIDGE: No number or precise description available; German-made, possibly Bing. Referred to in *Model Craftsman*, April 1948, p. 18. **NRS**

UNNUMBERED ACCESSORIES PICTURED WITH HAFNER TRAINS

TUNNEL: Catalogue lists it as "iron tunnel." **NRS**

BRIDGE: Produced from American Model Builders kit.

(A) 8" x 5⅛" x 4½" **5 10**

(B) 12" x 5⅛" x 4½" **10 20**

(C) 16" x 5⅛" x 4½" **15 25**

Note: Alan Littlejohn furnished the above measurements and noted that earlier bridges are not as wide. Two other AMB bridges actually found with old original Hafner sets measure:

(A) 12½" x 4¾" x 5⅛" **10 20**

(B) 16½" x 3½" x 5" **15 25**

TWO-ARM SEMAPHORE SIGNAL BRIDGE: Produced from American Model Builders kit; 10½" high. **NRS**

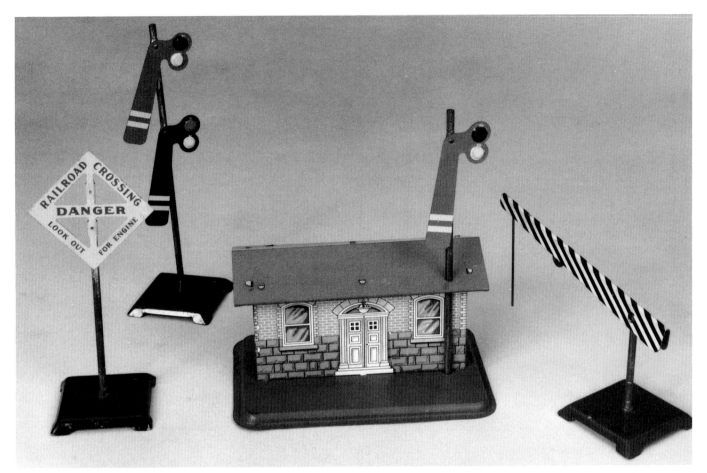

Hafner accessories used in the late 1920s and 1930s. Left to right: 121 danger signal, 125 double-arm semaphore, 400 Glen Ellyn passenger station with semaphore, 123 crossing gate. These accessories could be bought separately, but they were also sold together in the 1100 boxed accessory set.

	Gd	Exc
PASSENGER STATION: Produced by J. B. Chein Toy Co.	10	20

Note: The following six items were made by Fergusson: G-shaped bases. They came in a variety of colors, e.g., poles could be red, yellow, or white, or combine two colors.

	Gd	Exc
CROSSING GATE: Came with all-green or white/black striped gate with hanging red piece either in circle or lantern form.	2	5
WHISTLE SIGN	2	5
POLE WITH TWO SEMAPHORE ARMS	2	5
DANGER WARNING SIGN	2	5
CLOCK ATTACHED TO POLE: Number in Roman numerals; one red indicator hand arrow-shaped at end.	2	5
TELEGRAPH POLE	2	5

PASSENGER STATION: Described in the Fall 1927-Winter 1928 Sears catalogue as "6 by 4¼ by 3"". Although the measurements do not match, it appears from the drawing somewhat similar to the No. 400 Hafner Glen Ellyn Station. Dan Mordell believes the No. 400 station originated in 1930. Hafner advertised the Chein station in its 1928 and 1929 catalogue sheets, and this station appeared with Hafner sets in the Sears catalogues from 1924 to 1927. **10   20**

	Gd	Exc
TURNTABLE: This item and the two following accessories appear in the Fall 1929–Winter 1930 Montgomery Ward catalogue. They appear to be German-made, and it is theorized that Bing was probably the manufacturer.		NRS
SEMAPHORE WITH LADDER: One-arm type.		NRS
BRIDGE: Single span with two approaches.		NRS

HAFNER'S LATER ACCESSORIES

These are accessories actually made by Hafner or, in the case of the tunnels, produced specifically for Hafner. The pâpier-maché tunnels were made by Kramer in Chicago, who also sold similar tunnels to American Flyer.

	Gd	Exc
9 TUNNEL: 9" long; pâpier-maché.	4	8
50 TWO-PIECE ACCESSORY SET: Consists of danger sign and semaphore, which are also packed in the 1200 set. Complete boxed set.	20	40
65 TUNNEL: 8" long; pâpier-maché.	4	8
66 TUNNEL: 10" long; pâpier-maché.	4	8
67 TUNNEL: 12" long; pâpier-maché.	5	10
68 TUNNEL: 15" long; pâpier-maché.	6	12
69 TUNNEL: 18" long; pâpier-maché.		NRS

Hafner accessories of the late 1930s and 1940s. Left to right, rear: Freight station with sliding door, single-arm semaphore, passenger waiting platform. Foreground: Passenger station, danger signal. These accessories were sold together in the boxed 1200 accessory set. Note the elongated station style copied from Bing's freight station, and observe the base and lattice post similarity to Lionel's 68 warning signal and 62 semaphore.

	Gd	Exc

100 FLASHING SIGNAL: Square base; lattice pole; crossbuck lettered "Railroad Crossing" placed above a cross piece with flashing red lights; battery operated; pictured in ca. 1933 Hafner folder.   **NRS**

120 TELEGRAPH POLE: Silver pole; two yellow cross pieces; 8" high.

(A) Round lithographed wood-grained base.   3   6

(B) Same as (A), but unpainted pole with red cross pieces. R. Stekl collection.   2   5

(C) Same as (A), but with green base.   2   5

(D) Square green base with red cross pieces.   2   5

(E) Green base with silver cross pieces.   4   7

(F) Also came with dark gray and light gray round bases.   2   5

121 DANGER SIGNAL: Silver pole; "RAILROAD CROSS-ING / DANGER / LOOK OUT FOR ENGINE" lettered in black on white background; 6⅛" high.

(A) Round lithographed wood-grained base.   3   6

(B) Round green base.   2   5

(C) Square green base; red lettering; 6¾" high.   2   5

(D) Same as (C), but black lettering on gilt background.   3   6

(E) Square red base; black lettering.   2   5

122 CLOCK: Silver pole; black Roman numerals lettered on white background; "NEXT TRAIN LEAVES" lettered in black; movable hands, usually in red, but also found in gilt; 6⁵⁄₁₆" high.

(A) Round lithographed wood-grained base.   3   6

(B) Round green base.   2   5

(C) Square green base.   2   5

123 CROSSING GATE: Silver pole; black-and-white-striped arm with red circular warning piece attached to arm.

(A) Round lithographed wood-grained base.   3   6

(B) Square green base.   2   5

125 DOUBLE-ARM SEMAPHORE: Silver pole; red semaphore arm and green semaphore arm each with two white stripes; 8¼" high.

(A) Round lithographed wood-grained base.   3   6

(B) Square green base.   2   5

(C) Same as (B), but 9½" high. R. Stekl Collection.   5   10

	Gd	Exc

UNNUMBERED WHISTLE SIGN: Silver pole with "WHISTLE" lettered in black on white background; 6¼" high.

(A) Round lithographed wood-grained base. **3 6**

(B) Square green base. **2 5**

(C) Sam as (B), but "WHISTLE" lettered in brownish gold. **4 8**

200 WARNING BELL: Square base; lattice pole; lettered sign "RAILROAD CROSSING / DANGER / LOOK OUT FOR ENGINE"; bell attached at back of pole; battery operated; similar in appearance to Lionel No. 69 Warning Bell, but with only one bell; pictured in ca. 1933 Hafner folder. **NRS**

200 CURVE TRACK: The earlier catalogue listing was **C20.** In later advertisements Hafner used the No. **301;** still later the No. **911** was listed to designate a curve piece. Curve pieces came in regular size and were also eventually made in wide-radius form. **.10 .20**

201 STRAIGHT TRACK: The earliest listing had been No. **St.10.** Listed later by Hafner as No. **300** and still later as No. **910.** **.10 .20**

202 CROSSOVER: The earlier designation had been **X 12.** Listed later as No. **200** and then as No. **912** in the company's last years. The crossovers came in different degree forms. **.25 .50**

203 SWITCHES: Right and left switches always sold as a pair. Earlier listed as No. **Sw 16.** Hafner switches are later catalogued as No. **100,** and still later as No. **913.** **1.50 3.00**

400 PASSENGER STATION WITH SEMAPHORE ARM SIGNAL: Two windows and a center door lithographed on both the front and back of the station. "WAITING ROOM" lettered in black over the doors. One window and a clock lithographed on each end; "GLEN ELLYN" lettered in black over the clocks. Hole in base and roof to hold pole with semaphore arm, which comes in either red or green with two white stripes. The semaphore piece is frequently missing. In some instances the paint condition of the areas surrounding the holes suggests that on occasion the station was sold without the semaphore arm. 6⅝" by 3⁷⁄₁₆". This 400 station was sold throughout the 1930s and was copied from American Flyer's No. 90 station.

Note: In an interview given by John Hafner to Eric Buckley, Mr. Hafner noted that the "Glen Ellyn" name was chosen because he lived in that Chicago suburb and that the lithography was produced by the American Can Co. (*TCQ*, April 1969).

(A) Red base and roof; red brick litho; stone litho in cream. **10 20**

(B) Same as (A), but with green roof and orange brick lithography. **10 20**

(C) Same as (A), but with light gray stone lithography. **10 20**

(D) Same as (A), but with dark gray stone lithography. **10 20**

(E) Green base and roof; brick litho in orange; dark gray stone lithography. **10 20**

(F) Yellow base and roof; brick litho in orange; dark gray stone lithography. **12 24**

(G) Pea green base and roof; brick litho in fire red; dark gray stone lithography. **10 20**

(H) Dark chocolate base and roof; brick litho in orange; bluish gray stone lithography. **12 24**

(I) Orange base; dark blue roof; brick litho in light blue; light gray stone lithography. **10 20**

(J) Yellow base; pea green roof; brick litho in orange; light gray stone lithography. **12 24**

Note: Dan Mordell has observed that this station can also be found with roofs in gray or blue; base colors in tan or orange; brick litho in light blue; and stone litho in light aqua as well as in three shades of gray.

No. 500 BRIDGE: Red enamel truss bridge; 9½" long. Louis Hertz records that this bridge was first produced in 1940 (*Model Craftsman*, May 1940). **20 40**

1100 ACCESSORY SET: Hafner marketed a boxed accessory group consisting of the No. 400 Glen Ellyn passenger station with attached semaphore and three of their most popular accessories: No. 121 danger signal; No. 123 crossing gate; No. 125 double arm semaphore. These are the square-based Hafner products rather similar to the early Fergusson units but without the G-shaped bases.

Value for complete boxed set: **25 50**

1200 ACCESSORY SET: In the late 1930s Hafner produced its No. 1200 accessory set consisting of three new stations and a new danger signal and semaphore.

Value for complete boxed set: **50 100**

DANGER SIGNAL: Red base; yellow latticework mast, brass finial. "RAILROAD CROSSING / DANGER / LOOK OUT FOR ENGINE" lettered in black on white background; 8¾" high. **8 15**

Note: Base and lattice post of this accessory as well as of the accompanying semaphore appear to be duplicates of Lionel items. The danger signal resembles the Lionel No. 68 Warning Signal. Some train historians feel that Lionel may have made these two accessories for Hafner, but John Hafner contends that the similarity is a coincidence. The diamond-shaped signs of the two signals do differ in design and lettering. These two lattice post Hafner accessories appeared for the first time in 1939 (see *Model Craftsman*, June 1939).

SEMAPHORE: Red base; yellow latticework mast; brass finial; red semaphore arm with two white stripes; 8¾" high. Operates manually with lever on base. Similar to Lionel No. 62 Semaphore. **8 15**

PASSENGER STATION: Two doors and three twelve-pane windows lithographed on front; three twenty-pane windows lithographed on rear; "GLEN ELLYN" lettered in blue on off-white on each end; one circular window lithographed on each end; 9⅝" long, 3¼" high, and 3¼" wide.

(A) Blue, off-white lithography; red base and roof. **10 20**

(B) Same as (A), but with reddish cream lithography; plain red ends. **10 20**

(C) Same as (B), but with red and tan lithography; yellow base; light green roof. R. Stekl Collection. **10 20**

PASSENGER WAITING STATION: Roofed platform with two benches and three stanchions; 9⅝" long, 3¼" high, and 3⅛" wide.

(A) Red base and roof; gray benches; yellow stanchions. **10 20**

(B) Same as (A), but with red stanchions. **10 20**

	Gd	Exc
(C) Same as (B), but with gray benches.	10	20
(D) Same as (A), but with green roofs and benches; yellow stanchions.	10	20
(E) Yellow base; green roof; red benches and stanchions.	10	20
(F) Same as (A), but with gray benches and green stanchions.	10	20
(G) Same as (A), but with green benches and stanchions.	10	20

FREIGHT STATION: Red and yellow lithography; two lithographed twenty-pane windows on front, and three on back; large centered sliding door; "GLEN ELLYN" lettered in red on yellow background on each end; one circular window lithographed on each end; 9⅝" long, 3¼" high, and 3⅛" wide.

	Gd	Exc
(A) Red base and roof; red platform; silver door.	10	20
(B) Same as (A), but with red metallic platform.	10	20
(C) Same as (A), but with silver platform.	10	20
(D) Same as (A), but with light cream sides and copper platform.	10	20
(E) Same as (A), but with green platform.	10	20

	Gd	Exc
(F) Red and dark yellow lithography; two lithographed square eight-pane windows in front and two on back; punched-out door; plain red ends; yellow base; green roof; plain red platform.	10	20
(G) Same as (F), but with green base.	10	20
(H) Same as (F), but with silver door.	10	20

Note: Al McDuffie has pointed out to me in personal correspondence that the three narrow, elongated stations described above were Hafner's variation of Bing's No. 621 freight station.

START-STOP TRACK UNIT (Unnumbered): Advertised as making "switching and station stops possible for more realistic performance." Unit attaches to track and has hand lever which raises and lowers a square center piece to stop or release the locomotive. **1** **2**

3011 FENCE: Listed in a 1931 Hafner folder and described as having "30 pieces, nearly 12 feet; two gateways." The fence's purpose is to "keep the cows off your track." Further information requested about this accessory. **NRS**

CHAPTER TWELVE

★

THE WYANDOTTE TRAIN STORY

The All Metal Products Company of Wyandotte, Michigan, was organized in the autumn of 1920 by George Stallings and William F. Schmidt for the purpose of manufacturing automobile parts. The following year, however, the firm turned its attention to making toy pop guns and air rifles; thus, the "Wyandotte Toys" line was born. By the end of the 1920s the popularity of its products was so widespread that the company was then the world's largest manufacturer of toy guns.

Additional products — stamped-steel automobiles, trucks, airplanes, pull toys, etc. — were developed, and in 1935 the company produced more than 12,500,000 toys. Material from the Wyandotte Historical Society notes that the toys "were made from salvage sheets and strip metal sent directly from automobile manufacturers." It is further observed that the "factory used 1,000 tons of metal every month."

Pop gun-type pistols and rifles were very popular during the 1920s, 1930s, and 1940s as make-believe soldiers, cops and robbers, and cowboys and Indians shot it out with one another. All Metal also sold thousands upon thousands of cars, trucks, and airplanes. They produced a very collectible toy replica of the Ford coupe automobile and built several sets of various cars pulling miniature mobile homes. When Pan American Airways inaugurated the famous China Clipper flights to the Far East, All Metal sold a model of this plane that became another best seller. A later model of a United Airlines DC-4 Super Mainliner also had considerable appeal.

When World War II arrived, the supply of steel for toys was stopped so part of the company made wooden toys and the rest of the plant made clips for repeating rifles for the army. The firm received a citation from the War Department for its reliable military work.

In 1951 C. Lee Edwards, who had taken over the presidency of the company in 1932, sold his interest to others, and William Wenner became the president of All Metal. In the meantime a new policy of diversification was instituted, and in 1950 an additional plant was built in Piqua, Ohio, to produce die-cast and plastic toys. The purchase of Hafner trains in 1951 was in line with this philosophy of diversification to increase sales volume.

The May 1951 issue of *Playthings* (page 82) announced that Wyandotte had "acquired all rights to the well-known line of Hafner mechanical trains from the Hafner Manufacturing Co., Chicago."

The same issue of *Playthings* provided further details of the acquisition of Hafner: "The Hafner company decided to discontinue their manufacture and to liquidate its business by public auction at the end of March. For the past five years All Metal Products had been the sole distributor of Hafner mechanical trains and during that time it had an opportunity to analyze the line and its potential market; it came to the conclusion that it would be an excellent addition to its present lines of Wyandotte toys and Hopalong Cassidy guns and holster sets." Before Hafner's announced public auction could take place, All Metal purchased the company. It was announced that "Ultimately All Metal Products plans to produce the line in its own factory." The early 1950s were difficult for toy manufacturers because of the Korean War. The government put restrictions on the availability and use of raw materials, so All Metal Products in this respect did not purchase Hafner at the most ideal time.

Besides the track, Wyandotte continued at least six specific Hafner train items: the colorful No. 115041 yellow, blue, and silver streamlined-style locomotive, the matching 78100 tender, the 91746 sand car, two boxcars (the BX 32 and the 14825 Santa Fe), and the 41021 caboose.

For a time Wyandotte continued to use the same Hafner styles and lithography. The Hafner name was retained on all six pieces. After using up the Hafner inventory stock, Wyandotte added its own circular toy logo on the boiler front of the 115041 locomotive and on the sides of the sand car and caboose. To the end of its existence however, the Hafner name was so respected that even in boxed sets the lettering "HAFNER MECHANICAL TRAIN" was emphasized although the final set boxes added, "It's a Wyandotte Toy."

The most significant early change occurred when Wyandotte produced a new windup motor for the locomotive. This motor was narrower and ½ inch longer than the standard Hafner motor. The new slip-on key mechanism was shifted to the right side of the boiler, replacing the threaded key that wound the motor from the left side in traditional Hafner fashion. The motor was still attached by a screw at the top of the boiler, but since the motor was set back further, the brake lever now protruded from the cab roof instead of from the boiler top. The new Wyandotte motor, while serviceable, was more cheaply made than the reputable Hafner mechanism, so economics played the principal role in this change. Economy was achieved with die-cast gears replacing Hafner's machined brass counterparts.

At first Wyandotte used up the Hafner body and motor inventory on the 115041 locomotive; then it inserted its own motor, added its logo to the boiler front and soon deleted the lettering "BUILT BY / HAFNER TRAINS / CHICAGO, ILL. / USA" from near the bottom of the engineer's cab.

In 1955 Wyandotte produced its own totally new lithographed locomotive. The Hafner Hiawatha engine style remained the same; only the lithography was different. The new engine colors were black, red, and silver; "WYANDOTTE RAILWAY" was lettered on the boiler sides while "W.R.L. 970" was lettered under the cab. An Indian's head

Wyandotte set 2158 with 970 locomotive and 3689 bell tender. BX 32 Santa Fe boxcar, unnumbered sand car, and 41021 caboose. The box top was designed with a bend and a cut-out portion so that when the top was lifted it could be turned into an eye-catching display on a store counter.

surrounded by feather decorations was lithographed on the boiler front. This locomotive was initially produced with Hafner-type stamped metal, closed eight-spoke wheels, but eventually black plastic wheels were substituted as another economy measure. This engine came with and without a working battery-powered headlight. A matching black, red, and silver tender was designed to accompany the locomotive. The tender was lettered "W.R.L. 3689". This tender came with and without an underneath track-activated bell and clapper. Wyandotte's new slightly longer motor set further in the rear of the engine prevented the bell and clapper from being placed under the engineer's cab as had been the practice with Hafner bell locomotives. The W.R.L. 3689 tender first appeared with stamped-metal wheels, but later plastic wheels were used.

Wyandotte continued to sell trains as part of its toy line in the 1950s, but advertising emphasis was put on other toys, such as the Hopalong Cassidy outfits, and steel fire trucks, dump trucks, road graders, and moving vans. Wyandotte also stressed its toy lawn mowers, garden shovels, and rakes.

The Toy Yearbook for 1953–54, the official publication of the Toy Guidance Council, and called by *Forbes* magazine "The Social Register of Toyland," advertised and pictured a "Hafner Five-unit Mechanical Freight Train with Crossover." The advertisement, under a Wyandotte Toys heading, read: "Automatic start-stop attachment enables switching and stopping. Banked track prevents jumping of train. Engine has electric headlight and ringing bell. Sturdy metal construction, with special tempered steel spring clock mechanism. Complete with crossover, and 16 sections of

track — 4 straight, 12 curved. $4.95". Pictured were the 115041 engine and its matching color tender, the 91746 sand car, the 14825 Santa Fe boxcar, and the 41021 caboose. A four-unit set — without the boxcar — was also available. Unless the ad used is an old photo cut, the illustration and copy suggest that Wyandotte was still using the Hafner motor during these years. *The Toy Yearbook for 1955–56*, which pictures the set without the boxcar, indicates that the Wyandotte motor is now in use in the 115041 locomotive.

In order to save money and achieve a tax write-off, All Metal built a new plant in Piqua, Ohio, and shut down its operations in Wyandotte. An announcement in a 1955 issue of *Playthings* declared: "Now, Wyandotte, a great name in toys for more than 33 years — is consolidating all factories and general offices in one huge, greatly enlarged plant in Piqua, Ohio."

The All Metal Products Company carried on a vigorous advertising campaign in 1956, but again the emphasis was on its non-train toy items. Dump trucks, bulldozers, a super-tractor, and similar automotive toys were listed, and there was much ballyhoo for Robo, the robot pup, who wagged his tail, rolled his eyes, moved his jaw, and even yipped. The A. S. Groff store Christmas 1956 catalogue, however, pictures the five-unit train set and also advertises the same set without a boxcar.

A news item in the November 1956 issue of *Playthings* announced a heavy ad campaign to reach the Christmas toy market, including ads on station WPIX's TV show "Shain and Her Friends" (the story pictured Shain holding a puppet and a Wyandotte dump truck), and forty live spot notices on WABC-TV's "Romper Room" program. Charles A. Brethren, at one time the General Manager and Secretary-Treasurer of All Metal, relates the last part of the firm's history in a talk that was given at the Wyandotte Historical Society:

> In 1956, All Metal, whose worth was six and one half million, borrowed 2½ million without security. On Nov 1, 1956 the New York banks demanded their money at once. The Company could not meet these demands and was forced into bankruptcy. As a postscript to the All Metal saga, Mr. Harry Rouse, the last president of the company said there was absolutely no reason for the company to go into bankruptcy. The principal competitor of All Metals, at this time, was the Marx Toy Co. All Metals asked for five years to repay the loan. All the other banks were agreeable, except the Corn Exchange Bank of New York. The reason for this refusal was that a member of the Board of Directors of the Bank was one of the Marx family, who saw a golden opportunity to legally eliminate a competitor.[1]

On December 7, 1956, All Metal filed for protection under Chapter XI of the Bankruptcy Act. According to a news story in the *Wyandotte News-Herald*, All Metal's problems began when President William Wenner protested the replacement of the firm's sales manager, Al Smith, by Phil Haskill. Supposedly, this led Wenner to leave Wyandotte and join the Structo Toy Co.

Another view attributes the company's troubles to the construction of all the firm's facilities in Piqua, Ohio. Plant construction and deliveries were inadequate although sales levels were reputed as most satisfactory. In March of 1957 stockholders met to see if the company could be pulled out of

Gd Exc

its bankruptcy status, but the effort was unsuccessful. Thus, although an All Metal Products Company business card ad ran in the January, February, March, and April 1957 issues of *Playthings*, the Wyandotte toy story ended except for collectors of the toys themselves.

After the All Metal Company could not resolve its bankruptcy, the dies, tooling, and similar materials were, as recorded by Eric J. Matzke in his book *Greenberg's Guide to Marx Trains*, Vol. I (page 29), purchased by Marx and then shipped to Mexico. As Matzke observes, Louis Marx did not want this inventory falling into the hands of a competitor.

Several years ago Dr. Maurice Demers made a fascinating discovery in regard to this Marx takeover. As he reported in a *TTOS Bulletin* article (February 1980), he found at York a Wyandotte boxed set that contained a Marx number 37961 Pennsylvania "Merchandise Service" boxcar. This is the regular red PRR Marx boxcar, but in this case the car had Hafner upturned couplers. These couplers had been carried over by Wyandotte in its own line. This boxcar was obviously added by Marx when they bought out the Hafner-Wyandotte tools and dies to complete sets and reduce some leftover Wyandotte inventory. In his *Greenberg's Guide to Marx Trains*, Matzke records that this red Pennsylvania boxcar came in sixteen different number variations — from 37960 to 37975. Dr. Demers' car is lettered 37967, and the author has in his collection two other Marx PRR boxcars with Hafner couplers — a number 37961 and a 37971. Thus it appears likely that this car may have been produced by Marx with Hafner-Wyandotte couplers in all sixteen number variations and perhaps even in the unnumbered form (cf. *TTOS Bulletin*, November–December 1989). Marx also may have used some of its own track to complete Wyandotte sets. (cf. *TTOS Bulletin*, July 1992.)

So the Hafner coupler at least lived on for a time in the Marx line, and, as Eric Matzke points out, the Hafner-Wyandotte line appeared in limited form in Mexico as part of the Plastimarx production. Since windup trains were more popularly priced and also because of limited availability of electricity in various areas of Mexico in the 1950s, windup trains there had a special appeal. Undoubtedly, some of these trains can be found today still running at Christmas at least — south of the border, "down Mexico way."

115041 ENGINE

(A) Yellow, blue, and silver lithography; "HAFNER TRAINS" circular logo under engineer's cab, black lettering on white circle with pinkish orange circle in the middle; "HAFNER TRAINS" lettered in white on the boiler sides; "115041" lettered in white on the front of the boiler sides and also on the roof at the rear of the cab; "HAFNER TRAINS" circular logo lettered in black on the boiler front; "BUILT BY / HAFNER TRAINS / Chicago, Ill. / U.S.A." lettered in black at the bottom of the cab. "ON" and "OFF" lettered at the bottom of the boiler front on either sides of the lever which regulates the headlight. Hooded socket holding bulb at the top of the boiler front; battery holder attached to inner part of the boiler front; "KEEP OUT" lettered in black at bottom of cab door. Some engines had eyelets to hold shell and battery, and had silver headlight hoods. Some engines used rivets. Late 115041 locomotives usually had black headlight hoods.
                                                                    15   30

Gd Exc

Note: Wyandotte first used this locomotive with the Hafner motor; later when Wyandotte developed its own windup mechanism, their motor was put into the Hafner engine shell.

(B) Similar to (A), but "WYANDOTTE TOYS / MADE / IN / USA" herald lettered in black in circle on boiler front replacing "HAFNER TRAINS" lettering there; "BUILT BY / HAFNER TRAINS / CHICAGO, ILL / U.S.A." deleted; "ON" and "OFF" lettered at the bottom of the boiler front but no slit for light switch; no headlight and no opening for light at the top of the boiler front; no battery holder. First came with Hafner motor, later with Wyandotte motor.   **15   30**

(C) Same as (B), but with lighter blue striping.   **15   30**

(D) Same as (B), but has light switch protruding from the boiler front; hooded socket holding bulb at the top of the boiler front; battery holder attached to inner part of boiler front. First came with Hafner motor, later with Wyandotte motor.   **15   30**

970 WYANDOTTE ENGINE

(A) Black, dark red, and silver lithography with silver detailing; "WYANDOTTE RAILWAY" lettered in white on each side; "W.R.L. 970" lettered in white under engineer's cab; Indian head with feather decorations on each side of head on the boiler front; lithographed lens at the top of the boiler front; no battery.   **10   25**

(B) Same as (A), but has hooded socket holding bulb at the top of the boiler front. Lever at the bottom of the boiler front to turn light on and off. Battery holder attached to the inner section of the boiler front. Usually has two-piece lead weight riveted under the cab, but some engines added three or four lead weights. Some engines have no weights.   **15   30**

(C) Same as (A), but with black plastic wheels.   **15   30**

(D) Same as (B), but with black plastic wheels.   **15   30**

(E) Same as (C), but with either two-, three-, or four-piece lead weight riveted under the cab.   **15   30**

(F) Same as (A), but no motor; metal hook protrudes from two holes at the bottom of the boiler front. It is assumed that this locomotive was designed as a floor pull toy. Further verification needed.   **NRS**

Note: Some engines have frame held together with eyelets while other engines use panhead tubular rivets.

78100 TENDER: Yellow, blue, and silver tender matching colors of number 115041 locomotive; black frame; "78100" lettered in white on black in a silver-bordered rectangle; has coal load; Type VI coupler.   **4   8**

3689 TENDER

(A) Black-, dark red-, and silver-striped tender matching colors of Wyandotte number 970 locomotive; black frame; "W.R.L. 3689" lettered in black on the top front of each side; "RAIL / Wyandotte / LINES" lettered in white on red background in a circle centered on each side; the "W" is also enclosed in a separate circle; "LT WT 22000 / Built 4.6.55" lettered in white at the bottom front of each side; has coal load.   **4   8**

(B) Same as (A), but with pinkish red striping.   **4   8**

(C) Same as (A), but with bell and clapper underneath tender.   **7   15**

Note 1: All Wyandotte tenders have Type VI couplers.

Note 2: 3689 tenders first came with stamped-metal wheels, but later plastic wheels were used.

Top: Wyandotte 970 locomotive with matching 3689 tender. The metal piece hanging down between the wheels hits the crossties and activates the bell in the tender. This tender was also made without the bell. Middle: Hafner Bx32 Santa Fe boxcar sold by Wyandotte; unnumbered sand car with Wyandotte herald. Bottom: Hafner 41021 caboose with Wyandotte herald.

	Gd	Exc

Note 3: Although absolute verification is requested, it appears that Hafner's 90131 tender (described in Chapter Three) came with some of the Wyandotte trains sold by All Metal Products.

Bx 32 BOXCAR

(A) Orange sides, chocolate brown doors, roof, and frame; "Santa Fe" herald lettered in white on orange color background to the left of the sliding doors; "ATSF" lettered in white to the left of the doors and underneath the herald; "Bx 32" lettered in brown to left of doors; "The / Grand Canyon / Line" lettered in white to the right of the doors; circular "HAFNER / TRAINS" logo lettered in white at car ends; Type IX frame; Type VI couplers. **6 12**

(B) Same as (A), but with black doors. **6 12**

(C) Same as (A), but with doors deliberately omitted. **3 6**

14825 BOXCAR

(A) Chocolate brown sides, doors, roof, and frame; "Santa Fe" herald lettered in white to the left of the doors underneath the herald; "Bx 32" lettered in white to the left of the sliding doors; "The / Grand Canyon / Line" lettered in white to the right of the doors; circular "Hafner / Trains" logo lettered in white at car ends; Type IX frame; Type VI couplers. **6 12**

(B) Same as (A), but with doors deliberately omitted. **4 8**

(C) Same as (A), but with aluminum-colored doors. **8 16**

Note: The lettering "HAFNER TRAINS" appeared on both ends of the Wyandotte boxcars and was never removed. All the Wyandotte freights came in stamped-metal wheels and later in plastic wheels. Usually black plastic was used, but brown plastic wheels have also been found on some of the later cars.

91746 SAND CAR

(A) Dark yellow sides, bright yellow ends, black frame; "91746" lettered in red at far left side of car; "HAFNER TRAINS" lettered in red on car sides; circular "WYANDOTTE TOYS / MADE / IN / USA" herald lettered in black on silver background; herald is centered on sides; Type VIIIa frame; Type V coupler. **4 8**

(B) Same as (A), but Wyandotte herald on white background. **4 8**

(C) Same as (B), but with silver ends. **5 10**

(D) Same as (A), but with darker yellow ends. **4 8**

(E) Same as (A), but dark green sides; "91746" and "HAFNER TRAINS" lettered in black. **4 8**

(F) Same as (E), but using Wyandotte herald; unnumbered and "HAFNER TRAINS" lettering omitted; has dark green ends. **4 8**

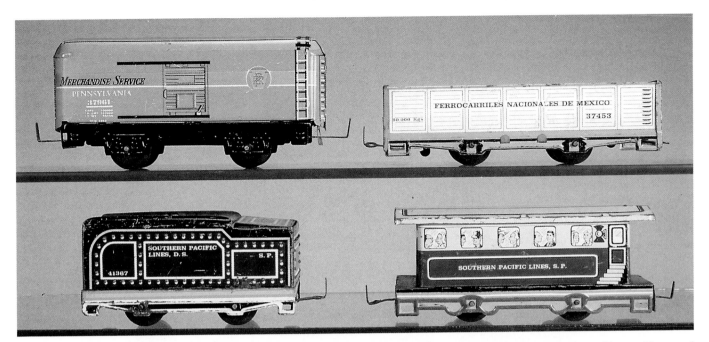

Top: Marx 37961 Pennsylvania boxcar equipped with Hafner-Wyandotte couplers. After purchasing Wyandotte, Marx sold unused Wyandotte boxed sets and filled out the boxes with partly Marx equipment when Wyandotte inventory was depleted; rare Plastimarx sand car sold in Mexico — the car's body is that created by Hafner and continued by Wyandotte. Bottom: Plastimarx Santa Fe tender; except for the color and lettering, the exact duplicate of Hafner's 90131 and 78100 tenders and Wyandotte's 3689 tender; Plastimarx's Santa Fe passenger car; the late Hafner-Wyandotte caboose body and frame was used, but the cupola was omitted. The three rare Plastimarx cars are from the J. Cirinelli Collection.

	Gd	Exc
(G) Same as (F), but has black ends.	4	8

(H) Same as (A), but silver lithography inside the car runs 3/16" the length of the car at the top of one side; obviously a factory production error. **NRS**

Note 1: The author has a number 91876 Hafner sand car lithographed gray and blue on the sides and dark red on the ends. This car was obtained with a Wyandotte set in unboxed form. The author would like to hear from collectors who may have this car in a boxed set; this would authenticate this Hafner 91876 gray, blue, and red car as also Wyandotte production — at least for a short time immediately after Wyandotte acquired Hafner and turned exclusively to the 91746 sand car and its unnumbered successor.

Note 2: Only on the unnumbered sand cars has the lettering "HAFNER TRAINS" been omitted from the lithography. Up to that point Wyandotte merely added its logo to the Hafner designation.

41021 CABOOSE

(A) Reddish orange sides, medium red roof, dark red frame, white and black detailing; "41021" lettered in white near the right corners of each side; "HAFNER TRAINS" lettered in white on sides; circular "Wyandotte Toys / Made in USA" herald, lettered in black on white background on sides; two trainmen lithographed in two of the four windows on each side; windows not punched out; Type IX frame; Type VI coupler. 4 8

	Gd	Exc
(B) Same as (A), but fire red sides and roof.	4	8
(C) Same as (B), but light red frame.	4	8

(D) Same as (B), but two lithographed windows on each cupola side and one lithographed window at cupola ends. 4 8

Note 1: On both cabooses Wyandotte merely added its logo; otherwise the caboose remained a Hafner car.

Note 2: Both the sand car and the caboose initially came with metal wheels, but later cars have plastic wheels.

Note 3: Some of the Wyandotte cabooses came with two couplers.

TRACK AND CROSSOVER

All Metal eventually made its own version of track with black ties for greater realism. All Metal's Wyandotte crossover is all black on the top and is much longer than Hafner's, measuring 7¼" by 7¼". Its four ends are U-shaped. No numbering is available for these Wyandotte units. The prices for straight and curve track would be the same as those given for Hafner track. The Wyandotte crossover is uncommon and would list for $5 in excellent condition.

NOTE

1. From an undated circular: "Historical Sketches of Wyandotte's Past: Toys Bring Wyandotte Fame" issued by the Wyandotte Historical Society, Wyandotte, Michigan.

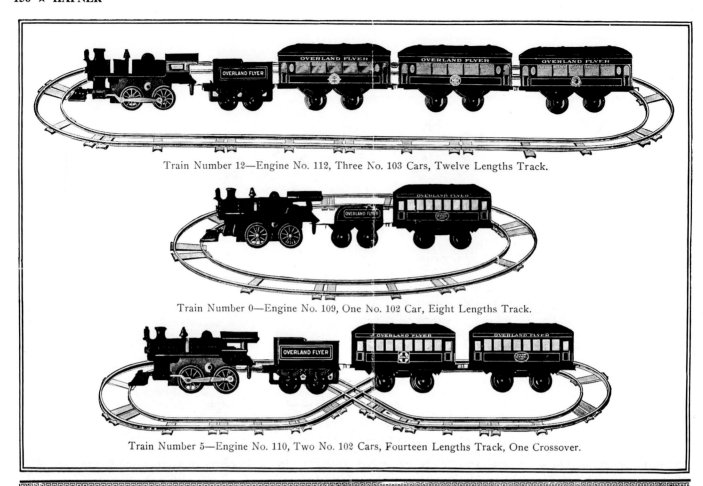

Train Number 12—Engine No. 112, Three No. 103 Cars, Twelve Lengths Track.

Train Number 0—Engine No. 109, One No. 102 Car, Eight Lengths Track.

Train Number 5—Engine No. 110, Two No. 102 Cars, Fourteen Lengths Track, One Crossover.

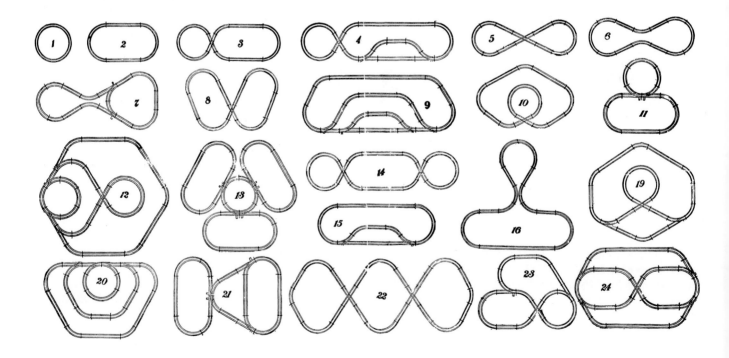

Two pages from an 8-page Hafner brochure

Cover of one of the few Hafner catalogues.

Carlton Norris McKenney

With the assistance of
Peter H. Riddle

CONTENTS

★

PREFACE 163

ACKNOWLEDGMENTS 164

ONE ★ Dorfan — A History of Its Innovations 165

TWO ★ Narrow Gauge Locomotives 170

THREE ★ Narrow Gauge Passenger Cars 180

FOUR ★ Narrow Gauge Freight Cars 193

FIVE ★ Wide Gauge Locomotives 199

SIX ★ Wide Gauge Passenger Cars 203

SEVEN ★ Wide Gauge Freight Cars 210

EIGHT ★ Accessories and Dealer Displays 212

NINE ★ Loco-Builder Kits, Dorfan sets, and Catalogues 220

GLOSSARY, SUMMARY OF TYPES, and INDEX appear at the end of this book

PREFACE

★

WHY DORFAN?

Why would a boy shopping for an electric train in the late 1920s choose a Dorfan train set rather than a Lionel, Ives, or American Flyer? Or, more importantly, what Dorfan features would appeal to the boy's dad, who was probably making the big decision and purchase?

Dorfan's late 1920s–early 1930s advertising emphasized realism, being modern, and well informed:

If you're a thinking boy who isn't satisfied with just "toys," then Dorfan is the engine for you. You'll get more fun, more thrills, more real enjoyment out of "the Engine that is designed by engineers." Talk it over with your Dad, and tell him you want a real train in miniature, not a toy; explain Dorfan's wonderful features to him — he'll understand." (1930 catalogue, *Dorfan Modern Electric Trains*, page 2.)

If a boy (or his father) wanted an engine that was rugged and could pull, Dorfan was the hands-down winner. Dealers had layouts featuring steep, 20 percent grade slopes, showing how a Dorfan train could pull its own weight up an incline. Ball bearings on the drive axles allowed more of the motor power to be used for pulling, and the company gave credit also to the new, nonmagnetic alloy used in its die-castings. Other alloys, it said, robbed a locomotive of from 15 to 45 percent of its tractive effort! (More will be said about the Dorfan alloy later.)

Other attractions of owning a Dorfan were the detailed figures seated in the passenger cars, the range of lines in all price ranges, and the *educational* play value of a model which could be opened up. A smiling young man, with screwdriver in hand, ready to assemble his Dorfan Take-Apart Locomotive, became the symbol of Dorfan trains during the late 1920s. The Dorfan Company sponsored a "take-apart" contest at Boy Scout Camp Nobebosco in North Bergen, New Jersey, in which every boy took apart and reassembled a Dorfan engine, including the motor and body parts, wiring, and gears, in less than four minutes!

Dorfan also offered a locomotive and motor kits brochure addressed to boys who were " . . . living in the age of Class and Speed!"; the copy suggested that a boy with an inquisitive mind and a Dorfan locomotive could make his own repairs. Parts could be purchased easily using the parts list in the Loco-Builder box.

With ball-bearing motors, great pulling power, Take-Apart engines, realistic passengers in the windows, and beautiful details, Dorfan trains offered many enticing features. These features provide a ready answer to the question "Why Dorfan?"

DESCRIBING DORFAN TRAINS

The chapters of listings of Dorfan productions are organized by gauge, with narrow first and wide second, and then often subdivided by car length. Peter Riddle has contributed descriptions of certain Narrow Gauge items, based on observations of the Carlton N. McKenney Collection. We invite readers to submit similarly detailed descriptions of items of either gauge that they have personally observed to Greenberg Publishing Company, 7566 Main Street, Sykesville, Maryland 21784.

Entries are listed by catalogue number, preceded by "No.". In those instances where the side-of-car number differs, car num-

bers observed are cited in the listing and are listed separately, in proper numerical order — although the reader is then referred to the full description under the catalogue number. In those cases where the catalogue number is the one appearing on the side of the car, the word "No." is placed in parentheses. The Index of Dorfan items, found in the back of this volume, lists both catalogue and car numbers.

It should be pointed out that most Dorfan items have no numbers on their sides. Some items were first produced with the catalogue number, but later variations got new catalogue numbers even though they retained the old embossed or lithographed numbers, which may simply have been cheaper than retooling. A classic example of number confusion is the Wide Gauge lithographed passenger car whose body was bent to a different shape to form an observation car; both items carry the same number. Dorfan collectors come to accept this confusion.

For each item we show the date or dates when the item appeared in the Dorfan catalogue. Bear in mind that a catalogue shows items intended for sale for Christmas of the catalogue year through the early part of the next. This is because the manufacturer's year was designed to begin with the Toy Fair held in New York City in February and to end with Christmas of that year. New models, prototypes, and manufacturing innovations were all presented at the Toy Fair. After orders were taken and manufacturers assessed interest, production was planned. If toys were not well received at the Toy Fair or encountered manufacturing problems, the manufacturer sometimes decided not to produce the toy even though it appeared in its catalogue. A study of toy train manufacturing and marketing reveals some catalogued items are indeed not available for the year of the catalogue and, on the other hand, some uncatalogued items *are* available. In cases where Dorfan catalogue information is not available, other documents — such as a flyer or catalogue insert — have been consulted to authenticate dates.

The color descriptions in the following chapters are based on observation if the item was available for inspection. In the more than sixty years since these cars were painted, the effects of light and aging have caused fading in the pigments. To verify a car's original color, remove a door or window frame. The color underneath should be closer to the original and not dulled by time or yellowed by the coat of lacquer Dorfan frequently used to protect finishes. Cars stored in an attic, subject to the extremes of heat and cold, may age even more dramatically.

If the item was not available, the listing is based on the catalogue's description or illustration. Any discussion of the color of Dorfan trains must include mention of the fact that, unlike Lionel, Dorfan used the same word to describe different shades of the same color. Consequently a Dorfan "brown" could be a leather brown or a dark metallic maroon. A Dorfan leather brown might appear slightly different on two cars because of differential aging.

Dorfan offered a "crackle" — or, more correctly, an "alligator" — finish on some passenger cars. There was an apple green undercolor covered with a black paint that "alligatored" into a crystalline pattern, allowing the green color to show through in the cracks. As Dorfan collector Richard Fletcher points out, there was also a tan undercolor sprayed with black on some Wide Gauge models; he has seen this on cars coming with stamped-steel chrome trucks (numbered 990, 991, and 992). Restorers who have tried to duplicate this finish have had more failure than success: humidity, temperature, thinners, and airbrush settings are critical to obtain the proper alligator pattern.

VALUES AND REPLACEMENT PARTS

For each item listed in the following chapters we provide three categories of values — Good, Excellent, and Restored. As mentioned in the Introduction, suggesting Dorfan values presents various challenges. One of the factors to be aware of is the fact that the two gauges, narrow and wide, are experiencing differing rates of change in value. Collectors have reported that generally Standard or Wide Gauge items have not been increasing in value at the rate enjoyed by Narrow Gauge Dorfan. On the other hand not very much really good all-original Dorfan is offered for public sale at meets, and therefore records of observed sales may not be widely available. Those suggested value guidelines offered here come from a panel of reader/collectors.

It should also be noted that Dorfan equipment often is found in deteriorated condition, primarily due to the alloy employed. Some hard-to-find equipment in very deteriorated condition will nevertheless be graded as "Good" for price evaluation by some buyers. A Dorfan buyer is usually willing to pay more for a Dorfan piece in less than good condition if he knows that replacement parts are available.

Some replacement parts have been fabricated. Dies, for example, were made to stamp out Narrow Gauge window frames.

When an original body is used as a pattern to make a replacement body, the replacement body is slightly smaller than the original due to shrinkage of the metal as it cools. Since cast Dorfan bodies served as the motor frames (except for steam locomotives), a replacement body made from an original will be slightly smaller than the original. Consequently, gears mounted on the replacement body will not properly mesh. The late Roger Loxley of Colorado experimented with the lost-wax process to make a few brass and bronze locomotive bodies and parts. Others have reproduced Wide Gauge truck frames. See Chapter Nine for a list of engine parts listed in the Loco-Builder kit.

The following are sources of replacement parts:

- Richard Fletcher, 60 Fredonia Road, Newton, New Jersey 07860, has Narrow and Wide Gauge bearings for axles and armatures and is planning production of some Standard Gauge decals.
- Al Franceschetti, 7910 Poplar Hill Drive, Clinton, Maryland 20735, has molded Dorfan wheels in epoxy.
- Ernie Noebel of New Haven, Connecticut, has offered reproduction No. 51 and No. 53 bodies.
- LaSalle Olsen, 2192 McKinley Avenue, Lakewood, Ohio 44107, has various replacement parts.
- Richard Trickel, 3015 Cardin Place, Norristown, Pennsylvania 19403, has cast numerous parts in soft metal, including working and dummy headlights, Standard Gauge truck sides, wheels, and gears.

This author feels that the best source is another Dorfan locomotive or car from which parts can be cannibalized.

Acknowledgments

Much of the information in this book was gathered over a period of about twenty years from collectors such as you. Nearly forty persons read the manuscript, supplied additions and comments, made diagrams, sent photographs, and telephoned information. Many of these contributions are specifically credited in the text that follows.

Particular thanks go to **Cal R. Avery, Gordon G. Blickle, James L. Bodeker, Charles Brasher, Morgan G. Brenner, Alfred C. Clarke, Steven A. Clarke, Paul Cole, Philip Engelder, Myron Erickson, William J. Farmer, George B. Fisher, Richard D. Fletcher, Ken Halverson, Tony Hay,** **John A. Horner, Larry House, Don Huovinen, Robert Ignasiak, Bill Kelishek, Robert E. Lakemacher, Donald C. Leo, William Lyon, Robert L. Mancus, James M. McAuliff, Sr., G. Dan McLain, Don Morman, Marvin S. Nauman, John Nolden, Jr.,** the family of the late **Harry Osisek, Jr., Bill Paul, Stuart Perlmutter, William M. Reed, Jr., Peter Riddle, Karl F. Schmidt, George L. Smith, Robert M. Stekl, William E. Stephens, Walter E. Stinger, Jr., Emmett T. Stouffer, Edwin T. Thompson,** and **Cornell M. Wing,** as well as **the family of the late Roger Loxley.**

Carlton N. McKenney

CHAPTER ONE

★

DORFAN — A HISTORY OF ITS INNOVATIONS

A DECADE OF DORFAN PRODUCTION

Dorfan's origin can be traced to Nürnberg, Germany, where Joseph Kraus & Company began making toys in 1910. At that time and until World War I, Nürnberg was the toy capital of Europe, and German toys, the most popular throughout the world, dominated the American market.

Two of Kraus' cousins, Milton and Julius Forchheimer, were associated with the company. It was their mothers, sisters Fanny and Dora, however, who "made history": their names were joined to create the "Fandor" line. When the Forchheimer brothers crossed the Atlantic in 1923, "Fandor" was reversed to create the "Dorfan" line.

The Forchheimer brothers brought Fandor's chief engineer, John C. Koerber, to direct the new factory which they set up in 1924 on the top two floors of a three-story commercial building at 137 Jackson Street in Newark, New Jersey. When Dorfan entered the toy train market, it faced strong competition. Although Nürnberg and the German toy industry had dominated the American toy market before World War I, the war and the resulting hiatus in the importation of European — primarily German — toys allowed American manufacturers, such as Lionel, American Flyer, Hafner, and Ives, to establish their own niches. Undaunted, and apparently knowing the industry well from its own German background, Dorfan quickly gained market share. It turned out that Dorfan entered the toy market at a propitious time and enjoyed rapid growth. In fact, the toy market, the stock market, and the real estate market all were bullish and expanding. Dorfan employed about 150 employees at its peak.

However, the Depression left an indelible scar on Dorfan, and it never recovered. Sales slowed, and the manufacture of Dorfan trains ended about 1934, although

A CORNER IN THE ASSEMBLING DEPARTMENT
of the Dorfan factory; where capable swift fingered young women are putting Dorfan cars together.

A glimpse of one end of the machine shop at the Dorfan Factory.

A CORNER OF OUR TESTING LABORATORY

showing a Dorfan Loco-Builder Engine in the course of one of the electrical tests. The dials register the results of these tests.

Where Loco-Builder Is Built

THE Dorfan Loco-Builder Engine and Dorfan Trains are strictly "Made in America" products. Every part is designed and made in our factory at Newark, New Jersey. Back of the Loco-Builder idea, and back of all Dorfan products, is the experience of many, many years in the making of metal toys. The men who design Dorfan toys and who superintend the making of them have spent a lifetime in the toy business. And they are in that business because of a love for it.

In the designing of the Dorfan toys, engineering skill of the highest type is employed in the endeavor to put into them the same conscientious effort employed in making real, lifesize locomotives.

The Dorfan factory located in a quiet street skirting the manufacturing section of Newark, is thronged with enthusiastic young workers who put heart and soul into the thought of producing something to bring keen pleasure to young America.

Every Dorfan product, whether electrical or otherwise, goes through a series of tests before leaving the factory that makes it proof against defect. And the Dorfan guarantee is a binding one.

trains were still available for sale until about 1936. Even in 1937 or 1938, Koerber and the Forchheimer brothers dreamed of manufacturing many new and improved trains; they hoped that the Dorfan line could be revived. But that was not to be. Eventually, they gave up the second floor of their building and the remaining business was headquartered in Koerber's office on the third floor. For a while they made toys for other manufacturers. Finally, the company was dissolved.

At this point the Unique Art Manufacturing Company, also of Newark, bought the Dorfan dies, but they did nothing with them for many years. Finally, when Unique brought out their train line, most of the items were based on new designs and dies. Dorfan enthusiasts were surprised, however, to see that Unique used the No. 493 passenger car body for its coaches. It was not an exact reproduction, but if you put the two cars side by side, you can see the similarities. Unique cars have four wheels and are lithographed, while most Dorfan cars have eight wheels and are painted. All of the Dorfan-inserted parts — such as window frames and handrails — were eliminated. Unique roofs were permanently attached to their bodies, while Dorfan roofs were separate units. The Dorfan dies were modified to provide for these changes.[1]

DORFAN'S CONTRIBUTIONS

Dorfan's marketing focused on a traditional theme of the toy train industry — the immediate and long-term educational value of toy trains. Toy trains helped a boy learn about electricity, then a new and exciting phenomenon; toy trains encouraged the development of self-reliance; and toy trains provided the groundwork for a career in railroad transportation. Never forgotten was the obvious play value of the trains themselves. But Dorfan added a new twist: being up-to-date and modern.

Dorfan Materials

When Dorfan began production, American toy trains were made from either stamped-steel pieces soldered and tabbed together or from cast iron. Dorfan innovated by utilizing the new metal-forming techniques of zinc alloy die-casting to make large body sections. Furthermore, Dorfan locomotives consisted of two halves; fewer parts dramatically reduced manufacturing costs. And Dorfan carried its technological advance one step farther by offering locomotives in simple kits to be assembled by the train buyer — an experience linked to the educational theme.

The catalogue made history in that it offered the first die-cast locomotive body made in America. The dies were designed under the watchful eyes of engineer Koerber and the casting was done by Doehler Die-Casting, using a special formula for the copper-zinc alloy to produce what was called a "Dorfan alloy." Dorfan attributed great qualities to its special alloy; it called the metal "unbreakable," as it was able to withstand much rough handling. For example, it has been reported that when new, a die-cast locomotive boiler could be thrown against a concrete floor and not break!

No one dreamt of the inherent limitations of the alloy, which began to appear within a few years. Impurities in the zinc alloy oxidized and the metal expanded and cracked. Today most Dorfan castings are cracked and deteriorated.

The Range in Two Gauges

As far as gauge was concerned, Dorfan followed the American Flyer tradition of Wide and Narrow Gauges, although Dorfan used a measuring system for O Gauge track, which was referred to as "ordinary 1⅜-inch track." Dorfan introduced its O Gauge trains in its first catalogue in 1925. Dorfan called these Narrow Gauge (as contrasted to the Wide Gauge trains it produced as *its* version of "Standard Gauge," 2¼-inch track).

In the mid-1920s American O Gauge equipment came in three price ranges: low, medium, and high. Rolling stock from low-priced sets was generally stamped from one piece of metal with only axles and wheels as additional parts. Dorfan, Hafner, and American Flyer offered low-priced sets in which the couplers were stamped as part of the body stamping. In the 1920s Lionel did not offer a line of low-cost stamped cars. That company's most economical sets simply contained fewer cars, but the quality of their construction was high.

Like the other manufacturers, Dorfan offered trains in several price ranges. Small (compared with cars in medium-to-deluxe categories) passenger cars in the cheapest sets were stamped from a single, lithographed sheet. Their forming die created a hook coupler on one end and a ring on the other. (See Chapter Six for discussion and illustration of Dorfan's more sophisticated coupling system.) To quickly complete the factory assembly of such a car, only the wheels and axles had to be pushed into place. In the 1920s Dorfan used hollow rivets to replace and/or supplement the older bent tab and soldering techniques on its rolling stock. American Flyer also started using hollow rivets at this time.

For the father who could afford bigger trains, beautiful Wide Gauge sets were available. The early cast 3930 locomotive had twelve wheels and a motorman (known as Dorfan Dan the Engine Man, who was featured in early Dorfan advertisements) in the cab of his large electric engine. Later lithographed freight cars were beauties, with plenty of bright brass trim. Passenger cars were offered both in a lithographed finish or painted with decals. Many of the cars were equipped with end marker lamps — clear magnifying lenses which beamed the interior illumination along the track.

In the more expensive Narrow Gauge train sets the cars were longer and contained more detailed parts and a variety of paints. Handrails were attached with two brass cotter pins, a method which did not allow assembly by machine. A recent disassembly of a No. 493 revealed 117 parts, not counting the decals. One can imagine the labor needed to assemble such a car which sold for about $3.75. Even the painting of the car could be labor-intensive.

Among collectors Dorfan is perhaps most fondly remembered for its clever placement of passengers. Passenger cars in the mid-price range had swivel couplers and most had rows of passengers, one in each window. The heads were stamped from a strip of lithographed metal which was then tabbed to the car floor. (Observation cars in this series are seldom found with passengers, even though the car floor is punched for their attachment.)

Deluxe passenger cars had passengers in each window, too, but they were not made from flat, lithographed metal.

Two versions of the famous Dorfan passenger strips

Rather, these passengers, made from cast metal, were three-dimensional and beautifully crafted and handpainted, much like expensive lead soldiers of the time. In the deluxe cars, the people had complete faces, buttons on their coats, hats with colored bands, and a variety of hair colors. In all there were six different figures. Only the heads and shoulders of the passengers showed at the open windows: this allowed Dorfan to attach the figures with flat tabs. The figures/tabs were riveted to a strip which in turn was riveted to the car floor. No boy protested that clones of these six people, dressed in identical outfits, rode in each of the cars — although he might notice an assembly error in which a lady and her twin sister were placed in adjacent windows!

Trains for Educational Play

Another innovation announced in the 1925 catalogue was the "Take-Apart" Narrow Gauge locomotive, also called "Loco-Builder" and "Constructive." The locomotive was patterned after the New York Central S-class electric engine. The Take-Apart locomotives were designed so that every "red-blooded boy" could easily answer his own question, "How does it work?" Pulling two pins plus the pantograph pin, if it were present, would separate the body halves; electrical connections were made with clips. Each part was marked with a number so that the beginner could easily refer to the drawing to reassemble his engine. Fortunately, there were only fifteen parts, so reassembly took only a few minutes. Neither painting nor detailed assembly was required; a screwdriver alone was needed.

Assuming that a boy would be thrilled by building his own locomotive "rather than just reassembling it" Dorfan produced a line of kits consisting of compartmentalized boxes with train parts. In a few minutes a boy could have his engine ready to run! Kits for the Nos. 51, 52, 53, 3920, 3930, and/or the Dorfan motor were offered (descriptions of each of these will be found in Chapter Nine).

Motors

Small electric motors like those used in toy trains have two axles and a central motor shaft. In most toy trains, the motor side frames support the axles and shaft. In premium quality motors, special bushings or bearings are mounted inside the holes to support the axles and shafts. When properly lubricated, the bearing material has a long life. Dorfan castings were cleverly designed to include holes which served as bearings to support the axles and motor armature shaft. The zinc alloy used for the bearing is naturally slick and serves well as a bearing if properly lubricated.

The Dorfan Company was innovative and constantly sought to make a better train set. Lionel, American Flyer, and Dorfan built series-wired motors to run on either AC or DC power. These motors would always run in the same direction unless the relationship of the two brushes to the field windings (stators) and the armature windings were reversed. Reversing the polarity of DC current in the track does not change the direction of a series motor.

In 1930 it offered both Narrow and Wide Gauge locomotives with "Distance Remote Control." Dorfan's control mechanism was innovative in that it allowed the engineer to circumvent the fixed sequence of locomotive action. Lionel, Ives, and American Flyer, by contrast, offered electromechanical devices to reverse locomotive direction. These devices automatically sequenced either forward-reverse-forward or forward-neutral-reverse-neutral-forward. Hence, if you turned the power off, the engine automatically sequenced to the next position, whether that was the direction you wanted or not.

Dorfan's engineers developed a rectifier and reversing switch that put DC power in the track and gave the engineer control of the engine's direction without having to go through a fixed sequence. The Dorfan reversing device included a bridge rectifier mounted inside the locomotive cab that was wired to the field winding. Its field current polarity was always the same, regardless of the polarity. Thus, under Dorfan's device, a train could go forward, stop, and then start forward again without having to go through one of the sequences described previously. It is presented in detail by Walter Stinger.

Description of the Sequence Reverse Unit

Drawings and description by Walter Stinger

The reverse unit was built on a die-cast frame mounted on top of the motor. A laminated-steel arm was attracted to the motor field core when power was applied to the locomotive. This arm, or armature, moved a rod through the unit against spring tension. This reversing device was different from other types in that it did its switching when the motor was

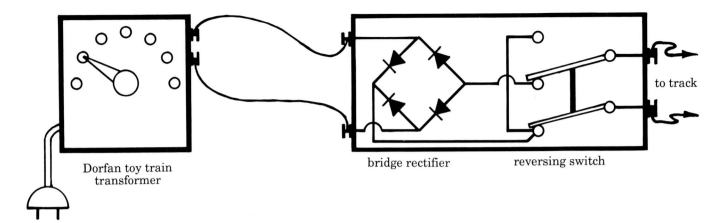

Dorfan "Distance Remote Control": power wiring schematic diagram

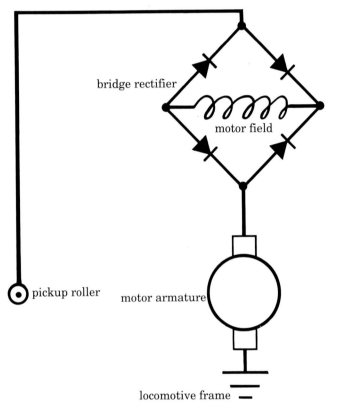

Dorfan "Distance Remote Control": locomotive motor wiring schematic diagram, showing bridge rectifier and motor field. DC power was put into the track.

de-energized. This avoided the contact burning, which would have occurred if switching had been done when power was applied.

When the power was turned off, the spring retracted the rod, and the movement caused a spring-centered toggle to engage one of two vertical pins on a reversing commutator. This moved the commutator and electrically swapped the armature leads (not the field leads), preparing the motor for travel in the reverse direction when power was again applied. Three small phosphor-bronze wiper arms made contact with the commutator top surface and were connected to the armature brushes and the motor field. A ground or frame connection was made to the commutator through its mounting rivet.

The commutator moved alternately about 45° clockwise and counter-clockwise with each removal of power, and there was no stop position in the cycle. The forces used in operation were quite small, making adjustment of spring tension critical, and it was important to keep dirt and dust from the mechanism. A dry lubricant, such as graphite, used on the moving parts would improve operation. If the toggle happened to contact both pins simultaneously, the commutator would assume a center position and prevent power flow to the motor. When this happened, the train operator would reach into the cab and move a metal tang back and forth to manually cycle the reverser. A lockout rod was provided in the cab to hold the commutator in the forward position and disable the automatic reverse.

The two sides of the reversing motor. Harry Osisek Collection; photograph by Gary Massat

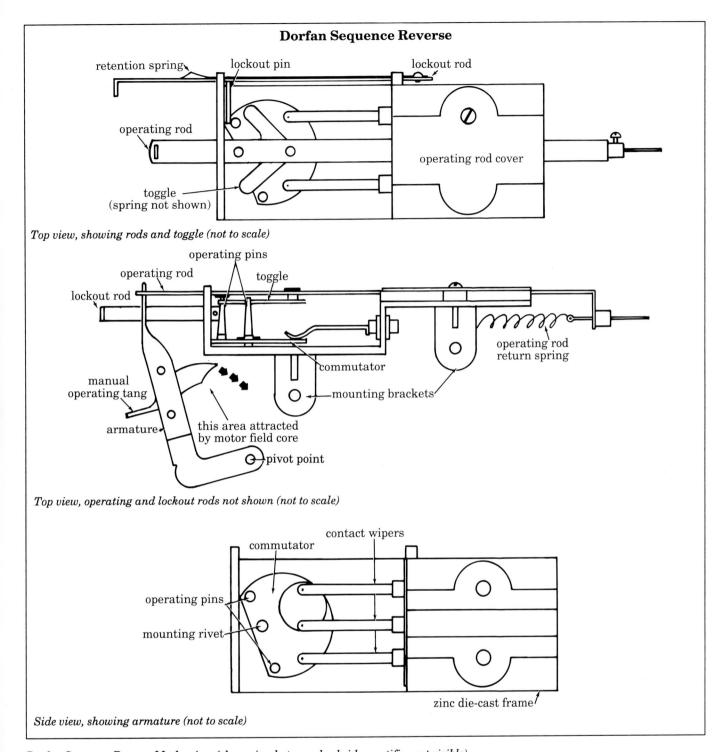

Dorfan Sequence Reverse

Top view, showing rods and toggle (not to scale)

Top view, operating and lockout rods not shown (not to scale)

Side view, showing armature (not to scale)

Dorfan Sequence Reverse Mechanism (shown in photographs; bridge rectifier not visible)

The reverse unit had the delicate appearance of a European-made device and may have been provided by Kraus.

Let us now turn to a closer examination of first the Narrow Gauge and then the Wide Gauge lines. Chapter Eight lists the accessories and dealer displays, and Chapter Nine describes the kits and the catalogued sets.

CHAPTER TWO

NARROW GAUGE LOCOMOTIVES

The smiling boy with screwdriver on the cover of the 1925 catalogue is taking apart a Dorfan locomotive. The engine was designed to be disassembled and put together in four minutes. Whether for maintenance or for the fun of it, to be able to dismantle an engine in only a few minutes is truly impressive.

These die-cast electric engines were called "Constructive," "Loco-Builder," or "Take-Apart" engines in the catalogues. To take an engine apart, one first removed the headlights, attached to long steel pins that slipped into the top of the body (see the diagram in Chapter Nine). These steel pins held the two sides of the frame snugly in place. With the pins removed, the body neatly separated and the remaining parts could be removed with a screwdriver. Electrical connections were made with Fahnestock clips or binding posts. After 1926 Loco-Builder engines were offered in the kit form (see the illustration and listings of kits in Chapter Nine), with the unassembled engine in a compartmentalized box containing all the parts to complete a locomotive. The catalogues did not list steam engines, which

Dorfan introduced after its electrics, as take-aparts, but the motors could be removed with a screwdriver.

With the exception of the No. 145 windup, the bodies and most wheels of the locomotives were die cast of the Dorfan alloy. Because of chemical imperfections in the alloy, many castings have become disfigured or have not survived at all. Some die-cast bodies suffered damage from impact because of poor pattern design. Frequently, steam engines are found without their pilots, dummy headlights, or coupler studs. Through the late 1920s engine patterns were improved, and the cast alloy was made thicker to produce a more rugged locomotive body. A possibility is that Dorfan improved the alloy.

Reproduction castings have been made of the Nos. 51, 52, 53, and 55 electric locomotive bodies. Collectors often salvage trim and motor parts from disintegrated locomotives to adorn the reproduction body castings.

DORFAN STEAM LOCOMOTIVES

Both electric and mechanical steam locomotives used similar body castings and tenders, and they are described below.

The smaller locomotive was 6½ inches long and painted in one color. "DORFAN" appeared in raised letters under the cab windows; the smokestack, bell, and dome were part of the casting. The motor assembly was hooked into the casting and secured with one screw.

The larger locomotive was 8¼ inches long. "DORFAN" appeared on a brass nameplate; the boiler bands, window frames, headlight socket, bell, and dome were nickel or brass and attached after the engine was painted. The motor

Label from the box of a No. 52 set

Steam Locomotive Types

Type I Boiler front had a cast, button-type number plate. This version was used for the larger 8¼-inch-long mechanical locomotives.

Type II Boiler front had a ½-inch opening for the electric headlight. The dummy headlight on top of the boiler had a crown on it; the cast tabs for the four motor-mounting screws were not reinforced.

Type III Boiler front had a ½-inch opening for the headlight. The dummy headlight on top of the boiler had a flat top; the cast tabs for the four motor-mounting screws were reinforced with additional cast flanges.

Tender Types

Type I 4 inches long with four wheels.

The floor had punched rings front and rear for coupling to the engine and train; had raised "bubbles" to clear the wheel flanges. Its three-sided body was tabbed to the floor and came with either stamped-steel or die-cast wheels. One version was all black, one was red with black floor, and one was black with number "160" in a red oval on the side.

Type II 5½ inches long with four wheels, it came with the mechanical locomotive.

The tender had a swivel coupler ring on the front and a riveted standard coupler on the rear, with a "DORFAN" decal. The wheels were either stamped steel or die cast.

Type III 6¼ inches long, designed for six wheels, it often was equipped with only four. It had a swivel ring coupler on the front and a riveted standard coupler on the rear. This tender was usually equipped with an imitation coal load consisting of a strip of metal embossed with lumps of coal. The tender's body was painted to match the locomotive's color and it had a "DORFAN" or "DORFAN LINES" decal. The floor was either black or painted yellow buff to match the engine's trim. **Note:** Richard Fletcher reports seeing a green mechanical set with red tender floor to match engine trim. Other color variations exist, but the author suspects that most were made as salesman samples and were not sold with the sets. Sometimes the centers of the wheels were painted. Gordon H. Blickle, George B. Fisher, and other collectors have discovered the word "GERMANY" stamped into the floor of the tender, under the coal load and covered by paint. Since Kraus offered an identical Fandor tender, except for the coupler and markings, it is assumed that Fandor manufactured these tenders.

assembly was secured with four screws. The larger body casting came in three versions.

MECHANICALLY POWERED LOCOMOTIVES

Dorfan sometimes called its mechanical engines "spring-winding." Whatever their name, Dorfan's windup motors were well built with long-running springs. An oscillating escapement held the train speed to a constant speed while it carried a variety of loads.

The cheapest mechanical locomotive had a spring motor without a brake. The wheels had to be restrained while the spring was wound with the key. Better motors had a brake lever projecting from the cab to engage a lock on the gear train so that the wheels could not turn while the motor was

being wound. Top-of-the-line motors were reversible, as described and illustrated in Chapter One. These motors switched direction using a gear shift lever, were imported from Germany, and were probably made by Kraus.

How about a complete train set for ONE dollar? Who could resist such a bargain, and a handsome one at that. **Set No. 99** cost only a dollar and included four sections of curved track (which made a complete circle), a No. 145 windup engine, and one passenger car. The little lithographed tinplate engine was 5¼ inches long, including the coupler and cowcatcher, but included a pantograph on the roof and was lithographed to look like an electric locomotive. Dorfan called it a novelty. A windup "electric" engine sounds like a contradiction in terms, but that is what Dorfan created with lithography. And, all for about a dollar, it was to become a classic toy train. No transformer needed!

Two side views of the windup motor (left) and the electric (right)

99-100. Note body fastened by eyelets and female coupler extending from frame. Tony Hay Collection

Set 100: No. 145 (A), clockwork motor and two Pullmans; note female coupler and body fastened by eyelets. Tony Hay Collection

Set with No. 145 (B). S. Bearn Collection

Top: Green windup No. 157 (B) engine. Bottom: Another version of the No. 55; compare locomotive and tender with the photograph at top of opposite page.

Top: Black No. 55 steam locomotive with red wheels, deluxe black 55 with extra valve gear. Bottom: Brass reproduction made by the late Roger Loxley.

Top: Red No. 55 with simplified motor unit. Middle: Blue 55 with circuit breaker shell. Bottom: Red 55 with circuit breaker mechanism.

	Gd	Exc	Rst

Set No. 100 cost fifteen cents more and came with two passenger cars (see color photos on page 172).

Besides its electric outline engines, Dorfan also manufactured 0-4-0 steam outline mechanical locomotives. Their die-cast bodies were similar or identical to Dorfan's small steam locomotives with electric motors.

Steam Outline

No. 154: 1929-30. Black; 10" long including tender; small body and Type I tender; die-cast, spoked wheels with side rods; motor has no brake. **150 200 125**
Note: Richard Fletcher reports seeing the No. 154 and the No. 157 in red and suspects the 156 came in red also.

No. 155: 1925-30. Die-cast bright red-enameled 6¼" body; clockwork motor; pressed-steel wheels, no drive rods; embossed "MADE IN U.S.A." under pilot; Type I tender. Similar to electrically powered No. 50. **125 175 100**

No. 156: 1928-30. Black; 11¼" long including tender; die-cast, large body and Type II tender; spoked wheels with side rods; motor had a brake lever for locking the gear train. **150 200 125**

No. 157: 1928-30. 13½" long including tender; reversible motor; no working headlight; knob on top of dummy headlight; Type III tender. A handsome locomotive; some even have a winding key painted in a matching color. Similar in appearance to No. 55; see **No. 55** for more details.
(A) Black body; buff trim. **175 225 160**
(B) Green body; red trim. **200 250 160**
Note: Gordon Blickle has (B) with brown boiler bands and cab window frames.
(C) Blue body; red trim. **225 275 175**
Note: Richard Fletcher reports seeing red body, yellow trim.

Electric Outline

99-100: See No. 145.

No. 145: 1925-(?). 5¼" long including pilot and coupler ring; lithographed tinplate body with printed ventilators, doors, and round windows with a pantograph attached to the roof to imitate a box-cab electric locomotive. This was Dorfan's "windup electric engine." Motor has no brake; the body was lettered "THE DORFAN LINES" and "99-100", which happens to be the numbers of the cheapest train sets.
(A) Orange body. **175 275 —**
(B) Red body. **175 275 —**

ELECTRICALLY POWERED LOCOMOTIVES

Steam Outline

No. 50: After 1930. Die-cast, bright red-enameled body; 6¼" (10" long including tender and its coupling ring); dummy headlight; detailed (beginning at boiler front) with embosssed rivets, stack, two rows of rivets, bell, rivets, steam dome, rivets, "DORFAN" on cab sides; bright yellow die-cast wheels;

	Gd	Exc	Rst

electric motor fastened with hooks and one screw drives front axle only, one pickup roller, no reverse; red or black Type I tender with folded sides tabbed to frame, hole in frame for locomotive post, one hook coupler, die-cast wheels.
Note: Uncatalogued economy model. **150 225 150**

No. 55: 1928-33. 0-4-0; die-cast shell with motor assembly fittted inside; 13½" including Type III tender. One-piece die-casting includes boiler, cylinders, pilot, cab, coupler pin, piping, rivet detail, dummy headlight; operating headlight projects through a hole in the boiler front; trim includes photoengraved brass plates with "DORFAN" on cab, window sash, brass or nickel dome, and smokestack and bell attached with machine screws. Three boiler bands in brass or contrasting color fit between rows of rivets. Some locomotives received additional trim when gold paint was hand-applied to piping, pilot, and cylinder heads, as well as to the tender.

The die-cast body appears in two versions, differing only in small detail: the Type II includes four semicircular bosses for attaching the motor and adds a button "hat" to the dummy headlight. The Type III has flat strips for the motor-mounting holes and lacks the "hat."

The motor assembly comes in two versions: more common is one with two pickup rollers and the armature driving both axles; a slide-type reversing switch is located inside the cab. The simplified motor has only one pickup roller and the armature drives only the forward axle; it has no reversing switch.

Carlton McKenney has in his collection a No. 55 with some electrical modifications. A fiber contact block is hidden behind a cylinder and connected to a buzzer mounted on the fmotor. It appears fabricated from Dorfan materials. Could this be a prototype "chugger"?

(See the tender description at the beginning of this chapter.)
(A) Type II body; blue with blue tender body, buff windows and boiler bands; blue, black or yellow tender frame with die-cast wheels; catalogued as 55-B (for blue).
175 325 175
(B) Same as (A), Type III casting. **175 325 175**
(C) 1930-33. Type II casting; black with black tender, yellow or red wheels; brass windows, boiler bands, and trim; gold-painted piping and cylinder heads; "DORFAN" on tender framed with yellow and red pinstripes; catalogued as 55-BK (for black). **225 350 200**
(D) Same as (C), Type III casting; no gold-painted trim or pinstripes on tender. **200 275 175**
(E) Type II casting; red with red tender body; brass trim; yellow wheels, black tender frame; catalogued as 55-R (for red). **225 325 200**
(F) Same as (E), Type III casting. **225 325 200**
(G) 1930-33. Type II casting; dark metallic maroon (catalogued as "brown") with matching tender body; buff windows, boiler bands, wheels, and tender frame; catalogued as 55-BR (for brown). **225 300 200**
(H) Same as (G), Type III casting. **225 300 200**
(I) Orange with orange tender body; green trim. **225 300 200**

No. 770: 1930-. A 4-4-0 steam-outline engine, which is discussed at the end of this chapter.

| | Gd | Exc | Rst |

Electric Outline

Dorfan's electric locomotives were powerful, particularly after the gearing was modified from single to double-reduction. The company claimed that its Dorfan alloy used in die casting was non-magnetic and therefore did not waste power.

The 51s, 52s, and 54s, as well as many of the 53s, used depressions in the body castings as bearings for armature and axles. This somewhat unorthodox design simplified the assembly of the Take-Apart engines (also catalogued, under different numbers, as Electric Constructive Locomotives). The field piece and brush holder fitted over pins, and electrical connections were made to Fahnestock clips or binding posts. Headlight wires simply plugged into the sockets. Two pins, part of the headlight (or dummy headlight) fixtures, plugged into the body to hold the two body halves, "A" and "B" sections, together. Dorfan's choice of 5-40 screws and 36-pitch gears has made restoration somewhat difficult. Neither the screw size or the gear pitch is commonly used today. (The gear pitch may have been a carryover from a German metric standard.)

(No.) 51 TAKE-APART LOCOMOTIVE: 1925-33. New York Central S-Class style enameled die-cast body with two dissimilar halves containing internal mounting posts for motor and gears, later versions with roof ridge covering seam between halves; embossed rivet detail; journal boxes, steps, one door and two windows per side; embossed side lettering "DORFAN LINES" on all and "NYC 51" on early versions, and "PAT. U.S. PAT. OFF. / JUNE 1924 / MADE IN U.S.A." on one end; slot for reverse lever; slots for two couplers (but only one mounted); two (early) or four (later) holes for handrails in ends; two headlights (both cast dummy or one dummy and one working, nickel-plated or black- and red-enameled with simulated number plates) mounted on rods to hold body halves together; brass handrails flanking doors; one twist shank coupler; one or two pickup rollers; two gear-driven axles; die-cast wheels; with or without enameled window frame inserts; brass handrails on ends, brass ventilator covers, decals, manual reverse; frequently demonstrated by dealers pulling two cars up a 20-percent grade.

(A) 1925; also catalogued as set No. 255; 6¼" body, 6½" overall, red; brass ventilator covers and end handrails; two dummy headlights; no reverse; no roof ridge; one pickup roller; solid wheels with embossed spokes.

| | 150 | 200 | 150 |

(B) 1925. Also catalogued as set No. 260; same as (A), but red, brown, maroon, or dark green; one nickel working headlight.

| | 150 | 200 | 150 |

(C) 1925-26. Same as (A), but two pickup rollers.

| | 150 | 200 | 150 |

(D) 1925-26. Same as (B), but turquoise, red, or orange; two pickup rollers.

| | 150 | 200 | 150 |

(E) 1926. Same as (D), but with manual reverse.

| | 150 | 200 | 150 |

(F) 1927-29. Similar to (D), but with new longer 6¾" body, 7¼" overall; red, orange, or olive green; roof ridge; no end handrails or reverse; no brass ventilator covers (but with

slots for them); one nickel or enameled (1928-29) working headlight.

| | 170 | 215 | 160 |

(G) 1927-29. Same as (F), but with end handrails, brass ventilator covers; 1929 version has open-spoke wheels.

| | 170 | 215 | 160 |

(H) 1930-33. Similar to (F), but with new longer 7" body, 7¼" overall; red or green; roof ridge; embossed "NYC" and "51" eliminated and replaced with decals lettered "DORFAN / LINES" at left of door and "-NO-/ 51" at right; decaled ventilator covers; four-pane window inserts; open-spoke wheels.

| | 175 | 225 | 175 |

No. 52 TAKE-APART LOCOMOTIVE: 1928-33. Catalogue number for No. 51 locomotive with hand reverse lever.

(A) 1927-28. Same as 51 (F), dark green, blue, orange, or olive green; brass ventilator covers and handrails; body castings embossed "51"; reverse switch.

| | 150 | 210 | 150 |

(B) 1929-33. Same as 51 (H), red or green; embossed "NYC" and "51" and ventilator covers eliminated and replaced by decals; brass handrails; reverse switch.

| | 175 | 225 | 175 |

(No.) 53 TAKE-APART LOCOMOTIVE 1927-33. C.M. & St. Paul bipolar electric-style enameled die-cast body with two dissimilar halves containing internal mounting posts for motor and gears; 8¼" body, 9¼" overall; embossed rivet detail, journal boxes, steps, one door and two windows per side; brass plates lettered "DORFAN"on left of door, "LINE" at right od door (in early version) "-NO-/ 53" at right (early) or decals (later); embossed on one end "MADE IN U.S.A." above "THE DORFAN / CO." at left and "NEWARK, N.J." at right on pilot, "PAT. U.S. PAT. OFF. / JUNE 24 1924" on opposite end; two headlights (nickel-plated in 1927 or black-and red-enameled with simulated number plates from 1928) mounted on rods to hold body halves together; brass handrails flanking doors; brass ventilator covers; pantograph centered on top of roof; flag sockets; reverse switch; one coupler fastened with shoulder rivet; two pickup rollers; single (early) or double (later) reduction gear drive; two gear-driven axles; die-cast wheels; with (early) or without (later) enameled window frame inserts; mounting holes and brass handrails on ends; ball bearings.

(A) 1927-28. Red, blue, or black; no window frame inserts; brass plates; lettering is "DORFAN" and "LINE".

| | 300 | 400 | 300 |

(B) 1928. Heavier body casting; black or apple green; red window frame inserts; brass handrails on ends; three-color decals ½" wide and ⅞" high under cab windows (instead of brass plates) lettered diagonally "DORFAN" at left and "LINES" at right, black and red headlights; appears once in 1928 catalogue only; scarce.

Note: The diagonal decals are quite rare, having been attached to the No. 53 for only one year; they do appear in the catalogue illustrations and on the Toytown station pictured in Chapter Eight.

| | 300 | 400 | 300 |

(C) 1929. Same as (B), but black or apple green; smaller black on gold decals ½" wide and ⅜" high lettered "DORFAN / LINES" at left and "-NO-/ 53" at right; double reduction gears.

| | 300 | 400 | 300 |

(D) 1930-33. Heavier body casting with recesses for five ball bearings (four for the axles and one for one end of the armature shaft); trim same as (C), but with slots for brass

An assortment of 51s and 52s. Note the shorter body of the locomotives on the top shelf.

No. 51 (B); note the all-too-common Dorfan deterioration. Pickens Collection.

	Gd	Exc	Rst

ladders and air tanks (installed on some models only) as used on No. 54.   **350   500   350**

No. 53-RC TAKE-APART LOCOMOTIVE: 1930-33. Same as 53 (D), but with Distance Remote Control.

(No.) 54 TAKE-APART BOX CAB LOCOMOTIVE: 1930-33. New Haven-style silver-blue-enameled die-cast body with two dissimilar halves containing internal mounting posts for motor and gears; 8¼" body, 9¾" over couplers; embossed rivet detail, journal boxes, and steps; brass door (similar to Type IIa passenger car door; see Chapter Three) and two brass window inserts per side; embossed on one end "MADE IN U.S.A." above "THE DORFAN / CO." at left and "NEWARK, N.J." at right on pilot, "PAT. U.S. PAT. OFF. / JUNE 24 1924" on opposite end; two black- and red-enameled headlights with simulated number plates mounted on rods to hold body halves together; brass handrails, ventilator covers, and flag sockets; some with brass air tanks and ladders; pantograph centered on top of roof, reverse switch through slot in casting; one coupler fastened with shoulder rivet, two pickup rollers, two gear-driven axles, die-cast wheels; three-color decals lettered in red "DORFAN" at top left and "LINES" at top right, "54" below each window.

	Gd	Exc	Rst
(A) With air tanks and ladders.	300	400	300
(B) Without air tanks and ladders.	250	350	240

(No.) 54(-RC) TAKE-APART BOX CAB LOCOMOTIVE: 1930-33. Same as 54, but with Distance Remote Control.

AN UNCATALOGUED STEAM ENGINE: THE 770

In an attempt to recover business lost during the growing Depression, Dorfan engineers designed several beautiful new steam engines in Narrow and Wide Gauge (see Chapter Five). One factory pre-production sample was a Wide Gauge 4-6-2 locomotive with eight-wheel tender. This beautiful engine was never produced. In the Narrow Gauge line, John Koerber and his staff constructed a 4-4-0 steam engine with an eight-wheel tender. Called the 770, the pre-production model was pictured on an insert sheet included with a later printing of the 1930 catalogue. However, the production model was a compromise. Driving wheels, side rods, brushplate, and other parts came from the No. 55 steam engine. The tender was the familiar six-wheel Type III sold with the 55.

One 770 was reported by Malcolm Berger in the January 1988 issue of the TCA *Quarterly*. Larry Nahagian reports he has seen several production models of the 770, and there is one in the Richard Fletcher Collection. This locomotive, made when Dorfan used Ives castings, is an Ives No. 1122 with eight-wheel tender, painted bright red with yellow trim and displaying "770" and "EXPRESS 770" decals. Further comments from collectors are sought.

Closeup of 54 air tanks

Closeup of ladder

A closeup of the No. 53 showing the brass nameplates just above the frame and cast-in-place window frames

Castings made by Roger Loxley. Top: No. 55 body casting and 51 brass reproduction locomotive. Middle left: 53 reproduction locomotive in brass, painted green; the headlights, pantograph, and wheels are also reproductions. Middle right: A 54 brass reproduction body: Dorfan in brass, a tribute to Roger Loxley! Bottom: Two halves of 53 reproduction body also in brass. This is the third version of this locomotive, and this view clearly shows the sockets for the axle ball bearings (left piece) and armature ball bearings (right piece).

Top: Silver blue No. 54 electric locomotive. Middle: Red 53 locomotive, the earliest version which had brass nameplates and cast-in-place window frames. This green 53 locomotive was the second version, which featured decals and was a thicker casting. Bottom: Green 53 locomotive, shown here because it was incorrectly numbered 51, and crackle green locomotive No. 53, the third version, which featured five ball bearing assemblies and lots of brass trim.

CHAPTER THREE

★

NARROW GAUGE PASSENGER CARS

By the mid-1920s, the market for O Gauge passenger cars was well established. The major manufacturers — Ives, Lionel, and American Flyer — offered four or five lines, from diminutive four-wheel cars with simple construction to slightly larger and more elaborate cars with either four or eight wheels; a large, deluxe eight-wheel line, to a super deluxe line approaching Standard Gauge in size. There were several other manufacturers including Bing from Germany and Hafner from Chicago with attractive trains.

Lionel's mid-1920s line consisted of enameled cars with brass plates, except for its small four-wheel cars. American Flyer produced lithographed passenger cars but in the late 1920s, following Lionel's lead, it started to replace lithographed-finished cars with enameled cars with brass plates. Ives, Bing, and Hafner were producing lithographed cars.

Dorfan rapidly gained a foothold in this market because of its technological innovations. Initially dividing its line into three classes — a small four-wheel class (5½ inches long), a medium-size four-wheel class (6¾ inches long), and a deluxe eight-wheel class (7¼ inches long) — Dorfan later added two super deluxe lines. Dorfan chose lithography for its two lower-priced lines and an enameled finish with decals for its deluxe lines.

Dorfan covered the wide and varied train market by manufacturing high-to-low-end pieces. Since American Flyer, Ives, and Bing were its principal competitors at the low end, the lithographed finish made sense both from the perspective of market niche and cost.

Dorfan chose an enameled finish with brass plates for its early trains to compete with the more expensive Lionel line. Brass plates are relatively expensive to produce and substantially increase the cost of car assembly. Dorfan, however, discovered how to match the appeal of Lionel's brass plates at a much lower cost. Its innovation was to substitute decals for brass plates. Moreover, printed decals allowed more elaborate designs than brass plates. This innovation was so effective and inexpensive that Ives, American Flyer, and Lionel all adapted it. Brass nameplates were used on the early painted cars, but it was not long before decals replaced them. Sometimes a brass plate was painted over and a decal put on top. A few inconsistencies will be noted in the choice of decals or selection of window frames; this could have resulted from parts shortages.

Second, Dorfan introduced window passengers, as illustrated in Chapter One. The toy train operator no longer

Decal placed over a painted plate

Earliest nameplate

The decal over a painted plate is partially gone, exposing the painted-over lettering.

had to imagine passengers inside the car because Dorfan put them in the windows. These passengers were not printed silhouettes on translucent film but metal heads and torsos in full color. The No. 490 Pullman cars used a strip of lithographed metal having eight different heads and torsos punched in profile; each passenger had different headgear and clothing. The larger cars had three-dimensional cast-metal people, like the upper parts of lead soldiers, which were attached to flat tabs and hand-painted in great detail. The word "Germany" is stamped on many of the tabs, indicating the origin of this painstaking labor. This innovation was not adopted by its competitors at the time but in 1950 Lionel added silhouettes to its deluxe Madison series passenger cars.

Finally, Dorfan addressed a source of annoyance to both real railroad and toy train passengers: flickering overhead lights. O Gauge toy train passenger cars were lighted with current from the center rail and from the two outside rails. Current is picked up from the center rail by means of a roller

Development of the pickup roller and car floor. Top to bottom: Car with center pickup; car with roller pickup and plate over center pickup hole; car without center hole and with roller pickup on truck.

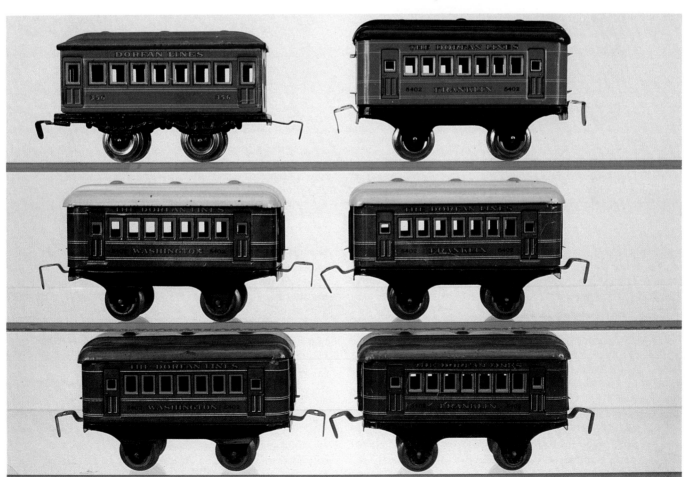

Top: No. 356 passenger and 5402 Franklin (catalogued as No. 470 in 1925–1930). The 356 differs from other Dorfan cars with its square corners rather than round corners and shows its Fandor ancestry. The 5402 dates from 1925 since it has red lithography and a black roof. It has a Type I vestibule with a pair of angles. Middle: Two 5402s with green bodies and yellow roofs from 1929 with Type II vestibule with protruding lip; it was also produced with "Jefferson" markings. Bottom: Two more 5402s but with green bodies and green roofs. These cars were not catalogued so dating is uncertain but it is likely that they were produced after 1930.

Top: The early four-wheel series came in both lithographed as well as enameled finishes (the previous plate showed the lithographed cars which were catalogued as 470s). The enameled brown passenger car shown on the top shelf was catalogued as a 480. Middle: Dorfan made orange 480s with brown doors and Type I vestibules and green doors and Type II vestibules. The author has not seen the reverse combination. Bottom: The No. 490 Pullman was introduced in 1925 painted dark green with brass plates and floor-mounted pickup roller. In the plates that follow, these features will change. The car on the right has the people reversed; this is uncommon.

assembly which was first mounted on the car floor and later on the truck frame. However, the ground side of the circuit which comes through the car wheels, axles, trucks, and body produces intermittent current flow, and this creates flickering lights.

To surmount this problem, Dorfan added an additional soldered connection from the truck to the car body. A flexible wire was soldered from the lamp bracket to the truck pivot screw, an innovation unique among American manufacturers (Lionel in the 1940s added ground circuits to its four driver locomotives from the tenders in an attempt to alleviate intermittent electrical connections).

Dorfan's smallest and earliest passenger cars (such as the No. 355) were punched and formed from a single sheet of lithographed tinplate and were offered in train sets in all catalogues. By comparison, the larger, more detailed cars, such as the No. 493 Pullman, used as many as 117 parts.

In 1928 Dorfan introduced its super deluxe 10-inch cars with die-cast wheels and three-part air tanks. Die-cast wheels had not been previously used on any O Gauge passenger cars. These may or may not have reduced

production costs since the required finishing probably was as expensive as the assembly of the traditional two-part stamped wheel. But these wheels gave Dorfan's line a distinctive quality in a crowded marketplace. By 1930 Dorfan offered five different classes of passenger cars. The more complex the line, the greater the production and marketing costs. On the other hand, the more complex or elaborate the line, the more market niches Dorfan could fill. Dorfan's expansion was exceptionally rapid.

Most Dorfan car wheels were of stamped, nickel-plated steel with a profile different from those used by American Flyer or Lionel trains. The 492-series cars, tenders, and some freight cars were fitted with die-cast metal wheels. Handrails of solid brass rods were attached by two brass cotter pins spread open inside the car body. Bodies of the smaller, cheaper cars were assembled with tabs in slots, while the better cars were assembled with eyelets. The coupler design (except the automatic coupler) allowed three methods of attachment to locomotives and cars. The end could be inserted in a slot in the car floor and twisted, an eyelet could be inserted in the hole in the coupler, or a

Gd   Exc   Rst

shoulder rivet could be attached for use on the die-cast electric locomotives. Depending on the method of attachment, Dorfan's car lengths (measured over extended couplers) varied. The observation car, having no rear coupler, was catalogued as shorter than its matching Pullman, though the body was the same length. All the truck frames on the double-truck cars had similar outlines, though some had holes for attachment of a pickup roller and/or slots for journal boxes.

Note: The No. 5 machine screw with forty threads per inch is not a common size, though screws and nuts can still be ordered through specialty stores. Dorfan used this screw, called the "5-40," for truck and roof assembly. The knurled nuts used to attach the roofs are very difficult to find, so collectors should be careful not to lose them.

TYPES USED IN DESCRIPTIONS OF NARROW GAUGE PASSENGER AND FREIGHT CARS

The designations in the boxes are used in this chapter and in Chapter Four.

DETAILED LISTINGS

5½" CARS (four wheels)

No. 355 PULLMAN: 1925-30. Lithographed body and roof, punched and formed from a single sheet of tinplate; coupler hook formed on one end and a large ring punched in the other; lettering shows "THE DORFAN LINES" and "PULLMAN", and window frames, door outlines, and "MADE IN USA" are lithographed too.

(A) Yellow body; orange roof, underframe, and lettering.

| | **35** | **50** | **—** |

Vestibule Types

Type I Unpainted or enameled tinplate pair of ⁵⁄₁₆" x ¾" angles with tabs; some had small punched holes, the purpose for which is undetermined.

Type II A rectangular, formed frame ¾" x 1⅜" with protruding lower lip.

Type III A rectangular, formed frame ¾" x 1⅝".

Door Types

Type I Flat, enameled with tabs top and bottom. ⁷⁄₁₆" x 1³⁄₁₆".

Type IIa Formed panel and frame with tabs top and bottom; brass or enameled. ½" x 1⅜".

Type IIb Brass only; same as II, but has additional tabs at window opening. These windows are used on the No. 54 locomotive.

Type III Formed panel and frame; brass or enameled with tabs top and bottom. ⁹⁄₁₆" x 2".

Left to right: Vestibule Types I, II, and III

Truck Frame Types

Type I Nickel-plated; not punched for journal boxes.

Type II Black-enameled; not punched for journal boxes.

Type III Black-enameled; punched for journal boxes, but no journals installed.

Type IVa Black-enameled; equipped with nickel journal boxes

Type IVb Black-enameled; equipped with brass journal boxes.

I

II

III

IV

Top: The No. 490 Boston and Seattle Pullman cars have the early style two-color decals which cover the brass plates found on the earlier cars. These new cars also have handrails but retain the floor-mounted pickup rollers found on the earlier models. Bottom: The No. 491 observation, constructed from a 480 Pullman with the addition of a brass platform and longer roof and floor, and the 490 Boston Pullman. The 490 has the later style three-color decals above the windows, the later handrails, and the truck-mounted rollers. However, the large hole in the floor is covered with a plate: obviously, the factory did not want to scrap the floors that had the holes punched, but the labor and materials cost of designing, stamping, and inserting the cover plate certainly exceeded the cost of scrapping the original floors, if you view this from today's engineering perspective.

	Gd	Exc	Rst

(B) Red body; black roof, underframe, and pin striping; yellow lettering and window frames.   **40**   **60**   —

(C) Orange body; black roof, underframe, and pin striping.   **40**   **60**   —

6¾" CARS (5¼" body; four wheels)

(No.) 356 PULLMAN: 1930. Folded and tabbed two-piece steel body with square corners (unlike rounded corners on all other Dorfan production), punched for seven main windows plus two door windows each side, door and two windows each end; dark red lithographed sides with yellow and black borders around windows and doors; double yellow pinstripes below windows enclosing "356" at each end, single yellow pinstripes enclosing "DORFAN LINES" in yellow with black borders above windows; dark red-enameled roof with sharp corners (unlike rounded corners on all other Dorfan production); four-wheel black-enameled frame with simulated steps and springs; no journals; extends ⅛" beyond body on all sides (appears identical to frame on Fandor caboose observed in McKenney Collection); stamped-steel wheels; hook couplers (appear identical to Fandor caboose); probably assembled partially from imported Fandor parts; listed only in the 1930 dealer catalogue in mechanical set No. 136.   **45**   **75**   —

No. 470 PULLMAN: 1925-30. Formed (with rounded corners) two-piece steel 5¼" body assembled with unpainted Type I or enameled Type II vestibules, tabbed to frame; punched for seven main windows plus two small door windows each side, not punched for windows at ends; lithographed sides with double pinstripes below windows enclosing "5402 FRANKLIN 5402" (alternate names

"HAMILTON", "WASHINGTON", "JEFFERSON"), single pinstripes enclosing "THE DORFAN LINES" above windows, "MADE IN / U.S.A." on each end at lower left; two lithographed portholes enclose door on each end; enameled roof; unembossed four-wheel black-enameled frame bent inward to hold axles; stamped-steel wheels; hook couplers.

(A) 1925. Dark red body; Type I vestibules; black roof; twist shank couplers.   **45**   **65**   —

(B) 1926-30. Dark red body and roof; Type I vestibules; twist shank couplers.   **45**   **65**   —

(C) 1929-30. Green body; yellow roof; Type II vestibules; couplers fastened with eyelets.   **45**   **65**   —

(D) 1930(?). Green body and roof; Type II vestibules; couplers fastened with eyelets.   **45**   **65**   —

No. 480 PULLMAN: 1925-27. Same construction as No. 470; enameled body and roof with brass plates lettered "DORFAN LINES" or decals lettered "PULLMAN" above windows, no other lettering or details; some versions with attached Type I doors tabbed at top and bottom; black-enameled frame.

(A) 1925. Brown or reddish-brown body and roof; brass plates; Type I vestibules; twist shank couplers.   **50**   **75**   **50**

(B) 1926-27. Orange body and roof; decals; Type II vestibules; green or brown doors; twist shank couplers.   **50**   **75**   **50**

5402: See No. 470.

7¼" CARS (6¼" body; eight wheels)

No. 490 PULLMAN: 1925-30. Formed two-piece 6¼" enameled steel body assembled with Type I or Type II vestibules, tabbed to frame; eight windows; some versions

Top: Restored red No. 490 Seattle Pullman with Type I vestibule. Middle: Restored red Atlanta and Boston Pullmans with Type II vestibules, handrails, no plates, and three-color 2-inch Pullman decals. Bottom: Restored red No. 491 observation and original 491 observation with three-color, 2¾-inch Pullman decals and no handrails.

	Gd	Exc	Rst

with handrails formed from bent metal rod inserted in body at top and held with cotter pins, some versions with attached Type I doors tabbed at top and bottom; lithographed steel figures in windows; brass plates or decals applied either to brass plates or body and lettered "PULLMAN", decals lettered "BOSTON", "SEATTLE", or "ATLANTA" in black on gold or red and black on gold; enameled 6¼" roof fastened with one 5-40 knurled nut on central stud projecting from heavy inner frame that contains light socket; stamped-steel wheels; enameled frame with central pickup roller mounted through holes on fiber plate, or with truck-mounted pickup roller and holes in frame covered by steel plates; hook couplers.

(A) 1925. Dark green body, roof and frame; brass "PULLMAN" plates; no handrails; Type I trucks; Type I vestibules; floor-mounted pickup. **50 75 50**

(B) Same as (A), but with brass handrails.
50 75 50

(C) 1926. Same as (B), but turquoise body, roof, and frame. **60 100 60**

(D) 1926. Olive green body, roof, and frame; brass handrails; 2" "PULLMAN" decals; Type I trucks; Type I vestibules. **35 45 25**

(E) 1927. Same as (D), but truck-mounted pickup; brass "PULLMAN" plates; no decals. **35 45 25**

(F) 1927. Turquoise body, roof and frame; brass handrails; 2¾" "PULLMAN" decals; Type I trucks; Type I vestibules; truck-mounted pickup. **35 45 25**

(G) 1927. Same as (F), but bright red body, roof, and frame; 2" "PULLMAN" decals. **35 45 25**

(H) 1928. Blue body, roof, and frame; red Type I doors; brass handrails; 2" "PULLMAN" decals; Type III trucks; Type II vestibules; truck-mounted pickup. **35 45 25**

(I) 1928-29. Olive green body, roof, and frame; red Type I doors; no handrails; 2¾" "PULLMAN" decals; Type I trucks; Type I vestibules; truck-mounted pickup. **35 45 25**

No. 491 OBSERVATION: 1926-29. Formed two-piece 5¼" enameled steel body (borrowed from 480-series cars, which were smaller in size) assembled with Type I or Type II vestibule and brass-painted observation platform, tabbed to 6¼" 490-series frame; seven windows; some versions with handrails formed from bent metal rod inserted in body at top and held with cotter pins at end opposite observation platform, some versions with attached doors tabbed at top and bottom; redundant doors at observation end (due to borrowed smaller 480-series body), likewise, unneeded slots for observation

Top: Grayish blue No. 490 Boston Pullmans with Type III trucks punched for journal boxes but without journals. People originally came with these cars (1928). Middle: The blue-green 495 Boston and Seattle Pullmans without people and lights have handrails but do not have separate doors, and came with mechanical sets or inexpensive electric sets. Note that the floor and roof are a contrasting maroon color. Bottom: 495 Seattle and Atlanta Pullmans without people and lights, and with doors but no handrails. Dorfan made cars with various combinations of features, but there are only about twenty combinations that have been observed out of the hundreds that could exist.

	Gd	Exc	Rst

platform in opposite end; no lithographed steel figures in windows (although shown with figures in catalogue and slots for them exist in the floor); brass plates or decals lettered "PULLMAN" in red and black on gold, decals lettered "OB-SERVATION" in black on gold; enameled 6¼" roof fastened with one 5-40 knurled nut on central stud projecting from heavy inner frame supporting light socket; stamped-steel wheels; enameled frame with central pickup roller mounted through holes on fiber plate, or with truck-mounted pickup roller and holes in frame covered by steel plates; hook couplers.

(A) 1926. Turquoise body, roof, and frame; brass "PULLMAN" plates; brass handrails; Type I trucks; Type I vestibules; floor-mounted pickup; matches 490 (C).

	60	115	60

(B) 1927. Same as (A), but with 2¾" "PULLMAN" decals; matches 490 (F).

	40	50	30

(C) 1927. Bright red body, roof, and frame; brass handrails; 2" "PULLMAN" decals; Type I trucks; Type I vestibules; truck-mounted pickup; matches 490 (G).

	40	50	30

(D) 1928. Blue body, roof, and frame; two red Type I doors at end opposite observation platform; brass handrails; 2" "PULLMAN" decals; Type III trucks; Type II vestibules; truck-mounted pickup; matches 490 (H).

	40	50	30

(E) 1928-29. Olive green body, roof, and frame; red Type I doors; no handrails; 2¾" "PULLMAN" decals; Type I trucks; Type I vestibules; truck-mounted pickup; matches 490 (I).

	40	50	25

No. 495 PULLMAN: Same construction as No. 490, but without lights, roller pickup, or figures in windows; 2" "PULLMAN" decals above windows and "SEATTLE", "BOSTON", or "ATLANTA" decals on sides; catalogued separately from 490 series and supplied with mechanical and low-priced electric sets.

(A) 1928. Maroon body, roof, and frame; yellow Type I doors; no handrails; Type III trucks; Type II vestibules.

	40	55	30

(B) 1929. Same as (A), but orange with bright red doors.

	40	55	30

Top: Orange No. 495 Boston Pullman with red attached doors and no handrails. Note the early style "Boston" decal with the large letters. Blue-green 495 Atlanta Pullman with red roof and floor, people, handrails but no lights. Middle: Red 498 Pullmans with handrails and yellow-painted inserted doors and windows. This series with 6¼-inch-long bodies was first offered in 1930 and represented a premium version of the four-wheel car. The older style four-wheel car, which was 5¼ inches long, was continued. Bottom: A comparison of a restored Atlanta, originally with Pullman decal above the window and an original Atlanta with "Dorfan Lines" above the window.

	Gd	Exc	Rst
(C) 1930. Blue body; maroon roof and frame; no doors; brass handrails; Type III trucks; Type I vestibules without holes in top piece.	40	55	30
(D) (?). Same as (C), but bright red roof and frame.	40	55	30
(E) (?). Red body, roof, and frame; no doors; brass handrails; Type I trucks; Type I vestibule.	40	55	30
(F) (?). Orange body, roof, and frame; green Type I doors; no handrails; Type I trucks; Type II vestibules.	40	55	30

No. 498 PULLMAN: 1930. Folded two-piece 6¼" enameled steel body assembled with Type II vestibules, tabbed to frame; four buff (dusty yellow) enameled window frame inserts usually divided by central post into two lights; handrails formed from bent metal rod inserted in body at top and held with cotter pins; Type IIa doors with embossed panels tabbed at top and bottom; most without lithographed steel figures in windows (although figures observed in some maroon cars only); 2" decals lettered "DORFAN LINES"

above windows on most examples, decals below windows lettered "BOSTON", "SEATTLE", or "ATLANTA" in red and black on gold; enameled 6¼" roof fastened with one 5-40 knurled nut on central stud projecting from heavy inner frame; not illuminated; 2"-wide four-wheel black-enameled frame with embossed steps, air tanks, and single-spring journals (very similar to Lionel 529-series frame), not bent inward as on 470 series and requiring eyelet spacers on axles between wheels and frame, stamped-steel wheels; hook couplers attached with eyelets.

	Gd	Exc	Rst
(A) Bright red body and roof; buff doors (matching window frames).	40	60	25
(B) Dark metallic maroon body (called "brown" in catalogue); buff roof and doors.	40	60	25
(C) Turquoise body and roof; buff doors.	40	60	25
(D) Olive green body and roof; red doors.	40	60	25

No. 499 OBSERVATION: 1930. Same construction as No. 498 with separate end panel at platform end; four buff-enameled window frames with or without central post to

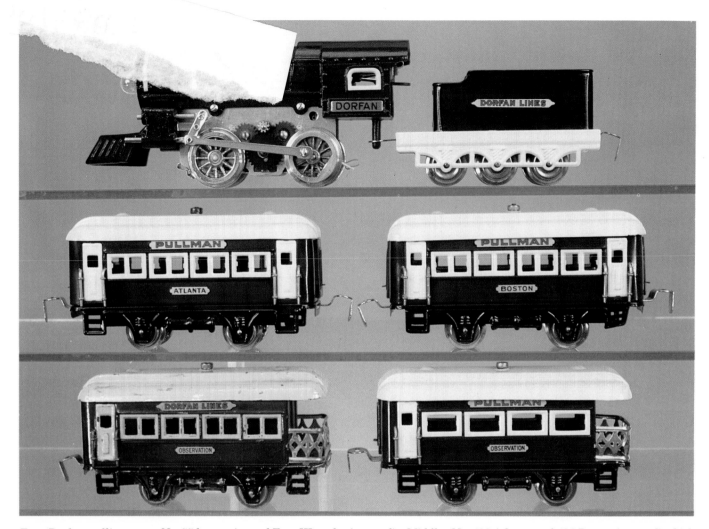

Top: Dark metallic maroon No. 55 locomotive and Type III tender (restored). Middle: No. 498 Atlanta and 498 Boston (restored) which accompanied the 55 locomotive and tender in a set advertised in 1930. Dorfan called this paint "brown." Bottom: Two 499 observations which demonstrate the variations in window style and decals.

	Gd	Exc	Rst

divide lights (an apparently random variation); unpainted brass observation platform, door to observation platform tabbed to separate body end panel; decals below windows lettered "OBSERVATION".

(A) Bright red body and roof; matches No. 498 (A).

	45	75	35

(B) Dark metallic maroon body (called "brown" in catalogue); buff roof and doors; matches No. 498 (B). **45 75 30**

(C) Turquoise body and roof; buff doors; matches No. 498 (C).

	45	75	30

(D) Olive green body and roof; red doors; matches No. 498 (D).

	45	75	30

9" CARS (7½" body; eight wheels)

No. 496 PULLMAN: 1929-30. 7½" enameled steel body assembled with Type III vestibules, fastened to frame with eyelets; four window frame inserts usually divided by central post into two lights; brass handrails; Type IIa doors tabbed at top and bottom; four three-dimensional hand-painted die-cast figures in windows on each side mounted on metal strips attached to frame by eyelets; decals lettered "PULLMAN"

above windows, decals lettered "BOSTON" or "SEATTLE" below windows; enameled roof fastened with two 5-40 knurled nuts on studs projecting from heavy inner frame containing light socket or two binding-head screws; Type IVa trucks (nickel journals) or IVb trucks (brass journals); stamped-steel wheels; truck-mounted brass pickup roller with nickel frame, fiber plate, and coil spring; hook couplers attached with eyelets.

(A) 1929. Blue body, roof, and frame; buff windows and doors; Type IVa trucks. **50 80 40**

(B) 1930. Dark red body, roof, and frame; brass windows and doors; Type IVb trucks. **70 90 60**

(C) 1930. Silver-blue body; bright red roof and frame; brass windows and doors; Type IVb trucks. **70 90 60**

(D) 1929. Silver-blue body, roof, and floor; brass windows and doors; Type IVb trucks; shown in 1929 catalogue, but not confirmed. **NRS**

No. 497 OBSERVATION: 1929-30. Same construction as 7½" No. 496; three window frames with or without central post to divide lights (an apparently random variation), one elliptical window frame at observation platform end;

Top: Red No. 499 observations that match the 498 Pullmans in the previous plate. Note that one is lettered "Pullman" and the other is lettered "Dorfan Lines" above the windows. A new stamping die was made for the observation. Middle: Olive green 499 observation with yellow windows and red doors. Bottom: Blue 498 Boston and 499 observation that have yellowed from a factory coat of lacquer; the original color is visible inside the car (blue model railroad paint is particularly susceptible to aging).

	Gd	Exc	Rst

unpainted brass or red-painted tinplate observation platform lighted by red bulb in socket in roof, three die-cast hand-painted figures per side; decals above windows lettered "PULLMAN" and below windows lettered "OBSERVATION".

(A) 1929. Blue body, roof, and frame; buff windows and doors; brass platform; Type IVa trucks; matches No. 496 (A).

	45	75	35

(B) 1930. Dark red body, roof, and frame; brass windows, doors, and platform; Type IVb trucks; matches No. 496 (B).

	60	80	40

(C) 1930. Silver-blue body; bright red roof and frame; brass windows, doors, and platform; Type IVb trucks; matches No. 496 (C).

	60	80	40

(D) 1929. Silver-blue body, roof, and frame; brass windows, doors, and platform; Type IVb trucks; matches No. 496 (D); shown in 1929 catalogue but not confirmed. **NRS**

(E) Date unknown. Same as (C), but with red-painted tinplate platform matching roof and frame.

	65	90	50

	Gd	Exc	Rst

10" CARS (1928–1930; 8¾" body; eight wheels)

(No.) 492 BAGGAGE: 1928-30. 8¾" enameled steel body assembled with Type III vestibules, fastened to frame with eyelets; two small bright red window frame inserts per side divided into five lights simulating bars; two bright red sliding baggage doors embossed with four indented panels and cut out for four window lights; large brass door handles (same as boxcar); individual gold letters and numbers spell "THE DORFAN LINES" at top, "492" in center and "AMERICAN RAILWAY EXPRESS" at bottom of sides; two three-piece black-enameled air tanks with nickeled ends fastened to frame by eyelets; enameled roof fastened with two 5-40 knurled nuts on studs projecting from heavy inner frame supporting light socket; Type IVa trucks (nickel journals), heavy die-cast wheels; truck-mounted nickel pickup roller with nickel frame, fiber plate, and coil spring; hook couplers attached with eyelets; electric interior lights.

(A) 1928-30. Apple green body, roof, and frame.

	50	100	40

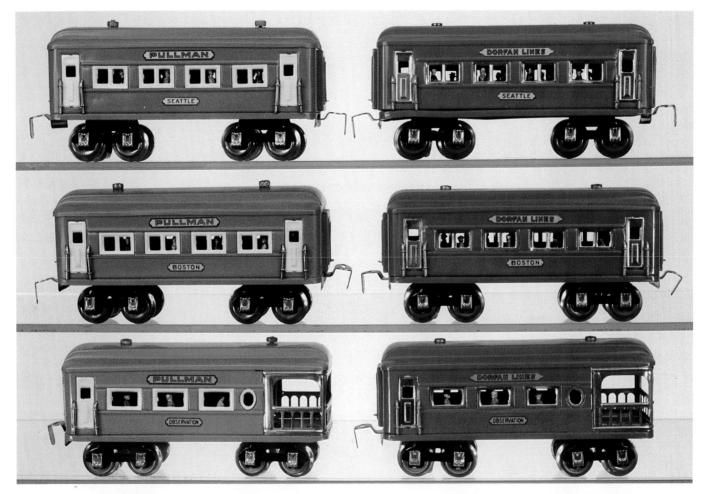

A new series of 7½-inch eight-wheel passenger cars was introduced in 1929. These cars featured three dimensional hand-painted passengers — a substantial improvement when compared with the two-dimensional lithographed figures used in earlier designs. Dorfan used ten eyelets to mount the car sides to the base. The cars glistened with trim — handrails, journal boxes, and brass observation platforms — and a red lamp lighted the observation platform. The blue cars were first catalogued in 1929 and have Type IVa trucks. The red cars were first catalogued in 1930 and have Type IVb trucks in addition to their brass doors and windows. Restored cars from the McKenney Collection.

	Gd	Exc	Rst

(B) 1929. Crackle green body and frame; bright red roof.

	50	100	40

(C) (?). Crackle green body; black roof. | 50 | 100 | 40 |

(No.) 493 PULLMAN: 1928-30. Same construction as No. 492; five bright red window frame inserts; brass handrails; bright red Type II doors tabbed at top and bottom; with five three-dimensional hand-painted die-cast figures in windows on each side mounted on metal strips attached to frame by eyelets; individual gold letters and numbers spell "THE DORFAN LINES" above and "493 SEATTLE 493" below windows; two three-piece black-enameled air tanks with nickeled ends fastened to frame by eyelets; enameled roof fastened with two 5-40 knurled nuts on studs projecting from heavy inner frame supporting light socket; Type IVa trucks (nickel journals); heavy die-cast wheels, truck-mounted nickel pickup roller with nickel frame, fiber plate, and coil spring; hook couplers attached with eyelets; electric interior lights.

(A) 1928-30. Apple green body, roof, and frame; window frames divided by central post into two lights; matches 492 (A). | 50 | 100 | 40 |

	Gd	Exc	Rst

(B) 1929. Crackle green body and frame; bright red roof; undivided window frames; matches 492 (B).

	50	100	40

(C) (?). Crackle green body; black roof; undivided window frames; matches 492 (C). | 50 | 100 | 40 |

(No.) 494 OBSERVATION: 1928-30. Same construction as No. 492; four bright red window frame inserts, elliptical window frame insert at platform end; brass handrails; brass observation platform lighted by red bulb in socket in roof; electric interior lights; bright red Type IIa doors tabbed at top and bottom at end opposite platform; with four three-dimensional hand-painted die-cast figures in windows on each side mounted on metal strips attached to frame by eyelets; individual gold letters and numbers spell "THE DORFAN LINES" above and "494 OBSERVATION 494" below windows; two three-piece black-enameled air tanks with nickeled ends fastened to frame by eyelets; enameled roof fastened with two 5-40 knurled nuts on studs projecting from heavy inner frame supporting light socket; Type IVa trucks (nickel journals); heavy die-cast wheels, truck-mounted nickel pick-

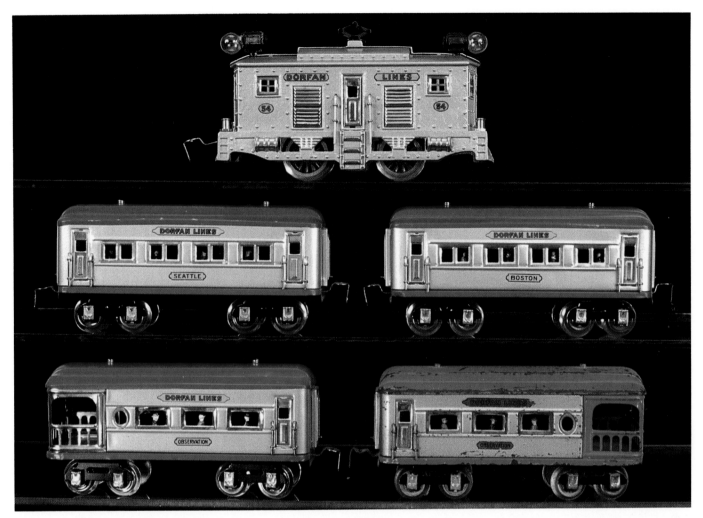

Top: No. 54 box cab electric locomotive resplendent in brass trim: ventilator covers, windows, doors, air tanks, flagholders, handrails, and ladders. Lionel and American Flyer made very similarly decorated engines at the same time. Middle: No. 496 Seattle and Boston Pullmans in silver blue, and red with brass trim. Dorfan did not make an Atlanta in this series. Bottom: Two No. 497 observations, one with brass platform and the uncommon version with red-painted tinplate observation railing. The set which consisted of the 54, two Pullmans, and one observation, was called Silver-Blue Arrow (set 256). The engine and three cars were restored by Carlton McKenney; the fourth car is original.

	Gd	Exc	Rst

up roller with nickel frame; fiber plate and coil spring; hook couplers attached with eyelets.

(A) 1928-30. Apple green body, roof, and frame; window frames divided by central post into two lights; matches No. 492 (A). **65 125 50**

(B) 1929. Crackle green body and frame; bright red roof; undivided window frames; matches No. 492 (B). **65 150 55**

(C) (?). Crackle green body; black roof; undivided window frames; matches No. 492 (C). **65 150 55**

(No.) 496 PULLMAN: Uncatalogued; 8¾" body, same as No. 493, but lettered "496 BOSTON 496" below windows; sold in four car sets only; differs from 7½" No. 496 Pullman described in the preceding section.

(A) 1928-30. Apple green body, roof, and frame; window frames divided by central post into two lights, matches No. 492 (A). **70 125 60**

(B) 1929. Crackle green body and frame; bright red roof; undivided window frames; matches No. 492 (B). **80 140 70**

(C) (?). Crackle green body; black roof; undivided window frames; matches No. 492 (C). **80 140 70**

In 1928 Dorfan introduced its longest Narrow Gauge rolling stock. The new series of 8¾-inch passenger cars were catalogued as Nos. 492, 493, 494, and 496 and marked with their catalogue numbers, a major breakthrough in product merchandising. This series featured Dorfan's first American Railway Express car, new die-cast wheels for better weight distribution, and three-piece air tanks. Top and second: Uncatalogued crackle green cars with black roofs that were packed with a black No. 53 locomotive. Third and bottom: Crackle green cars with red roofs which were packed with matching crackle green 53 locomotive. This set was apparently not catalogued.

CHAPTER FOUR

★

NARROW GAUGE FREIGHT CARS

Dorfan's 1926 catalogue introduced the first of the Narrow Gauge freight trains. The biggest set was "Big Bill" train 241, which had an engine and seven new lithographed freight cars. For this series standard equipment included 6¼-inch-long black floors, black ladders, and brakewheel stands, as well as black sliding-door hardware on the boxcars.

Lithography on the cars was quite realistic. Two of the boxcars had lithographed wood siding, while the yellow New York Central car showed riveted steel plating. The bodies (with some exceptions) were assembled from two identical lithographed stampings tabbed to each other to form a rectangle, and the assembly was then riveted to the car floor. The two body halves were identical except that one had additional slots punched for the tabs of the brakewheel stand and the ladder. Sometimes two identical car sides were selected for assembly and both had punched slots; this resulted in a finished car which appeared to be missing some parts.

Couplers were attached to some of the cars by twisting the ends, but later all the couplers were attached with eyelets. Later versions of these freight cars had trucks attached with eyelets instead of screws and nuts. With the exception of a four-wheel caboose, which resembled a Fandor caboose, all had eight wheels in trucks that were attached with 5-40 machine screws and hex nuts.

The No. 607 eight-wheel caboose appeared in the 1928 catalogue. It was not included with train sets but was only available as an extra car. By 1929 it was joined by the 610 derrick and the 609 flatcar, or lumber car, with its load of wood. The lumber car is the scarcest of all the Narrow Gauge freight cars, possibly because the lumber load was easily lost and the fragile stake sides often were bent or broken. A car in this condition might have been discarded.

The derrick car, on the other hand, was (and is) prized by its owners. Its three-color lithographed cab was equipped with two crankwheels, one for swinging the red boom and one for lifting a load with the hook.

A careful look at the freight train sets in the 1930 catalogue will reveal the first (and last) illustration of the use of Type IVb trucks on freight cars. These cars were not only fitted with trucks with brass journal boxes but, in Dorfan's last years of production, brass sliding door hardware, ladders, and brakewheels were added. Later still came automatic couplers (see Chapter Six) and the use of die-cast wheels on the freight cars, but these refinements appeared after the last catalogue.

Except for the No. 606 caboose, all the following listings are of 7½-inch cars (1926–1930; 6¼-inch body, eight wheels). For explanations of truck types, see the box at the beginning of Chapter Three. Side-of-car numbers for Narrow Gauge freight cars appear at the end of each category of car for cross-reference to the proper listing by catalogue number.

BOXCARS

No. 601 N.Y.C. BOXCAR: 1926-30. Folded and tabbed tan-two-piece steel body; black-enameled frame; black-enameled brakewheel platform tabbed to one end, nickel or brass brakewheel; stamped-steel wheels except version (E); tan enameled roof; five-step ladder; lithographed sliding doors with large handles and "NYC" at center; upper and lower door guides tabbed to sides; tan lithographed sides with elliptical "NEW YORK / CENTRAL / LINES" logo at upper right, simulating riveted steel construction; lettered at left "N.Y.C. / 3182999 / CAP'Y 110000 LBS. / WT. 46000 NEW 9-22 / DORFAN LINES" and at right "HGT. AT EAVES 12 FT. 8 IN. / WTH. AT EAVES 9 FT. 2 IN. / LGT. INSIDE 40 FT. 6 IN. / WDTH. INSIDE 8 FT. 6 IN / HGT. INSIDE 8 FT. 7 IN. / CAP'Y 2955 CU. FT.", lettered on both ends "N.Y.C. / S-182999 / MADE IN U.S.A. / TYPE D COUPLER SHANK 6X8 / FRICTION DRAFT GEAR / FORGED YOKE 6X1-1/2 KEY / K-2 TRIPLE".

(A) Type I trucks fastened with screws; black trim; nickel brakewheel; twist shank couplers.   **35   45   —**

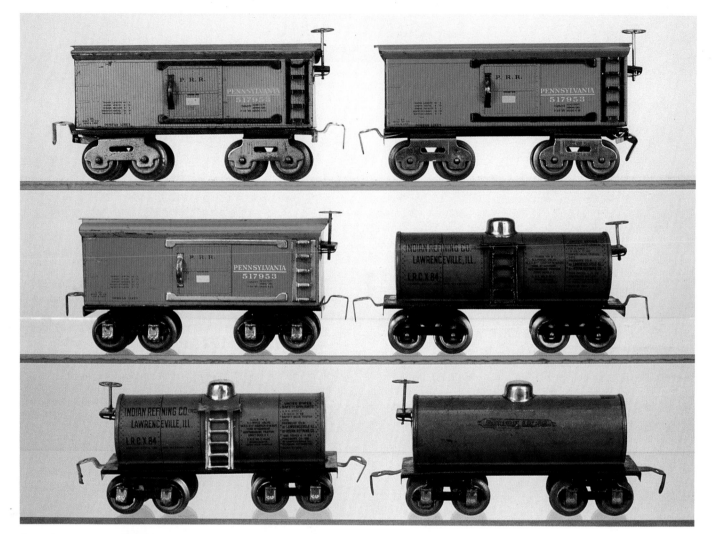

Top: Two No. 603 PRR boxcars, each trimmed in black and fitted with Type I trucks. The car on the left has faded from orange to yellow. Middle: 603 PRR boxcar with brass trim and fitted with Type IVb trucks; No. 604 oil tank car with black trim and fitted with Type III trucks. Bottom: 604 (D) oil tank car fitted with a yellow ladder; on the right, version (F) with "Dorfan Lines" decal, and on top a locomotive decal 3931 — a car evidently assembled at the Dorfan factory by an employee with a sense of humor.

	Gd	Exc	Rst

(B) Type II trucks fastened with screws; black trim; nickel or brass brakewheel; couplers fastened with eyelets.

| | 35 | 45 | — |

(C) Type III trucks fastened with screws or eyelets; black trim; brass brakewheel; couplers fastened with eyelets.

| | 35 | 45 | — |

(D) Type IVb trucks and couplers fastened with eyelets; brass trim, brass brakewheel.

| | 40 | 60 | — |

(E) Same as (D), but equipped with uncatalogued automatic couplers and die-cast wheels.

| | 60 | 90 | — |

No. 602 UNION PACIFIC BOXCAR: 1926-30. Folded and tabbed two-piece steel body; black-enameled frame; black-enameled brakewheel platform tabbed to one end, nickel or brass brakewheel; stamped-steel wheels except version (E); green-enameled roof; five-step ladder; lithographed sliding doors with large handles and "UP" at upper center and "TACK CARD-HERE" at center; upper and lower door guides tabbed to sides; green lithographed sides simulating outside braced wooden construction, lettered at left "UNION PACIFIC / UP / 126432 / CAPACITY 3412 CU.

Comparison of No. 606 Dorfan caboose with No. 3677 Fandor caboose

Top: Yellow No. 600 gondola with Type IVb trucks; this car has been specially fitted with die-cast wheels, brass brakewheel, and automatic couplers. Bottom: No. 601 New York Central boxcar trimmed in black and fitted with Type III trucks and No. 602 Union Pacific boxcar, trimmed in black and fitted with Type I trucks.

Top: Fandor caboose, with wood-grain detailing. Middle: No. 606 (A) and (B). Bottom: 605 coal hoppers.

	Gd	Exc	Rst

FT. / 100000 LBS. / WT. 46700 NEW 5-27 / DORFAN LINES" and at right "HEIGHT AT EAVES 13 FT. 4 IN. / WIDTH AT EAVES 10 FT. 0-1/2 IN. / LENGTH INSIDE 40 FT. 6 IN. / K-2 TRIPLE VALVE / DIRT COLLECTOR / D-COUPLER SHANK 6X8 / FRICTION DRAFT GEAR / NO. 2 BRAKE BEAMS", lettered on both ends "U.P. / 126432 / MADE IN U.S.A.".

(A) Type I trucks fastened with screws; black trim; nickel brakewheel; twist shank couplers. **35 45 —**

(B) Type II trucks fastened with screws; black trim; nickel or brass brakewheel; couplers fastened with eyelets. **35 45 —**

(C) Type III trucks fastened with screws or eyelets; black trim; brass brakewheel; couplers fastened with eyelets. **35 45 —**

(D) Type IVb trucks and couplers fastened with eyelets; brass trim; brass brakewheel. **40 60 —**

(E) Same as (D), but equipped with uncatalogued automatic couplers and die-cast wheels. **40 90 —**

No. 603 PENNSYLVANIA BOXCAR: 1926-30. Similar to No. 602, but lithographed body color is described as "pink" or "red," depending on which catalogue is being consulted, and usually found faded to pale orange; the enameled roof is terra cotta in color. Simulated outside braced wooden construction is lettered at left "INSIDE LENGTH 40-5 / INSIDE WIDTH 8-5 / INSIDE HEIGHT 9-1 / HEIGHT AT EAVES 12-10 / WIDTH AT EAVES 9-2 / X 25 / BUILT 10-25 / PFW & CRW DORFAN LINES", and at right "PENNSYLVANIA / 517953 / CAPACITY 3243 CU. FT. / 100000 LBS. / P99 WT. 49100 422", lettered on both ends "P.R.R. / 517953 / A.R.A. NO. 2 BRAKE BEAMS / k-2 TRIPLE VALVE / MADE IN U.S.A."

(A) Type I truck frames; black trim. **35 45 —**

(B) Type II truck frames; black trim. **35 45 —**

(C) Type III truck frames; black trim. **35 45 —**

(D) Type IVb truck frames; brass ladder and trim. **40 60 —**

(E) Same as (D), but with die-cast wheels and automatic couplers. **60 110 —**

126432: See No. 602.

517953:. See No. 603.

3182999: See No. 601.

CABOOSES

No. 606 CABOOSE: 1926-30. Folded and tabbed 5" two-piece steel body; punched with four windows per side, two windows plus door window in ends; enameled roof, brass or lithographed cupola punched with two windows per side and three windows in each end and with enameled roof; black-enameled frame embossed with simulated coil springs; stamped-brass or black-enameled end platforms with railings (embossed with small dome in floor to clear coupler mounts) clamped to ends of frame; stamped-steel wheels; red lithographed sides with rivet detail and black-bordered yellow windows; lettered "N5 / BUILT 8.14. / P.R.R." at lower left, "PENNSYLVANIA / 486751" in center, and "DORFAN LINES" at lower right, ends lithographed with door and window detail and lettered "MADE IN U.S.A."; twist shank hook couplers.

	Gd	Exc	Rst

(A) Light brown roof and cupola roof; lithographed cupola; black railings. **45 75 —**

(B) Dark red roof and cupola roof; brass cupola and railings. **45 75 —**

Note: Richard Fletcher reports this version with green roof and dark red cupola roof.

(C) Fandor model, similar but with detailed frame (same as No. 356 Pullman) stamped "FANDOR / MADE IN GERMANY / N", sides and cupola lithographed with wood-grain detail; olive green-enameled roof, dark red-enameled cupola roof; wire railings attached to metal platform clamped to ends of frame; smaller dome over coupler mounts, Fandor couplers; lettered "NEW YORK / CENTRAL / AND / HUDSON RIVER" in center, "3677" at left and right, and "FANDOR" at top of ends; not Dorfan production, although produced for the American market, suggesting Dorfan used Fandor tooling for some parts. **45 75 —**

Note: Larry Nahagian reports other road names being available.

(No.) 607 CABOOSE: 1928-30. Folded and tabbed 6¾" two-piece steel body; punched with two windows per side divided into four panes, one door window with four panes in ends, embossed lower door in ends (strangely disconnected from upper window); green-enameled roof, brass cupola punched with two windows per side and three windows in each end and with green, red- or brown-enameled roof; black-enameled frame; stamped-brass end platforms with railings (embossed with small dome in floor to clear coupler mounts) clamped to ends of frame; stamped-steel wheels; red lithographed sides with rivet detail and green windows and belt-line stripe; lettered "N.6 / BUILT 9-28" at left and "DORFAN LINES / 607" in center, "MADE IN U.S.A." on ends; short couplers with original eyelet hole area cut off and new hole punched nearer to hook; one of only two Dorfan freight cars to bear catalogue number (see No. 610 derrick).

(A) Type III trucks fastened with screws; green cupola roof. **65 90 —**

(B) Type IVb trucks fastened with eyelets; green cupola roof. **65 90 —**

(C) Same as (B), but dark red cupola roof. **65 90 —**

(D) Same as (B), but brown cupola roof. **65 90 —**

3677: See No. 606.

486751: See No. 606.

DERRICK AND LOAD CARS

No. 609 LUMBER CAR: 1929-30. Black-enameled steel frame; three red-enameled stake assemblies fastened to frame with eyelets, center portion raised to lift lumber load above truck tabs and coupler mounts; holes punched in tops of stakes but no chain or wire retainers provided; no brakewheel; hook couplers fastened with eyelets; carries four rectangular pieces of lumber.

(A) Type III trucks. **65 125 —**

(B) Type IVb trucks. **65 125 —**

Note: Richard Fletcher comment: The 609 also came with Type IVb trucks and automatic couplers.

	Gd	Exc	Rst

(No.) 610 DERRICK CAR: 1929-30. Folded and tabbed gray lithographed steel cab; punched window and embossed door on each side with red and green lithographed details; black-enameled steel frame; green-enameled roof with embossed panels tabbed to cab; red boom fastened to large gear with eyelets; stamped-steel hook attached to cord wound around wooden spool; two ¾" wheels (similar to largest hopper control wheel but with longer crank handles) extend from back of cab to raise hook and swivel boom; large screw serves as axle for boom gear and also secures front truck through a spring clip, back truck and couplers fastened with eyelets; stamped-steel wheels; lettered "DERRICK / No. 610 / DORFAN LINES" on sides and "DORFAN LINES" in curved line above "No. 610 / MADE IN U.S.A." on end; one of only two Dorfan freight cars to bear catalogue number (see No. 607 caboose).

	Gd	Exc	Rst
(A) Type III trucks.	75	200	—
(B) Type IVb trucks.	85	225	—

GONDOLA

No. 600 GONDOLA: 1926-30. Folded and tabbed yellow two-piece steel body, folded over at top and embossed with ribs for rigidity; black-enameled frame; black-enameled brakewheel platform tabbed to one end, nickel or brass brakewheel, stamped-steel wheels except version (E); lithographed in shades of tan and yellow with elliptical "NEW YORK / CENTRAL / LINES" logo at upper right; ribs and gears with ratchets; lettered at center of sides "C.C.C. & St.L. / 140 48 / CAPY. 100000 LBS. / WT. 433000 NEW 8-22 / DORFAN LINES", lettered below logo "LENGTH 41 FT. 6 IN. / CAP'Y 1819 CU. FT. / TYPE D COUPLER SHANK 6X8 / FRICTION DRAFT GEAR / FORGED YOKE 6X1-1/2 KEYS / K-2 TRIPLE"; lettered on ends "MADE IN U.S.A.".

	Gd	Exc	Rst
(A) Type I trucks fastened with screws; nickel brakewheel; twist shank couplers.	30	45	—
(B) Type II trucks fastened with screws; nickel or brass brakewheel; couplers fastened with eyelets.	30	45	—
(C) Type III trucks fastened with screws or eyelets; brass brakewheel, couplers fastened with eyelets.	30	45	—
(D) Type IVb trucks and couplers fastened with eyelets; brass brakewheel.	35	55	—
(E) Same as (C), but equipped with die-cast wheels and uncatalogued automatic couplers; male end with track trip, female end with loop and spring-loaded top plate.	65	95	—

14048: See No. 600.

HOPPER

No. 605 COAL HOPPER CAR: 1926-30. Folded and tabbed gray two-piece steel body with top edges folded over for rigidity, fastened to frame with eyelets; black-enameled frame; black-enameled brakewheel platform tabbed to one end, nickel or brass brakewheel, nickel or brass hopper control wheel on one side (either same as brakewheel, or larger with crank handle and recessed center) attached to

shaft (with or without collars as spacers between sides) with soldered or pressed-on cam that opens two hopper doors in frame; one-piece flat brass spring fastened with eyelet between hopper doors to keep them closed; five-step ladder on same side as hopper control wheel; stamped-steel wheels except version (E); gray lithographed sides with four simulated ribs and numerous simulated rivets, twist shank couplers or short couplers with original eyelet hole area cut off and new hole punched nearer to hook; lettered "PENNSYLVANIA" at upper left, "P.R.R. / 11201" in center above hopper control wheel and "DORFAN LINES" below, "CAP'Y 110000 LBS. / WT. 4 00 NEW 9-20 / BUILT 9-20" at left, "LENGTH 40 FT. 6 IN. / CAP'T 1890 CU. FT. / COUPLER SHANK 6-8 / FRICTION DRAFT GEAR / CAST STEEL YOKE / 6 1-1/2 KEY / K 2 TRIPLE" at right, "P.R.R. / 11201" on ends at upper right.

	Gd	Exc	Rst
(A) Type I trucks fastened with screws; black ladder; nickel brakewheel; small nickel hopper control wheel; soldered cam; no collar on control shaft; twist shank couplers.	35	45	—
(B) Type II trucks fastened with screws; black ladder; nickel brakeheel; small nickel hopper control wheel; soldered cam; collar on one-half of shaft; couplers fastened with eyelets.	35	45	—
(C) Type III trucks fastened with screws or eyelets; black ladder; nickel or brass brakewheel; small nickel hopper control wheel; soldered cam; collar on one-half of shaft; couplers fastened with eyelets.	35	45	—
(D) Type IVb trucks and couplers fastened with eyelets; brass ladder; brass brakewheel; large hopper control wheel; pressed-on cam; collars on both halves of shaft.	40	60	—
(E) Same as (D), but equipped with uncatalogued automatic couplers and die-cast wheels.	60	90	—
(F) Same as (D), with Type IVb trucks, but probably earlier production, with small nickel hopper control wheel; soldered cam and half collar.	40	60	—

11201: See No. 605.

TANK CAR

84: See No. 604.

No. 604 OIL TANK CAR: 1926-30. Folded and tabbed red lithographed three-piece steel tank tabbed to frame with ends also tabbed at top; black-enameled frame; black-enameled brakewheel platform tabbed to one end, nickel or brass brakewheel; five-step ladder; nickel dome tabbed to top center; stamped-steel wheels except version (E); deep red lithographed sides with four simulated bands and eight rows of simulated rivets; lettered at left "INDIAN REFINING CO. (INC.) / LAWRENCEVILLE, ILL. / L.R.C.X. 84 / CAPACITY 60000 LBS. MTC. WT. 29400 11/2 20 / DORFAN LINES / MADE IN U.S.A.", at near right "CLASS TM 2 / K.I. TRIPLE VALVE / A.R.A. 5X7 COUPLER 9-1/8 BUTT. / YOKE ATTACHMENT / WESTINGHOUSE FRICTION / DRAFT GEAR D 2 / A.R.A. NO. 2 PLUS / BRAKE BEAMS / CAST IRON WHEELS", and at far right "UNITED STATES / SAFETY APPLIANCE / A.R.A. SPEC. 2 / I.R. CO. 11 17 22 / SAFETY VALVE TESTED / DATE / PRESSURE 25# / AT LAWRENCEVILLE ILL. / BY INDIAN REFINING CO. /

Top: No. 610 derrick; middle 609 lumber; bottom: 607 cabooses; note cupola roof variations.

Gd   Exc   Rst

TANK TESTED 4 14 25 / PRESSURE 60 LBS. / AT LAWRENCEVILLE ILL. / BY INDIAN REFINING CO. / BUILT-5-1910".

(A) Type I trucks fastened with screws; black ladder; nickel brakewheel; twist shank couplers.   **35   45   —**

(B) Type II trucks fastened with screws; black ladder; nickel or brass brakewheel; couplers fastened with eyelets.

35   45   —

(C) Type III trucks fastened with screws or eyelets; black ladder; brass brakewheel; couplers fastened with eyelets.

35   45   —

(D) Type IVb trucks and couplers fastened with eyelets; brass ladder; brass brakewheel.

Gd   Exc   Rst

Note: Richard Fletcher reports this version also with black ladders.   **35   60   —**

(E) Same as (D), but equipped with uncatalogued automatic couplers and die-cast wheels.   **60   90   —**

(F) Type IVb trucks fastened with eyelets; red-enameled tank; black brake platform, oversized ¾" brass brakewheel; yellow ladder; "DORFAN LINES" decal in black-bordered red letters on gold background on side opposite ladder; rectangular black on gold Wide Gauge locomotive decal "3931" on top near one end; probably unique, and may have been an experiment or joke; reader comments invited.

NRS

3931: See No. 604.

CHAPTER FIVE

★

WIDE GAUGE LOCOMOTIVES

In 1926 Dorfan introduced its first Wide Gauge trains pulled by the big twelve-wheel No. 3930 engine, patterned after the Pennsylvania Railroad's new L-5 electric locomotive, which was built between 1925 and 1928. "3930" was the actual number of one of the L-5s which operated on the railroad not far from the Dorfan factory. A year later, in 1927, the four-wheel 3920 joined the fleet, and those two engines furnished all the Wide Gauge Dorfan motive power. The 3920 was designed to resemble the Chicago Milwaukee and St. Paul bipolar electric locomotive which pulled trains through the Cascade Mountains of Washington. The train had considerable appeal; American Flyer, Lionel, and Ives each made models of it.

Both locomotives were classed as Loco-Builders and could be purchased in kit form with parts in a compartmentalized box so a child could assemble them (see the instructional brochure reproduced in Chapter Nine). Variations in catalogue numbers, such as 3919 and 3931, have appeared and probably designated some minor changes in the locomotives, such as non-ball bearing locomotives, during the period when some had ball bearings.

Toy locomotives usually have a sleeve-type axle bearing. The sleeve is a piece of steel or brass in which the axle turns. Sleeve bearings create a considerable amount of friction since the axle is in contact with the interior surface of the bearing. Ball bearings, therefore, were an improvement because the balls turned freely and provided less surface against which the axle would rub. However, this improvement, although great ad copy, was not as important as one might think, because the speed at which the axle turned and the weight of the engine did not readily wear out the sleeve-type axle bearing anyway (if properly lubricated).

Ball bearing models can be readily distinguished by the circular recesses in the body which hold the ball bearing assemblies. Locomotives without ball bearings only have axle recesses in their bodies. Collectors pay a premium for the ball bearing models.

No. 1134: See page 201.

No. 3920 LOCO-BUILDER ENGINE: 1927-30. 13" long body in a number of variations.

	Gd	Exc	Rst
(A) 1927-30. Orange body. In 1930, this engine was catalogued as No. 3919, possibly to distinguish it from those with ball bearings.	300	600	300
(B) 1928. Olive green body with red window frames.	375	600	350
(C) 1928-29. Red body with green window frames.	325	550	300
(D) 1929-30. Same as (B), but equipped with six ball bearings.	375	600	350
(E) 1929-30. Same as (C), but equipped with six ball bearings.	375	600	350

The rarely seen No. 3930 is featured in this promotional piece.

Dorfan's quick adoption of the Pennsylvania Railroad's new L-5 locomotive was commendable. Dorfan departed from the focus of American Flyer, Lionel, and Ives on the New York Central S-type electric and Minneapolis, St. Paul Olympian. Photograph courtesy Alvin F. Staufer.

The CM & St.P Olympian, which inspired Dorfan's No. 3920. This four-wheel engine was sometimes called the "whaleback." Two headlights, two pantographs, brass nameplates, and automatic couplers were standard equipment. Ball bearings were added in 1929.

	Gd	Exc	Rst

(F) 1929-30. Red body with brass trim and equipped with six ball bearings. **400 600 350**

(G) 1930. Maroon body with yellow window frames and equipped with six ball bearings. **375 600 350**

(H) Uncatalogued; ivory body with red roof and brass window frames, air tanks, and ladders. **600 900 450**

(I) (?). Gray body with orange window frames.

Note: Richard Fletcher has version (I) with red window frames as well and reports medium green and mustard colors with red windows. **325 550 350**

No. 3930 LOCO-BUILDER ENGINE: 1926-30. This Take-Apart engine had four leading and four trailing wheels (similar in size and design to the Narrow Gauge locomotive wheels), and the motor drove the four large spoked drivers. Some minor changes were made in the castings and trim parts during the years of production. Ball bearings were added to axle and armature shafts in 1928, while the body castings were made longer and heavier, particularly in the area of the pilots. Also in 1928, separate window inserts with mullions were added and Dorfan Dan, the little lithographed engineer, disappeared from the cab — although with the new window design, he could not have been seen anyway.

(A) 1926. Orange body with nickel-plated headlights; solid leading and trailing wheels (with simulated spokes); engineer in the cab window; no wire handrails. **750 1200 650**

(B) 1927. Olive green body with black headlights; spoked leading and trailing wheels, and added wire handrails; engineer in cab window. **750 1200 650**

(C) 1927. Similar to (B), but gray body with red wheels. **750 1200 650**

(D) 1927. Similar to (B), but black body with yellow wheels. **750 1200 650**

(E) 1928-30. Black body with yellow window frames and yellow wheels. The casting was heavier, slightly longer, and allowed for six ball bearings and window inserts; no engineer. **850 1500 700**

(F) (?). Same as (E), but with red wheels and window frames. **850 1600 700**

(G) 1928-29. Similar to (E), but blue body with yellow window frames and wheels. **900 2000 700**

(H) 1928-30. Similar to (E), but medium green body with red window frames and wheels. **850 1600 700**

	Gd	Exc	Rst

(I) 1930. Same as (E), but equipped with Distance Remote Control. **850 1600 700**

(J) 1930. Same as (E), but medium green body with red window frames and wheels; equipped with Distance Remote Control. **850 1600 700**

No. 3931 LOCO-BUILDER ENGINE: 1930 (shown only in 1930 catalogue). It is difficult to distinguish the 3930 and 3931 models. Dorfan was inconsistent in labeling its L-S production and few locomotives have 3931 markings. Locomotives with both ball bearings and Distance Remote Control are probably 3931, even if not so marked.

(A) 1930. Colonial Ivory body with red window frames and wheels; heavier, slightly longer type; later casting with ball bearings. **1250 3000 750**

(B) 1930. Same as (A), but equipped with Distance Remote Control. **1250 3000 750**

No. 3932 LOCO-BUILDER ENGINE: 1927. Black body with red window frames and wheels. **NRS**

UNCATALOGUED STEAM LOCOMOTIVE: No. 1134

In Chapter Two we discussed the uncatalogued Narrow Gauge locomotive, No. 770. Dorfan's Wide Gauge, die-cast, uncatalogued steam locomotive was the No. 1134. Using the Ives 1929-model 4-4-2 locomotive, and fitting the tenders with Dorfan die-cast trucks and wheels, Dorfan offered the engine in two colors: black with red trim and green with red trim.

The Ives version had the high, brass-colored headlight and hand reverse in the cab. Dorfan decals appeared where the Ives brass plates would normally have been applied. The green 1134 locomotive and tender were offered in a set known as the Palmetto Limited. The 995 baggage (numbered 770), the 994 Pullman (numbered 772), and the 996 observation (numbered 773) were painted green with red windows and trim. The observation car displayed a drumhead sign reading "PALMETTO LIMITED — DORFAN LINES".

Note: The Palmetto Limited was also catalogued as set 915, consisting of a green No. 3930, the 994, 995, and 996.

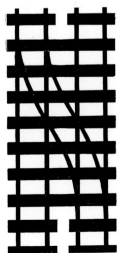

KING-O'-THE-RAILS No. 892
Wide Gauge—(Red)

Passenger Train—Includes Dorfan die cast take apart engine reversible No. 3920-R with 6 ball bearings. Die cast wheels and trucks on engine and cars. Engine trimmed with brass hand rails, radiators, head and tail light. Beautifully finished in red, trimmed with green. Train consists of baggage car No. 788 with sliding doors, pullman car No. 787 with green doors, windows, hand rails and observation car No. 789 all-brass trimmed with observation platform and red and white awning. Journal boxes on cars and real steps. A life-like passenger in every seat and electric lighted throughout. Complete with track terminal, eight pieces curved and two pieces straight track. Length of train 58 inches. Packed in individual box. Shipping weight 24 pounds. Retail price, each **$34.50**

Maroon No. 3920 and Chicago and Washington passenger cars

3920 (H). George Smith Collection. H. Lew photograph.

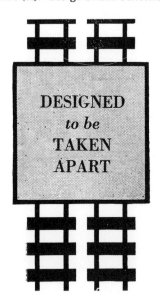

DESIGNED
to be
TAKEN
APART

THE TRAVELFAST No. 893
Wide Gauge—(Green)

Passenger Train—Includes Dorfan die cast take apart engine reversible; No. 3930-G with 6 ball bearings, die cast wheels and trucks on engine and cars. This engine has twelve wheels and is trimmed with brass hand rails with head and tail light. Cars are trimmed with flashy red on doors and windows. Train consists of baggage car No. 995 with two sliding red doors, pullman car No. 994 and observation car No. 996 with brass platform and awning. A passenger in every seat, brass hand rails on cars and real steps. Electric lighted throughout. All cars are equipped with automatic couplers. The roofs on cars are removeable so that the interior can be reached easily. Complete with track terminal, eight pieces curved and four pieces straight track. Length of train 59½ inches. Packed in individual sturdy box. Shipping weight, 27 pounds Retail price, each **$47.50**

CHAPTER SIX

★

WIDE GAUGE PASSENGER CARS

Dorfan, the "new kid on the block," as well as the innovator, was able to mix and match features from Ives, American Flyer, and Lionel — the big three toy train manufacturers — and then offer youngsters the best features of each.

To compare Dorfan features with those of the other "big three" manufacturers, it is interesting to note that although Lionel provided tables and chairs as well as lavatories for passengers in its top-of-the-line sets, its mid-1920s cars lacked passengers, as did Ives and American Flyer cars. Passengers were a Dorfan innovation.

Some Dorfan cars were lithographed, others were painted or enameled. American Flyer offered both lithographed and painted (or enameled) passenger cars, as did Lionel and Ives, and featured a crackle finish on some passenger cars. Lionel also featured a crackle finish, but only on some of its locomotives. By the mid-1920s, Lionel had adopted an enameled finish, brass plates, and rubber stampings for its Standard Gauge passenger cars. Lionel did not lithograph its Standard Gauge passenger cars, nor did it use decals. Ives produced enameled cars with rubber stampings, and by the late 1920s introduced brass plates.

The orange Pullman No. 890, Dorfan's first Wide Gauge passenger car, made its appearance in the 1926 catalogue. It had brass window inserts and passengers (who were usually die-cast but sometimes lithographed) in the windows. Since the observation car was not ready for production, a modified Pullman No. 891 was equipped to protect the rear of the train; it had two red bull's eye lenses on the rear which projected the interior illumination down the track.

Bull's eye lenses were added to other cars in later years, when clear lenses were used on both ends of the Pullman and even on the front end of the observation car. However, some budget-priced cars lacked passengers and bull's eye lenses in the round windows.

Early truck frames were stamped steel with formed steel wheels; in 1928 the die-cast truck frame with die-cast wheels was introduced. This heavier truck also had nickel journal boxes. Painted vestibule doors appeared in 1928. Three-piece air tanks (described as water tanks in the catalogue) were riveted under the floors of most passenger cars. Window inserts were brass or painted in a contrasting color.

An observation car arrived in 1927 and in 1928 a four-door baggage car was added. According to catalogue illustrations, passenger cars produced before 1928 had the word "Pullman" either lithographed on the car sides or printed on 4-inch decals. Later years had "The Dorfan Lines" in individual letter decals. Lithographed cars were named "Pleasant View" or "Mountain Brook", while the painted cars were "Chicago", "Washington", "San Francisco", and

"Observation". A lithographed observation car? Not in the catalogue, but a maroon No. 790 Pleasant View Pullman was shortened behind the fifth window, and fitted with a brass observation rail to complete the train set. Perhaps other examples of shortened observation cars exist?

Car bodies were all 13¼ inches long, although Dorfan catalogued these cars as 13¼ inches, 14 inches, and 15¼ inches, depending on whether the measurement extended over the couplers or not. The couplers, incidentally, were the Dorfan-patented Wide Gauge automatic type which were unidirectional. The cars were all lighted, and the observation car had an additional light on the rear platform.

The development of Dorfan passenger cars has intrigued many collectors. We are indebted to Alfred Clarke for the following detailed information, which applies to the cars listed in this chapter; indeed, it makes unnecessary the repetition of commonly found construction details at the beginning of the listings that follow.

CLOSE STUDY OF WIDE GAUGE PULLMAN CARS

by Alfred C. Clarke

Dorfan Wide Gauge Pullman cars were truly impressive. They were essentially rivet-constructed, and in a very real sense over-built. This method of construction gave these cars an overall strength that may not have been equaled by competing manufacturers. But this labor-intensive method was also expensive and probably contributed to the early demise of the Dorfan Company.

Since the construction of these cars is so intricate, a discussion of their distinguishing features may be helpful. Additional descriptions of specific details are also included in this chapter, along with photographs illustrating specific models.

While the abundant use of rivets [Author's Note: these are hollow rivets, known to the contemporary trade as "eyelets."] resulted in a high-quality product, this feature is not fully appreciated until one closely examines the way these cars were put together. The following paragraphs describe this level of workmanship at close range and summarize the major characteristics these models have in common.

In the overall construction of the more expensive cars, an excess of thirty rivets would normally be used. Wide Gauge Pullman cars were formed by two metal sections, with wraparound ends. They had symmetrical sides, 13½ inches long, which were riveted to the floor. Windows were accentuated by separate metal insert units painted a color that was different from that of the car body. They were

Male (above) and female (below) automatic couplers

The ornate observation platform of a No. 773; note the "Palmetto Limited" drumhead. A.Clarke Collection and photograph

attached with tabs that did not go through the sides but folded, unseen, around the inside window edge, pressing the window frame firmly to the car body. Door handrails, heavier than those used by competing companies, were held in place with two brass cotter pins. The sides of some cars were lithographed while others had a duco lacquer finished with decal lettering. A few sets had crackle finish.

The roof was attached with two knurled nuts threaded on vertical posts soldered to 1-inch metal spanners. Stamped-metal trucks and steel wheels were used on the earlier cars. These trucks frequently had a black lacquer finish, while others were nickel-plated. Later, die-cast wheels were used along with die-cast trucks and journal boxes — the trucks and journal boxes were all one piece.

Replacement die-cast trucks are, however, made with slots for the tabs of metal journal boxes. The rear area of observation cars were fitted with a large platform, often featuring a read and white awning extending around the top of the platform area. In some instances the awning was left its natural brass color, and not all sets displayed this ornamental trim. Most cars had at least two overhead lights. Some, however, had additional bulbs illuminating two large circular marker lamps containing red lenses, located on the upper part of the card end sections. Sometimes a car had a set of red lenses at one end and clear lenses at the other.

Couplers were male-female type and were attached to the floor frame ends. It is interesting to note that Lionel and Ives did not use this precision-type slot hook-on coupler, which involved two separately machined parts. In addition, there was a double reinforcing of the coupler bar, consisting of an underside lip unit riveted to the main coupler section for greater stability and precision. In this intricate design we see again Dorfan's emphasis on high-quality, solid construction.

Air tanks consisted of three pieces of pressed steel, comprising a cylindrical metal tank section, painted black, with separate ends riveted to the car floor. Pickup units were also constructed in a complex manner, involving more than a dozen time-consuming assembly operations. They consisted of a roller in a frame, riveted in two places to a fiber strip — either red or black — which was fastened with two screws to the underside of the truck section. The roller tension spring was placed between the fiber strip and the top of the roller frame. Dorfan cars normally had an attractive gold oval decal glued to the underframe between the air tanks. The edges were outlined with detailed scrollwork and the word "Dorfan" was printed in bold red script in the center area.

Interestingly, at both ends of the floorplate there were eight 3/16-inch holes. Six were used to hold the stair steps in place, but the other two are a mystery as to function.

To the left, closeup details of Dorfan passenger car construction. Above, the interior of a Washington Pullman with the roof removed, showing the stud for mounting the roof and individually tabbed windows. The floor had a depressed area along the wall and hollow eyelets fastening the body.

The comparison of the undersides of passenger cars shows the Washington on the left, with steps and eyelet-mounted coupler, and the Mountain Brook on the right, with soldered stud-mounted coupler, similar to Lionel's, and no steps.

The more expensive passenger cars had figures appearing in each window. They were three-dimensional head-and-shoulder representations with hand-painted features. Both male and female passengers were depicted in superb detail, including coat buttons, assorted designs of hats, neckware, jackets, and dresses. Twelve figures appeared in the coaches, six along each side, while observation cars, with fewer windows, had ten passenger figures. In typical Dorfan fashion, these figures were riveted to an L-shaped metal strip which, in turn, was riveted to the car floor. It is important to remember that work of this order was not done by a machine. One can only imagine the amount of time, energy, and skill needed to create these handcrafted figures and to place each one in a separate car window. This was indeed labor-intensive construction!

Note: Remember, numbers on the car sides (if any) were not always the catalogue numbers. Catalogue numbers were changed to designate small differences in color or a part, but catalogue descriptions and illustrations of specific cars are not always reliable indications of side-of-car numbers. Personal observation is the best approach; readers are invited to submit their detailed observations for inclusion in future editions.

770 BAGGAGE: See No. 995.

771 PULLMAN: See Nos. 994 and 997.

772 PULLMAN: See No. 994.

Compare the observation car on the left (George Smith Collection; H. Lew photograph) with the six-window Pleasant View Pullman in the photo below. No. 990 (E) on right from Richard Fletcher Collection.

This photograph illustrates the variance in the dark red/maroon painting of Dorfan passenger cars. No. 789 (B), top right, is a brighter red than the No. 996 (D) beneath it.

Shown here are the versions of lettering on Dorfan Wide Gauge passenger cars.

	Gd	Exc	Rst

773 OBSERVATION: See No. 996.

No. 780 PULLMAN: 1928-30. Lithographed body; steel truck frames, steel wheels; no passengers.

(A) 1928. Red body; yellow trim.	80	125	—
(B) 1930. Orange body; brown trim.	80	150	—
(C) 1930. Buff body; green trim.	80	150	—

Set with variation (A) of Nos. 995, 994, and 996 cars

	Gd	Exc	Rst

No. 781 PULLMAN: 1928. Lithographed red body; yellow trim; steel truck frames; steel wheels; no passengers; red bull's eye lenses on rear end. **90 150 —**

No. 785 PULLMAN: 1928-29. Olive (Nile) green-painted body; red doors and windows; die-cast trucks and wheels; passengers in the windows; bull's eye windows in both ends.

90 150 60

	Gd	Exc	Rst

No. 786 OBSERVATION: 1928-29. Olive (Nile) green-painted body; red doors and windows; die-cast trucks and wheels; passengers in the windows; bull's eye windows in front. **100 160 70**

No. 787 PULLMAN: 1928-30. Red-painted body; green doors and windows; die-cast trucks and wheels; passengers in the windows; bull's eye windows in ends. **100 160 60**

No. 788 BAGGAGE: 1928-30. Red-painted body; green doors; die-cast trucks and wheels; bull's eye windows in ends. **120 160 70**

(No.) 789 OBSERVATION: 1928-30.
(A) 1928; red-painted body; green windows and doors; "789" on side; die-cast trucks and wheels; passengers in the windows; bull's eye windows in front ends. **120 180 70**
(B) 1929-30. Same as (A), but awning fringe on rear platform. **125 180 75**

(No.) 789 MOUNTAIN BROOK PULLMAN: (?). Lithographed body; steel truck frames; stamped wheels; no passengers; no bull's eye windows; carries the name "DORFAN LINES" and number "789" in black ovals on car sides. Note duplicate catalogue number.
(A) (?). Maroon body; green roof; buff windows. **100 175 —**
(B) (?). Maroon body and roof; chartreuse windows. **100 175 —**
(C) (?). Mustard body; orange windows; ovals were brown instead of black. **100 175 —**
(D) (?). Orange body; green roof and windows. **100 175 —**

(No.) 790 PLEASANT VIEW PULLMAN: 1927-. Lithographed body; steel truck frames; stamped wheels; no bull's eye windows; no passengers; carries the name "DORFAN LINES" and number "790" in black oval on car sides.
(A) (?). Maroon body; green roof; yellow windows. **100 175 —**
(B) 1927. Orange body and roof; brown windows. **100 175 —**
(C) 1928. Red body and roof; yellow windows. **100 175 —**
(D) (?). Orange body; green roof and windows. **100 175 —**
(E) (?). Maroon body and roof; chartreuse windows. **100 175 —**

(No.) 790 PLEASANT VIEW OBSERVATION: (?). Lithographed maroon body; green roof; yellow windows; steel truck frames; stamped-steel wheels, no bull's eye windows, no passengers; wraparound brass railing complete with awning fringe; carries the name "DORFAN LINES" and number "790" in black ovals. This car was apparently constructed by using the printed sides from 790 Pullman described above. **150 225 —**

No. 791 PULLMAN: 1928. Red body; yellow windows; identical to 790 Pullman (and is numbered "790"), except that two bull's eye windows with red lenses were added to the rear end; interior illumination was projected down the track. **100 175 —**

No. 890 PULLMAN: 1926-28. Orange-painted body and roof; brass window frames, handrails, and steps; 4" "PULLMAN" decals, 2¼" name decals; flat lithographed passengers in the windows; steel truck frames, stamped-steel wheels; names are "WASHINGTON" or "CHICAGO". **100 175 —**

No. 891 SAN FRANCISCO PULLMAN: 1926. Orange body and roof; brass trim; identical to 890 Pullman, except that two bull's eye windows with red lenses were added to the rear end; named "SAN FRANCISCO". **125 175 —**

No. 990 PULLMAN: 1927-28. Painted body; steel truck frames; stamped-steel wheels; no passengers; 4" "PULLMAN" decals; 2¼" name decals are "WASHINGTON" or "CHICAGO".
(A) 1927. Gray body; brass window frames. **100 175 50**
(B) 1927. Olive green body; brass windows. **100 175 50**
(C) 1927. Crackle brown body; black roof; yellow or brass windows. **100 175 70**
(D) 1927. Maroon body; green windows and doors. **100 175 50**
(E) (?). Gray body; orange window frames. **100 175 50**

No. 991 PULLMAN: 1927. Gray body; brass windows; same as 990, except that two bull's eye windows with red lenses were added to the rear end; named "SAN FRANCISCO".
(A) 1927. Gray body; brass windows. **125 200 70**
(B) (?). Gray body; orange windows. **125 200 90**

No. 992 OBSERVATION: 1927-28. Painted body; steel truck frames; stamped-steel wheels; no passengers; 4" "PULLMAN" decals, 2¼" name decal; no awning fringe on open platform.
(A) 1927. Gray body; brass windows. **120 200 75**
(B) 1927. Olive green body; brass windows. **120 200 75**
(C) 1927. Crackle brown body; black roof; yellow windows. **120 200 75**
(D) (?). Crackle brown body; black roof; brass windows; brown doors. **130 200 90**
(E) 1927. Maroon body; green windows and doors. **120 200 90**
(F) (?). Gray body; orange windows. **120 200 90**

No. 992 PULLMAN: 1928-29. Blue-painted body and roof; yellow windows and doors; die-cast wheels and truck frames; decals read "THE DORFAN LINES"; passengers in the windows; bull's eye windows in both ends. Note duplicate catalogue number. **300 750 100**

No. 993 OBSERVATION: 1928-29. Blue-painted body and roof; buff windows and doors; die-cast wheels and truck frames; decals read "THE DORFAN LINES" and "OBSERVATION"; passengers in the windows; bull's eye windows in front; no awning fringe on open platform. **300 750 100**

No. 994 PULLMAN: 1928-30. Painted body and roof; die-cast wheels and trucks; decals read "THE DORFAN LINES", with "772" and "WASHINGTON" or "771" and "SAN FRANCISCO"; bull's eye windows in both ends; passengers in

	Gd	Exc	Rst

the windows.(A) 1928-30. Green body and roof; red doors and windows. **125 200 80**

(B) (?). Red body and roof; green doors and windows. **125 200 80**

No. 995 BAGGAGE: 1928-30. Painted body and roof; die-cast wheels and trucks; decals read "THE DORFAN LINES", "770", and "AMERICAN RAILWAY EXPRESS"; four sliding doors; bull's eye windows in both ends.

(A) 1928-30. Green body and roof; red doors and window rings. **150 250 100**

(B) (?). Red body and roof; green doors and window rings. **150 250 100**

No. 996 OBSERVATION: 1928-30. Painted body and roof; die-cast wheels and truck frames; decals read "THE DORFAN LINES", "773", and "OBSERVATION"; bull's eye windows in front; passengers in the windows.

(A) 1928. Green body and roof; red doors and windows. **90 175 80**

(B) (?). Red body and roof; green doors and windows. **90 175 80**

(C) 1929-30. Same as 996 (A), except that awning fringe was added to the open platform. **90 175 90**

(D) (?). Maroon body and roof; chartreuse windows. **90 175 90**

No. 997 PULLMAN: 1928-30. Painted body and roof; die-cast wheels and trucks; decals read "THE DORFAN LINES" with "771" and "SAN FRANCISCO" or "772" and "WASHINGTON"; bull's eye windows in both ends; passengers in the windows.

(A) 1928. Crackle green body; black roof; red doors and windows. **90 150 70**

(B) 1929-30. Crackle green body; red roof, doors, and windows. **90 150 70**

(C) 1930. Catalogued as **997-I** for the FLORIDA LIMITED; ivory body; red roof; brass windows and doors. **300 750 70**

No. 998 BAGGAGE: 1928-30. Painted body and roof; die-cast wheels and trucks; decals read "THE DORFAN LINES", "770", and "AMERICAN RAILWAY EXPRESS"; bull's eye windows in both ends; four sliding doors.

(A) 1928. Crackle green body; black roof; red doors. **90 150 75**

(B) 1929-30. Crackle green body; red roof and doors. **90 150 75**

(C) 1930. Catalogued as **998-I** for the FLORIDA LIMITED; ivory body; red roof and doors. **300 750 75**

No. 999 OBSERVATION: 1928-30. Painted body and roof; die-cast wheels and trucks; decals read "THE DORFAN LINES" and "OBSERVATION"; bull's eye windows in front ends.

(A) 1928. Crackle green body; black roof; red doors and windows. **90 150 80**

(B) 1929-30. Crackle green body; red roof, doors, and windows; less intricate awning fringe on platform. **90 150 85**

(C) 1930. Catalogued as **999-I** for the FLORIDA LIMITED; ivory body; red roof; brass windows and doors; awning fringe on rear platform. **300 750 85**

CHAPTER SEVEN

WIDE GAUGE FREIGHT CARS

Wide Gauge freight cars were made for only three years — 1928 through 1930 — but a substantial number survive today. Their survival suggests successful marketing in a well-developed market.

To understand the remarkable success of Dorfan's 1928 Wide Gauge freight cars, we need to look at its competitors. Lionel, for example, in 1925 introduced a new line of Standard Gauge freight cars to replace its outdated line of 1906. The new cars were painted with bright automotive enamels and featured brass plates and trim. Although very attractive toys, these cars bore little resemblance to real trains.

American Flyer's initial Wide Gauge freight cars (1926) were Lionel's discontinued early design 10-series freight cars. These cars were painted in drab prototypical colors and were finished with realistic rubber-stamped markings with real railroad names and car numbers. American Flyer adopted Lionel's "modern look" in 1927 and produced very brightly painted cars with brass plates. American Flyer's colors were even more dramatic than Lionel's and their cars were substantially larger than Lionel's, yet they sold for less.

Ives, on the other hand, adapted its 1 Gauge designs from the 1910s for its Wide Gauge freight car line of the 1920s. Ives cars were finished in realistic, drab enamels and featured hand-soldered construction and very realistic rubber stampings for road names and car numbers. The Ives cars were very expensive to produce because of their numerous parts, when compared to the number of parts in Lionel and American Flyer.

Dorfan designers ignored the market consensus and made a bold move by adapting lithography for its new designs. Dorfan's Wide Gauge cars are, consequently, the most realistic large size American toy trains ever made. It is a pleasure to study the subtle details of these cars — the brake mechanisms, the road names, the car's technical markings. Many of the construction details are similar to those given in Chapter Four. It is likely that Dorfan's designs were based on the drawings from the *Car Builders Cyclopedia*.

Five beautiful lithographed freight cars appeared in Dorfan's 1928 catalogue, which introduced die-cast wheels and truck frames, although some cars were assembled with stamped-steel wheels. Dorfan said the new truck frame kept the axles in line and the deep flanges on the die-cast wheels kept cars on the track even though they were "whizzing along at a high speed." Plated journal boxes, brass ladders and brakewheels, and bright colors added to the realistic prototype railroad lettering and logos. The automatic couplers required that cars be headed in the proper direction, and some finger work was necessary to lift or drop the latch hook.

Car body lengths were 14 inches, but some catalogues showed the car lengths as 15½ inches because Dorfan often remeasured its cars to include the extended couplers.

The No. 809 lumber car appeared a year later, but no crane car. The cab and boom of the stationary crane which appeared in 1929 would have made a great Wide Gauge crane car, but none was built.

	Gd	Exc	Rst

No. 800 GONDOLA: 1928-30. Construction similar to No. 600 Gondola listed in Chapter Four, Narrow Gauge Freight Cars, except two brakewheels, one at each end; orange color (catalogued as "tan"); ribbed sides and ends; lettered "N.Y.C. / 253761 / CAP'Y. 100000 LBS. / WT. 43300 NEW 8-22", with gears and ratchet logo at bottom; same lettering an and other markings as in No. 600, Narrow Gauge.
Note: Richard Fletcher comments this came in two versions, one with brace riveted to interior floor, reinforcing both sides, and one without. **125 275 —**

No. 801 BOXCAR: 1928-30. Roof attached with two screws; the car had four ladders (one each side, one each end), two brakewheels, and two sliding doors on each side; black lettering on right-hand sliding door "A.T. & S.F. / 121499 / TACK CARD HERE"; black lettering near ladder EH 9'8" / EW 12'-8½" / IL 40'-6" / IW 8'-7½" / CU. FT 3005 / BLT. 5-26 Bx-S"; black and white Santa Fe logo to left of sliding door, underneath is white-lettered "A.T. & S.F. / 121499" and beneath this in black "CAPY. 100000 / LD. LMT. 122600 / LT. WT. 46400 NEW 5-26" and "DORFAN LINES"
(A) Green body; red roof. **150 275 —**
(B) Green body; green roof. **150 275 —**

No. 804 TANK CAR: 1928-30. Robin's-egg blue tank, red tank cradle; brass dome, tank bands, ladders, railings, and brakewheels; lettered at left of ladder in white "UTLX 29325", underneath in black "CAPACITY 100000 LBS. / WT. 50900 NEW 7-23 / MADE IN U.S.A."; right of ladder in white "UNION TANK CAR CO.", underneath in black "DORFAN LINES", and at far right "UNITED STATES / SAFETY APPLIANCES / STANDARD / A.R.A. SPEC. 111 / U.T.C. CO. 7-27-23 / SAFETY VALVE / TESTED 7-27-23 / PRESS. 25 LBS. / AT BUTLER PA. BY S.S.C. CO. / TANK / TESTED 7-29-23 / PRESS. 60 LBS. / AT BUTLER PA. / BY S.S.C. CO. / BUILT 7-23" **150 275 —**

No. 800

Gd Exc Rst

No. 805 HOPPER: 1928-30. Deep red body with raised ribs; four brass ladders and two brakewheels; "PENNSYLVANIA" in white lettering on far left panel, "CAP'Y. 110000 LBS. / WT. 4 00 NEW 9-20 / BUILT 9-20" on second left panel, "P.R.R. / 11701" in white lettering on middle two panels of car, with "DORFAN LINES" underneath, and on second right, "LENGTH 10 FT. 6 IN. / CAP'Y. 1890 CU. FT. / COUPLER SHANK 6-8 / FRICTION DRAFT GEAR / CAST STEEL YOKE / 6 1 ½ KEY / K 2 TRIPLE"; hopper doors were opened with a wheel on the side of the car.   **150 325 —**

No. 806 CABOOSE: 1928-30. Roof was attached with two machine screws; window inserts the same ones used on the passenger cars; brass platform railings; interior lighting and two taillights on the rear platform shone through red bull's eye lenses; "PENNSYLVANIA / 486751" in green lettering on middle of car, "DORFAN LINES" to right, "N. 5. / BUILT 8.14. / P.R.R." on left.

(A) Brown body; blue-green roof; red cupola and cupola roof; yellow window inserts.   **150 275 —**

(B) Brown body; brown cupola, red main and cupola roofs; green window inserts.   **150 275 —**

(C) Dark brown-painted body; blue-green roof; red cupola and cupola roof; decal "3931". This reminds us of the strange 604 (E) oil tank car described in Chapter Four. Are there any leads on the source?   **175 300 —**

No. 804

Nos. 806 and 801

No. 805

Comparison of Dorfan tank cars with prototype model. The car in the middle is a handmade prototype model of Dorfan's Wide Gauge tank car; the final production version, No. 804, is shown at the top and the red earlier Narrow Gauge car at bottom. Interestingly, the name "Indian Refining Co., Inc." does not appear on the Wide Gauge version. The tank cradle is the same, but the darker prototype tank color was changed to the familiar robin's-egg blue. Handrail eyelets on the prototype have been moved to the tank band area on the production model. The base unit holding the brakewheel was not redesigned, but a handwheel knob has been added to the production car wheel. Further, the trucks on the prototype are steel and painted black with brass journal boxes. These trucks are essentially the same type of truck frames that were used on some of the earlier Wide Gauge Dorfan passenger cars. Automatic couplers are normal, and die-cast wheels appear on both the prototype and the production models. A. Clarke Collection, photograph, and comments.

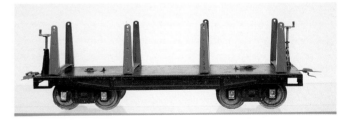

No. 809 without load

Gd Exc Rst

No. 809 LUMBER CAR: Similar to No. 609 in Chapter Four, Narrow Gauge Freight, except longer length allows four red-enameled stake assemblies per side; load consisted of six pieces of wood, ¾" square and 11⅝" long.   **425 700 —**

11701: See No. 805.

29325: See No. 804.

121499: See No. 801.

253711: See No. 800.

486751: See No. 806.

CHAPTER EIGHT

★

ACCESSORIES AND DEALER DISPLAYS

Dorfan produced a remarkably complete line of accessories in a very few years. Operating accessories were usually offered in two versions, Narrow Gauge and Wide Gauge, and these were the same except that the track connector or special track section and connector were different. In many instances Dorfan accessories, like its other areas of production, had a distinctive style that set Dorfan apart from its competitors and helped foster the company's remarkable growth and development.

The line included several stations. One was the magnificent No. 427 introduced in 1930 which was 18½ by 8 by 9½ inches. It had two clock faces, high rectangular windows, and was lighted. Dorfan's 427 surpassed Lionel's largest station and terrace, the 128, which was only 18 by 31½ inches, and sold for $25 in 1928, as well as Ives large lithographed station which measured 18½ by 8 inches, and American Flyer's short-lived 110 Union Station which measured 17¾ by 29 inches, and sold for $15 or $16.50 west of the Mississippi. The Flyer station was manufactured in 1928 only and was made of a framework of thin, clear pine with heavy composition board walls.

Other accessories included block signals, semaphores, and signal bridges. The block signals and semaphores were introduced with automatic train-stopping devices. This device consisted of a detection unit, a special piece of track with an insulated outside rail and a circuit-breaking switch or relay that was operated by the train. When the train passed over the special track section, it picked up current from the outside rail and transmitted it through the axles and wheels to the specially insulated section. A wire from the insulated outside rail to the relay allowed power to go to the relay or switch which would then open and prevent the current from completing its circuit, so that the train on the track would not operate. Lionel introduced its first train control in 1921 and used a similar switch for its train-control devices.

In the late 1920s the power house and switch signal towers were very popular accessories. Big towers were introduced by Dorfan and Lionel in 1926. Dorfan's was manufactured for two years, 1926 and 1927, and was 9½ by 8¾ by 4½ inches, while Lionel's 437 switch signal tower was 10¼ by 8⅜ by 8⅞ inches. Lionel's tower was manufactured from 1926 through 1937. American Flyer's 108 switch tower house was 11⁵⁄₁₆ by 9 inches and was manufactured from 1929 through 1934. The typical switch tower was modeled on a yard switch tower and had a series of knife switches mounted on one side. The switches could be operated by the engineer who could turn lights and even turn trains on and off by throwing one of the switches.

Parts of at least two Dorfan accessories, the Nos. 421 (1421) and 416 (1416), were quite similar to those of Lionel: the crossing gate arm and the brass warning diamond. A newly published Greenberg's guide to Lionel prewar accessories, by Peter Riddle, documents the full Lionel production and demonstrates that Dorfan and Hafner both had pieces which were of Lionel origin. The warning signals are among them but have some differences. We should note here that the Dorfan factory was only two miles from Lionel's, thus increasing the likelihood of interaction. For example, Dorfan sold the Ives 1134, which was purchased from either Lionel or Lionel and American Flyer. If the 1134 was sold in 1929, then it was Lionel and AF production; if sold in 1930 or later it was Lionel production.

CRANE, SIGNALS, LIGHTS, AND CROSSING GATES

Note that there is duplication of catalogue numbers amongst some items in this chapter. The listings do not

Closeups of the controls of the stationary crane, which is pictured on page 214. Harry Osisek Collection; photograph by Gary Massat

strictly follow one number sequential but are given in logical groupings, with a derivative item following the appropriate listing.

No. 70 ELECTRIC CRANE: 1929-30. This impressive accessory stands 20" high with a 10¼" x 10¼" base and cost as much as Dorfan's top-of-the-line Narrow Gauge train set — $19.50. It towers above everything on the layout except the No. 432 American flag. Buff cab with Dorfan decals; maroon windows and doors; red roof and base; green boom and girders; bug-eye glass lights on front of cab. An electric motor on the die-cast base is equipped with a worm drive and two gear-shift levers. With the controls, the cab and boom can be turned in a complete circle and the hook could be raised and lowered. Dorfan said it could lift any toy engine on the market! The 5" cab and 13" boom might have been used to construct a Wide Gauge crane car, but such a car was never manufactured. Listing details provided from to the crane in G. Blickle Collection.   **1200   2500   500**

Note: This piece has been especially subject to casting problems and has become a rare item. Should an owner be willing to sell, it could command very high prices if in Good condition.

No. 400 AUTOMATIC BLOCK SIGNAL (Narrow Gauge): 1925-30. With die-cast round base, described by some as a very sturdy traffic signal; supplied with several track sections which have insulated outer rails; painted dark red and oversprayed with black in a blending pattern, or blue with maroon overspray; two-piece die-cast head with red and green celluloid disks: signal aspect changes when the train passes.   **35   70   40**

No. 401 CONTROL BLOCK SIGNAL (Narrow Gauge): 1926-30. Same as No. 400 block signal, except revised wiring

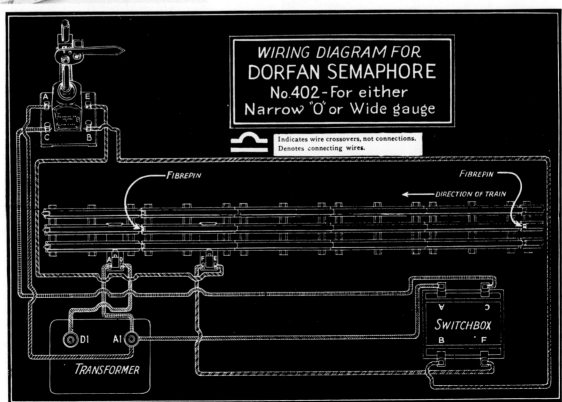

Instruction sheet diagram for No. 402 semaphore. Courtesy Richard Fletcher

Stationary electric crane, No. 70. Robert Ignasiak Collection

No. 419, hooked up. Harry Osisek Collection

	Gd	Exc	Rst

plan allows the train operator to control his signals and stop his train with a switch box; three-piece tabbed sheet-metal control housing stamped "A", "B", "C", and "F" above four terminal clips.

35 70 40

No. 1401 CONTROL BLOCK SIGNAL (Wide Gauge): 1929-30. Same as 401, but supplied for use with Wide Gauge track.

35 70 40

No. 402 SEMAPHORE (Narrow Gauge): 1927-30. Die-cast; olive green with red steel arm and red and green glass lenses inside round orange frames; 12" high; semaphore position and train stop are controlled from the "switch box"; insulated pins are provided to break connection to the center rail in the track and create a control block for this accessory; four knurled nuts on the base.

35 60 40

No. 1402 SEMAPHORE (Wide Gauge): 1929-30. Same as 402, but supplied with Wide Gauge track terminals.

35 60 40

	Gd	Exc	Rst

No. 405 SWITCHBOARD: 1925-26. A stand-up control board 6½" high and 8½" long with six single-pole knife switches supplied from a common bus; connections are made with Fahnestock clips. This design was replaced by No. 407.

15 40 20

No. 406 POWER SWITCH HOUSE: 1926-27. A switch tower house 9½" high, 8¾" long, and 4½" deep; contains the same knife-switch control board as the No. 405; six knife switches are supplied from a common bus.

175 350 150

No. 407 SWITCHBOARD: 1926-30. An improved version of the 405 switchboard, this one has six single-pole knife switches which are electrically separate; connections are made with Fahnestock clips.

15 40 20

No. 406 BELL SIGNAL (Narrow Gauge): 1928-30. 8½" high, double-gong electric bell mounted on the post of a grade-crossing warning signal. (Note reuse of catalogue number formerly assigned to power switch house.)

20 50 30

No. 1406 BELL SIGNAL (Wide Gauge): 1929-30. Same as No. 406, but boxed with connectors for Wide Gauge track.

20 50 20

No. 408 HEADLIGHT BULB (14 volt): 1928-30. For headlights and signals; available as a replacement part before it was listed in the 1928 catalogue.

NRS

No. 409 FROSTED BULB (14 volt): 1928-30. A teardrop-shaped lamp for lamp posts and the illuminated bridges.

NRS

No. 416 WARNING SIGNAL (Narrow Gauge): 1927-30. 8½" high; a pair of red lights mounted on the post of a grade-crossing warning sign to flash when train passes.

20 30 20

No. 1416 WARNING SIGNAL (Wide Gauge): 1927-30. Same as No. 416, but boxed with connectors for Wide Gauge track.

20 50 20

No. 417 POSITION-LIGHT SIGNAL: 1930. A mast with a round signal target containing five lamps; possibly a copy of the light-position block signals used on the Pennsylvania Railroad, except that the Dorfan signal does not have the "Approach" aspect, or 45-degree position; a control is included with this accessory.

40 85 40

No. 418 SIGNAL BRIDGE WITH ONE POSITION-LIGHT SIGNAL: 1930. There is space under the bridge for two tracks, but only one signal (similar to No. 417) is mounted on it; a control is included.

200 400 200

No. 419 SIGNAL BRIDGE WITH TWO POSITION-LIGHT SIGNALS: 1930. A signal bridge with signals for two tracks.

250 450 250

No. 420 BOULEVARD LIGHT: 1925-30. 7"-high street-lighting fixture of the "goose-neck" style; frosted lamp inserted below the reflector; red pole with red or black reflector and blue pole with blue reflector; yellow base.

10 20 10

No. 421 AUTOMATIC CROSSING GATE (Narrow Gauge): 1929-30. A crossing warning sign plus a striped arm gate which lowers as the train approaches.

20 50 20

	Gd	Exc	Rst

No. 1421 AUTOMATIC CROSSING GATE (Wide Gauge): 1929-30. Same as No. 421, but supplied with connectors for Wide Gauge track.   **20   50   20**

No. 430 LAMP POST (14 volt): 1925-30. A straight lamp post 8½" high with frosted lamp pointing up.   **10   20   10**

No. 431 LAMP POST (110 volt): 1930. 13½" high, much taller goose-neck style lamp wired for use on house voltage, AC or DC; lamp is inserted below the reflector. If the circuit breaker trips, this accessory will light up the layout and assist in finding the trouble.   **15   40   15**

No. 433 LAMP POST (14 volt): 1930. 13½" high; the same lamp post as No. 431, but wired for toy train voltage.   **15   40   15**

BRIDGES, TRACK, CROSSOVERS, AND SWITCHES

The most distinctive feature of Dorfan track was the operating lever on the manual switches. Instead of a slide knob or turn lever, Dorfan used a throw lever on an erect stand. The Dorfan bridges all included approach ramps, and single or double center spans. The "Electra" bridge featured lamp posts at the four corners.

For 1925 and 1926 Dorfan supplied some special track sections with an insulated outer rail to operate the semaphore and block signal. By 1927 signals were changed to stop the train. The special track was no longer needed, and only some wooden pins were supplied for insulating the center (control) rail.

A few minor catalogue errors have resulted in some confused catalogue numbers for the mechanical track; both numbers are shown.

Mechanical (Two-Rail) Track and Bridges, 1925–1930

No. 300 (310): 30" bridge; single center span.   **20   30   20**

No. 350 (360): 10" straight track section.   **NRS**

No. 360: 10" curved track section; one-eighth circle.   **NRS**

(No catalogue number): 14" curved track section; one-quarter circle (packed with the smallest sets).   **NRS**

No. 375: Crossover; 45-degree.   **5   10   5**

No. 385: Pair of manual switches.   **10   20   10**

Narrow Gauge Electric (Three-Rail) Track and Bridges

No. 403 TRACK TERMINAL: 1925-30. A spring-loaded clip to make connections to the center and outer rail.   **NRS**

No. 410: 1925-30. 30" (overall length) three-piece bridge for Narrow Gauge; single green center span; orange deck; red girders forming sides; tabbed and soldered sheet steel construction; two green approach tracks attached.

Note: Appears identical to bridge shown in 1906 Ives catalogue; possibly made with same tooling. Richard

No. 421, with diamond crossing signal. Richard Fletcher Collection

Variety of lamp posts on top shelf; Station House No. 425 on bottom. Richard Fletcher Collection.

No. 410

	Gd	Exc	Rst

Fletcher reports Nos. 410 and 411 come with tan girders also and believes there is a blue version matching the color of the No. 55 locomotive; verification requested.   **25   50   25**

No. 411: 1926-30. 40" bridge for Narrow Gauge; double center span.   **40   100   40**

No. 412: 1927-30. 40" "Electra" bridge for Narrow Gauge; double center span; lights on four corner posts.   **100   175   100**

No. 450: 1925-30. 10" straight track section.   **NRS**

A Word About Dorfan Tracks

IT IS highly important that the tracks on which any electric or mechanical train is to run are strongly built as they are expected to stand more careless handling than almost any other part of the train outfit. Dorfan track is built of unusually heavy gauge steel. It is pressed into hollow track form with just the right amount of base to give a firm foundation. It doesn't bend easily and will stand rough treatment. The cross ties are securely fastened and all pieces are accurate and uniform in length and width, or gauge. We supply three types of track—Narrow Electric, Wide Electric and Non-electric (for spring winding trains). The cuts below show the different units in which Dorfan track may be purchased.

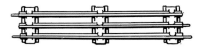

NARROW ("O") GAUGE DORFAN ELECTRIC TRACK, No. 450
1 ⅜ inches wide. In 10¼ inch straight sections.

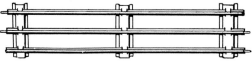

WIDE GAUGE DORFAN ELECTRIC TRACK, No. 850
2¼ inches wide. In straight sections of 14 inches.

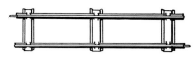

NARROW GAUGE DORFAN MECHANICAL TRACK, No. 350
For spring winding trains. 1 ⅜ inches wide. In straight lengths of 10¼ inches

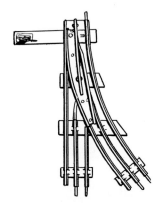

DORFAN LEFT-HAND SWITCH SECTION

With switch operating mechanism. 10¼ inches long. Supplied in pairs for narrow gauge electric and mechanical.
No. 485, electric.
No. 385, mechanical.

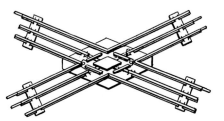

DORFAN CROSS-OVER SECTION

Supplied in narrow gauge, electric and mechanical tracks
No. 475, electric. No. 375, mechanical.

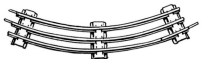

DORFAN CURVED SECTION TRACK

In all three types of track. Mechanical, No. 360, length 10 inches. Narrow gauge, electric, No. 460, length 11¼ inches. Wide gauge, electric, No. 860, length 16 inches.

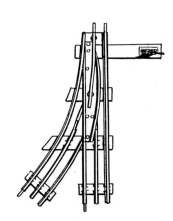

DORFAN RIGHT-HAND SWITCH

Sold in pair with switch shown on opposite side of page, but reverse in direction.
No. 485 electric.
No. 385 mechanical.

Strip of track with track terminal

	Gd	Exc	Rst
(No catalogue number): 1925-26. 10" straight track section with insulated outer rail.			NRS
No. 460: 1925-30. 11" curved track section; one-eighth circle.			NRS
(No catalogue number): 1925-26. 11" curved track section with insulated outer rail.			NRS

	Gd	Exc	Rst
No. 465: 1928-30. Dozen track binders (clips). **Note:** Fit both Narrow and Wide Gauge.			NRS
No. 475: 1925-30. Crossover; 45-degree.	10	15	10
No. 485: 1925-30. Pair manual switches.	25	40	25
No. 485-L: 1927-30. Pair manual switches with signal lights.	30	50	30

Wide Gauge Electric (Three-Rail) Track and Bridges

	Gd	Exc	Rst
No. 404: 1928-30. Track connector.			NRS
No. 413: 1927-30. 42" bridge; single center span.	40	100	40
No. 414: (?-1930). 56" bridge; double center span.	50	125	50
No. 414-L: 1929-30. 56" "Victory" bridge; double center span with four lights on corner posts. (A very impressive accessory.)	125	350	125
No. 465: (?-1930). Track binders (clips).			NRS
No. 850: 1926-30. 14" straight track section.			NRS

	Gd	Exc	Rst

(No catalogue number): 1926. 14" straight track section with insulated outer rail. **NRS**

No. 860: 1926-30. 16" curved track section; one-eighth circle. **NRS**

No. 875: 1927-28. Crossover; 45-degree. **10 15 10**

No. 875: 1929-30. Crossover; 90-degree. (Note duplicate catalogue number.) **10 15 10**

No. 885: 1927-30. Pair manual switches. **30 45 30**

No. 885-L: 1927-30. Pair manual switches with signal lights. **35 50 35**

No. 886-L: 1930. Pair remote-control switches. **40 60 40**

STATIONS

Dorfan's stations made extensive use of lithography. Their style of architecture and the use of large clock faces over the entrances resemble features of German stations, in spite of the fact that some of them were named for New Jersey cities; possibly these were indeed of German manufacture.

No. 417 NEWARK CENTRAL STATION: 1927-29 / **No. 426 STATION:** 1930. Three-story lithographed building, electrically lighted; 9½" high and 12½" long; mansard roof, covered platform, arcade, clock dial; named for the home office of the Dorfan company. **150 400 —**

No. 418 MONTCLAIR STATION: 1927-29 / **No. 424 STATION:** 1930. 7½" long and 5" high; two-story station lithographed to resemble stone; named for a suburban town not far from Newark; arched entrances, with a clock face over the entrance; unlighted. **50 125 —**

No. 419 STATION: 1929. Same size as No. 418/424, but different styling; lights are connected to large binding posts on the end wall. **50 125 —**

No. 425 STATION: 1930. 8¾" long and 5" high; modern single-story station with high windows; flag mounted on the roof; a clock protrudes between the two center windows in front and is easily broken off; two entrances with awnings; cream or bluish gray with red roof; lighted. **50 125 —**

Note: Richard Fletcher reports there is a station similar to the No. 425, but completely lithographed, and that it was sold with a green roof in some early windup sets.

No. 427 STATION: 1930. At 18½" long, 8" high, and 9½" deep; Dorfan's largest station; cream with red trim windows; two green benches between entrances; displays *two* clock faces and has high, rectangular windows; fenced roof is topped with a flagpole; chains are looped across the entrance doors; lighted. **500 900 400**

? STATION: Small, 5½" long and 5" high lithographed station named "Toytown"; packed with a train set sold in the early 1930s; "AMERICAN RAILWAY EXPRESS" appears above the baggage window; also decorated with two Dorfan locomotive decals. This station is uncatalogued and unlighted. **20 40 —**

Two views of toy station with unusual Dorfan decals. We wonder who built the station.

	Gd	Exc	Rst

TUNNELS, TELEGRAPH POLES, AND NON-ELECTRIFIED ACCESSORIES

Equally appropriate for mechanical or electric train layouts, these accessories added realism. The diamond-shaped warning sign listed below in the simple pole form was also used on more elaborate electrified accessories (see other listings), and the folding tunnels were cleverly designed to be packed in the boxed train sets.

No. 310 TUNNEL: 1925-30. Lithographed metal; folding tunnel; measures 7⅜" long, 5" wide, and 5" high; two embossed halves are identical; each side displays a road passing a number of large rocks; a house is shown near a hairpin turn at the bottom of the hill. **15 35 —**

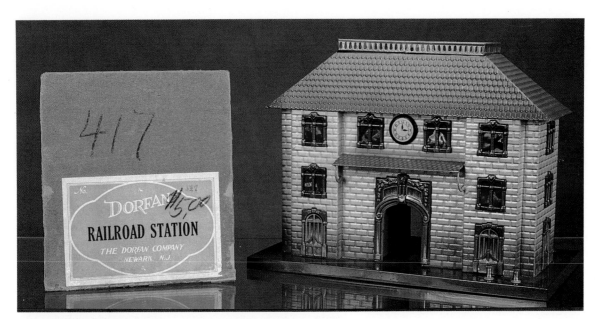

No. 426 Station House. Walter Kielkowski Collection.

No. 320 tunnel

	Gd	Exc	Rst

No. 319 TUNNEL: 1930. Made of composition material, this tunnel measures 8¼" long, 8" high, and 8" wide; embossed and decorated. **10 20 —**

No. 320 TUNNEL: 1925-30. Lithographed tunnel; unfolds to 8" long, 6½" wide, and 6½" high; embossed road on each side has its hairpin turn at the top of the hill, while a horse-drawn farm wagon climbs the hill past grazing cattle; sign at the bottom of the road points to "DORFAN HEIGHTS". **15 25 —**

No. 321 TUNNEL: 1927-30. Composition tunnel; similar to No. 319, but measuring 11¼" long, 8" wide, and 8¼" high. **10 20 —**

No. 322 TUNNEL: 1927-30. Made of composition material; same as Nos. 319 and 321, but measuring 12¼" long, 8½" wide, and 11¾" high. **15 30 —**

No. 323 TUNNEL: 1927-30. Largest of the composition tunnels; 14¼" long, 10" wide, and 12" high. **20 35 —**

	Gd	Exc	Rst

No. 330 SEMAPHORE: 1925-27. 7" high; a stiff control wire at the base positions the semaphore arm in the upper quadrant. **5 15 5**

No. 340 DANGER SIGNAL: 1925-30. 7" high; a diamond-shaped warning sign lettered "RAILROAD CROSSING", "LOOK OUT FOR LOCOMOTIVE" is attached to the mast; this same sign also appears on several electrified accessories. **5 10 5**

No. 350 TELEGRAPH POLE: 1925/370 TELEGRAPH POLE: 1926-30. 7" high; two insulators are mounted on the crossarm; catalogue number was changed to 370 in 1926. **5 13 5**

No. 351 LAMP POST: 1925. 7" high; this nonelectrified street light was offered only one year. **5 13 5**

No. 380 ACCESSORY SET: 1925-30. A box containing one each No. 310 tunnel, 340 warning sign, and 370 telegraph pole. **NRS**

No. 390 ACCESSORY SET: 1925-30. A box containing one No. 330 semaphore, one 340 warning sign, and two 370 telegraph poles. **NRS**

No. 395 ACCESSORY SET: 1925. A box containing one each No. 330 semaphore, 340 warning sign, 350 telegraph pole, and 351 lamp post. **NRS**

No. 415 TELEGRAPH POLE: 1927-30. 8½" high; taller than the 350/370 pole; die-cast. **5 10 5**

No. 415-B BOX OF POLES: 1928-30. A box of six No. 415 telegraph poles. **NRS**

No. 432 FLAG POLE: 1930. 20½" high; American flag can be raised or lowered; outsized accessory. **15 30 15**

TRANSFORMERS, CIRCUIT BREAKER, AND ROTARY CONVERTER

Some Dorfan train sets were packed with transformers which carried the "Jefferson Electric Co." nameplate. Jefferson also manufactured transformers sold by American

Gd Exc Rst

Flyer. It is quite likely that Jefferson also made many of the transformers that carried the Dorfan nameplate.

Dorfan was quite proud of its circuit breaker and gave full-page coverage of this small accessory in its catalogue. A solenoid would trip and open the track circuit in the event of an overload or short circuit. It was reset by a lever.

Back in the 1920s and as late as the 1940s, some apartments and houses were supplied with direct current (DC) from the local electric utility, rather than the alternating current (AC) that we expect today. A transformer could not be used to reduce the DC voltage to operate electric trains. Resistance-type voltage reducers were sometimes used; they would run the train, but they introduced some potentially lethal hazards. Dorfan recommended using storage batteries to run toy trains. In 1928 it offered a rotary converter to change the DC to AC, but this proved to be too heavy for practical home use.

Still other residences were supplied with 25 Hz electric power. This was a popular alternating frequency for real long-distance electric trains as well as the metal-smelting industry. Dorfan supplied some toy train transformers designed for 25 Hz. (Amtrak still uses 25 Hz on its northeast corridor, and connecting commuter railroads in the Philadelphia area tie into the system, but houses and industry have changed to 60 Hz.)

No. 440 TRANSFORMER: 1925. 60 Hz, 55 watts; knob on top; five voltage taps.

No. 440 TRANSFORMER: 1926. 60 Hz, 100 watts; lever on side; six voltage taps.

No. 441 TRANSFORMER: 1926. 60 Hz, 50 watts; lever on side; five voltage taps.

No. 442 TRANSFORMER: 1927-30. 60 Hz, 50 watts; lever on side; five voltage taps.

No. 443 TRANSFORMER: 1927. 60 Hz, 75 watts; lever on top; seven voltage taps.

No. 443 TRANSFORMER: 1928-30. 60 Hz, 100 watts; same transformer, upgraded.

No. 444 TRANSFORMER: 1927-28. 25 Hz, 75 watts; like No. 443, but for 25 Hz.

No. 444 TRANSFORMER: 1929-30. 25 Hz, 50 watts; note, downgraded in watts.

No. 445 TRANSFORMER: 1928-30. 25 Hz, 100 watts; an upgraded No. 444.

No. 446 CIRCUIT BREAKER: 1928-30. Green die-cast housing with two large squeeze-type terminal clips; a sensitive solenoid inside will trip on overload or short circuit.

20 30 20

No. 447 TRANSFORMER: 1930. 60 Hz, 150 watts; lever on side with six voltage taps; four fixed-voltage terminals.

No. 448 ROTARY CONVERTER: 1928. 110 volts DC to 110 volts 60 Hz AC. This accessory weighs *47 pounds!* Some houses and apartments were supplied with direct current, but operating toy trains with a DC voltage reducer is hazardous. Although a DC voltage reducer would produce low voltage direct current, it also created a potential 110 volts in the track. In 1928 the company offered this rotary converter to safely change the DC to AC which could then

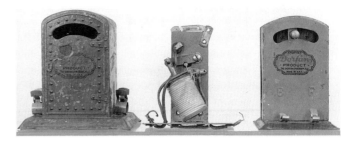

Green circuit breaker case, circuit breaker mechanism, and red controller

supply a normal toy-train transformer. By modern electric standards, this accessory is called a rotary inverter, since it is powered by direct current and produces alternating current. It consists of a DC motor and an AC generator on the same shaft. Evidently, not many were sold, because the rotary converter was dropped from the catalogue the following year.

No. 448 TRANSFORMER: 1930. 60 Hz, 50 watts, 220 volts; same as No. 442, but wired for use on the higher voltage.

No. 449 TRANSFORMER: 1930. 60 Hz, 50 watts, 220 volts; same as No. 443, but wired for use on the higher voltage.

DEALER DISPLAYS

In 1930 Dorfan issued a dealer catalogue in which there were centerfold illustrations of five prefabricated displays for Dorfan trains. The smallest display required a space about 3 by 5 feet and the largest required 4 by 15 feet! Mountains, tunnels, and bridges were in place, and electrical accessories were pre-wired. The displays needed only transformers and trains (which were *not* included). A dealer willing to spend from $50 to $100 for a ready-built layout could order one from Dorfan. This was in the midst of the Depression, and one wonders how many were sold.

No. 550/0 DISPLAY PIECE: 64" long, 36" wide, and 30" high; has a mountain in the center through which two Narrow Gauge trains pass on separate tracks; includes a lake and trees.

No. 550/1 DISPLAY PIECE: 96" long and 40" wide; similar to 550/0, but larger in order to allow two Wide Gauge trains to operate.

No. 551 DISPLAY PIECE: 60" long, 60" wide, and 40" high; truly a mountain layout; two Narrow Gauge trains and one Wide Gauge train can be run on separate tracks along the mountain ledges; lamp posts and a lighted station.

No. 552/0 DISPLAY PIECE: 144" long, 44" side, and 30" high; designed for one Narrow Gauge train; includes two mountains with tunnels, two bridges, a semaphore, a block signal, lamp posts, and a lighted station.

No. 552/1 DISPLAY PIECE: 180" long and 48" wide; almost identical to 552/0, but larger for operating a Wide Gauge train.

CHAPTER NINE

LOCO-BUILDER KITS, DORFAN SETS, AND CATALOGUES

Gd   Exc   Rst

KITS

In addition to the Take-Apart engines listed in Chapter Two, Dorfan offered a line of locomotive and motor kits, which are described below. These kits would require original packaging to distinguish them from the assembled versions. Any kits that may exist would bring a very substantial premium over the value of an assembled item without the kit packaging.

The following is a list of engine parts printed in the Loco-Builder Kits, as offered for Nos. 51, 52, and 53 and for Nos. 3920 and 3930 in the 1929–1930 retail price list:

- Right Half Engine, Gear Side
- Left Half Engine, Brush Holder Side
- Roller Contact
- Brushes
- Wheels with Gear Axle
- Connecting Pin
- Headlight Pin with Socket
- Armature
- Electric Field
- Field Screw
- Stud Collar
- Gear
- Gear Screw

- Headlight Pin Wire
- Headlight Bulb
- Reverser
- Coupler
- Four-Wheel Trucks (3930-type only)
- Motor Connecting Pin
- Small Gear

Note that the instructional brochure for Loco-Builder Kits is reproduced on pages 226–229.

No. 1000 NARROW GAUGE LOCO KIT: 1926-30. Parts to build the No. 51 Narrow Gauge locomotive; kit was upgraded through the years as the locomotive was improved.

NRS

No. 1001 NARROW GAUGE LOCO KIT: 1926-30. Parts to build the **reversing** 51 (later called 52); kit was upgraded as the locomotive was improved.

NRS

No. 1002 MOTOR KIT: 1926-30. Dorfan motor is 5¼" long, 2½" wide, and 2¾" high; consists of a pair of die-cast shells, a gear train, brushplate, pulley, and a motor armature which is identical to the one used in the locomotive. **NRS**

No. 1003 COMBINATION KIT: 1926-30. Parts to build the 51 Narrow Gauge locomotive **or** the Dorfan motor; only one armature is included, so a boy has to choose between the two. **NRS**

	Gd	Exc	Rst

No. 1004 MOTO-BUILDER KIT: 1926-30. Kit to build the Dorfan motor; complete with the armature. **NRS**

No. 1005 MOTOR HOUSING: 1926. Die-cast shells, gear train, and pulley for the stationary motor; the armature has to be borrowed from a Dorfan locomotive; available only one year. **NRS**

No. 1006 WIDE GAUGE LOCO KIT: 1926-30. Parts to build the No. 3930 locomotive; the kit was upgraded when the locomotive was improved. **NRS**

No. 1007 WIDE GAUGE LOCO KIT: 1927-30. Parts to build the No. 3920 locomotive. **NRS**

No. 1008 NARROW GAUGE LOCO KIT: 1927-30. Parts to build the No. 53 locomotive. **NRS**

CATALOGUED SETS

Because Dorfan's marketing emphasized train sets from the outset, our coverage of Dorfan production would not seem complete without documentation of the range offered. The following lists are based on catalogues examined. Readers are invited to send in additional information.

Narrow Gauge Mechanical

No. 99: No. 145, No. 355 Pullman, four pieces curved track.

No. 100: Same as No. 99, but with two 355 Pullmans.

No. 110: No. 155 with tender; No. 355 Pullman; four pieces curved track.

No. 112: No. 155 with tender; two No. 355 Pullmans; eight pieces curved track.

No. 120: No. 155 with tender; two No. 355 Pullmans; four pieces curved and two pieces straight track.

No. 130: No. 155 and tender; No. 355 Pullman; No. 310 tunnel; No. 340 signal; four pieces curved and two pieces straight track.

No. 135: No. 155 with tender; two No. 355 Pullmans, red and black; four pieces curved and two pieces straight track. Includes No. 310 tunnel and No. 340 signal.

No. 136: No. 155 with tender; two No. 356 Pullmans, eight pieces curved and two piece straight track; No. 310 tunnel; No. 340 signal; No. 424 station.

No. 140: No. 155, three No. 355 Pullmans, red; eight curved and two pieces straight track.

No. 142: No. 154 with tender; three No. 355 Pullmans; eight pieces curved and two pieces straight track.

No. 150: No. 155 and tender; two No. 355 Pullmans; fourteen pieces curved and two pieces straight track; No. 375 crossover.

No. 170: Same as No. 140, plus No. 310 tunnel, No. 418 station, and No. 330 semaphore.

No. 179: No. 156, with brake and tender; two No. 470 Pullmans, green, red, and yellow; eight pieces curved and four pieces straight track; No. 320 tunnel; No. 424 station; No. 340 signal; No. 330 semaphore.

No. 180/182: No. 156, with brake and tender, two No. 470 Pullmans, green or red; eight pieces curved and two pieces straight track.

No. 183: Same as No. 180, except has one additional Pullman and two additional pieces straight track.

No. 184: No. 157 engine with brake and reverser and triple-acting pistons, tender; two No. 495 Pullmans, light blue and red, with passengers; eight pieces curved and four pieces straight track.

No. 185: Same engine and tender as No. 184, but with freight cars (Nos. 600, 604, 606); eight pieces curved and four pieces straight track.

No. 191: No. 157 steam-type locomotive, reversible, and tender; with freight cars (No. 600, 604, 606); eight pieces curved and four pieces straight track.

Narrow Gauge Electric Passenger

No. 210 "Big Three": No. 51; two No. 470 Pullmans; eight pieces curved track, track terminal. Loco-Builder Outfit.

No. 215 "Heavy Duty": Red, green; No. 51; two No. 470 Pullmans; one track terminal, eight pieces curved track. Loco-Builder Outfit.

No. 215 "Dorfan Special": Same as above, but yellow and black.

No. 220 "Hurricane": Orange; No. 51; three No. 480 Pullmans; eight pieces curved, two pieces straight track. Loco-Builder Outfit.

No. 225 "Hurricane": Orange; No. 51; two No. 495 Pullmans; track terminal, eight pieces curved and two pieces straight track. Loco-Builder Outfit.

No. 230 "Western Special": Green; No. 51, reversible; two No. 490 Pullmans; eight pieces curved and two pieces straight track. Loco-Builder Outfit.

No. 235 "Western Special": Olive green; No. 52, reversible; one No. 490 Pullman; one No. 491 observation; illuminated; track terminal, eight pieces curved and two pieces straight track.

No. 240 "Blue Diamond": Blue; No. 51; two No. 490 Pullmans; one No. 491 observation; eight pieces curved and four pieces straight track. Loco-Builder.

No. 245: Blue and buff; steam-type locomotive, reversible, and six-wheel tender; two No. 496 Pullmans; No. 497 observation; illuminated; track terminals, eight pieces curved and four pieces straight tracks.

No. 253 "The Red Flash": Red; No. 52, with headlight and reverse; two No. 498-R Pullmans; No. 499-R observation; track terminal, eight pieces curved and two pieces straight track.

No. 254 "Scenic Limited": Brown; No. 55-B, reversible, with headlight and tender; No. 498-B Pullman; No. 499-B observation; track terminal, eight pieces curved and two pieces straight track.

No. 255 "Blue Diamond" Express: No. 52; two No. 490 Pullmans; No. 491 observation; track terminal, eight pieces curved and four pieces straight. Loco-Builder.

No. 256 "Silver-Blue Arrow": Pastel blue with red and black; No. 54 with head and taillight, reversible; two No. 496-S Pullmans; No. 497-S observation; track terminal, eight pieces curved and four pieces straight track.

No. 258 "The Starlight Flyer": Red; No. 55-R with tender; two No. 496-R Pullmans; No. 497-R observation; track terminal, eight pieces curved and four pieces straight track.

No. 259 "The Trans-Mountain Limited: Green; No. 53-G with head and taillight, reversible; No. 492-G baggage; No. 493-G Pullman; No. 494-G observation; track terminal, eight pieces curved and four pieces straight track.

No. 265 "Blue Streak": Blue; No. 52, reversible; two No. 496 Pullmans; No. 497 observation; illuminated; track terminal, eight pieces curved and four pieces straight track.

No. 275 "Manhattan Limited": Green with red; No. 53, reversible; No. 492 baggage; No. 493 passenger; No. 494 observation, illumiated; track terminal, eight pieces curved and four pieces straight track.

No. 285 "Bar Harbor Express": Crackle green with red; No. 53, reversible; No. 492 baggage; two No. 493 passenger cars; No. 494 observation; illuminated; track terminal, eight pieces curved and four pieces straight track.

Narrow Gauge Electric Freight

No. 211 "Hobo 'Leven": No. 51; gondola, tank car, caboose; track terminal, eight pieces curved and two straight pieces track. Loco-Builder.

No. 221 "Transcontinental": No. 52, reversible; gondola, tank car, hopper, boxcar, caboose; track terminal, eight pieces curved and four pieces straight track. Loco-Builder.

No. 231: Work train; No. 52, reversible; derrick, flat, caboose; track terminal, eight pieces curved and two straight pieces track.

No. 251 "Big Bill": No. 53, reversible; gondola, boxcars, tank car, coal car, caboose; track terminal, eight pieces curved and eight pieces straight track.

No. 252 "Fast Freight": No. 51; gondola, tank car, caboose; track terminal, eight pieces curved and two pieces straight track.

No. 255 "Speedster Wreck Train": No. 55B-K, reversible, with tender; derrick, flatcar, caboose; track terminal, eight pieces curved and two pieces straight track.

No. 257 "Speed Demon Freight Express": No. 55 B-K, reversible; gondolas, boxcar, lumber car, tank car, coal car, caboose; track terminal, eight pieces curved and six pieces straight track.

Wide Gauge Electric Passenger

No. 700 "Olympian": Red; No. 3920, reversible; two No. 790 Pullmans; illuminated; track terminal, eight pieces curved and two pieces straight track.

No. 701 "Chief": Same as No. 700, but has additional passenger cars equipped with red taillights.

No. 705 "Sunshine Special": Olive green; No. 3920, reversible, No. 785 Pullman; No. 786 observation; illuminated; track terminal, eight pieces curved and two pieces straight track.

No. 715 "Spirit of St. Louis": Red; No. 3920, reversible; No. 787 Pullman; No. 788 baggage; No. 789 observation; illuminated; track terminal, eight pieces curved and two pieces straight track.

No. 800 "Liberty Express": No. 3930; Nos. 890 and 891 Pullmans; eight pieces curved and two pieces straight track. Loco-Builder.

No. 801 "Congressional Limited: Same as No. 800, but with additional No. 891 Pullman with taillights, and four additional pieces straight track.

No. 890 "Champion Limited": Orange; No. 3919, reversible; two No. 780 Pullmans; track terminal, eight pieces curved and two pieces straight track.

No. 892 "King-O'-the-Rails": Red; No. 3920-R, reversible; No. 788 baggage; No. 787 Pullman; No. 789 observation; track terminal, eight pieces curved and two pieces straight track.

No. 893 "The Travelfast": Green; No. 3930-G, reversible; No. 995 baggage; two No. 994 Pullmans; No. 996 observation; track terminal, eight pieces curved and four pieces straight track.

No. 896 "New York Flyer Limited": Crackle finish, same as No. 897, except for finish and engine No. 3930BK.

No. 897 "Florida Limited": Ivory; No. 3931, reversible; No. 998-I baggage; two No. 997-I Pullmans; No. 999-I observation; track terminal, eight pieces curved and six pieces straight track.

No. 905 "Blue Bonnet": Blue; No. 3930, reversible; No. 992 Pullman; No. 993 observation; track terminal, eight pieces curved and two pieces straight track.

No. 915 "Palmetto Limited": Green; No. 3930, reversible; No. 994 Pullman; No. 995 baggage; No. 996 observation; track terminal, eight pieces curved and four pieces straight track.

No. 925 "The Dorfan Limited": Crackle finish green; No. 3930, reversible; two No. 997 Pullmans; No. 998 baggage; No. 999 observation; track terminal, eight pieces curved and six pieces straight track.

Wide Gauge Electric Freight

No. 711 "Seaboard Special": No. 3920, reversible; gondola, tank car, caboose; eight pieces curved and four pieces straight track.

No. 721 "Big Four Express": No. 3920; gondola, tank car, boxcar, caboose; track terminal, eight pieces curved and six pieces straight track.

No. 891 "Speed-Power Freighter": No. 3920-R; lumber car, tank car, caboose; track terminal, eight pieces curved and four pieces straight track.

No. 894 "All-Star Freight Limited": No. 3930-BK, reversible; boxcar, gondola, coal car, tank car, caboose; track terminal, eight pieces curved and eight pieces straight track.

No. 921 "Merchants' Dispatch": No. 3930, reversible; gondola, boxcar, tank car, coal car, caboose; track terminal, eight pieces curved and eight pieces straight track.

CATALOGUES AND PROMOTIONAL MATERIALS

Following is a listing of known Dorfan catalogues; the cover of the 1929 catalogue is shown below. Being exceptionally promotion-minded and focusing on the low end of the market, Dorfan issued quite a range of sales support and consumer-directed items; samples of some of these are reproduced on the pages that follow. Some of the catalogues are quite handsome, with tinted photographs to show the various colors in the lines of locomotives and cars.

- 1925. 24 pages plus covers; 5½" x 9½"
- 1926. 24 pages plus covers; 7¾" x 7"
- 1927. 10 pages; 8½" x 11"
- 1928. 12 pages; 15¼" x 11"
- 1929. 16 pages; 9" x 12"
- 1930 (small). 16 pages; 6" x 9"
- 1930 (large). 24 pages plus covers; 11" x 8"

The Modern Electric Trains Dorfan

Boys, you're living in the age of Class and Speed!

Between towering cities, great trains speed over rivers, plains and mountains. Thrill to this Speed-power, boys, in your own home. Run the trains that are modeled after the real transcontinental express. Own **DORFAN** the modern ELECTRIC TRAIN

Passenger Train—Wide Gauge No. 715 (Red). Includes Dorfan Engine No. 3920 with 6 ball bearings; reversible; one pullman car No. 787; one baggage car No. 788; one observation car No. 789; illuminated; track terminal; eight pieces of curved and two straight track. Length of train, 58 inches. Shipping weight, 23 lbs. $32.50
Similar Train (No. 275), but narrow gauge..........$18.00

SOLD BY

THE HUB,

W. J. B. GWINN
121 So. Wabash St.
WHEELING, W. VA.

DEC 7 1929

MARVELOUS RAILROAD FACTS

Read this fascinating story of the romance of American railroads

then answer the questions on the Official Entry Blank

WIN A PRIZE....YOU CAN!

HOW would you like to sit in the cab of the biggest locomotive in the world, pulling a swift limited passenger train for thousands of miles over all the railroads on the globe?

What would you see? You'd go racing over the long curve on the Hellgate Bridge — 3½ miles long in the Bronx, New York. Then travel on one of the star long-distance trains of railroad travel, the 20th Century Limited that leaps the distance from New York to Chicago in 20 hours. In Chicago, you know, you're in the greatest railroad center on earth, with 4300 passenger and freight trains leaving and arriving every day.

On, on you go through the Middle West — over the plains where 59 years ago the first cross-continent railroad was built while the workmen had to fight off the warlike Indians and Buffalo Bill shot buffaloes to provide meat for the railroad builders to eat.

Now switch up to the great Chicago, Milwaukee & St. Paul with 600 miles of electrified road over the Rocky and Cascade Mountains. While in the midst of these towering peaks in your giant-powered electric engine, just think of the progress made since the first locomotive was built. For this first puffing, buggy-like engine made only 10 miles an hour and a man on horseback rode ahead of the train waving a red flag! This first locomotive to haul passengers and goods was the invention of

George Stephenson who dreamed and worked as a boy to prepare himself for his great achievement. While very young he worked as a cowherd, and though still unable to read and write at the age of seventeen, he attended night school and forged his way upward to the immortal place his name holds to this day.

Keep on going! Let that roaring loco duck into the longest tunnel on the

RULES

1. This Contest is open to any boy between 7 and 16 years of age, in the United States and its possessions and Canada.
2. Read "Marvelous Railroad Facts" in this folder, then just write down your short answers to the four questions on the Official Entry Blank, on which all replies must be written to be considered.
3. First four questions can be answered in two to five words. Then write no more than 100 words answering Question 5.
4. Neatness and accuracy count; just be careful. All answers must be in handwriting; typewritten replies not accepted.
5. In case of ties, each tying contestant will be awarded the full prize tied for.
6. Contestants agree to accept the decisions of the judges as final.
7. No manuscripts will be acknowledged and no manuscripts will be returned.
8. Employees of the Dorfan Company are not eligible.
9. Contest opens November 1, 1928, and closes January 10, 1929.
10. Prizes will be awarded February 1, 1929.

American continent—the $12,000,000 Moffatt Tunnel—more than 6 miles of darkness for your powerful headlight to penetrate.

While you're at it, take a run over the longest line on earth, the Siberian Railroad stretching 4073 miles across Asia — Vladivostock to Cheliabinsk. See Europe too, and see how it feels to go through the Simplon Tunnel, the longest in the world boring under the Alps for 12⅓ miles. Soon you get the thrill of riding over the highest railroad bridge ever built, the Fades Viaduct rising 435 feet above the Liousle River at Pay-de-Dome, France.

Back in America again, you won't really see what power a locomotive can have till you feel it pull an almost unbelieveable number of freight cars. One of the longest and heaviest trains ever hauled was on the Erie Railroad— 120 cars laden with coal; a total weight of 8850 tons, and a length of 4888 feet or over 9/10 of a mile long. Some train!

Those are some of the marvelous railroad facts that have made the world a faster, more progresive place to live in. Now, you can tell somebody a few of those facts, can't you? If you were asked "Who shot the buffaloes for the railroad builders?" You'd answer, right off, "Buffalo Bill." Well, that's one of the easy four "Railroad Fact" questions on the Official Entry Blank of the Dorfan $2000.00 Prize Contest. And to be able to answer the 5th question, just read the next two pages. Then you can write out your own ideas on these,

JUDGES

Dr. George J. Fisher. *National Field Director, Boy Scouts of America.*

John E. McCrady, *The Dorfan Company, Newark, N.J.*

Milton A. Stoddard, *Blaker Advertising Agency, Inc., New York.*

- 2 -

How to Take Apart the

Dorfan

LOCO-BUILDER ENGINE
WIDE GAUGE MODEL

Study the pictures of the various parts and see what each looks like, so that you will know them by name as well as number.

1. Pull out the two little overhead trolleys or "Pantographs" (14-14).

2. Disconnect two Lighting Wires (12-13) by pulling out plugs at back of Headlights (11-11).

3. Draw Headlights (11-11) out of engine body, this unfastening the two halves of the body. The light Bulbs (M-M) may be unscrewed or left in, as desired.

4. Lay engine down with Reversing Lever toward you and carefully separate the two halves of the body, removing Pony Wheels (10-10) from channels 10-10 in body, and slipping out the couplers (7-7A).

5. Lift out Armature (4).

6. Disconnect Roller Contact (5) by releasing wire (9A) from spring clip at end, and remove from channels in body.

7. Remove Field (8) by removing Field Screw (8A) which holds Field to Body, and loosening red and green wire from spring clips on Reverser.

(N. B.) Be sure never to unwind or disconnect any of the wire that is around the Field or Armature. If you do, these parts will be ruined and you will have to get new ones. Remember, these are the most important members of your motor.

8. Remove Reverser (9) by loosening screw underneath that holds it in Channel (9), and releasing wire from clip Y.

(N. B.) If you wish, you may disconnect the three wires attached to the spring clips B, F, and X, on Reverser, but it is wise to leave them connected, as it will save time when you put your Loco-Builder together again.

9 Slip off the Stud Collar (6A) which keeps Brush-holder (6) in position.

10. Remove Brush-holder by lifting from Stud, or post (6).

11. Remove Gear (2) and wheels (1-1) from body half B by unscrewing Gear Screw (2A).

Care of your Loco-Builder

Keep all parts clear of dust, especially the Armature (4).

Never oil the brushes (the small black tips on the hinged arms on Brush-holder (6), nor the commutator, (the smooth copper surface of the armature). The brush-holder is equipped with a new type of *self-lubricating* brushes, which will never cut or wear the commutator. When, after long use, these brushes begin to show wear, simply pull them out of their sockets and replace with new ones, which, like all Loco-Builder Parts, may be secured promptly by ordering direct from our factory.

Dear Owner:

Loco-Builder is designed to give you pleasure for a long, long time. If you do not find our instructions clear enough, or if you have any kind of trouble at any time, write and tell us what your difficulty is, and we will help you. Then if you find that you cannot remedy the trouble yourself, ship your Loco-Builder to us and we will restore it to running condition.   *With our best wishes,*

THE DORFAN COMPANY
Factory and General Offices,   Newark, New Jersey

How to Operate
Dorfan
ELECTRIC TRAINS

DORFAN Electric Trains are built to operate on an electric current of six to eight volts. The electric current supplied in most homes is 110 volts. In order to operate your train on the house current it is necessary to reduce the strength of that current to six or eight volts.

Now there are two kinds of electric current—Alternating Current and Direct Current. The kind of current supplied to most homes is Alternating.

To Operate on Alternating Current

it is necessary to use a Transformer. This transformer, attached to a 110 volt fixture, will give you, by a process known in electricity as inductance, the low voltage current you require. It is essential, however, for the safety of your engine, to know that your transformer is a dependable one. And we recommend a Dorfan Transformer, because it is designed with special regard to the requirements of Dorfan engines.

A transformer, however, will *not operate on Direct Current*. So, before connecting any transformer with your house current be absolutely sure that you know what *kind of current it is*. If it happens to be direct current the transformer will burn out at once, if connected. If necessary, ask the company that supplies your electricity. If you find that it is direct current, instructions further down on this page will tell you what to do.

How to Set Up Your Track

ALL sections of Dorfan Electric Track are designed to fit together evenly. If you will take good care of your track when not in use, and see that it does not become bent, you will always be able to make smooth, even joints.

1. After selecting an open space on floor or carpet for laying out the track, slip the sections together carefully, being sure that the connecting pins fit closely into the ends of the corresponding rails. If these pins become bent, straighten them carefully with pliers *before fitting the rails together,* instead of trying to do so after they are in position, as that is likely to bend the rails.

2. Attach the two connecting wires, which come with your set or with your transformer, to the transformer and to the spring clips on the track terminal, following the instructions which come with same.

3. See that the connecting key on the transformer is turned to the lowest number on its scale. Insert the plug attached to the wire leading from the transformer in electric socket of your house current, first seeing that socket is turned *off*.

4. After making sure that every one of the above instructions has been carefully followed, turn the current on and your engine will light up and run immediately. You can increase or decrease the speed of the train by moving the handle or key on the transformer up or down the scale.

If your engine fails to start, give the track system a careful test, as follows: Take the track apart, section by section; disconnect the two wires from the track terminal and touch one to center rail of the section of track you are testing and the other to outside rail. If sparks form, section is defective and must be replaced with another before train will operate. If no sparks are formed, the section is O. K. Repeat this process with each section of track, until you are convinced that they are all good or that you have found out where the trouble comes.

If the track is found O. K. and the train still fails to run, remove the cars and see if locomotive will run alone. If it does not run, take it off the track and test the locomotive. Touch one transformer wire to the roller conductor and the other wire to one of the wheels. The wheels should turn immediately. If they do not, inspect the engine carefully according to instructions "How to Put Together," being sure that all wires are firmly connected and that the brushes rest on the commutator.

If You Have Direct Current

it is necessary to use what is called a Direct Current Reducer, in order to bring the current down to the required 6 or 8 volts. There are several makes of Direct Current Reducers on the market, and your electrical dealer may be depended upon to recommend a reliable one.

Usually, however, where the house current is direct, we recommend the use of a Storage Battery, such as is used for automobiles or radio sets. Such a battery gives a six volt current, so that no transformer or reducer is necessary. When a storage battery is used, a home charging apparatus is advisable, such as the "trickle" charger so commonly used with radio sets.

CAUTION: Do not attempt to use a Transformer on Direct Current as it will be burned out and rendered useless.

If you lose or break any part of your engine, you can secure a new part to replace it promptly by ordering direct from the factory. Simply write us the *name* of the part and the type of your engine (wide gauge or narrow) and we will advise you of the cost.

THE DORFAN COMPANY, NEWARK, NEW JERSEY

How to Put Together the
Dorfan
LOCO-BUILDER ENGINE
WIDE GAUGE MODEL

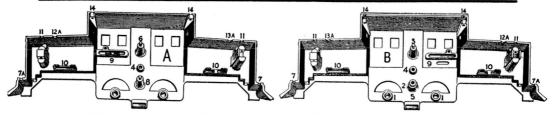

Note Difference in the Two Sides.

Before starting to put your Loco-Builder together, place the two halves of the body side by side on the table. The first one you use is the "Brush-holder Side," marked A.

In following the instructions, remember that all Dorfan parts are built to *fit together evenly*. If you seem to have to force any part into place, stop and read the instructions again, to be sure you are right. A screw driver is the only tool you need to build a Dorfan engine.

1—Where the Brush-Holder Goes

Place the Brush-holder (part 6) in position, by slipping it over the "stud," or post, 6 on Body. The side of Brush-holder marked 6 should be uppermost. The two hinged arms should rest around Bearing Hole 4.

Brush-holder (6)

2—The Collar Comes Next

Stud Collar (6 A)

Slip the Collar (part 6A) over the top of Stud. You will notice that the hole in the Collar is larger at one end. The large end belongs downward. Be sure to push the collar down close to Brush-holder.

3—Now the "Field"

Place Field (part 8), numbered side uppermost, over Studs 6 and 8 on body, so that hole 8 on field is over hole in stud 8, and opposite hole on field rests over stud 6. Insert Screw (part 8A) in hole 8 and tighten same.

Field Screw (8A)
8A
RED WIRE
GREEN WIRE
Electric Field (8)

4—Connect Reverser

Pick up Reverser (part 9) and attach wire now coming from Brush-holder (part 6) to clip marked Y on Reverser. Attach *red* wire from Field to clip U on Reverser. Connect *green* wire from Field to clip O on Reverser. Pick up *long* wire (part 9 A, see picture at bottom of page) and connect one end to clip X on Reverser. Hold Reverser with clip side away from you and black handle pointing up. Slip the end of the flat red part into the Channel 9 in body, having screw rest in slot over figure 9 on body. Fasten by tightening this screw. Bend all wires into the space above Field, under roof of locomotive, and shape long wire 9A around the *wire-wound* end of Field, down to bottom of body. (See diagram at top of next page).

Reverser (9)

5—Insert the Armature

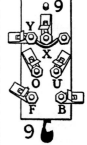

Place Armature (part 4) in center of Field, slipping the shaft, which runs through Armature into the bearing hole in Body, first putting a bit of vaseline into the hole. The gear on Armature should be uppermost. The Brushes—the little black tips on the Brush-holder—must rest against the commutator, which is the round copper surface of Armature.

Armature (4)

6—Connect up the Lighting System

12 *Short Lighting Wire (12)*

13 *Long Lighting Wire (13)*

Pick up *short*, thin, black Lighting Wire (part 12) and attach *plain* end to clip F on Reverser, and lay wire in groove 12A on body. Pick up *long* Lighting Wire (part 13) and attach *plain* end to clip B on Reverser. Carry this wire back above field and fit into groove 13A on body.

9A *Connecting Wire (9A) See Instructions 4 and 10*

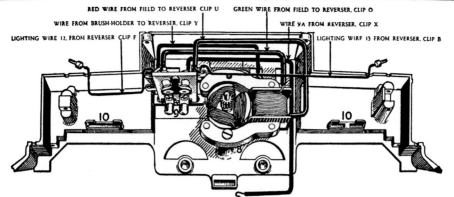

RED WIRE FROM FIELD TO REVERSER CLIP U   GREEN WIRE FROM FIELD TO REVERSER, CLIP O

WIRE FROM BRUSH-HOLDER TO REVERSER, CLIP Y   WIRE YA FROM REVERSER, CLIP X

LIGHTING WIRE 12, FROM REVERSER CLIP F   LIGHTING WIRE 13 FROM REVERSER, CLIP B

If the foregoing instructions have all been followed correctly, Body Side A will now appear as shown in this picture, and you are ready to go ahead with Body Side B.

7—Insert Wheels, Gear End Down

Take *other half* of body, marked B, and put a little vaseline in bearing holes, 4, 1, 1. Place Wheels (part 1-1) in position, by inserting the *geared* wheel ends in holes 1-1.

8—The Gear Drives the Wheels

Put a bit of vaseline around stud 2 and fit Gear (part 2) over same. Fit or "mesh" the teeth of gear and wheels in place, and fasten gear with large headed Screw (part 2A). Wipe teeth with vaseline.

Gear Screw (2 A)

9—Close Engine Body Together

Put a little vaseline in bearing holes for the wheel axles in body half A, and fit the two halves of Body carefully together, making sure that Reverser handle projects through open slot in body. End of red base on Reverser must fit into Channel 9 that runs parallel to Reverser slot. End of Armature shaft must rest in bearing hole 4 and ends of wheel axles in corresponding bearing holes.

10—Roller Contact is an Underground Trolley

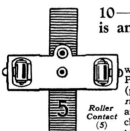

Lay engine on table with *plain wheels down* Place Roller Contact (part 5) on table with *numbered side down* and end having spring clip toward engine. Attach wire 9A (see bottom of preceding page) to this clip. Turn Roller Contact over, and holding the halves of the Body together with one hand, place Roller Contact in position (roller side outward, as in picture) by inserting projection 5 into Channel 5 in body, and opposite projection in Channel on opposite side of body.

11—Next Come the "Pony" Wheels

Hold Pony Wheels (parts 10-10) with wheels upward and slip the flat plate into Channels 10-10 in ends of body. The notches in these plates must fit around corresponding projections in channels.

Pony Wheels (10) There are two parts like this.

12—The Couplers Join the Cars

Holding sides firmly, slip the rivet end of Coupler (part 7) through hole 7 in end of Body and Coupler (part 7A) through hole 7A.

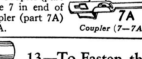
Coupler (7—7A)

13—To Fasten the Sides Together

Headlights (11-11)

Slip the pins on Headlights (parts 11-11) through holes 11-11 in top of Body, and push straight down through.

14—The Finishing Touches

Insert the metal plugs on Lighting Wires (12 and 13), now projecting through holes 12A and 13A into holes in back of Headlights, and screw the electric Bulbs (parts M-M) in Headlights.

Bulbs M-M)

Slip the two little overhead trolleys or pantographs (parts 14-14) into holes 14-14 in roof.

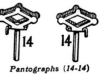
Pantographs (14-14)

If you have followed all the above directions correctly, your Loco-Builder Engine is now ready to run when placed on the electric track. To make it go forward, switch the projecting black handle toward front of engine. To go backward, shift handle toward rear. If engine fails to run when you place it on the track and turn on the current, take the engine apart, according to the directions you will find on the next page, and rebuild it again, paying close attention to all the directions until you succeed.

GLOSSARY

★

armature: rotating part of the electric motor, consisting of center shaft, the rotor poles and their windings, and a commutator

articulated train: two or more sections are connected by movable joints, or a streamline-style train where all the units are closely linked by vestibules or vestibule-like substitute attachments; the trucks are under the couplers instead of the cars

brushes: graphite or copper electrical conductors that make a sliding contact between moving and stationary parts of a motor; brushes rub on the commutator portion of a rotating armature

bumper band: type of coupler used by Carlisle & Finch; a U-shaped wire fit over the bumper to connect two cars

clerestory: raised center section of passenger car roof with actual or simulated windows or openings on the sides

clockwork: windup motor that is powered by a spring, gear, or other feature of clockwork; very common before widespread use of electricity

commutator: rotating part of a locomotive motor that contacts stationary carbon brushes and completes the circuit. There are flat types in most toy train locomotive motors, but some of the older types had a drum type.

compromise joints: term used by real railroads to connect two pieces of rail of different sizes or weights

corrugations: ridges in pressed metal, such as frequently found on Carlisle & Finch items

cowcatcher: more properly, the pilot on the front of a steam locomotive

cupola: raised structure on the roof of a caboose to permit a forward view of the whole train

decal: thin transparent adhesive-backed film that transfers lettering to toy trains and accessories

die-casting: method of making smooth and accurate castings by forcing molden metal into a die or mold

drawbar: the large hook-like device that attaches a steam locomotive to its tender

embossed: a surface raised by stamping which is often ornamented or decorated

eyelet: actually a hollow rivet; when stuck in a hole, it leaves a ring around the hole

Fahnestock clip: a quickly connected or disconnected spring fastener for wires

field winding: wire on the field magnet

frog: intersection of two railway tracks, resembling frog's spread legs

Gramme ring: large-diameter type of armature, which acts as a flywheel, enabling the engine to make smooth starts and stops

grommet: eyelet usually held in place by a metal washer

herald: insignia or logo of a particular railroad or company

japanning: process using natural Japanese lacquer to coat metal

journal box: box that encloses the journal or the part of an axle that runs in a bearing

lithography: printing on sheets of metal, usually in multiple colors with elaborate designs. The sheets are then cut and folded to make the individual engine or cars desired

Loco-Builder: take-apart engines offered by Dorfan

mechanical train: term for a train powered by a windup spring. See **clockwork**

Narrow Gauge: Dorfan's version of O Gauge, which it called "ordinary 1⅜" track"; compare with **Wide Gauge**

nonarticulated train: one in which cars are joined by couplers; each car can be seen as a distinct separate unit as opposed to the caterpillar-like continuity of the **articulated train**

pantograph: sprung diamond-shaped device with large sliding shoe at the top for the collection of electrical power from overhead wire

pole: one of the opposing parts of a battery or other power source, each attracting the other to induce the flow of current; also a slender rounded piece of wood or metal, such as a trolley pole or lineside trolley wire pole

Pullman: specific type of passenger car originally designed by George Pullman; often used as a generic term for better-grade passenger cars

rectifier: a device that allows electrical current to flow in only one direction. Alternating current coming into the rectifier is changed to direct current coming out.

rollers: small cylindrical devices attached to a bracket to collect electric current from the center rail in tinplate layouts, to power motorized or lighted cars or locomotives

semaphore: railroad signaling device that conveys to an engineer the presence of a train on the track ahead by the position of a movable arm

shroud: term for a cowl

solenoid: electrical device, an electromagnet with a metal rod inside its core. The rod moves with the flow of current and thus moves anything attached to it.

split insulated axles: a Carlisle & Finch device; steel axles were split into two parts connected by fiber tubes or bushings to provide insulation

streamlined: locomotives and other trains featuring aerodynamic design; highly popular in the 1930s

strip-steel rail: track using thin, narrow steel strips pressed into wooden ties as rails, the track being assembled and shaped by the customer; used by Carlisle & Finch, early Lionel 2⅞-inch gauge, and others

TCA: Trains Collectors Association; their publication is the *TCQ*

Tee-Rail: Carlisle & Finch's term for its tubular rail

three-rail track: current is transmitted to car or engine motor through contact with the center third rail, the return being through the wheels on the running rails

tinplate: toys made from tin-coated steel; the tin prevented rust

TTOS: Toy Train Operators Society

turnout: proper term for "switch"; a track section with movable pivotal rails to transfer trains from track to track. The turnout is actually the entire arrangement by which a train can be turned out to the side of a rail line; the switch is the arrangement by which movable "points" of rail can be set to accomplish the turning.

CARLISLE & FINCH INDEX
to Listings of Trolleys, Locomotives, Cars, Toys, and Accessories

The descriptive listings in the Carlisle & Finch section of this volume are organized according to catalogue number. In this index, all catalogue and side-of-car numbers are given in one sequence, except that all preproduction samples described by F. O. Loveland are listed at the end. Sets or "outfits" that are included in this book through reproduction of Carlisle & Finch catalogue descriptions and illustrations are listed below, even though we do not provide formal listings of all the Carlisle & Finch offerings. It should be pointed out that individual car numbers were often derived from the advertised number for a set including that item. In this index, catalogue numbers are not given in parentheses, but side-of-car numbers are followed by "(S)". Remember that Carlisle & Finch often used the same number for various versions, some markedly different, of an item. Note the brief descriptors in the entries below as an aid to distinguishing items. The page numbers provided below indicate the page where descriptions of the variations begin.

ITEM	PAGE(S)
1 (Four-Wheel Trolley, Two-Rail)	25
1 (Four-Wheel Unpowered Trailer)	25
1-R Four-Wheel Trolley, Reversing)	25
2 (Eight-Wheel Trolley)	28
2 (Eight-Wheel Unpowered Trailer)	28
2 (Early Large Eight-Wheel Inter-urban, 1903)	28
2 (Late Large Eight-Wheel Interurban)	29
2-S (Eight-Wheel Trolley)	28
3 (Coal Mining Locomotive, 1897)	31
3 (Coal Mining Locomotive, 1899)	31
3 (Fixed-Bucket Coal Mining Cars)	32
3 (Coal Mining Locomotive and Train Outfit)	33
3 (S)	43
4 (Steam Outline Locomotive)	34
4 (Electric Locomotive and Freight Train)	47
4 (Inclined Plane Railway)	61
5 (Bridge)	54
6 (Strip-Steel Track Crossing)	53
T-6 (Tee Rail Track Crossing)	53
7 (Hand-powered Dynamo)	59
7-S (Larger Dynamo)	59
8 (Water Power Plant)	59
9 (Station)	55
10 ("Y" Switch)	53
10-R, 10-L (Early Switches)	53
10-R, 10-L (Late Switches)	54
11 (Small Gondola or Flat)	46
12 (Small Boxcar)	49
13 (Small Coach)	42
13B (Small Baggage Car)	43
14 (Track Connector)	52
16 (Larger Water Generator)	59
17 (Side-dumping Coal Mining Cars)	33
17 (Coal Mining Locomotive and Dump Cars Outfit)	31
18 (Large Four-Wheel Trolley)	28

ITEM	PAGE(S)
19 (Large Four-Wheel Summer Trolley)	28
19 (Electric Automobile)	61
20 (Tank-type Switch Engine)	35
20 (Double-ended "Suburban" Locomotive	37
20 (Electric Torpedo Boat)	61
26 (S)	43; 47
29 (S)	43
32 (Electric Locomotive and Passenger Train Outfit)	42
34 (Medium-sized 4-4-2 Locomotive)	40
42 (Early Four-Wheel Trolley, 1902)	25
42 (Unpowered Four-Wheel Trailer)	25
42 (Late Four-Wheel Trolley, 1909)	25
45 (Early 4-4-2 Road Locomotive, 1903)	37
45 (Late 4-4-2 Locomotive, 1909)	40
46 (Small Caboose)	49
47 (Small Coal Hopper)	50
48 (Small Cattle Car)	50
49 (Small Oil Tank Car)	50
50 (Small Flatcar)	50
51 (Large Baggage Car)	43
52 (Large Coach)	43
53 (Operating Derrick)	46
54 (Piers for Elevated Railway)	29
55 (Loading Platform and Derrick)	56
56 (Truss Bridge)	55
57 (Suspension Bridge)	55
58 (Transformer)	59
58 (Direct Current Reducer)	60
58-R, 58-L (Switches)	54
59 (Medium-sized Baggage Car)	44
60 (Medium-sized Coach)	45
68 (S)	45
70 (Electric Locomotive and Wrecking Train Outfit)	51
82 (S)	38; 40
85 (Bumper Post)	52

ITEM	PAGE(S)
87 (Vestibuled Pullman Parlor Car)	43
89 (Electric Locomotive and Freight Train	47
90 (Large Gondola)	50
90 (Medium-sized Gondola)	51
91 (Large Boxcar)	50
91 (Medium-sized Boxcar)	51
92 (Large Caboose)	50
92 (Medium-sized Caboose)	51
93 (Tee Rail Track)	53
94-RT, 95-LT (Switches)	54
96 (Freight Depot with Derrick)	56
97 (Passenger Terminal)	56
98 (Elevated Railway)	29
99 (Four-Wheel Trolley, Overhead Pole)	28
100 (Four-Wheel Summer Trolley, Overhead Pole)	28
103 (Lineside Trolley Wire Poles)	29
108 (Passenger Station, Locomotive, and Passenger Car Set)	40
109 (Electric Telegraph Set)	62
111 (S)	43
131 (S)	35; 37; 41; 46
171 (S)	34; 37; 45; 49; 51
683 (S)	34
868 (S)	49
1141 (S)	47
8681 (S)	47
Unnumbered Sectional Tee Rail Track	53
Unnumbered Strip-Steel Track	52

Preproduction Samples:

ITEM	PAGE(S)
75 (Set, 7000 Locomotive and Tender)	64
83 (Burlington Zephyr Set)	64
273 (C & NW Boxcar)	65
7000 (Atlantic-type Locomotive)	64
Erie Gondola	65
Ohio Passenger Car	65
Pennsylvania Caboose	66

HAFNER INDEX
to Listings of Locomotives, Cars, and Accessories

The descriptive listings in the Hafner section of this volume are organized by the number on the side of the car, whenever that number exists, with the catalogue numbers that are available cited in the body of the listing. In this index, all side-of-car and catalogue numbers are given in one sequence. Catalogue numbers are found in parentheses. Many Hafner locomotives and cars had no car numbering nor catalogue number, but items without side-of-car numbering will always be found under type or road name. The index includes accessories. When there are two or more different items carrying the same number or name, these entries are separated by a semi-colon.

ITEM	PAGE(S)	ITEM	PAGE(S)	ITEM	PAGE(S)
1	123	(121)	148	(913)	149
(9)	147	(122)	148	919	116
(10)	146	(123)	148	970	153
St.10	149	(125)	148	1000	123
(12)	146	(127)	86	1000K	146
X 12	149	(192)	146	1010 Locomotive	89
(16)	146	(200)	149	1010 Tanker	139; 140
SW 16	149	(201)	149	1010 Tender	99
(20)	146	(202)	149	(1100)	149
C 20	149	(203)	149	1110 (Locomotive)	89
(24)	146	(300)	149	1110-style Locomotive (Unnumbered)	89
(29)	146	(301)	122; 149	(1180) (Early Large)	96
BX32	141; 154	(302)	123	1180 (Later Small)	97
(49)	146	(303)	123	(1181)	97
(50)	147	(304)	123	(1190)	97
(62)	146	(305)	123	(1200)	149
(65)	147	(306)	123	X 1357	90; 141
(66)	147	(307)	123	X1357-90	141
PHILLIPS 66	140	(308)	123	2000	92
(67)	147	(309)	123	2000-style Locomotive (Unnumbered)	92
(68)	147	(310)	108	(3011)	150
(69)	147	(400) (Accessory)	149	3057 (Long)	137
(70)	146	(400) (Freight Car)	137	3057 (Short)	140
(80)	124	(401)	136	(3115)	146
(81)	124	(402)	137	(3259)	146
(82)	125	(403)	139	3689	153
(83)	125	(404)	137	4226	
86	109	(405)	132	(4514)	146
(87)	111	(406)	133	4610	123
(88)	110	(407)	137	4825	140
(90)	119	(500)	149	5933	123
(96)	112	(506)	146	7300	122
(97)	114	(508)	146	M-10000	129
(98)	112	528	123	10205	123
(100) (Accessory)	148; 149	529	109	13788	137
(100) (Locomotive)	88	(619)	146	13789	137
(102)	108	(621)	146	14825	141; 154
(103)	112	(644)	146	15731	140
(109) (Early)	86	(654)	146	31230	136
(109) (Late)	88	(655)	146	31280	124
(110) (Early)	86	(673)	146	31320	124
(110) (Late)	88	(900)	146	31400	125
(112) (Early)	86	(910)	149	32001	123
(112) (Late)	88	(911)	149	41021	141; 155
(120)	148	(912)	149	62425	126

ITEM	PAGE(S)
78100	99; 153
81932	141
90131	99
91746	139; 154
91876	137
102151	135
115041	93; 153
115041-style Locomotive (Unnumbered)	92
614333	143
1350141	136
2110471	133

Unnumbered Items:

Locomotives:

Chicago "Century of Progress Special"	89
Union Pacific (Zephyr Power Unit)	129
Stamped-Steel, ca. 1917-20	87
1110-style	89
2000-style	92
115041-style	92

Tenders:

Type III, copper-plated	98
Type IVa	99
Type Va	99

Passenger Cars:

Baltimore & Ohio	108
Canadian Flyer	108
Canadian Flyer (One-piece Coach)	117

ITEM	PAGE(S)
"Century of Progress Special"	116
Chicago & North Western	108
Erie	108
Hafner's Streamliners	132; 133; 135
Illinois Central	112
New York Central	109
New York Central Observation	108
New York Flyer	109
New York Flyer (One-piece Coach)	117
Northern Pacific	112
Overland Flyer (5⁷⁄₁₆" Coach)	116
Overland Flyer (One-piece Coach)	117
Overland Flyer Observation	116
Pennsylvania	109
Pittsburg Flyer	109
Santa Fe	109
Southern Pacific	112
Sunshine Special	118-120
Toy Manufacturers	109
Union Pacific	112
Union Pacific (Later Observation)	133
Union Pacific (Later Pullman)	132
Union Pacific (Streamliner)	129; 130
Type I Observation	110
Type I Passenger	109
Unlettered Observation (Later)	133; 135
Unlettered Pullman (Later)	132

Baggage Cars:

Adams Express Company (5½-inch)	111

ITEM	PAGE(S)
Adams Express Company (6¼-inch)	114
American Express Co. (5½-inch)	111
Overland Flyer	111; 116
Union Pacific	114
Wells Fargo	114

Freight Cars:

Overland Refrigerator Car	140
Overland Flyer Caboose	125; 126
Overland Flyer Sand and Gravel Car	126
Overland Freight Caboose	136
Phillips 66 Tank Car	140
Unlettered Lumber Car	126
Unlettered Tank Car	140

Streamliner Sets:

M-10000	130
Zephyr	130

Accessories:

Bridge	146; 147
Clock	147
Crossover	155
Gate	147
Pole	147
Semaphore	147
Sign, Signal	147; 149
Station	147; 149; 150
Track Unit	155; 159
Tunnel	146
Turntable	147

SUMMARY OF HAFNER TYPES

Frames for No. 1110-Style Locomotives

Type I A raised platform rests on the top of the frame shelf. The platform runs the length of the frame as well as the front and back of the engine. It is designed to elevate the shell to make room for the battery holder which was inserted over the top of the motor.

Type II Does not have the platform. Since there are no batteries in this type of engine, extra room at the top of the casing is not needed. The frame shelf is bent downward so that a side strip runs the entire length below the frame shelf. The section of the frame under the cab representing firebox sides is slightly shorter in Type II.

Type III Similar to Type II, but the frame shelf is not bent downward on the sides so there is no side strip running the entire length.

No. 1010 Types

Type I Steamlined cowl on roof; sideboards run the length of the engine.

Type II Streamlined cowl discarded; smokestack, bell, and two domes now visible.

Type III Similar to I, but has embossed ridge on sideboards.

Type IV Similar to I, but sideboards extend only 2½ inches from the front; "HAFNER" stamped on sideboards.

Coupler Types

Type I Hook with straight shank and tab end

Type II Hook end is inverted T-shape; banjo-shaped hole

Type III Similar to Type II, but with notch at front of banjo-shaped hole

Type IV T-shaped hook turned upward; banjo-shaped hole without notch

Type V Upturned hook coupler; small hole and thin hook

Type VI Upturned hook coupler; similar to Type V, but longer; fits into floor frame rather than end piece

Tender Types

Type Ia 1180 (Large) Larger of the two earliest tenders; usually lettered "OVERLAND FLYER" but has been found with "CANADIAN FLYER" and "NEW YORK FLYER" lettering

Note: Numbering changed from "1180" to "1190" in the late 1920s for the following four subtypes:

Type Ib Red sides, black frame; lithographed with iridescent gold heralds of various railroads

Type Ic Black sides and frame; various railroad heralds on sides

Type Id Green or red sides, black frames; "HAFNER'S / OVERLAND FLYER / RAILWAYS" bar and circle herald on sides

Type Ie Green, red, or blue sides, red or black frame; has extended front floor piece with hole rather than usual sliding coupler

Type IIa 1181 Smaller size of earliest tenders; "OVERLAND FLYER" lettered on sides, "1181" lettered in black; also came in no lettering and no number versions

Type IIb 1180 (Small) Lettering changed from "1181" to 1180 in the late 1920s; usually has railroad herald on sides; "HAFNER'S / OVERLAND FLYER / RAILWAYS" bar and circle herald on some tenders; also came with no lettering

Type III Copper-plated body with green rounded end pieces; no lettering; high triangular pedestal trucks

Type IVa Center body unit with rounded end pieces; various colors; coffin-style without high pedestal trucks; "HAFNER" is embossed on sides

Type IVb Similar to IVa, but "HAFNER TRAINS" lettering centered on sides; center body unit comes in gray, gold, or cream; "1010" lithographed to the left of center on both sides; "Made in U.S.A." lettered on bottom at right

Type Va Square shape without separate end pieces; winglike top sides curving inward; black or blue sides; unnumbered; "HAFNER" embossed on center of both sides

Type Vb Similar to Va, but yellow, blue, orange, and gray lithography on sides or plain black sides; usually numbered either "90131" or "78100" on top front of sides

Passenger, Baggage, and Freight Frame Types

Type I Length, journal box configuration, air tank style, and frame notches similar to AF's Type 3 frame

Type II Length and high journal box styling followed the arrangement used by AF for its early 6⅜-inch herald cars

Type III Integral bottom for one-piece cars

Type IV Eight-wheel frame with truss rod, vertical post, and open space on both sides of post

Type V Low-slung frame used on only a few of the 5⅞-inch passenger cars

Type VI High triangular axle supports; come in short and long versions

Type VII Streamliner frame for cars pulled by the M-10000 and Zephyr power units; comes in articulated and nonarticulated versions

Type VIII Used with streamliner-style post-1938 freight and passenger cars

Type IX Square corner frame used on several late-production freight cars

SUMMARY OF LOCOMOTIVE TYPES

I 109 (Early)
Lowest-priced engine in Hafner's first line
Cast iron
No brake or drive roads
6½ inches long

II 110 (Early)
Similar to the 109, but equipped with brake and drive rods

III 112 (Early)
Larger than 109 and 110 (7 inches long)
Usually has two silver boiler bands
Has brake and drive rods
Used with higher-priced sets

IV 127
Most impressive Hafner engine
Copied from Ives No. 17 engine of the 1912–1914 period
8 inches long with impressive detailing, including horizontal rivets
Powerful motor, used to pull eight-wheel cars
Only Hafner engine with winding key on right side
Very rare

V
Unnumbered stamped steel
World War I production
Antiquated nineteenth-century styling
Small (6 inches long)
No drive rods or brake

VI 100
Used with lower-priced sets
6 inches
No brake or drive rods

VII 109 (Late)
a: Very detailed cast iron
6 inches long
Three domes
No brake or drive rods
b: Identical to VIIa, but has two domes and is ½ inch shorter
Probably devised to save on shipping costs

VIII 110 (Late)
Similar to VIIa, but came with driving rods and brake

IX 112 (Late)
Cast-aluminum shell
Rectangular two-part window
No window stripe

Later models had extra-long brake lever
8 inches long

X Century of Progress Special Unnumbered Locomotive
Stamped steel
Red boiler front
Battery-operated headlight bulb
Bell under cab
7 inches long

XI 1110 Lithographed Locomotive
Stamped steel
Number lettered under cab windows
Usually came with No. 1110 Type II frame, although can have Type I frame with headlight, or Type III
Came in red, blue, or green with gold piping
7 inches long

XII Unnumbered 1110-style Locomotive
Similar to IX
Usually came with black boiler, although also produced with copper or red boiler
No battery headlight; usually has simulated headlight hooded cover

XIII 1010 Locomotive
Stamped steel
7 inches long
"1010" usually embossed on engine
Came in four distinct types (see text)

XIV Unnumbered 2000, 115041-style Locomotive
Stamped steel
Punched-out cab windows
Punched-out lower section of door
All black
No lettering
Battery-operated headlight and bell
8½ inches long

XV 2000 Locomotive
Stamped steel
Colorfully lithographed in either black, silver, and red, or in blue, red, and silver
"2000" lettered under cab
Came with and without battery-operated headlight
8½ inches long

XVI 115041
Stamped steel
Yellow, blue, orange, and silver lithography
"115041" lettered on boiler front and at rear of cab roof
Came with battery-operated headlight and bell
8½ inches long

DORFAN INDEX
to Listings of Locomotives, Cars, Kits, and Accessories

The detailed listings in the Dorfan section of this volume are organized according to catalogue number. In this index, all catalogue and side-of-car numbers are given in one sequence; any side-of-car number is followed by "(S)", even if it is also the catalogue number. Brief listings of catalogued Dorfan sets will be found on pages 221–223 but are not included in the following index.

ITEM	PAGE(S)
50 (Steam Outline Locomotive)	174
51 (S)	175
52 (Take-Apart No. 51-style Locomotive)	175
53 (S)	175
53-RC (No. 53 with Distance Remote Control)	176
54 (S)	176
54-RC (No. 54 with Distance Remote Control)	176
55 (Steam Outline Locomotive)	174
70 (Electric Crane)	213
84 (S)	197
99-100 (S)	174
145 (Electric Outline Locomotive)	174
154 (Steam Outline Locomotive)	174
155 (Steam Outline Locomotive)	174
156 (Steam Outline Locomotive)	174
157 (Steam Outline Locomotive)	174
300/310 (Bridge)	215
310 (Tunnel)	217
319 (Tunnel)	218
320 (Tunnel)	218
321 (Tunnel)	218
322 (Tunnel)	218
323 (Tunnel)	218
330 (Semaphore)	218
340 (Danger Signal)	218
350/360 (Track)	215
350/370 (Telegraph Pole)	218
351 (Lamp Post)	218
355 (Pullman, Narrow, 5½")	183
356 (S)	184
360 (Track)	215
375 (Crossover)	215
380 (Accessory Set)	218
385 (Switches)	215
390 (Accessory Set)	218
395 (Accessory Set)	218
400 (Automatic Block Signal)	213
401 (Control Block Signal)	213
402 (Semaphore, Narrow)	214
403 (Track Terminal)	215
404 (Track Connector, Wide)	216
405 (Switchboard)	214
406 (Power Switch House)	214

ITEM	PAGE(S)
406 (Bell Signal, Narrow)	214
407 (Switchboard)	214
408 (Headlight Bulb)	214
409 (Frosted Bulb)	214
410 (Bridge, Narrow)	215
411 (Bridge, Narrow)	215
412 (Bridge, Narrow)	215
413 (Bridge, Wide)	216
414 (Bridge, Wide)	216
414-L (Bridge, Wide)	216
415 (Telegraph Pole)	218
415-B (Box of Poles)	218
416 (Warning Signal, Narrow)	214
417 (Position-light Signal)	214
417/426 (Newark Station)	217
418 (Signal Bridge, One Position-light Signal)	214
418/424 (Montclair Station)	217
419 (Signal Bridge, Two Position-light Signals)	214
419 (Station)	217
420 (Boulevard Light)	214
421 (Automatic Crossing Gate, Narrow)	214
425 (Station)	217
427 (Station)	217
430 (Lamp Post)	215
431 (Lamp Post)	215
432 (Flag Pole)	218
433 (Lamp Post)	215
440 (Transformer)	219
441 (Transformer)	219
442 (Transformer)	219
443 (Transformer)	219
444 (Transformer)	219
445 (Transformer)	219
446 (Circuit Breaker)	219
447 (Transformer)	219
448 (Rotary Converter)	219
448 (Transformer)	219
449 (Transformer)	219
450 (Track, Narrow)	215
460 (Track, Narrow)	216
465 (Clips, Wide)	216
470 (Pullman, Narrow, 6¾")	184
475 (Crossover, Narrow)	216

ITEM	PAGE(S)
480 (Pullman, Narrow, 6¾")	184
485 (Switches, Narrow)	216
485-L (Switches, Narrow)	216
490 (Pullman, Narrow, 7¼")	184
491 (Observation, Narrow, 7¼")	185
492 (S)	189
493 (S)	190
494 (S)	190
495 (Pullman, Narrow, 7¼")	186
496 (Pullman, Narrow, 9")	188
496 (S)	191
497 (Observation, Narrow, 9")	188
498 (Pullman, Narrow, 7¼")	187
499 (Observation, Narrow, 7¼")	187
550/0 (Display Piece)	219
550/1 (Display Piece)	219
551 (Display Piece)	219
552/0 (Display Piece)	219
552/1 (Display Piece)	219
600 (Gondola, Narrow)	197
601 (N.Y.C. Boxcar, Narrow)	193
602 (UP Boxcar, Narrow)	194
603 (PRR Boxcar, Narrow)	196
604 (Oil Tank Car, Narrow)	197
605 (Coal Hopper, Narrow)	197
606 (Caboose, Narrow)	196
607 (S)	196
609 (Lumber Car, Narrow)	196
610 (S)	197
770 (Steam Outline Locomotive)	174; 177
770 (S)	209
771 (S)	208; 209
772 (S)	208; 209
773 (S)	209
780 (Pullman, Wide)	207
781 (Pullman, Wide)	207
785 (Pullman, Wide)	207
786 (Observation, Wide)	208
787 (Pullman, Wide)	208
788 (Baggage, Wide)	208
789 (S; Observation, Wide)	208
789 (S; Pullman, Wide)	208
790 (S; Pullman, Wide)	208
790 (S; Observation, Wide)	208
791 (Pullman, Wide)	208

800 (Gondola, Wide)	210	
801 (Boxcar, Wide)	210	
804 (Tank Car, Wide)	210	
805 (Hopper, Wide)	211	
806 (Caboose, Wide)	211	
809 (Lumber Car, Wide)	211	
850 (Track, Wide)	216	
860 (Track, Wide)	217	
875 (Crossover, Wide)	217	
885 (Switches, Wide)	217	
885-L (Switches, Wide)	217	
886-L (Switches, Wide)	217	
890 (Pullman, Wide)	208	
891 (Pullman, Wide)	208	
990 (Pullman, Wide)	208	
991 (Pullman, Wide)	208	
992 (Pullman, Wide)	208	
992 (Observation, Wide)	208	
993 (Observation, Wide)	208	
994 (Pullman, Wide)	208	
995 (Baggage, Wide)	209	
996 (Observation, Wide)	209	

997 (Pullman, Wide)	209	
998 (Baggage, Wide)	209	
999 (Observation, Wide)	209	
1000 (Loco Kit, Narrow)	220	
1001 (Loco Kit, Narrow)	220	
1002 (Motor Kit)	220	
1003 (Combination Kit)	220	
1004 (Moto-Builder Kit)	221	
1005 (Motor Housing)	220	
1006 (Loco Kit, Wide)	221	
1007 (Loco Kit, Wide)	221	
1008 (Loco Kit, Narrow)	221	
1134 (S)	201	
1401 (Control Block Signal)	214	
1402 (Semaphore)	214	
1406 (Bell Signal, Wide)	214	
1416 (Warning Signal, Wide)	214	
1421 (Automatic Crossing Gate, Wide)	215	
3677 (S)	196	
3920 (Loco-Builder, Wide)	199	
3930 (Loco-Builder, Wide)	201	

3931 (Loco-Builder, Wide)	201	
3931 (S)	211	
3932 (Loco-Builder, Wide)	201	
5402 (S)	184	
11201 (S)	197	
11701 (S)	211	
14048 (S)	197	
29325 (S)	210	
121499 (S)	210	
126432 (S)	194	
253761 (S)	210	
486751 (S)	196; 211	
517953 (S)	196	
3182999 (S)	193	
Unnumbered Track (Two-Rail)	215	
Unnumbered Straight Track (Three-Rail, Narrow)	216	
Unnumbered Straight Track (Three-Rail, Wide)	217	
Unnumbered Curved Track (Three-Rail, Narrow)	216	

SUMMARY OF DORFAN TYPES

Steam Locomotive Types

Type I Boiler front had a cast, button-type number plate. This version was used for the larger 8¼-inch-long mechanical locomotives.

Type II Boiler front had a ½-inch opening for the electric headlight. The dummy headlight on top of the boiler had a crown on it; the cast tabs for the four motor-mounting screws were not reinforced.

Type III Boiler front had a ½-inch opening for the headlight. The dummy headlight on top of the boiler had a flat top; the cast tabs for the four motor-mounting screws were reinforced with additional cast flanges.

Tender Types

Type I 4 inches long with four wheels.

The floor had punched rings front and rear for coupling to the engine and train; had raised "bubbles" to clear the wheel flanges. Its three-sided body was tabbed to the floor and came with either stamped-steel or die-cast wheels. One version was all black, one was red with black floor, and one was black with number "160" in a red oval on the side.

Type II 5½ inches long with four wheels, it came with the mechanical locomotive.

The tender had a swivel coupler ring on the front and a riveted standard coupler on the rear, with a "DORFAN" decal. The wheels were either stamped steel or die cast.

Type III 6¼ inches long, designed for six wheels, it often was equipped with only four. It had a swivel ring coupler on the front and a riveted standard coupler on the rear. This tender was usually equipped with an imitation coal load consisting of a strip of metal embossed with lumps of coal. The tender's body was painted to match the locomotive's color and it had a "DORFAN" or "DORFAN LINES" decal. The floor was either black or painted yellow buff to match the engine's trim. **Note:** Richard Fletcher reports seeing a green mechanical set with red tender floor to match engine trim. Other color variations exist, but the author suspects that most were made as salesman samples and were not sold with the sets. Sometimes the centers of the wheels were painted. Gordon H. Blickle, George B. Fisher, and other collectors have discovered the word "GERMANY" stamped into the floor of the tender, under the coal load and covered by paint. Since Kraus offered an identical Fandor tender, except for the coupler and markings, it is assumed that Fandor manufactured these tenders.

Truck Frame Types

Type I Nickel-plated; not punched for journal boxes.

Type II Black-enameled; not punched for journal boxes.

Type III Black-enameled; punched for journal boxes, but no journals installed.

Type IVa Black-enameled; equipped with nickel journal boxes

Type IVb Black-enameled; equipped with brass journal boxes.

Vestibule Types

Type I Unpainted or enameled tinplate pair of 5⁄16" x ¾" angles with tabs; some had small punched holes, the purpose for which is undetermined.

Type II A rectangular, formed frame ¾" x 1⅜" with protruding lower lip.

Type III A rectangular, formed frame ¾" x 1⅝".

Door Types

Type I Flat, enameled with tabs top and bottom. 7⁄16" x 1³⁄16".

Type IIa Formed panel and frame with tabs top and bottom; brass or enameled. ½" x 1⅜".

Type IIb Brass only; same as II, but has additional tabs at window opening. These windows are used on the No. 54 locomotive.

Type III Formed panel and frame; brass or enameled with tabs top and bottom. 9⁄16" x 2".

ABOUT THE AUTHORS

★

W. Graham Claytor, Jr. is chairman and president of the National Railroad Passenger Corporation, better known as Amtrak, in Washington, D.C., which operates some 230 trains daily over 23,000 route-miles, reaching approximately 500 cities and towns in the United States. A native of Roanoke, Virginia, he received his B.A. from the University of Virginia, and graduated with a J.D. summa cum laude from Harvard Law School. His early years in the law profession saw him clerking for Judge Learned Hand and Justice Louis Brandeis. A commanding officer in the Navy during World War II, he went on to become CEO of Southern Railway System for a period of ten years, and his service to government includes being Secretary of the Navy, Acting Secretary of Transportation, and Deputy Secretary of Defense during the time from 1977 to 1981. Since receiving a Lionel Standard Gauge set at age 10 he steadily developed an interest in toy trains and has been actively collecting for forty-five years, operating many of them to the delight of his two children. Member of the Train Collectors Association, the Toy Train Operating Society, and the Antique Toy Collectors of America, he has written articles for *Train Collectors Quarterly*.

Paul A. Doyle first developed an interest in railroading and its history because his father, grandfather, and great-grandfather all worked for the Delaware and Hudson Railroad. Born in Carbondale, Pennsylvania, he received a Ph.D. from Fordham University and is Professor of English at Nassau College, State University of New York at Garden City, Long Island. He is the author and/or editor of eighteen previous books on literary figures, poetry, and English composition, and has written over one hundred articles for numerous literary journals on both sides of the Atlantic. Starting out as a Lionel Standard Gauge collector, he saw only more and more reproductions being made and instead turned his attention to lithographed trains, especially Hafner, Marx, and early O Gauge American Flyer. As a former college history major, he was fascinated by the living John Hafner, a link to the earliest train production in America, and began corresponding with him and emphasizing Hafner in a collection he has been building for almost twenty-five years. Also a member of TCA and TTOS, he belongs as well to the Toy Train Collectors Society and has contributed articles on Hafner to many collector publications.

Carlton Norris McKenney, P.E. has been collecting trains for forty-five years as part of a life that has included the far-ranging interests of racing sailboats, flying airplanes, operating and riding streetcars and trains, communications, and writing. Now a consulting engineer in his hometown of Richmond, Virginia, he received his B.S. in Electrical Engineering from Princeton University and after the many required years of apprenticeship and rigorous board exams earned his license as professional engineer. He is also licensed as a multiengine pilot and an FCC radiotelephone operator. His professional training has meshed well with his avocation. In the 1920s he operated an O Gauge layout using choke cables to operate manual switches from the control panel; signals and operating accessories were homemade. Although virtually all of his toy trains disappeared during World War II (he suspects scrap metal drives), two Dorfan cars survived. Four sons provided good excuses to build a collection of toy trains, and Dorfan has remained the favorite. He is the author of *Rails in Richmond* and a member of the National Railway Historical Society and TCA, as well as the Instrument Society of America, E.R.A., and C.E.R.A.

Franklin O. Loveland is a Dartmouth College graduate who earned his Ph.D. in Anthropology from Duke University; he is now Associate Professor of Anthropology at Gettysburg College. A Christmas gift of a Lionel Scout Set in 1949 in Cincinnati (also home to Carlisle & Finch) set him on the collecting trail, which for the past fourteen years has focused on Carlisle & Finch, Voltamp, early wooden toys with paper lithography, Japanese tin, and Marx tin toys. With his background in anthropology he has written about collecting as an activity and has written extensively for *TCQ*. When Bruce Manson ran a request in that publication for information about the Carlisle & Finch company, he went back to Ohio, got to know Brent Finch, and has been studying original records as well as past and current operations of the firm.

Peter H. Riddle has earned three academic degrees in the fields of music and education and is currently administrator of the School of Music at Acadia University in Nova Scotia. He is originally from Long Branch, New Jersey, and received his Ph.D. from Southern Illinois University. He has had a lifelong interest in model railroading and has written two books on layout wiring for Greenberg (the second soon to be published) as well as a new Greenberg Guide to Lionel Prewar Accessories and a book based on his 13- by 16-foot layout, entitled *Trains from Grandfather's Attic*. He especially enjoys collecting and restoring Prewar O Gauge from American Flyer, Ives, and Lionel, when his work as band director, composer, and specialist in music education allows. A member of TCA, TTOS, and LCCA, as well as many music organizations, he is a regular contributor to *Classic Toy Trains* magazine.